THE VISTA HIGHER LEARNING

Introductory Spanish

Pocket Dictionary
& Language Guide

VISTA
HIGHER LEARNING

Boston, Massachusetts

ISBN 1-59334-387-6

Library of Congress Control Number: 2004106252

5 6 7 8 9 B 09 08 07 06

CONTENTS

Introduction

The Vista Higher Learning Introductory Spanish Pocket Dictionary & Language Guide was created to complement your Vista Higher Learning introductory Spanish textbook. Its Spanish-English and English-Spanish dictionaries contain all of the active words and expressions taught in these texts:

- *VISTAS*
- *PANORAMA*
- *AVENTURAS*
- *INVITACIONES: Primera parte y Segunda parte*

Besides active vocabulary, the dictionaries also incorporate several thousand additional words, expressions, and idioms chosen because of their high-frequency and their usefulness to students who are using these Vista Higher Learning introductory textbooks to learn Spanish.

The dictionaries are followed by *Useful Expressions*, a storehouse of contextualized sentences illustrating new vocabulary, idioms, and grammatical structures that can help you make your Spanish more natural and expressive. These sentences are related to the themes presented in your Vista Higher Learning textbook. Verb conjugation tables containing all of the verbs taught in your textbook follow the *Useful Expressions* section.

The Pocket Dictionary & Language Guide then closes with the *Reference* section. It contains lists of specialized vocabulary on a variety of topics, such as country names, adjectives of nationality, academic subjects, foods, numbers, sayings, false friends, and so forth.

We hope that you will find the *Vista Higher Learning Introductory Spanish Pocket Dictionary & Language Guide* to be a useful language learning resource and that it will help you to increase your Spanish language skills in a productive, enjoyable fashion.

The Vista Higher Learning Editorial Staff

Note on Alphabetization

For purposes of alphabetization, the Spanish language contains one more letter, **ñ**, than English. **Ñ** follows **n**; therefore, the word **dañar**, for example, appears after **danza**.

Abbreviations Used in This Dictionary

adj.	adjective	*L.A.*	Latin America
adv.	adverb	*loc.*	set expression
art.	article	*m.*	masculine
aux.	auxiliary	*n.*	noun
conj.	conjunction	*obj.*	object
def.	definite	*p.p.*	past participle
dem.	demonstrative	*pl.*	plural
d.o.	direct object	*poss.*	possessive
f.	feminine	*prep.*	preposition
fam.	familiar	*pron.*	pronoun/pronominal
form.	formal		nal
i.	intransitive	*recip.*	reciprocal
impers.	impersonal	*refl.*	reflexive
indef.	indefinite	*sing.*	singular
inf.	infinitive	*subj.*	subject/subjunctive
interj.	interjection	*t.*	transitive
i.o.	indirect object	*v.*	verb
irreg.	irregular		

Español-Inglés
Spanish–English

A

a *prep.* at; to
a la(s) + (time) at + (time)
abadía *f.* abbey
abajo *adv.* down
  ¡Abajo! Down (with it/him/her/them)!
abatido/a *adj.* dejected
abeja *f.* bee
abeto *m.* fir tree
abierto *p.p. of* **abrir** opened
abierto/a *adj.* open
abogado/a *m. f.* lawyer
abonar *v.t.* (*soil*) to fertilize
abono *m.* fertilizer
abortar *v.i.* to have a miscarriage
  abortar de manera provocada to have an abortion
aborto *m.* (espontáneo) miscarriage; (provocado) abortion
abrazar *v.t.* to hug; to embrace
abrazarse *v. pron.* (*recip.*) to hug; to embrace each other
abrazo *m.* hug; embrace
abrebotellas *m.* bottle opener
abrelatas *m. sing.* can opener
abreviar *v.t.* to abbreviate
abreviatura *f.* abbreviation
abridor *m.* opener
abrigo *m.* coat; overcoat; jacket
abril *m.* April
abrillantador (para pisos/suelos) *m.* (*floor*) polish

abrillantar *v.t.* to polish
abrir *v.t.* to open
abrirse *v. pron.* to open
  La ventana se abrió de golpe. The window opened suddenly.
absorbente *adj.* absorbent
absorber *v.t.* to absorb
absurdo/a *adj.* absurd
abuelo/a *m.* grandfather; *f.* grandmother
abuelos *m., pl.* grandparents
aburrido/a *adj.* bored; boring
aburrir *v.t.* to bore
  Este libro me aburre. This book bores me.
aburrirse *v. pron.* to get bored
  Espero que hoy no se aburran. I hope you don't get bored today.
acá *adv.* here
  ¡Ven acá! Come here!
acabar *v.t.* to finish
  Acabé la tarea. I'm done with my homework.
acabar de (+ inf.) *v.i.* to have just done something
  Acabo de limpiar. I've just finished cleaning.
acampada *f.* camp; camping
  ir de acampada to go camping
acampar *v.i.* to camp
acantilado *m.* cliff
acariciar *v.t.* to caress; (*hair, pet*) to stroke, to pet
acaso: por si acaso *loc.* just in case
accesorio *m.* accessory
accidentado/a *adj.* (*terrain*) rugged; (*person*) hurt, injured

3

accidente *m.* accident
  accidente laboral industrial accident
acción *f.* action
  ...de acción action (*genre*)
accionar *v.t.* (*machine*) to operate; to activate
aceite *m.* oil
  aceite de oliva olive oil
aceituna *f.* olive
acelerador *m.* accelerator (*pedal*)
acelerar *v.t.* to accelerate
  ¡Acelera! Hurry up!
aceptar *v.t.* to accept
acera *f.* sidewalk
acerca de *prep.* about
  Leí un artículo acerca de Sevilla. I read an article about Seville.
acercarse (a) *v. pron.* to approach, to come closer (to)
acero *m.* steel
  acero inoxidable stainless steel
ácido *m.* acid
  ácido fólico folic acid
ácido/a *adj.* acid; (*flavor*) tart, tangy
acogedor(a) *adj.* cozy
acolchado/a *adj.* padded
acompañar *v.t.* to go with, to accompany
acondicionado *adj.* conditioned
aconsejar *v.t.* to advise
acontecimiento *m.* event
acordar (o:ue) *v.t.* to agree
acordarse (de) (o:ue) *v. pron.* to remember

acostarse (o:ue) *v. pron.* to go to bed
acostumbrarse (a) *v. pron.* to be accustomed to
acrobacia *f.* acrobatics
acróbata *m., f.* acrobat
activar *v.t.* to activate
actividad *f.* activity
activo/a *adj.* active
acto *m.* act
  en el acto *loc.* immediately, right away
  acto seguido *adv.* immediately after
actor *m.* actor
actriz *f.* actor
actual *adj.* current, present
actualidades *f., pl.* news; current events
acuarela *f.* watercolor (*painting*)
acuario *m.* aquarium
acuático/a *adj.* aquatic
acuerdo *m.* agreement
  de acuerdo con according to
  llegar a un acuerdo to reach an agreement
adaptación *f.* adaptation
adaptarse (a) *v. pron.* to adapt; to adjust (to)
adelantar (a un vehículo) *v.t.* to pass (*a vehicle*)
adelante *adv.* forward, ahead
  La librería Porté está un poco más adelante. The Porté Bookshop is a little farther ahead.
adelgazar *v.i.* to lose weight; to slim down
además (de) *adv.* furthermore; besides; in addition (to)

adentro *adv.* inside
aderezar *v.t.* (*food*) to season; (*salad*) to dress
aderezo *m.* seasoning; dressing
adicción *f.* addiction
adicional *adj.* additional
adicto/a *m., f.* addict; *adj.* addicted
adiós *m.* good-bye
aditivo *m.* additive
adivinanza *f.* riddle
adivinar *v.t.* to guess
adjetivo *m.* adjective
administración *f.* management, administration
　administración de empresas business administration
administrar *v.t.* (*business*) to manage; to run
adolescencia *f.* adolescence
adolescente *m., f.* teenager, adolescent
adolorido/a *adj.* sore
¿adónde? *adv.* (*destination*) (to) where?
adornar *v.t.* to decorate; (*food*) to garnish
adorno *m.* ornament, decoration
　de adorno for decoration
　Se puso un lazo de adorno en el pelo. She wore a ribbon in her hair for decoration.
adquirir (i:ie) *v.t.* to acquire
adquisición *f.* acquisition
adrede *adv.* intentionally, on purpose
aduana *f.* customs
adulación *f.* flattery

adulador(a) *m., f.* flatterer
adular *v.t.* to flatter
advertencia *f.* warning
advertir (i:ie) *v.t.* to warn; to notice
　Por fin alguien advirtió mi presencia. Finally someone noticed I was there.
aéreo/a *adj.* air
　correo aéreo air mail
aeróbico/a *adj.* aerobic
aerolínea *f.* airline
aeroplano *m.* airplane
aeropuerto *m.* airport
afectado/a *adj.* affected
afectar *v.t.* to affect
afeitarse *v. pron.* to shave (*oneself*)
afición *f.* hobby
aficionado/a *adj.* fan
aficionarse (a) *v. pron.* to become a fan (of); (*hobby*) to take up
afinar *v.t.* (*musical instrument*) to tune
afirmativo/a *adj.* affirmative
africano/a *adj./m., f.* African
afuera *adv.* outside
afueras *f., pl.* suburbs; outskirts
agachar *v.t.* (*head*) lower
agacharse *v. pron.* to squat
agencia *f.* office; agency
　agencia de viajes travel agency
agente *m., f.* agent
　agente de viajes travel agent
agosto *m.* August
agotado/a *adj.* (*person, supplies*) exhausted; (*commerce*) out of stock; (*tickets*) sold out

agotamiento *m.* exhaustion
agotarse *v. pron.* (*provisions, supplies*) to run out
agradable *adj.* (*person*) pleasant, nice; (*situation*) enjoyable
agradecer (c:zc) *v.t.* to thank, to be grateful
Te agradezco tu ayuda. Thank you for your help.
agradecido/a *adj.* grateful
agrícola *adj.* agricultural
labor agrícola farm labor
agricultor(a) *m., f.* farmer
agricultura *f.* agriculture, farming
agridulce *adj.* bittersweet
agrio/a *adj.* sour
agrupar *v.t.* to group
agruparse *v. pron.* to get into groups
agua (el) *f.* water
agua bendita holy water
agua dulce fresh water
agua mineral mineral water
agua potable drinking water
agua salada salt water
aguacate *m.* avocado
aguafiestas *m., f.* party pooper
aguantar *v.t.* to endure, to put up with; (*Spain*) to hold
aguante *m.* endurance
águila (el) *f.* eagle
aguja *f.* needle
agujerear *v.t.* (*material*) to make holes; (*ear*) to pierce
agujero *m.* hole
ahijado/a *m.* godson; *f.* goddaughter
ahogado/a *adj.* drowned

ahogar *v.t.* to drown
Ahoga sus dudas leyendo. He drowns his doubts by reading.
Ahoga sus penas trabajando. She drowns her sorrow with work.
ahogarse *v. pron.* to drown
Se ahogó en el río. He drowned in the river.
ahora *adv.* now
ahora mismo right now
de ahora en adelante from now on
ahorrador(a) *adj.* frugal
ahorrar (dinero) *v.t.* to save (*money*)
ahorros *m.* savings
aire *m.* air
aire acondicionado air conditioning
al aire libre in the open air
aislante *adj.* insulating
aislar *v.t.* to isolate; to insulate
ajedrecista *m., f.* chess player
ajedrez *m.* chess
ajo *m.* garlic
al (*contraction of* a + el) to the, at the
al contado in cash
al (+ *inf.*) upon, on
Al llegar a San Juan, fuimos a la playa. Upon arriving in San Juan, we went to the beach.
ala (el) *f.* wing
ala delta (*vehicle*) hang glider; (*sport*) hang gliding
practicar el ala delta to hang glide

alardear (de) *v.i.* (*Spain*) to boast (about)
Alardeaba de haber ganado. He was boasting about having won.
alarmante *adj.* alarming
albahaca *f.* basil
albañil *m.* builder; bricklayer
albañilería *f.* (*profession*) building; bricklaying
albaricoque *m.* apricot
alberca *f.* (*Mexico*) swimming pool
albergue *m.* hostel
albergue juvenil youth hostel
alcachofa *f.* artichoke
alcalde, alcaldesa *m., f.* mayor
alcaldía *f.* city hall
alcoba *f.* (*L.A.*) bedroom
alcohol *m.* alcohol
alcohólico/a *adj.* alcoholic
aldea *f.* village
alegrarse (de) *v. pron.* to be happy
alegre *adj.* happy; joyful
alegría *f.* joy; happiness
alejado/a *adj.* remote
alemán *m.* (*language*) German
alemán, alemana *adj./m., f.* German
alérgico/a *adj.* allergic
aleta *f.* (*fish*) fin; (*swiming*) flipper
alfabeto *m.* alphabet
alfombra *f.* carpet; rug
alga (el) *f.* seaweed
algarabía *f.* rejoicing, jubilation; noisy commotion
algo *pron.* something; anything
algodón *m.* cotton
de algodón (made of) cotton
alguien *pron.* someone; somebody; anyone
algún, alguno/a(s) *adj.* any; some
alguna vez ever
aliento *m.* breath
dar aliento to encourage
alimentación *f.* diet
alimentar *v.t.* to feed
alimentarse *v. pron.* to feed oneself
alimento *m.* food
aliñar *v.t.* (*food*) to season; (*salad*) to dress
aliño *m.* seasoning; dressing
aliviar *v.t.* to ease; alleviate; (*pain*) to relieve
aliviar el estrés/la tensión to relieve/reduce stress/tension
aliviarse *v. pron.* (*pain*) to let up; (*person*) to get better
alivio *m.* relief
allí *adv.* there
allí mismo right there
alma (el) *f.* soul
almacén *m.* department store
almacenamiento *m.* storage
almacenar *v.t.* to store
almeja *f.* clam
almendra *f.* almond
almendro *m.* almond tree
almíbar *m.* syrup
almohada *f.* pillow
almorzar (o:ue) *v.i.* to have lunch
almuerzo *m.* lunch
¿Aló? *interj.* Hello? (*on the telephone*)
alojado/a *adj.* guest
alojamiento *m.* lodging

alojar (a alguien) *v.t.* to lodge, to put up

alojarse *v. pron.* (*hotel*) to stay

alpinismo *m.* (*mountain*) climbing

alpinista *m., f.* (*mountain*) climber

alquilar *v.t.* to rent

alquiler *m.* rent (*payment*)

alrededor (de) *prep.* around
  Hay una muralla alrededor de la ciudad vieja. There is a wall around the old city.

alrededor *adv.* around
  una mesa con cuatro sillas alrededor a table with four chairs around it

alrededores *m., pl.* outskirts, surrounding area
  en los alrededores de Barcelona on the outskirts of Barcelona

altavoz *m.* loudspeaker

alternador *m.* alternator

alternativa *f.* alternative

altillo *m.* attic

alto/a *adj.* tall; high

alto *m.* halt, stop
  señal de alto stop (*sign*)

altura *f.* height

aluminio *m.* aluminum
  de aluminio (*made*) of aluminum

alumno/a *m., f.* (*elementary school*) pupil, student

ama: el ama *m., f.* **de casa** housekeeper; caretaker; housewife; home-maker

amable *adj.* nice; friendly; kind

amanecer *m.* dawn

al amanecer at dawn

amanecer (c:zc) *v. impers.* to dawn; (*person*) to wake up (*in the morning*)
  Amanecí con dolor de cabeza. I woke up with a headache.

amapola *f.* poppy

amante *m., f.* lover; fan; *adj.* loving
  amantes del jazz jazz lovers
  su amante esposa his loving wife
  amante de la buena conversación fond of good conversation

amar *v.t.* to love

amargo/a *adj.* bitter

amarillento/a *adj.* yellowish

amarillo/a yellow

amarse *v. pron.* (*recip.*) to love each other

ambición *f.* ambition

ambicionar *v.t.* to aspire to

ambicioso/a *adj.* ambitious

ambientador *m.* air freshener

ambiente *m.* (*natural*) environment; (*created by people, decoration*) atmosphere

ambos/as *adj.* both
  Sujetó la pelota con ambas manos. He held down the ball with both hands.

ambulancia *f.* ambulance

amenaza *f.* threat

amenazar *v.t.* to threaten

amígdala *f.* tonsil

amigo/a *m., f.* friend
  hacer amigos to make friends

amistad *f.* friendship
amistades *m., pl.* friends
  **Martina tiene muchas
  amistades en Cartagena.**
  Martina has lots of friends
  in Cartagena.
amistoso/a *adj.* friendly
amor *m.* love
amortiguador *m.* shock
  absorber
amueblado/a *adj.* furnished
amueblar *v.t.* to furnish
analfabeto/a *m., f.* illiterate
  person; *adj.* illiterate
analista *m., f.* analyst
anaranjado/a *adj.* (*color*) orange
anarquía *f.* anarchy
anárquico/a *adj.* anarchic
anatomía *f.* anatomy
anatómico/a *adj.* anatomical
ancho/a *adj.* wide
anchoa *f.* anchovy
anciano/a *adj.* elderly; *m.*
  elderly man; *f.* elderly woman
andar en bicicleta to ride bikes
andar en patineta to skateboard
anestesia *f.* anesthesia
anestesiar *v.t.* anesthetize
anestesiólogo/a *m., f.*
  anesthesiologist
anfitrión *m.* host
anfitriona *f.* hostess
anglosajón, anglosajona
  adj./m., f. Anglo-Saxon
anguila *f.* eel
ángulo *m.* angle
anillo *m.* ring
  anillo de bodas wedding ring
  anillo de compromiso
  engagement ring

animado/a *adj.* (*person*) in
  good spirits; (*party*) lively
animal *m.* animal
animar *v.t.* to cheer up; to
  encourage
animarse *v. pron.* to cheer up
aniversario (de bodas) *m.*
  (wedding) anniversary
anoche *adv.* last night
anormal *adj.* abnormal
ansia *f.* longing
ansiar *v.t.* to crave for, to long
  for
anteayer *adv.* the day before
  yesterday
antepasado/a *m., f.* ancestor
antes *adv.* before
  antes de *prep.* before
  antes (de) que *conj.* before
antibiótico *m.* antibiotic
anticipación *f.* anticipation;
  (*business*) advance
  con anticipación ahead of
  time; beforehand
anticonceptivo *m.*
  contraceptive
anticuado/a *adj.* old-fashioned
antideportivo *adj.*
  unsportsmanlike
antídoto *m.* antidote
antifaz *m.* mask
antigüedades *f., pl.* antiques;
  antiquities
antiguo/a *adj.* old; ancient
antipatía *f.* dislike
antipático/a *adj.* unpleasant,
  irritating, hasty
antojo *m.* whim
antología *f.* anthology
antorcha *f.* torch

anular *v.t.* to cancel
anunciar *v.t.* to announce; to advertise
anuncio *m.* (*newspaper*) advertisement
anzuelo *m.* hook
  morder el anzuelo (*loc.*) to swallow the bait; to bite
añil *adj.* indigo
año *m.* year
  el año pasado last year
añoranza *f.* yearning
añorar (a alguien) *v.t.* to long for (someone); to miss (someone)
apagar *v.t.* (*TV, radio*) to turn off; (*fire*) to put out, to extinguish
apagón *m.* power failure, blackout
aparato *m.* appliance
  aparato circulatorio circulatory system
  aparato digestivo digestive system
  aparato doméstico household appliance
  aparato respiratorio respiratory system
aparecer (c:zc) *v.i.* to appear
apartamento *m.* apartment
apellido *m.* last name
apenas *adv.* hardly; scarcely; barely; just
  Apenas le conozco. I barely know him.
  Apenas te oigo. I can hardly hear you.
aperitivo *m.* appetizer
apilar *v.t.* to stack
apio *m.* celery

aplaudir *v.t./v.i.* to applaud, to clap
aplauso *m.* applause
aplazamiento *m.* postponement
aplazar *v.t.* to postpone, to put off
apodo *m.* nickname
apoyar *v.t.* to support
apoyo *m.* support
apreciar *v.t.* to appreciate
aprecio *m.* esteem
aprender (a + *inf.*) *v.t.* to learn
apresurarse *v. pron.* to hurry
aprobado *m.* passing grade, C
aprobar (o:ue) *v.i.* to pass
aprovechar *v.t.* to make good use of
aprovecharse (de) *v. pron.* to take advantage (of)
aptitud *f.* aptitude, competence
apto/a *adj.* fit (*to practice a profession*); suitable
  No es apto para ejercer la psicología. He's not fit to practice psychology.
apuñalar (a alguien) *v.t.* to stab (somebody)
apurarse *v. pron.* to hurry; to rush
aquel, aquella, aquellos/as *dem. adj.* that (over there); those (over there)
aquél, aquélla, aquéllos/as *dem. pron.* that (over there); those (over there)
aquello *dem. neuter pron.* that; that thing; that fact
aquí *adv.* here
  aquí está here (he/she/it) is

aquí estamos en... here we are in . . .

aquí mismo right here

árabe *m.* (*language*) Arabic

árabe *adj.* Arabian; *m., f.* Arab

araña *f.* spider; (*light*) chandelier

árbitro/a *m.* referee; umpire

árbol *m.* tree
  árbol frutal fruit tree
  árbol genealógico family tree

arboleda *f.* grove

arbusto *m.* shrub, bush

archipiélago *m.* archipelago

archivar *v.t.* to file

archivo *m.* file

arcilla *f.* clay

arco *m.* arch; (*sport*) bow
  arco iris *m.* rainbow

ardilla *f.* squirrel

arena *f.* sand

arete *m.* (*L.A.*) earring

argumentar *v.t.* to argue

argumento *m.* (*reasoning*) argument; (*literature, film*) plot

arisco/a *adj.* unfriendly

aristocracia *f.* aristocracy

aristócrata *m., f.* aristocrat

arma (el) *f.* weapon, arm

armar (un rompecabezas) *v.t.* to assemble (a puzzle)

armario *m.* closet

aroma *m.* scent

arqueólogo/a *m., f.* archaeologist

arquitecto/a *m., f.* architect

arrancar *v.t.* (*car*) to start; (*sheet of paper*) to tear out

arrastrar *v.t.* to drag

arrastrarse (por el piso/suelo) *v. pron.* to crawl (on the ground)

arrecife *m.* reef

arreglado/a *adj.* tidy

arreglar *v.t.* to fix; to arrange; to neaten; to straighten up
  El profesor arregló la situación. The professor fixed the situation.
  La modista me arregló el vestido. My dressmaker fixed my dress.

arreglarse *v. pron.* to do oneself up; to get ready
  Tarda mucho en arreglarse. He/She takes forever getting ready.

arrepentido/a *adj.* repentant, feeling sorry

arrepentirse *v. pron.* to be sorry; to regret

arrestado/a *adj.* arrested; under arrest
  estar arrestado/a to be under arrest

arrestar *v.t.* to arrest

arresto *m.* arrest

arriba *adv.* up
  ¡Manos arriba! Hands up!
  Me miró de arriba abajo. He/She looked me up and down.

arriesgarse *v. pron.* to take the risk

arroba *f.* @ symbol

arrogante *adj.* arrogant

arroz *m.* rice

arte *m.* art

arteria *f.* artery

artes *f., pl.* arts

artes marciales martial arts
artesanía f. craftsmanship; crafts
articulación f. joint, articulation
artículo m. article; item
artículos m., pl. (business) goods
artículos de cocina kitchenware
artículos de deporte sporting goods
artículos de piel leather goods
artículos de punto knitwear
artista m., f. artist
artístico/a adj. artistic
arveja m. pea
asa (el) f. (cup, serving dish) handle
asado m. roast
asado de cordero roast lamb
asado p.p. of **asar** roasted; **asado/a** adj. roast(ed)
castañas asadas roasted chestnuts
asador m. barbecue
asar v.t. to roast
ascender v.t. (temperature, prices) to rise; v.i. (employee) to be promoted
ascenso m. rise; (at work) promotion
ascensor m. elevator
asco m. nausea
¡Qué asco! How revolting! How disgusting!
asegurar v.t. to assure, to guarantee
asegurarse v. pron. to make sure

asesinato m. murder; assassination
asesino/a adj./m., f. murderer; assassin
asfalto m. asphalt
así adv. thus; so (in such a way); like this
Debe hacerse así. It must be done like this.
así así so-so
asiático/a adj. Asiatic; m., f. Asian
asiduo/a m., f. (client) regular; adj. frequent
asiento m. seat
asiento delantero front seat
asiento trasero rear seat
asignación f. (Mexico) homework
asistencia f. assistance
asistencia médica health care
asistir (a) v.i. to attend
asociación f. association
asociar v.t. (ideas, words) to associate
asociarse (con) v. pron. to collaborate (with)
asombroso/a adj. amazing, astonishing
aspecto m. appearance
áspero/a adj. (surface, skin) rough
aspiradora f. vacuum cleaner
aspirante m., f. candidate; applicant
aspirina f. aspirin
asqueroso/a adj. (food, smell) disgusting, revolting; (place) filthy

Esta cocina está asquerosa.
This kitchen is filthy.

astrología *f.* astrology

astrólogo/a *m., f.* astrologist

astronauta *m., f.* astronaut

astronomía *f.* astronomy

astrónomo/a *m., f.* astronomer

astuto/a *adj.* shrewd

asumir *v.t.* to assume

atajo *m.* short cut

ataque *m.* attack

  ataque al corazón heart attack

  ataque cardíaco heart attack

  ataque de nervios panic attack

atardecer *m.* dusk

  al atardecer at dusk, at twilight

ataúd *m.* coffin

ateísmo *m.* atheism

atención *f.* attention; care

atender *v.i.* to pay attention

  atender a los clientes to take care of clients

atentado *m.* assault, attack; crime

  atentado terrorista terrorist attack; assassination attempt

atentar (contra) *v.t.* to attempt to assassinate (*somebody*); to attack (*something*)

ateo/a *adj.* atheistic; *m., f.* atheist

aterrizaje *m.* landing

aterrizar *v.i.* to land

atleta *m., f.* athlete

atlético/a *adj.* athletic

atletismo *m.* athletics; track and field

atontado/a *adj.* stunned, dazed

atracar *v.t.* (*bank*) to hold up; (*person*) to mug

atracción *f.* attraction

atraco *m.* robbery, holdup

atractivo/a *adj.* attractive

atractivo *m.* attraction; appeal, charm

  No entiendo su atractivo. I don't understand his appeal.

atraer *v.t. irreg.* (**yo atraigo**) to attract

atragantarse *v. pron.* to choke

atrás *adv.* behind

atravesar *v.t.* to cross

atreverse *v. pron.* to dare

atrevido/a *adj.* (*dress*) daring, provocative; (*person*) brave; daring, cheeky.

  ¿No te da miedo viajar sola? Eres muy atrevida. You're not afraid of traveling all by yourself? You're really brave.

atrevimiento *m.* nerve

atropellar (a alguien con un vehículo) *v.t.* to run over (someone with a vehicle)

atroz *adj.* atrocious, awful

atún *m.* tuna

audición *f.* hearing; (*test*) audition

auditorio *m.* auditorium; audience; theater

auge *m.* peak

  estar en auge to be on the increase

aula *f.* classroom; lecture hall

  aula magna main lecture hall

aumentar *v.t.* to increase

  aumentar de peso to gain weight

aumento *m.* increase
  aumento de sueldo (*pay*)
  raise
aunque *conj.* although, even
  though
auricular *m.* headphone;
  (*telephone*) receiver
ausencia *f.* absence
ausentarse *v. pron.* to go away
ausente *adj.* absent
australiano/a *adj./m., f.*
  Australian
auténtico/a *adj.* real
autobús *m.* bus
autodidacta *m., f.* self-taught
  person; autodidact
auto(e)stop *m.* hitchhiking
  hacer auto(e)stop to
  hitchhike
auto(e)stopista *m., f.* hitchhiker
autógrafo *m.* autograph
automático/a *adj.* automatic
automóvil *m.* automobile
automovilismo *m.* motor racing
automovilista *m., f.* motorist
autonomía *f.* autonomy
autónomo/a *adj.* (*government*)
  autonomous; *m., f.* (*work*)
  self-employed worker,
  freelancer
autopista *f.* highway; freeway,
  expressway
autor(a) *m., f.* author
  autor intelectual (*L.A.*)
  mastermind (*of a crime*)
autoritario/a *adj.* authoritarian
autoritarismo *m.*
  authoritarianism
autorretrato *m.* self-portrait
auxiliar *v.t.* to help
  ¡Auxilio! *interj.* Help!

avance *m.* advance
avanzado/a *adj.* advanzed
avanzar *v.i.* to advance; to
  move forward
avaricia *f.* avarice
avaricioso/a *adj.* greedy,
  avaricious
avaro/a *m., f.* miser
ave (**el**) *f.* bird
avellana *f.* hazelnut
avellano *m.* hazel tree
avenida *f.* avenue
aventura *f.* adventure
  ...de aventuras adventure
  (*genre*)
aventurero/a *adj.* adventurous;
  m., f. adventurer
avergonzado/a *adj.*
  embarrassed
avergonzar (o:ue) *v.t.* to shame,
  to embarrass
avergonzarse (o:ue) *v. pron.* to
  be ashamed
avería *f.* (*Spain*) (*automobile,
  mechanical*) breakdown
averiado/a *adj.* (*Spain*) broken
  down, out of order
averiarse *v. pron.* (*Spain*) to
  break down
averiguar *v.t.* to find out; to
  check
aversión *f.* aversion, dislike
avestruz *m.* ostrich
avión *m.* airplane
  viajar en avión to travel by
  plane
avioneta *f.* light aircraft
avisar *v.t.* to warn, to inform
aviso *m.* warning, notice
avispa *f.* wasp
axila *f.* armpit

¡Ay! *interj.* Oh!, Ouch!, Yikes!
  ¡Ay, qué dolor! Ouch, it
  hurts!/Oh, what pain!
ayer *adv.* yesterday
ayudar (a) *v.t.* to help (to)
ayudarse *v. pron. (recip.)* to
  help each other
ayunar *v.i.* to fast
ayuno *m.* fast
ayunas: salir en ayunas to go
  out without breakfast
ayuntamiento *m.* city hall
azafrán *m.* saffron
azar *m.* chance; coincidence
  al azar at random, randomly
azúcar *m.* sugar
azucarero *m.* sugar bowl
azul *adj./m.* blue
  azul celeste sky blue
  azul marino navy blue
azulado/a *adj.* bluish
azulejo *m.* (*ceramic*) tile

B

babero *m.* bib
bacalao *m.* cod, codfish
bahía *f.* bay
bailar *v.t.* to dance
bailarín, bailarina *m., f.* dancer
baile *m.* dance
bajar *v.i.* to go down
bajar(se) de (un vehículo) *v.
pron.* to get off/out of (a
vehicle)
bajo/a *adj.* (*person*) short;
(*volume, light, temperature*)
low
  Por favor, hablen más bajo.
  Please speak quietly.
bajo/a *prep.* under

bajo cero below zero
bajo control under control
bajo ningún pretexto under
no circumstances
bajo juramento under oath
balanza *f.* (*for weighing*) scale
balcón *m.* balcony
baldosa *f.* (*floor*) tile
ballena *f.* whale
ballet *m.* ballet
balneario *m.* spa, resort
baloncesto *m.* basketball
balonmano *m.* handball
banana *f.* banana
banco *m.* bank; bench
banda *f.* (*music*) band
  banda sonora sound track
bandera *f.* flag
banquero/a *m., f.* banker
bañarse *v. pron. (refl.)* to
bathe; to take a bath; to
shower
bañera *f.* bathtub
baño *m.* bathroom
baraja (de cartas/naipes) *f.*
deck (of cards)
barato/a *adj.* cheap
barba *f.* beard
barbero *m.* barber
barbudo/a *adj.* bearded
barco *m.* ship
barra (de pan) *f.* (*Spain*) loaf
(of bread)
barrer (el suelo/el piso) *v.t.* to
sweep the floor
barriga *f.* stomach
barrio *m.* neighborhood
barro *m.* mud
barroco/a *adj.* baroque
báscula *f.* scale

bastante *adj.* enough; sufficient; rather
bastar *v.i.* to be enough
  Con esto basta y sobra. This is more than enough.
  Con ocho basta. Eight is enough.
  Dos semanas no bastan para completarlo. Two weeks are not enough to finish it.
bastón *m.* walking stick
basura *f.* trash
basurero *m.* garbage dump; garbage can
basurero/a *m., f.* garbage collector
bata *f.* robe
  bata de baño bathrobe
batidor *m.* whisk
batidora *f.* (*Spain*) blender, mixer
batir *v.t.* to whisk; to beat
  batir un récord mundial to break a world record
baúl *m.* trunk
bautizar *v.t.* to baptize; to name
bautizo *m.* baptism
bazo *m.* spleen
bebé *m., f.* baby
beber *v.t./v.i.* to drink
bebida *f.* drink
  bebida alcohólica *f.* alcoholic beverage
beca *f.* grant; scholarship
béisbol *m.* baseball
belleza *f.* beauty
bello/a *adj.* beautiful
  bellas artes *f., pl.* (fine) arts
bendecir *v.t. irreg.* (**yo bendigo**) to bless
bendición *f.* blessing

beneficiarse *v.t.* to benefit
beneficio *m.* benefit
beneficioso/a *adj.* beneficial
benigno *adj.* benign
berenjena *f.* eggplant
bermellón *m.* vermilion
berrinche *m.* tantrum
besar *v.t.* to kiss
besarse *v. pron.* (*recip.*) to kiss each other
beso *m.* kiss
betabel *f.* (*Mexico*) (*sugar*) beet
biblioteca *f.* library
bibliotecario/a *m., f.* librarian
bicarbonato *m.* baking soda
bicicleta *f.* bicycle
bien *adj.* good; well
bienes raíces *m., pl.* real estate
bienestar *m.* well-being
bienvenida *f.* welcome
  dar la bienvenida to welcome
bienvenido/a *adj.* welcome
bigote(s) *m.* (*pl.*) moustache
bikini *m.* bikini
bilingüe *adj.* bilingual
bilingüismo *m.* bilingualism
billete *m.* (*Spain*) ticket; paper money
  billete de ida y vuelta round-trip ticket
  Vale muchos billetes. It costs a lot of money.
billón *m.* trillion
  Un billón es un millón de millones. One trillion is a million millions.
biodiversidad *f.* biodiversity
biogenética *f.* genetic engineering

biografía *f.* biography
biográfico/a *adj.* biographical
biología *f.* biology
biólogo/a *m., f.* biologist
biosfera *f.* biosphere
bisabuelo/a *m.* great-grandfather; *f.* great-grandmother
bisagra *f.* hinge
bisnieto/a *m.* great-grandson; *f.* great-granddaughter
bistec *m.* steak
bisturí *m.* scalpel
blanco/a *adj.* white
bluejeans *m., pl.* (*L.A.*) jeans
blusa *f.* blouse
boca *f.* mouth
  boca abajo face-down
  boca arriba face-up
bocina *f.* (*automobile*) horn
boda *f.* wedding
  boda concertada arranged marriage
bodega *f.* (*house*) cellar; (*store*) wine cellar
boina *f.* beret
boletín *m.* bulletin, report
  boletín de notas school report
  boletín informativo newsletter
boleto *m.* (*L.A.*) ticket
boliche *m.* bowling
bolígrafo *m.* pen
bolsa *f.* purse; bag
  la Bolsa the stock market
bolsillo *m.* pocket
  libro de bolsillo paperback book
bolsista *m., f.* stockbroker
bolsita *f.* (*diminutive*) small bag

bolsita de té teabag
bolso *m.* shoulder bag
bomba *f.* bomb
bombero/a *m., f.* firefighter
bonito/a *adj.* pretty
bordar *v.t.* to embroider
bordo: a bordo aboard, on board
  ¡Todos a bordo! All aboard!
borracho/a *adj.* drunk
borrador *m.* eraser
borrar *v.t.* to erase
bosque *m.* forest
  bosque nuboso cloud forest
  bosque tropical tropical forest; rain forest
bota *f.* boot
  botas de agua rubber boots
  botas de montar riding boots
botánica *f.* botany
botánico/a *m., f.* botanist; *adj.* botanical
botar *v.t.* (*L.A.*) to throw away
botella *f.* bottle
  botella de vino bottle of wine
botiquín *m.* medicine cabinet
  botiquín de primeros auxilios first-aid kit
botón *m.* button
  botón de rebobinado rewind button
botones *m., sing.* bellhop
boxeador(a) *m., f.* boxer
boxear *v.i.* to box
boxeo *m.* boxing
bragas *f., pl.* (*Spain*) panties
brasier *m.* (*L.A.*) bra
brazo *m.* arm
  Es su brazo derecho. He's her right-hand man.
breve *adj.* brief; short

en breve *adv.* shortly, soon
brevedad *f.* brevity
brillar *v.i.* to shine
brillo (para zapatos) *m.* (*shoe*) polish
brindar *v.t.* (*drink*) to toast
brindis *m.* toast
brisa *f.* breeze
brócoli *m.* broccoli
broma *f.* joke
  broma pesada practical joke
  bromas aparte joking aside
  en broma in jest, as a joke
  hacer bromas to make jokes
bromista *m., f.* joker
bronce *m.* bronze
bronceado/a *adj.* sun-tanned
bronceador *m.* suntan lotion
broncear *v.t.* to tan
broncearse *v. pron.* to (get a) tan
buceador(a) *m., f.* (*underwater*) diver
bucear *v.i.* to scuba dive
budista *adj./m., f.* Buddhist
buen, bueno/a *adj.* good
  Buen viaje. Have a good trip.
  Buena idea. Good idea.
  Buenas noches. Good evening.; Good night.
  Buenas tardes. Good afternoon.
  buenísimo/a *adj.* (*superlative*) extremely good
  ¿Bueno? Hello? (*on telephone*)
  (No) Es bueno que ... It's (not) good that ...
  (No) Es bueno que corras. It's (not) good that you run.
  Buenos días. Good morning.

bueno *adv.* well
bufanda *f.* scarf
búho *m.* owl
buitre *m.* vulture
bujía *f.* spark plug
bulevar *m.* boulevard
bulto *m.* bundle, package
buque *m.* boat, ship
burbuja *f.* bubble
buscar *v.t.* to look for
búsqueda *f.* search
buzón *m.* mailbox

C

caballero *m.* gentleman
caballo *m.* horse
  montado/a a caballo on horseback
cabaña *f.* cabin
cabello *m.* hair
caber *v.i. irreg.* (**yo quepo**) to fit
  Esta mesa no cabe aquí. This table doesn't fit here.
  Esta falda no me cabe. This skirt doesn't fit me.
  no cabe duda (de) que... there's no doubt that...
cabeza *f.* head
cable *m.* cable
  echarle un cable a alguien *idiom.* to help somebody out
cada *adj.* each
cadáver *m.* corpse
cadena *f.* chain
  cadena perpetua life imprisonment; life sentence
cadena *f.* channel (TV)
cadera *f.* hip
caer *v.t. irreg.* (**yo caigo**) to fall
caerse *v. pron. irreg.* (**yo me caigo**) to fall (down)

café *m.* (*place*) café, coffee shop; (*drink*) coffee; (*color*) brown
cafeína *f.* caffeine
cafetera *f.* coffee maker
cafetería *f.* cafeteria
caída *f.* fall
   caída libre free fall
caído *p.p. of* caer fallen;
   caído/a *adj.* fallen
caja *f.* box; cash register
   caja de música music box
   caja fuerte safe
cajero/a *m., f.* cashier
   cajero automático automatic teller machine (ATM)
calabaza *f.* pumpkin
calamar *m.* squid
calavera *m.* skull
calcetín *m.* sock
calculadora *f* calculator
calcular *v.t.* to calculate, to work out
cálculo *m.* calculation, estimate
caldo *m.* broth, soup
   caldo de patas (Ecuador) beef soup
   caldo de gallina chicken soup
   caldo de res beef soup
calefacción *f.* heating
calendario *m.* calendar
calentador *m.* heater
calentar (e:ie) *v.t.* to heat
calentarse (e:ie) *v. pron.* to warm up
calidad *f.* quality
caliente *adj.* hot
calificación *f.* grade
calificar *v.t.* to grade

calificarse *v. pron.* to qualify
callado/a *adj.* (*person*) quiet
calle *m.* street
callejón *m.* alley
   callejón sin salida dead end, blind alley
calor *m.* heat
caloría *f.* calorie
calvo/a *adj.* bald
calzado *m.* shoes
calzar *v.t.* to take size . . . shoes
   Calzo un 38. I take size 38.
calzarse *v. pron.* to put one's shoes on
calzoncillos *m., pl.* men's underwear
   calzoncillos largos long underwear
cama *f.* bed
camara *f.* camera
   cámara digital *f.* digital camera
   cámara de video video camera
camarero/a *m.* waiter; *f.* waitress
camarón *m.* shrimp
camarote *m.* (*ship*) cabin
cambiar (de/en) *v.t.* to change
   cambiar de casa to move
   cambiar de marcha to shift gears
cambio *m.* change; exchange rate
   a cambio de in exchange for
   cambio de marchas gearshift
   cambio de moneda currency exchange
   cambio de velocidades gearshift

en cambio on the other hand

camello m. camel

camerino m. (*theater*) dressing room

camilla f. stretcher

caminar v.i. to walk

camino m. road, path

De camino a casa, me perdí. On my way home, I got lost.

camión m. truck

camionero/a m., f. truck driver

camioneta f. pickup truck

camisa f. shirt

camiseta f. t-shirt

campana f. bell

campeón, campeona m., f. champion

campeonato m. championship

campestre adj. rural

campo m. countryside; field

la gente del campo country people

campo de fútbol soccer field

campo de golf golf course

cana f. gray hair

echar una cana al aire idiom. to let one's hair down

canadiense adj./m., f. Canadian

canal m. (TV) channel

canario m. canary

cancha f. court, field

canción f. song

candidato/a m., f. candidate

candidato a la presidencia presidential candidate

canela f. cinnamon

cangrejo m. crab

canguro m. kangaroo

cansado/a (de + inf.) adj. tired (of + gerund)

Estoy cansado de esperar. I'm tired of waiting.

cansancio m. fatigue

cansarse v. pron. to tire oneself out

cantante m., f. singer

cantar v.t. to sing

cantidad f. amount

cantimplora f. water bottle, canteen

caña f. cane

caña de azúcar sugar cane

caña de pescar fishing rod

cañería f. pipe

capacitación f. training

capilla f. chapel

capital m. (*finance*) capital

capital f. capital city

capítulo m. chapter

capó m. (*car*) hood

capricho m. whim

cápsula f. capsule

capturar v.t. to capture

cara f. face

cara a cara face to face

¡Caramba! interj. Darn! Shoot! Gosh!

caracol m. snail

caradura adj./m., f. cheeky (*person*)

¡Qué cara más dura tienes! You've got some nerve!

caravana f. trailer

carbohidrato m. carbohydrate

carbón m. coal

carburador m. carburator

cárcel f. prison, jail

cardiología f. cardiology

carencia f. lack, (*supplies, food*) shortage

caribeño/a *adj./m., f.* Caribbean (person)

caricia *f.* caress

caries *f.* (*sing. or pl.*) cavity, cavities

cariño *m.* affection

cariñoso/a *adj.* affectionate, loving

carisma *m.* charisma

carne *f.* meat

  carne de res beef

  carne picada/molida ground beef

carnicería *f.* butcher shop

carnicero/a *m., f.* butcher

carnívoro/a *adj.* carnivorous; *m.,* carnivore

caro/a *adj.* expensive

carpeta *f.* folder

carpintería *f.* carpenter's workshop; (*activity*) carpentry

carpintero/a *m., f.* carpenter

carrera *f.* (*profession*) career; (*sports*) race

  a la carrera on the run

  carrera ciclista bicycle race

  carrera contra reloj time trial

  carrera de caballos horse race

  carrera de fondo long-distance race

  carrera de obstáculos obstacle course

  carrera de relevos relay race

  carrera pedestre foot race

  Está en la cima de su carrera. She's at the peak of her career.

carretera *f.* highway

carretilla *f.* wheelbarrow

carril *m.* (*highway*) lane

carro *m.* (*L.A.*) automobile, car; (*Spain*) cart

  carro de bomberos fire engine

  carro de carreras racecar

  carro deportivo sports car

carroza *f.* (*carnival*) float

carta *f.* letter; (*playing*) card

cartel *m.* poster

cartera *f.* wallet

cartero/a *m., f.* mail carrier

casa *f.* house; home

  casa de apartamentos apartment building

  en casa at home

casado/a *adj.* married

casar *v.t.* to marry

casarse (con) *v. pron.* to get married (to)

cascanueces *m., sing.* nutcracker

casco *m.* helmet

casero/a *adj.* (*meal*) homemade, home style

casi *adv.* almost

caso *m.* case

  el caso es que the thing is that

  en caso de in case of

caspa *f.* dandruff

castaña *f.* chestnut

castaño/a *adj.* (*hair, eyes*) brown

castellano *m.* (*language*) Spanish, Castilian

castellano/a *adj./m., f.* Castilian

castigar *v.t.* to punish

castigo *m.* punishment

castillo *m.* castle

casualidad *f.* chance, coincidence
por (pura) casualidad by (sheer) chance
¡Qué casualidad! What a coincidence!

catarata *f.* waterfall

catarro *m.* cold

catástrofe *f.* catastrophe

catastrófico/a *adj.* catastrophic

catedral *f.* cathedral
como una catedral (*fam.*) huge, enormous
una mentira como una catedral a whopper of a lie

catedrático/a *m., f.* professor; department head

categoría *f.* category
de categoría fine, first-rate, excellent
un restaurante de categoría a first-rate restaurant
un escritor de poca categoría a second-rate writer

católico/a *adj./m., f.* Catholic

catorce fourteen

cava *m.* sparkling wine

caverna *f.* cavern

cavernícola *adj./m., f.* cave dweller; caveman

caza *f.* (*sport*) hunting

cazador(a) *m., f.* hunter

cazar *v.t.* to hunt

cazuela *f.* casserole

cebolla *f.* onion

cebra *f.* zebra

paso cebra (*Spain*) crosswalk

ceder *v.t.* to give in; to give way
ceder el paso to yield (the right of way)
Discutieron hasta que el más sensato cedió. They argued until the most sensible one gave in.

cederrón *m.* CD-ROM

cedro *m.* cedar

ceja *f.* eyebrow

celebrar *v.t.* to celebrate

celos *m., pl.* jealousy
Tiene celos de su hermanita. She is jealous of her little sister.

celoso/a *adj.* jealous

célula *f.* cell

celular *adj.* (*phone*) cellular

celulitis *f.* cellulite

cementerio *m.* cemetery

cemento *m.* cement

cena *f.* dinner, supper

cenar *v.i.* to have dinner, to dine
¿Qué hay para cenar? What's for dinner?

cenicero *m.* ashtray

ceniza *f.* ash

censo *m.* census

censura *f.* censorship; censure

censurar *v.t.* to censor; to censure

centro *m.* center; (*city*) downtown
centro comercial shopping mall/center
centro de gravedad center of gravity

centro de atención center of attention
cepillar *v.t.* to brush
cepillarse (el pelo/los dientes) *v. pron.* to brush one's hair/teeth
cepillo *m.* brush
  cepillo de dientes toothbrush
  cepillo de pelo hairbrush
cera *f.* wax
cerámica *f.* pottery
ceramista *m., f.* ceramist
cerca de *adv.* near
cercano/a *adj.* near; (*relative*) close
  Cercano Oriente Near East
cerdo *m.* (*animal*) pig; (*meat*) pork
cereales *m., pl.* cereal; grains
cerebro *m.* brain
cereza *f.* cherry
cerezo *m.* cherry tree
cerilla *f.* match
cero *m.* zero
cerrado *p.p. of* **cerrar** closed
cerrado/a *adj.* closed
cerrajero/a *m., f.* locksmith
cerrajería *f.* locksmith's shop
cerrar (e:ie) *v.t.* to close
cerrarse (e:ie) *v. pron.* to close
  La puerta se cerró lentamente. The door closed slowly.
cerrojo *m.* (*lock*) bolt
  correr/echar el cerrojo to bolt the door
certeza *f.* certainty
cerveza *f.* beer
césped *m.* grass

cesta *f.* basket
ceviche *m.* marinated fish dish
  ceviche de camarón marinated shrimp
chal *m.* shawl
chaleco *m.* vest
champán *m.* champagne
champiñón *m.* mushroom
champú *m.* shampoo
chantaje *m.* blackmail
chantajear *v.t.* to blackmail
chantajista *m., f.* blackmailer
chaqueta *f.* jacket
charlatán, charlatana *m., f.* chatterbox; *adj.* talkative
chau *fam.* bye
cheque *m.* (*bank*) check
  cheque de viajero traveler's check
  cheque en blanco blank check
chequeo (médico) *m.* (*L.A.*) physical exam
chévere *adj., fam.* terrific, great, cool
chicle *m.* chewing gum
chico/a *m.* boy; *f.* girl
chimenea *f.* chimney; fireplace
chino *m.* (*language*) Chinese
chino/a *adj./m., f.* Chinese
chismes *m., pl.* gossip
chiste *m.* joke
chistoso/a *adj.* funny, amusing
chocar (con, contra) *v.i.* to crash, to collide; to run into; to hit (*a car*); to dislike (**me choca**)
chocolate *m.* chocolate
chofer/chófer *m.* chauffeur, driver

choque *m.* collision; (crash) car accident
chuleta *f. (food)* chop
  chuleta de cerdo pork chop
cibercafé *m.* cybercafé
cicatriz *f.* scar
cicatrizar *v.i.* to scar, to heal
ciclismo *m.* cycling
ciclista *m., f.* cyclist
ciego/a *adj.* blind
  a ciegas *adv.* blindly
cielo *m.* sky; heaven
  ¡Cielos! Good heavens!
cien(to) one hundred
  cientos de miles hundreds of thousands
  por ciento percent
  Es cien por cien(to) algodón. It's pure cotton.
ciénaga *f.* swamp
ciencia *f.* science
  (…de) ciencia ficción science-fiction *(genre)*
  ciencias exactas exact sciences
científico/a *adj.* scientific; *m., f.* scientist
cierto/a *adj.* certain; true
  (No) Es cierto. It's (not) true.
  por cierto by the way
ciervo *m.* deer
cifra *f. (arithmetic)* figure, number
cigüeña *f.* stork
cilindro *m.* cylinder
cima *f.* top, summit; peak
cimientos *m., pl. (house, building)* foundations
cinco five
cincuenta fifty

cine *m.* movie theater; movies
  cine mudo silent movies
  cine negro film noir
cineasta *m., f.* filmmaker, director
cinta *f. (audio)* tape; ribbon
  Siempre lleva una cinta en el pelo. She always wears a ribbon in her hair.
cinta caminadora *f.* treadmill
cintura *f.* waist
cinturón *m.* belt
  cinturón de seguridad seat belt
ciprés *m.* cypress
circo *m.* circus
circuito *m. (electric)* circuit
  circuito en serie series circuit
  circuito cerrado closed circuit
circulación *f.* circulation; traffic
  circulación sanguínea blood circulation
círculo *m.* circle
ciruela *f.* plum
cirugía *f.* surgery
cirujano/a *m., f.* surgeon
cisne *m.* swan
cita *f.* date; appointment
cítrico/a *adj.* citrus
ciudad *f.* city
  ciudad natal hometown
ciudadanía *f.* citizenship
ciudadano/a *m., f.* citizen
civilización *f.* civilization
civilizado/a *adj.* civilized
claro/a *adj.* clear; (color) light
  ¡Claro! *interj.* Of course!

¡Claro que sí! *(fam.)* Of course!
clase *f.* class
  clase de ejercicios aeróbicos aerobics class
  clase alta/baja upper/lower class
  clase media middle class
  clase trabajadora working class
clásico/a *adj.* classical
clausura *f.* closing
  ceremonia de clausura closing ceremony
clavado *m.* (*L.A.*) (*high*) dive
clavel *m.* carnation
clavícula *f.* clavicle
clavo *m.* nail
  dar en el clavo *idiom.* to hit the nail on the head
cliente/a *m., f.* customer
clientela *f.* clientele, customers
clima *m.* climate
climatizado/a *adj.* (*place, room*) air-conditioned
climatología *f.* climatology
clínica *f.* clinic
cloaca *f.* sewer
cloro *m.* chlorine
clorofila *f.* chlorophyll
clóset *m.* closet
coartada *f.* alibi
cobarde *adj.* coward
cobardía *f.* cowardice
cobertizo *m.* shed
cobija *f.* (*L.A.*) blanket
cobrar *v.t.* (*check*) to cash; (*rent*) to charge for; (*salary*) to earn
  El dueño de mi casa no me cobra la electricidad. My landlord doesn't charge me for electricity.
  Cobro una miseria. I earn a pittance.
cobre *m.* copper
cocer (o:ue) (c:z) *v.t.* to boil, to cook
  cocer a fuego lento to simmer
coche *m.* (*Spain*) car; automobile
  coche bomba car bomb
  coche cama sleeper, sleeping car
cocina *f.* kitchen; (*Spain*) stove
cocinar *v.t.* to cook
cocinero/a *m., f.* cook; chef
coco *m.* coconut
codo *m.* elbow
codorniz *f.* quail
cofre *m.* (*car*) hood
cohete *m.* rocket
  cohete espacial space rocket
coincidencia *f.* coincidence
  ¡Qué coincidencia! What a coincidence!
coincidir *v.i.* to coincide, to match up
cojín *m.* cushion
cojo/a *adj.* (*person*) lame
col *f.* (*Spain*) cabbage
cola *f.* line; (*animal*) tail
  cola de caballo pony tail
  hacer cola to line up; to stand in line
colaboración *f.* collaboration
colaborar *v.i.* to collaborate
colador *m.* colander

colar (o:ue) *v.t.* to strain, to drain; **colar café** (*L.A.*) to make coffee

colarse (o:ue) (en una fiesta) *v. pron.* to crash (a party)

colchón *m.* mattress
colchón de agua water bed
colchón de muelles spring mattress

coleccionar *v.t.* to collect (*as hobby*)

coleccionismo *m.* collecting

coleccionista *m., f.* collector

colegio *m.* school

colesterol *m.* cholesterol

colgar (o:ue) *v.t.* to hang

colibrí *m.* humming bird

cólico *m.* colic

collar *m.* necklace

colmillo *m.* fang; (*in humans*) eye tooth

colmo: ¡Esto es el colmo! *loc.* That's the last straw!

colocación *f.* placing; arrangement

colocar *v.t.* to place, to put; to arrange

colonia *f.* cologne

colonización *f.* colonization, settling

colonizar *v.t.* to colonize

colono *m.* colonist; settler

coloquio *m.* discussion, talk

color *m.* color

colorear *v.t.* to color

columna *f.* column
columna vertebral spinal column, spine

combustible *m.* fuel

comedia *f.* comedy; play

comedor *m.* dining room

comenzar (e:ie) *v.t./v.i.* to begin

comer *v.t./v.i.* to eat; to have lunch

comercial *adj.* (*movie*) commercial; (*district, operation*) business-related; *m.* (*L.A.*) commercial, advertisement

comestible *adj.* edible

comestibles *m., pl.* groceries

cometa *f.* kite; *m.* comet

comida *f.* food; meal
comida basura junk food
comida rápida fast food

comienzo *m.* beginning
a comienzos de at the beginning of
al comienzo at first, in the beginning

comisaría (de policía) *f.* police station

como *prep.* like, as
Anda despacio como una tortuga. She walks as slowly as a turtle.
Es tan alto como su padre. He's as tall as his father.
Quiero un carro como el tuyo. I want a car like yours.

¿cómo? *adv.* how?; what?
¿Cómo es...? What's . . . like?
¿Cómo está Ud.? *form.* How are you?
¿Cómo estás? *fam.* How are you?
¿Cómo les fue…? *pl.* How did . . . go for you?
¿Cómo se llama Ud.? (*form.*) What's your name?

¿Cómo te llamas (tú)? (*fam.*)
What's your name?
cómoda *f.* chest of drawers,
dresser
cómodo/a *adj.* comfortable
compañerismo *m.* camaraderie
compañero/a *m., f.* companion;
partner; mate
  compañero/a de clase
  classmate
  compañero/a de cuarto
  roommate
compañía *f.* company; firm
  El perro me hace compañía.
  My dog keeps me company.
comparación *f.* comparison
  en comparación con
  compared to/with
comparar *v.t.* to compare
compartir *v.t.* to share
compás *m.* (*tool*) compass;
(*music*) beat, rhythm
competencia *f.* (*L.A.*)
competition, contest
competente *adj.* competent
competidor(a) *m., f.* competitor
competir (e:i) *v.i.* to compete
competitivo/a *adj.* competitive
complejo/a *adj.* complex
completamente *adv.*
completely
complicar *v.t.* to complicate, to
make difficult
cómplice *m., f.* accomplice
comportamiento *m.* behavior
comportarse *v. pron.* to behave
oneself
compositor(a) *m., f.* composer
compra(s) *f.* buy, purchase
  ir de compras to go shopping

  la lista de la compra the
  shopping list
  una buena/mala compra a
  good/bad buy
comprar *v.t.* to buy
comprender *v.t.* to understand
comprensión *f.* understanding
comprobar *v.t.* (o:ue) to check
comprometerse (a/con) *v.*
pron. to promise (to); to get
engaged (to)
  Se comprometió a limpiar
  todas las ventanas. He
  promised to clean all the
  windows.
compromiso *m.* commitment;
engagement
computación *f.* computer
science
computadora *f.* computer
  computadora portátil
  portable computer; laptop
común *adj.* common, shared
comunicación *f.*
communication
comunicar *v.t.* to communicate
comunicarse (con) *v. pron.* to
communicate (with)
comunidad *f.* community
con *prep.* with
  Con él/ella habla. This is
  he/she. (*on the telephone*)
  con tal (de) que provided
  (that)
conciencia *f.* conscience
  a conciencia *adv.*
  conscientiously
concierto *m.* concert
concordar (con) *v.i.* to agree
(with)

concreto *m.* (*L.A.*) concrete

concursar *v.i.* (*contest*) to participate, to take part

concurso *m.* contest; game show

condensar *v.t.* to condense

conducir (c:zc) *v.i.* to drive

conducta *f.* conduct, behavior

conductor(a) *m., f.* chauffeur; driver

conejo *m.* rabbit

conferencia *f.* lecture

confiado/a *adj.* (*person*) trusting

confianza *f.* confidence; trust
  en confianza *adv.* in confidence
  No le tengo mucha confianza. I don't trust him much.
  Es una persona de confianza. She's a trustworthy/reliable person.

confiar (en alguien) *v.t.* to trust (somebody)
  Confía en mí. Trust me.

confirmación *f.* confirmation

confirmar *v.t.* to confirm
  confirmar una reservación to confirm a reservation

confort *m.* comfort

confortable *adj.* comfortable

confundido/a *adj.* confused

confundir *v.t.* to confuse

confusión *f.* confusion

confuso/a *adj.* (*idea, text*) confused, hazy
  Su explicación fue muy confusa. His explanation was very confused.

congelador *m.* freezer

congestionado/a *adj.* (*medicine*) congested; stuffed-up

congreso *m.* conference

conmemoración *f.* commemoration, remembrance
  en conmemoración de in memory of

conmemorar *v.t.* to commemorate

conmigo with me

conocer (c:zc) *v.t.* to know; to be acquainted with; to meet

conocido/a *adj.* (well-)known; familiar

conquista *f.* conquest

conquistador(a) *m., f.* conqueror

conquistar *v.t.* to conquer

consecuencia *f.* consequence
  en consecuencia *adv.* consequently, as a result, therefore; (*to act*) accordingly

conseguir (e:i) *v.t.* to get; to obtain

consejero/a *m., f.* counselor; advisor

consejo *m.* advice
  dar consejos to give advice

consenso *m.* consensus

consentido/a *adj.* spoiled (person)

consentimiento *m.* consent, permission

consentir (e:ie) *v.t.* to consent to, to permit

conserje *m., f.* (*hotel*) receptionist

conservación *f.* (*culinary*) preserving; (*environment*) conservation, protection

conservador(a) *adj./m., f.* conservative

conservar *v.t.* (*culinary*) to preserve; to conserve

considerado/a *adj.* (*person*) considerate

constelación *f.* constellation

constitución *f.* constitution

constructor(a) (de obras) *m., f.* builder, building contractor

construir (y) *v.t.* to build

consulado *m.* consulate

consultar *v.t.* (*dictionary, facts*) to look up

consultorio *m.* doctor's office

consumidor(a) *m., f.* consumer

consumir *v.t.* consume
  consumir alcohol to consume alcohol

consumo *m.* consumption, intake

contabilidad *f.* accounting

contador(a) *m., f.* accountant

contagiar *v.t.* (*disease*) to pass on

contagio *m.* contagion

contagioso/a *adj.* contagious

contaminación *f.* pollution; contamination
  contaminación del aire/del agua air/water pollution

contaminado/a *m., f.* polluted

contaminar *v.t.* to pollute

contar (o:ue) *v.t.* to count; to tell
  Contamos contigo. We count on you.

contemplar *v.t.* to contemplate, to gaze at

contemporáneo/a *adj.* contemporary

contentarse (con) *v. pron.* to be pleased (with), to be happy (with)

contento/a *adj.* happy; content

contestadora *f.* answering machine

contestar *v.t.* to answer

contigo with you
  Contigo o sin ti. With or without you.

continuar *v.t.* (*yo continúo*) to continue
  La novela continúa en el segundo tomo. The novel continues in the second volume.

contra *prep.* against
  dos contra uno two against one
  Estoy totalmente en contra. I'm totally against it.
  Chocó contra un árbol. He crashed into a tree.

contradecir (a alguien) *v.t. irreg.* (*yo contradigo*) to contradict (somebody)

contradecirse *v. pron. irreg.* (*yo me contradigo*) to contradict oneself

contradicción *f.* contradiction

contraponer *v.t. irreg.* (*yo contrapongo*) to contrast

contrario *m.* contrary, opposite; *adj.* opposite
  al contrario *adv.* on the contrary, quite the opposite

contrarreloj *adj.* timed
  a contrarreloj against the
  clock
contraseña *f.* password
contratar *v.t.* to hire
contrato *m.* contract; lease
contrincante *m., f.* opponent
control *m.* control
  control de natalidad birth
  control
  control remoto remote
  control
controlar *v.t.* to control
convencer (c:z) *v.t.* to convince
convento *m.* convent
conversación *f.* conversation
conversar *v.i.* to talk, to
  converse, to chat
convertirse (e:ie) (en) *v. pron.*
  to become; to turn into
  convertirse en rana to turn
  into a frog
  convertirse en realidad to
  come true
convicción *f.* conviction
convincente *adj.* convincing
convivencia *f.* coexistence
convivir *v.i.* (*people*) to live
  together; (*ideas, ideologies*)
  to coexist
copa *f.* wineglass; goblet
copiar *v.t.* to copy
coqueta *f.* flirt, coquette
coquetear *v.i.* to flirt
corazón *m.* heart
corbata *f.* tie
corcho *m.* cork
cordero *m.* lamb
cordillera (montañosa) *f.*
  (mountain) range

cordón *m.* shoelace
coro *m.* choir, chorus
corpulento/a *adj.* (*person*)
  hefty
correa *m.* belt
corrección *f.* correction;
  correctness
correcto/a *adj.* correct
corredor(a) (de bolsa) *m., f.*
  stockbroker
corregir (e:i) (g:j) *v.t.* to correct
correo *m.* post office; mail
  correo electrónico e-mail
correr *v.i.* to run; to jog
correspondencia *f.* mail
corrido *p.p. of* **correr** run
corrida (de toros) *f.* bullfight
corriente *f.* (*electricity*) current
  corriente alterna alternating
  current, AC
  corriente continua direct
  current, DC
  corriente eléctrica electric
  current
  contra corriente aginst the
  tide
  estar al corriente to be up to
  date
  ponerse al corriente to catch
  up
  **seguirle la corriente (a
  alguien)** to humor
  (somebody), to play along
  with (somebody)
cortacésped *f.* lawnmower
cortar *v.t.* to chop; to slice; to
  cut
  cortar el pasto to mow the
  lawn
corte *f.* cut; (*L.A.*) court (of law)

corte longitudinal lengthwise section

Corte Suprema Supreme Court

corte transversal cross section

cortés *adj.* courteous

cortesía *f.* courtesy

cortina *f.* curtain

correr las cortinas to draw the curtains

corto/a *adj.* short (*in length*)

cortocircuito *m.* short circuit

cosa *f.* thing

cosecha *f.* harvest

cosechar *v.t.* to harvest

coser *v.t.* to sew

costa *f.* coastline, coast

costar (o:ue) *f.* to cost

costar un ojo de la cara *idiom* to cost an arm and a leg

costero/a *adj.* coastal

costilla *f.* rib

costumbre *f.* habit, custom

cotillear *v.i.* (*Spain*) to gossip

cotilleo *m.* (*Spain*) gossip

cráneo *m.* skull

cráter *m.* crater

creador(a) *m., f.* creator

crear *v.t.* to create

creativo/a *adj.* creative

crecer (c:zc) *v.i.* to grow

creciente *adj.* increasing, growing

crecimiento *m.* growth

crédito *m.* credit

creer (en) *v.t.* to believe (in); to think

Creo que no. I don't think so.

no creer not to believe

creído *p.p. of* **creer** believed

crema *f.* cream

crema antiarrugas anti-wrinkle cream

crema de afeitar shaving cream

crema hidratante moisturizer

cremallera *f.* zipper

cremoso/a *adj.* creamy

crepúsculo *m.* (*evening*) twilight; (*morning*) dawn

criar *v.t.* (*children*) to raise, to bring up

crimen *m.* crime; murder

crisis *f.* crisis

crisis de los cuarenta midlife crisis

crisis nerviosa nervous breakdown

crisis respiratoria respiratory failure

cristal *m.* crystal; glass

cristalería *f.* glassware

cristiano/a *adj./m., f.* Christian

criticar *v.t.* to criticize

crítico/a *m., f.* critic

crítico de arte art critic

cronometrar *v.t.* to time

cronómetro *m.* chronometer; stopwatch

cruce *m.* crossroads

crucero *m.* cruise

crucigrama *m.* crossword

cruda *f.* (*Mexico*) hangover

tener cruda to have a hangover

crudo/a *adj.* (*food*) raw

crujiente *adj.* crunchy; (*bread*) crusty

cruz *f.* cross
  Cruz Roja Red Cross
cruzar *v.t.* to cross
cuaderno *m.* notebook
cuadra *f.* (city) block
cuadrado *m.* square
cuadrilátero *m.* (*boxing*) ring; (*baseball*) home run
cuadro *m.* picture
  cuadros, (de) *m., pl.* plaid
  una falda de cuadros a plaid skirt
¿cuál(es)? *pron.* which?; which one(s)?; what?
  ¿Cuál te gusta más? Which one do you like best?
  ¿Cuál es la fecha (de hoy)? What is the date (today)?
cuando *conj.* when
  Cuando estoy triste, canto. When I'm sad, I sing.
  de cuando en cuando *loc.* every so often
  de vez en cuando *loc.* now and then; from time to time
¿cuándo? *adv.* when?
  ¿Cuándo terminas? When do you finish?
  No sé cuándo termina. I don't know when he finishes.
cuanto: cuanto antes as soon as possible
  Envíemela cuanto antes. Send it to me as soon as possible.
¿cuánto/a? *adv.* how much?
  ¿Cuánto cuesta? How much does it cost?
  ¿Cuánto tiempo hace que esperas? How long have you been waiting?

  ¿cuántos/as? *adv.* how many?
  ¿Cuántos años tienes? How old are you?
cuarenta forty
cuarto *m.* room
  cuarto de baño bathroom
cuarto/a *adj., m.* fourth
cuatro four
cuatrocientos/as four hundred
cubertería *f.* cutlery
cubierto *p.p. of* **cubrir** covered
cubiertos *m., pl.* silverware
cubrir *v.t.* to cover
cucaracha *f.* cockroach
cuchara *f.* (*table or large*) spoon
cucharita *f.* teaspoon
cucharón *m.* ladle
cuchillo *m.* knife
cuello *m.* neck
cuenta *f.* bill; account
  a fin de cuentas all things considered, after all
  A fin de cuentas, es mejor esperar que irse. All things considered, it's better to wait than to leave.
  A fin de cuentas, ¿a quién le importa? After all, who cares?
  cuenta corriente checking account
  cuenta de ahorros savings account
  en resumidas cuentas to make a long story short
  por mi cuenta on my own
cuentakilómetros *m., sing.* odometer, speedometer
cuento *m.* short story

cuerda *f.* rope
cuero *m.* leather
cuerpo *m.* body
cuestión *f.* issue, matter
  Es un experto en cuestiones de historia medieval. He's an expert in matters of medieval history.
cuestionar *v.t.* to question
cuestionarse *v. pron.* to ask oneself
  Tenemos que cuestionarnos si es válida la conclusión. We have to ask ourselves if the conclusion is valid.
cuidado *m.* care; *interj.* Watch out!
cuidar *v.t.* to take care of
cuidarse *v. pron.* to take care of oneself
culpa *f.* fault
  echar la culpa a alguien to blame someone
  tener la culpa to be to blame
culpable *adj.* guilty; *m., f.* guilty person
culpar *v.t.* to blame
cultivar *v.t.* to grow
cultura *f.* culture
  Tiene mucha cultura. She's a highly educated person.
culturismo *m.* bodybuilding
cumpleaños *m., sing.* birthday
cumplir años *v.t.* to have a birthday
  ¿Cuántos años cumples? How old are you?
cumplir (con) *v.i.* (*duty*) to carry out
  Cumplí con mi deber. I did my duty.

cuna *f.* cradle
cuñado/a *m.* brother-in-law; *f.* sister-in-law
cura *f.* cure; *m.* priest
curar *v.t.* to cure
curita *f.* adhesive bandage
currículum *m.* (*Spain*) résumé; curriculum vitae
curso *m.* course
curva *f.* curve, bend
  curva peligrosa sharp bend
custodiar *v.t.* to guard
cutis *m.* skin, complexion
  limpieza de cutis skin cleansing

D

dados *m., pl.* (*game*) dice
dama *f.* lady
damas (chinas) *f., pl.* (*game*) checkers
danza *f.* dance
dañar *v.t.* to damage; to harm; to break down
dañarse *v. pron.* to get damaged; (*food*) to go bad
dañino/a *adj.* harmful
daño *m.* damage, harm
dar *v.t. irreg.* (**yo doy**) to give
  dar a luz (a) to give birth (to)
  dar de comer to feed
  dar direcciones to give directions
  dar en el clavo *idiom* to hit the nail on the head
  dar lo mismo to not matter
  dar un consejo to give advice
  dar un paseo to go for a walk
  dar vuelta to turn

Me da lo mismo si vienes o no. It doesn't matter to me if you come or not.

dardos *m., pl.* (*game*) darts

darse con *v. pron. irreg.* to bump into; to run into
darse cuenta de (que) to realize, to become aware of
Gustavo se dio cuenta de que tenía que salir por la puerta de atrás. Gustavo realized he would have to leave by the back door.
darse prisa to hurry (up); to rush
darse vuelta to turn

de *prep.* of; from
¿de quién(es)? whose?
¿De dónde eres? *fam.* Where are you from?
¿De dónde es Ud.? *form.* Where are you from?
¿De parte de quién? Who is calling? (*on telephone*)
de ida y vuelta roundtrip
de repente suddenly, all of a sudden

debajo de *prep.* below; under

debate *m.* debate

debatir *v.t.* to debate

deber (+ inf.) *v. aux.* to have to; should; must
Deberías salir más temprano. You should leave earlier.

deber *m.* responsibility; obligation; duty
Tu deber es esperar aquí. Your duty is to wait here.

deberes *m., pl.* homework

debido *adj.* appropriate
a su debido tiempo in due course
con el debido respeto with all due respect
debido a (que) *loc.* due to, owing to (the fact that); because of
No hubo partido debido a la lluvia. There was no match because of the rain.

débil *adj.* weak

década *f.* decade
la década de los sesenta the sixties

decadencia *f.* decadence; decline

decaer *v. irreg.* (**yo decaigo**) to decay, to decline; to deteriorate

decano/a *m., f.* (*university*) dean

decepcionado/a *adj.* disappointed

decepcionarse *v.t.* to be disappointed

decidido *p.p. of* **decidir** decided

decidido/a *adj.* (*person*) determined

decidir (+ inf.) *v.t.* to decide

decidirse *v. pron.* to make up one's mind
¡Decídete de una vez! Come on, make up your mind!

décimo/a *adj.* tenth

decir *m.* a saying
Es sólo un decir. It's just a manner of speaking.

decir *v.t.* (**e:i**) to say; to tell

¿Diga? Hello? (*on the telephone*)

No me diga(s). You don't say.

decisión *f.* decision
  tomar una decisión to make a decision

declarar *v.t.* to declare; to say

decorado *m.* (*theater*) set

decorar *v.t.* to decorate; (*food*) to garnish

dedicación *f.* dedication

dedicar *v.t.* to dedicate

dedicatoria *f.* dedication

dedo *m.* finger; (*del pie*) toe

defecto *m.* fault, defect

defectuoso/a *adj.* faulty, defective

defender *v.t.* to defend, to protect

defensa *f.* defense
  defensa personal self-defense

deficiencia *f.* deficiency, shortcoming

déficit *m.* deficit

definición *f.* definition

definir *v.t.* to define

deforestación *f.* deforestation

defunción *f.* death

dejar *v.t.* to let; to quit; to leave (behind); to drop off; to allow
  dejar una propina to leave a tip

dejar de (+ inf.) *v.i.* to stop (*doing something*)

del (*contraction of* de + el) of the; from the

delantal *m.* apron

delante de *prep.* in front of

deleite *m.* delight

delfín *m.* dolphin

delgado/a *adj.* thin; slender

delicioso/a *adj.* delicious

delincuencia *f.* crime, delinquency

delincuente *m., f.* criminal

delineante *m.* draftsman, *f.* draftswoman

delinear *v.t.* to deliniate; to outline

delito *m.* crime, offense

demás (lo/los/las) *pron.* the rest

demasiado *adv.* too much

democracia *f.* democracy

demócrata *m., f.* democrat

democrático/a *adj.* democratic

demostración *f.* proof

demostrar *v.t.* to prove

densidad *f.* density

dentadura *f.* teeth
  dentadura postiza false teeth
  tener buena/mala dentadura to have good/bad teeth

dentista *m., f.* dentist

dentro *adv.* (*space*) inside

dentro de within
  Llámame dentro de dos horas. Call me within two hours.

denuncia *f.* report

denunciar *v.t.* (*crime*) to report

departamento *m.* department

depender (de) *v.t.* to depend (on)
  Eso no depende de mí. That doesn't depend on me.

dependiente/a *m., f.* clerk

depilarse *v.t.* (*eyebrows*) to pluck; (*legs*) to shave, to wax

deporte *m.* sport

deportista *m., f.* sports person

deportivo/a *adj.* sports-loving, sports-related

depositar *v.t.* to deposit

depósito *m.* tank

   depósito de gasolina gas tank

depredador(a) *adj.* predatory

depredador *m.* predator

depresión *f.* depression

deprimido/a *adj.* depressed

deprimirse *v. pron.* to get depressed

derecha *f.* right

   a la derecha (de) to the right (of)

derecho/a *adj.* straight

derecho *adv.* straight (ahead)

   (todo) derecho straight ahead

   Siga (todo) derecho. Keep on going straight.

derechos *m., pl.* rights

deriva *f.* drift

   a la deriva adrift

dermatólogo/a *m., f.* dermatologist

derramar *v.t.* (*liquid*) to spill

derramarse *v. pron.* (*liquid*) to spill over, to run over

derrame *m.* spillage; (*medical*) hemorrhage

derretir *v.t.* to melt

   El calor derritirá la mantequilla. The heat will melt the butter

derretirse *v. pron.* to melt

   El helado se derritió. The ice cream melted.

derrota *f.* defeat

derrotar *v.t.* to defeat, to beat (*an opponent*)

desactivar *v.t.* to defuse

desafiar *v.t.* to challenge

desafinado/a *adj.* out of tune

desafío *m.* challenge

desafortunadamente *adv.* unfortunately

desagradecido/a *adj.* ungrateful

desagüe *m.* wastepipe, drainpipe

desanimado/a *adj.* downhearted

desaparecer *v.t.* to disappear

desaparecido/a *adj.* missing

desaparición *f.* disappearance

desarreglado/a *adj.* unkempt, messy

desarrollar *v.t.* to develop

desarrollo *m.* development

desastre *m.* disaster

   desastre natural natural disaster

desastroso/a *adj.* disastrous

desatascar *v.t.* to unblock, to clear

desayunar *v.t.* to have breakfast

desayuno *m.* breakfast

descafeinado/a *adj.* decaffeinated

descalificación *f.* (*sports*) disqualification

descalificar *v.* (*sports*) to disqualify

descalzarse *v. pron.* to take off one's shoes

descampado *m.* open ground

en un descampado in/on open ground
descansar *v.i.* to rest
descanso *m.* rest
descapotable *adj./m.* (*automobile*) convertible
descarga *f.* (*electricity*) discharge
  descarga eléctrica electric shock
descargar *v.t.* to download
descarrilamiento *m.* derailment
descarrilar *v.t.* to derail
descender *v.i.* to descend
descendiente *m., f.* descendant
descenso *m.* descend; (*temperatures, prices*) fall, decline, decrease
descifrar *v.t.* to decipher, to decode
descompuesto/a *adj. (L.A.)* not working; out of order
desconfiado/a *adj.* distrustful
desconfiar (de alguien) *v.i.* distrust
descontar *v.t.* to discount; to give a discount
descremado/a *adj.* (*dairy products*) skimmed
describir *v.t.* to describe
descrito/a *p.p.* of **describir** described
descubierto *p.p. of* **descubrir** discovered
descubrimiento *m.* discovery
descubrir *v.t.* to discover
descuento *m.* discount
desde *prep.* from; *conj.* since

Les llamé desde Japón. I called them from Japan.
  ¿Desde cuándo lo sabes? Since when have you known it?
desear *v.t.* to wish, to desire
desechable *adj.* disposable
desechar *v.t.* (*leftovers*) to throw away
desembocadura *f.* (*river*) mouth
desempacar *v.t./intrans.* to unpack
desempleo *m.* unemployment
desengañar *v.t.* to disillusion
desengaño *m.* disappointment
desenvolver (o:ue) *v.t.* to unwrap
deseo *m.* desire, wish
desértico/a *adj.* pertaining to the desert, desert-like
desesperación *f.* desperation
desesperado/a *adj.* desperate
desesperanza *f.* despair
desesperar *v.t.* to exasperate
  La lentitud del tren le desesperó. The slowness of the train exasperated him.
desesperarse *v. pron.* to despair, to give up hope
  No te desesperes; todo saldrá bien. Don't give up hope; everything will be fine.
desfavorable *adj.* unfavorable
desfile *m.* parade
desgraciado/a *adj.* unhappy, unfortunate; *m., f.* wretch
desgracia *f.* misfortune
desgraciadamente *adv.* unfortunately

37

deshelar (e:ie) *v.t.* to defrost

deshelarse (e:ie) *v. pron.* (*ice*) to melt; (*river, lake*) to thaw

deshidratar *v.t.* to dehydrate

deshielo *m.* thaw

deshonesto/a *adj.* dishonest

desierto *m.* desert

desigualdad *f.* inequality

desilusionado/a *adj.* disappointed

desinfectante *adj./m.* disinfectant

desinfectar *v.t.* to disinfect

desintoxicación *f.* detoxification

desintoxicar *v.t.* to detoxify

desmayarse *v. pron.* to faint

desnatado/a *adj.* (*dairy products*) skimmed

desobedecer *v.t.* to disobey

desodorante *m.* deodorant

desordenado/a *adj.* disorderly

despacio *adv.* slowly

despedida *f.* farewell; good-bye

despedir (e:i) *v.* to fire

despedirse (de) (e:i) *v. pron.* to say good-bye (to)

despegar *v.i.* (*airplane, rocket*) to take-off

despegue *m.* (*airplane, rocket*) takeoff

despeinado/a *adj.* disheveled, unkempt

despejado/a *adj.* (*sky*) clear

despensa *f.* pantry

despertador *m.* alarm clock

despertarse (e:ie) *v. pron.* to wake up

despistado/a *adj.* absent-minded, forgetful; *m., f.* scatterbrain

desplazamiento *m.* movement; trip

desplazarse *v. pron.* to move (*from one place to another*); to travel

después (de) *adv.* afterwards; then

  después de after

  después de que after

destacar *v.t.* to emphasize, to stress

destino *m.* destination, destiny

destornillador *m.* screwdriver

destrucción *f.* destruction

destruir (y) *v.t.* to destroy

desventaja *f.* disadvantage

desvestirse (e:i) *v. pron.* to get undressed, to undress

detalle *m.* detail

detallista *adj./m., f.* perfectionist

detención *f.* arrest

detener *v.t. irreg.* (**yo detengo**) (*vehicle*) to stop; (*person*) to arrest

detenido *p.p. of* **detener** arrested

detenido/a *adj.* detained; under arrest

  estar detenido to be under arrest

detractor(a) *m., f.* detractor; critic

detrás de *adv.* behind

devolución *f.* (*purchase*) return; (*money*) refund

devolver (o:ue) *v.t.* to take back; to return (*merchandise*)

día *m.* day

  día de fiesta holiday

día laborable work day
diabetes *f.* diabetes
diabético/a *adj./m., f.* diabetic
diagnosticar *v.t.* to diagnose
diagnóstico *m.* diagnostic
diálogo *m.* dialogue
diamante *m.* diamond
diapositiva *f.* slide
diario *m.* diary; newspaper
diario/a *adj.* daily
diarrea *f.* diarrhea
dibujar *v.t.* to draw
dibujo *m.* drawing
  dibujos animados *m., pl.* (*animated*) cartoons
diccionario *m.* dictionary
dicho *m.* saying
dicho *p.p. of* **decir** said
diciembre *m.* December
dictador(a) *m., f.* dictator
dictadura *f.* dictatorship
diecinueve nineteen
dieciocho eighteen
dieciséis sixteen
diecisiete seventeen
diente *m.* tooth
dieta *f.* diet
  a dieta on a diet
  comer una dieta equilibrada to eat a balanced diet
diez ten
diferencia *f.* difference
  a diferencia de in contrast to, unlike
diferente *adj.* different
difícil *adj.* hard; difficult
dificultad *f.* difficulty, hardship
dificultar *v.t.* to make difficult
difunto/a *m., f.* deceased (*person*)
Diga. Hello. (*on telephone*)

diligencia *f.* errand
dimisión *f.* resignation
dimitir *v.i.* to resign
dinamita *f.* dynamite
dinamitar *v.t.* to dynamite
dinastía *f.* dynasty
dinero *m.* money
dinosaurio *m.* dinosaur
Dios *m.* God
  ¡Dios me libre! *loc.* Heaven forbid!
diplomático/a *adj.* diplomatic, tactful; *m., f.* diplomat
dirección *f.* address
dirección electrónica *f.* e-mail address
direcciones *f., pl.* directions
directo *adj.* (*fly*) direct, nonstop
  en directo *adv.* (*radio, TV*) live
director(a) *m., f.* director; (*musical*) conductor
dirigir *v.t.* to direct
disciplina *f.* discipline; (*university*) subject
disco *m.* (computer) disk
  disco compacto compact disc; CD
discoteca *f.* disco(teque)
discreto/a *adj.* discreet, discrete
discriminación *f.* discrimination
disculpa *f.* apology
  pedir disculpas to apologize
disculpar *v.t.* to excuse
disculparse (por) *v. pron.* to apologize for
discurso *m.* speech
discusión *f.* argument

39

discutir *v.t.* to argue; to discuss
diseñador(a) *m., f.* designer
diseño *m.* design
disfraz *m.* costume
disfrazarse de… to wear a… costume
disfrutar (de) *v.t.* to enjoy; to reap the benefits (of)
disfunción *f.* dysfunction
disgusto: a disgusto *adv.* against one's will
   Fui, pero a disgusto. I went, but against my will.
disimular *v.t.* to hide; to conceal; to pretend
disminución *f.* decrease
disminuir (y) *v.i.* (*number*) to decrease; *v.t.* (*price, speed*) to reduce
   Ha disminuido el número de parados. The number of unemployed people has decreased.
   Debes disminuir la velocidad. You have to reduce your speed.
disparar *v.t./v.i.* to shoot, to fire
disparo *m.* shot, gunshot
disponibilidad *f.* availability
disponible *adj.* available
distancia *f.* distance
distinguido/a *adj.* distinguished
distinguir *v.t.* (**yo distingo**) to distinguish
distribución *f.* distribution
distribuir (y) *v.t.* to distribute
divergencia *f.* difference
divergente *adj.* (*opinions*) differing

divergir (e:i) (g:j) *v.i.* to differ
diversión *f.* fun activity; entertainment; recreation
divertido/a *adj.* fun
divertir (e:ie) *v.t.* to entertain
   Pepe nos divirtió con sus historias. Pepe entertained us with his stories.
divertirse (e:ie) *v. pron.* to have fun
divisar *v.t.* to sight
divorciado/a *adj.* divorced
divorciarse (de) *v. pron.* to get divorced (from)
divorcio *m.* divorce
divulgación *f.* spreading
divulgar *v.t.* (*news, information*) to spread
   El chismoso divulgó la noticia por toda la universidad. The gossip spread the news around the whole university.
doblar *v.t.* (*paper, clothes*) to fold; (*corner*) to turn; (*movie*) to dub
doble *adj.* double
doce twelve
docena *f.* dozen
doctor(a) *m., f.* doctor; physician
doctorado *m.* doctorate; Ph.D.
documental *m.* documentary
documentar *v.t.* to document; to provide evidence for
   Estos artículos no documentan nada. These do not provide any evidence.
documentarse *v. pron.* to do research

Tuve que documentarme muy bien para escribir la tesis. I had to do a lot of research to write the thesis.

documento *m.* document

documentos de viaje travel documents

dólar *f.* dollar

doler (o:ue) *v.i.* to hurt

Me duele mucho. It hurts a lot.

dolor *m.* ache; pain

dolor de cabeza headache

doméstico/a *adj.* domestic

dominar *v.t.* to dominate; to master

Aún no domino muy bien el español. I haven't quite mastered Spanish yet.

dominarse *v. pron.* to restrain, to control oneself

domingo *m.* Sunday

dominó *m.* (game) dominoes; (game piece) domino

don/doña title of respect used with a person's first name Mr.; sir/Mrs.; ma'am

dona *f.* donut

donante *m., f.* donor

donde *conj.* where

Están donde las dejaste. They are where you left them.

¿dónde? *adv.* where

¿Dónde está…? Where is…?

¿Dónde están las llaves? Where are the keys?

donjuán *m.* womanizer

dorado/a *adj.* gold, golden

dormir (o:ue) *v.i.* to sleep

dormirse (o:ue) *v. pron.* to go to sleep; to fall asleep; to oversleep

Llego un poco tarde; me dormí. I'm a bit late; I overslept.

dormitorio *m.* bedroom

dos two

dos veces twice; two times

doscientos/as two hundred

drama *m.* drama; play

dramático/a *adj.* dramatic

dramaturgo/a *m., f.* playwright

droga *f.* drug

drogadicto/a *adj.* drug-addicted; *m., f.* drug addict

ducha *f.* shower

ducharse *v. pron.* to shower; to take a shower

duda *f.* doubt

poner en duda to question, to doubt

Nadie pone en duda su talento. Nobody questions his talent.

sin duda undoubtedly, without a doubt

dudar *v.t.* to doubt

no dudar not to doubt

dueño/a *m., f.* owner; landlord

dulce *adj.* sweet

dulces *m., pl.* sweets; candy

duna *f.* dune

duradero/a *adj.* lasting

durante *prep.* during

durar *v.i.* to last

¿Cuánto dura la película? How long is the movie?

El dinero no duró mucho. The money didn't last long.

¿Dura más la piel? Does leather last longer?

durazno *m. (L.A.)* peach

duro/a *adj.* hard

E

e *conj. (used instead of* **y** *before words beginning with* **i** *and* **hi**) and
  Javier e Inés Javier and Inés
  masaje e hidratación massage and moisturizing

ebrio/a *adj.* inebriated, drunk

echar *v.t.* to throw
  echar chispas *idiom* to be hopping mad
  echar la casa por la ventana *loc.* to go overboard, to pull out all the stops
  echar una carta al buzón to put a letter in the mailbox; to mail
  echarle flores a alguien *idiom* to flatter someone

eclipse *m.* eclipse

ecología *f.* ecology

ecológico/a *adj.* ecological; *(food)* organic

ecologista *m., f.* environmentalist, ecologist

economía *f.* economics

ecosistema *m.* ecosystem

ecoturismo *m.* ecotourism

ecuador *m.* equator
  cruzar el ecuador to cross the equator

ecuatoriano/a *adj.* Ecuadorian

edad *f.* age
  edad de piedra Stone Age
  edad media Middle Ages

No nos dijo su edad. He didn't tell us his age.

edificio *m.* building
  edificio de apartamentos apartment building

educado/a *adj.* polite, well-mannered

educador(a) *m., f.* educator

efectivo *m. (money)* cash
  en efectivo (in) cash

efecto *m.* effect
  bajo los efectos del alcohol under the influence of alcohol
  efectos especiales special effects
  efecto invernadero greenhouse effect
  efecto secundario side effect
  en efecto in fact

eficacia *f.* effectiveness

eficaz *adj.* effective

eficiencia *f.* efficiency

eficiente *adj.* efficient

egoísmo *m.* selfishness

egoísta *adj.* selfish

ejemplo *m.* example

ejercicio *m.* exercise
  ejercicios aeróbicos aerobic exercise
  ejercicios de estiramiento stretching exercises
  ejercicios de portugués Portuguese exercises
  hacer ejercicio to exercise, to work out

ejército *m.* army

el *m., sing., def. art.* the

él *pron. m. sing.* he; him

elástico/a *adj.* elastic

elección, elecciones *f.* election

electorado *m.* electorate
electricista *m., f.* electrician
electrocutarse *v. pron.* to be electrocuted
electrodoméstico *m.* electric appliance
electrólisis *f.* electrolysis
electrónica *f.* electronics
elefante *m.* elephant
elegante *adj.* elegant
elegir (e:i) (g:j) *v.t.* to elect
elemental *adj.* (*course, level*) elementary
   Elemental, amigo Watson. Elementary, my dear Watson.
elevado/a *adj.* (*quantity*) large; (*price*) high
   un elevado número de personas a large number of people
   un precio elevado a high price
eliminación *f.* elimination
eliminar *v.t.* to eliminate
ella *pron. fem. sing.* she; her
ellos/as *pron. m., f. pl.* they; them
   Dáselo a ellos. Give it to them.
elocuencia *f.* eloquence
elocuente *adj.* eloquent
elogiar *v.t.* to praise
elogio *m.* praise
embajada *f.* embassy
embalse *m.* reservoir
embarazada *adj.* pregnant
embarcadero *m.* jetty, wharf
embarcar *v.i.* (*passengers*) to board (*a ship*)
embargo: sin embargo however; yet

embotellamiento (de tráfico) *m.* (*Spain*) traffic jam
embrague *m.* clutch (*pedal*)
embriagado/a *adj.* inebriated, drunk
embudo *m.* funnel
emergencia *f.* emergency
emigración *f.* emigration
emigrante *m., f.* emigrant
emigrar *v.i.* emigrate
emitir *v.t.* to broadcast
emocionado/a *adj.* excited
emocionante *adj.* exciting
empacar *v.t.* to pack
empacharse *v. pron.* to get an upset stomach
empatar *v.i.* (*sports*) to tie
empate *m.* (*sports*) tie
empeorar *v.t.* to get worse; to make worse
   Esto empeora la situación. This makes the situation worse.
empezar (e:ie) *v.t.* to begin; to start
   para empezar to begin
empleado/a *m., f.* employee
empleo *m.* job, employment
empobrecer (c:zc) *v.t.* to impoverish, to make poor
   Las guerras empobrecen los países. Wars impoverish countries.
empobrecerse (c:zc) *v. pron.* to become impoverished, poor
empresa *f.* company; firm; business
empresario/a *m., f.* entrepreneur
empujar *v.t.* to push
en *prep.* in; on

43

en caso (de) que in case (that)

en cuanto *conj.* as soon as

en qué in what; how

¡En marcha! Forward ho/march!

¿En qué puedo servirles? How may I help you?

en resumidas cuentas *loc.* to make a long story short, in short

en un dos por tres *idiom* in a jiffy

enamorado/a (de) *adj.* in love (with); beloved

enamorarse (de) *v. pron.* to fall in love (with)

encantado/a *adj.* delighted; pleased to meet you

encantador(a) *adj.* charming

encantar *v.t.* to like very much; (*inanimate things*) to love; to enchant

encanto *m.* charm

encarcelar *v.t.* to imprison, to jail

encargar *v.t.* to order

encargo *m.* order

encendedor *m.* lighter

encender *v.t.* to light, to turn on

encerar *v.t.* to polish, to wax

encía *f.* (*dental*) gum

encima de *adv.* on top of

por encima *adv.* (*read*) superficially

encontrar (o:ue) *v.t.* to find

encontrarse (o:ue) *v. pron.* to meet each other; to run into each other; to find each other

encuesta *f.* poll; survey

energía *f.* energy

energía (nuclear/solar) (nuclear/solar) energy

enero *m.* January

énfasis *m.* emphasis

enfatizar *v.t.* to emphasize

enfermarse *v. pron.* to get sick

enfermedad *f.* illness

enfermería *f.* health center

enfermero/a *m., f.* nurse

enfermo/a *adj.* sick

enfocar *v.t.* (*a topic*) to focus on, to look at

El problema enfoca el problema de la falta de vivienda. The program looks at the problem of homelessness.

enfoque *m.* approach

enfrentamiento *m.* clash

enfrentar *v.t.* to confront, to face

Hay que enfrentar la realidad. It's necessary to face reality.

enfrentarse (con) *v. pron.* to confront

El ejército se enfrentará con el enemigo. The army will confront the enemy.

enfrente *prep.* across from, in front of

enfrente de *adv.* opposite; facing

El ayuntamiento está enfrente de la catedral. The town hall is opposite the cathedral.

enfriar *v.t.* to chill

engañar *v.t.* to deceive, to cheat on

engaño *m.* deception

engordar *v.i.* to gain weight
que no engorda *adj.* non-fattening

engreído/a *adj.* conceited

enigma *m.* enigma, mystery

enigmático/a *adj.* enigmatic, mysterious

enloquecer (c:zc) *v.i.* to go crazy

ennegrecer (c:zc) *v.t.* to blacken

ennegrecerse (c:zc) *v. pron.* to go black, (*sky, clouds*) to darken

enojado/a *adj.* mad; angry; upset

enojar *v.t.* to annoy, to make angry

enojarse (con) *v. pron.* to get angry (with)

enredadera *f.* climbing plant

enriquecer (c:zc) *v.t.* to enrich, to make rich
La lectura enriquece la imaginación. Reading enriches imagination.

enriquecerse (c:zc) *v. pron.* to get rich

ensalada *f.* salad

ensaladera *f.* salad bowl

ensayar *v.t.* to rehearse

ensayo *m.* essay; rehearsal

enseguida *adv.* right away

enseñanza *f.* learning

enseñar *v.t.* to teach; to show

ensuciar *v.t.* to dirty; to get (something) dirty

entender (e:ie) *v.t.* to understand

entierro *m.* burial

entonces *adv.* then

entrada *f.* entrance; (*Spain*) ticket

entrar (en) *v.i.* to enter, to come in

entre *prep.* between; among
entre tú y yo between you and me
entre la multitud among the crowd
entre semana on weekdays

entregar *v.t.* to turn in, to deliver

entremeses *m., pl.* hors d'oeuvres; appetizers

entrenador(a) *m., f.* trainer; coach

entrenamiento *m.* coaching; training
El boxeo requiere mucho entrenamiento. Boxing requires a lot of training.
El entrenamiento duró seis horas. The training lasted six hours.

entrenarse *v. pron.* to practice; to train

entretener *v.t. irreg.* (**yo entretengo**) to entertain

entretenerse *v. pron. irreg.* (**yo me entretengo**) to amuse oneself; to hang about
No te entretengas camino a la escuela. Don't mess around on the way to school.

entretenido/a *adj.* entertaining

entrevista *f.* interview

entrevistador(a) *m., f.* interviewer
entrevistar *v.t.* to interview
entusiasmado/a *adj.* enthusiastic
entusiasmo *m.* enthusiasm
envase *m.* container
envejecer (c:zc) *v.i.* to age, to grow old
envejecimiento *m.* aging
enviar *v.t.* to send; to mail
  Te enviaré los libros por correo. I'll mail you the books.
envidioso/a *adj.* envious, jealous
envolver (o:ue) *v.t.* to wrap
  papel de envolver wrapping paper
enyesar *v.t.* (*medicine*) to put in a cast
  El médico me enyesó el brazo. The doctor put my arm in a cast.
  Tengo el brazo enyesado. My arm is in a cast.
equilibrado/a *adj.* balanced
equipado/a *adj.* equipped
equipaje *m.* luggage
equipo *m.* team
  equipo local home team
  equipo visitante visiting team
  equipo de técnicos team of technicians
equitación *f.* (horse) riding
equivalencia *f.* equivalence
equivaler *v.i.* to be equivalent to
equivocación *f.* mistake

equivocado/a *adj.* mistaken; wrong
equivocarse *v. pron.* to make a mistake, to be mistaken
  ¿Me equivoco al pensar que mientes? Am I mistaken in thinking you're lying?
  Nos equivocamos de camino. We went the wrong way.
eres *fam.* you are
ermita *f.* chapel
ermitaño/a *m., f.* hermit
eructar *v.i.* to belch, to burp
eructo *m.* belch, burp
erupción *f.* eruption
  hacer erupción (*volcano*) to erupt
es he/she/it is; *form.* you
  Es de... He/She is from...
  Es la una. It's one o'clock.
  Es obvio que... It's obvious that...
escalada *f.* (*mountaineering*) climb, ascent
escalador(a) *m., f.* (*mountaineering*) climber
escalar *v.t.* to climb
  escalar montañas to climb mountains
escalera *f.* stairs; stairway
  escalera de incendios fire escape
  escalera mecánica escalator
escalofrío *m.* shiver
  tener escalofríos to be shivering; to have the chills
escalón *m.* step, stair
escandaloso/a *adj.* loud; outrageous

escapada *f.* getaway

escaparate *m.* (*Spain*) shop window

escarcha *f.* frost

escayola *f.* (*Spain*) plaster cast

escayolar *v.* (*Spain*) *trans.* to put in a cast

escenario *m.* stage

escoba *f.* broom

escoger (g:j) *v.t.* choose

esconder *v.t.* to hide

escondidillas *f.* hide-and-seek

escondite, (al) *m.* hide-and-seek

escorpión *m.* scorpion

escribir *v.t./v.i.* to write
  escribir a máquina to type
  escribir un mensaje electrónico to write an e-mail message
  escribir una (tarjeta) postal to write a postcard
  escribir una carta to write a letter

escrito *p.p. of* **escribir** written
  por escrito *adv.* in writing

escritor(a) *m., f.* writer

escritorio *m.* desk

escuchar *v.t.* to listen (to)
  escuchar la radio to listen to the radio
  escuchar música to listen to music

escuela *f.* school

escuela pública *f.* public school

escuela de niños/as *f.* all-boys/girls school

esculpir *v.t.* to sculpt

escultor(a) *m., f.* sculptor

escultura *f.* sculpture

escurrir *v.t.* (*dishes*) to drain; (*clothes*) to wring out

ese, esa, esos, esas *dem. adj.* that (by you); those (by you)

ése, ésa, ésos, ésas *dem. pron.* that (one by you); those (by you)

esfera *f.* sphere

esforzarse (o:ue) *v. pron.* to try hard
  Debes esforzarte más. You must try harder.

esfuerzo *m.* effort

esgrima *f.* (*sport*) fencing

esgrimidor(a) *m., f.* fencer

esmeralda *f.* emerald

esnob *adj.* snobby; *m., f.* snob

esnobismo *m.* snobbery

esnórkel *m.* snorkel

eso *dem. pron. neuter.* that (by you)

esófago *m.* esophagus

espacio *m.* space

espagueti *m.* spaghetti

espalda *f.* back
  No me importa que hablen a mis espaldas. I don't mind them talking behind my back.

España *f.* Spain

español *m.* (*language*) Spanish

español(a) *adj./m., f.* Spanish

espárrago *m.* asparagus

espátula *f.* spatula

especialista *m., f.* specialist

especialización *f.* major (field of study or interest); specialization

especializarse *v. pron.* to specialize

especie *f.* (*biology*) species; type

especie en peligro de extinción endangered species

especie protegida protected species

espectacular *adj.* spectacular

espectáculo *m.* show

espectador(a) *m., f.* spectator

espejo *m.* mirror

esperanza *f.* hope

esperanza de vida life expectancy

esperar (+ inf.) *v.t.* to wait (for); to hope; to wish; to expect

espina *f.* (*fish*) bone; (*plant*) thorn

espinaca *f.* spinach

espolvorear *v.t.* (*sugar*) to sprinkle

esponja *f.* sponge

esponjoso/a *adj.* (*pastry*) spongy, soft; (*fabric*) fluffy

espontáneo/a *adj.* spontaneous

esposo/a *m.* husband; *f.* wife; *m., f.* spouse

espuma *f.* foam

esqueleto *m.* skeleton

esquema *m.* outline

esquí (acuático) *m.* (water) skiing

esquiador(a) *m., f.* skier

esquiar *v.i.* to ski

esquina *f.* corner

establecer (c:zc) *v.t.* to establish

establecer una marca mundial to set a world record

establo *m.* stable

estación *f.* station; season

estación de autobuses bus station

estación del metro subway station

estación de tren train station

estacionamiento *m.* parking lot; parking; parking space

estacionar *v.t.* to park

estacionarse *v. pron.* to park

estadio *m.* stadium

estado *m.* state

estado civil marital status

Estados Unidos *m. pl.* (EE.UU.; E.U.) United States

estadounidense *adj./m., f.* from the United States

estafador(a) *m., f.* fraud, con artist

estafar *v.t.* to defraud

estampado/a *adj.* print(ed), patterned

estampilla *f.* stamp

estancia *f.* stay

Nuestra estancia en La Coruña fue magnífica. Our stay in La Coruña was magnificent.

estanque *m.* pond (*man-made*)

estante *m.* bookcase; bookshelf, bookshelves

estar *v.i.* to be

Está bien. That's fine. It's okay.

(no) está nada mal it's not at all bad

estar a (veinte kilómetros) de aquí to be (twenty kilometers) from here

estar a dieta to be on a diet

estar a régimen to be on a diet

estar aburrido/a to be bored
estar afectado/a (por) to be affected (by)
estar bajo control to be under control
estar cansado/a to be tired
estar contaminado/a to be polluted
estar de acuerdo (con) to be in agreement with
estar de acuerdo to agree
no estar de acuerdo to disagree
estar de moda to be in fashion
estar de vacaciones *f., pl.* to be on vacation
estar de vuelta to be back
estar en buena forma to be in good shape
estar en las nubes to be daydreaming
estar enfermo/a to be sick
estar listo/a to be ready
estar perdido/a to be lost
estar roto/a to be broken
estar seguro/a to be sure
estar torcido/a to be twisted; to be sprained
estatua *f.* statue
este *m.* east
al este to the east
este, esta, estos, estas *dem. adj.* this; these
éste, ésta, éstos, éstas *dem. pron.* this (one); these
Éste/Ésta es… This is… *(introducing someone)*
estéreo *m.* stereo
estéril *adj.* sterile
esterilizar *v.t.* to sterilize

esteticista *m., f.* beautician
estetoscopio *m.* stethoscope
estiércol *m.* manure
estilo *m.* style; *(swimming)* stroke, style
algo por el estilo something like that
estilo braza *(Spain)* breaststroke
estilo espalda backstroke
estilo libre freestyle
estilo mariposa butterfly
estilo pecho *(L.A.)* breaststroke
estiramiento *m.* stretching
estirar *v.t.* to stretch
esto *dem. pron. neuter* this; this thing
estómago *m.* stomach
estornudar *v.i.* to sneeze
estrecho/a *adj.* narrow, tight
estrella *f.* star
estrella *m., f.* **de cine** movie star
estrella fugaz shooting star
estrellado/a *adj.* starry
estrenar *v.t.* to wear for the first time; to début
estreno *m.* *(film, play)* premiere
estreñido/a *adj.* constipated
estreñimiento *m.* constipation
estrés *m.* stress
estresado/a *adj.* under stress
estresante *adj.* *(situation)* stressful
estropear *v.t.* to damage
estropearse *v. pron.* *(automobile)* to break down
estudiante *m., f.* student
estudiantil *adj.* student
estudiar *v.t.* to study

estudioso/a *adj.* studious
estufa *f. (L.A.)* stove
estupendo/a *adj.* stupendous
etapa *f.* stage; step
 las etapas de la vida the
 stages of life
ética *f.* ethics
ético/a *adj.* ethical
euforia *f.* euphoria, elation
eufórico/a *adj.* euphoric
Europa *f.* Europe
europeo/a *adj.* European
evadir *v.t.* (*danger, problem*) to
 avoid; (*taxes*) to evade
evadirse *v. pron.*
 (*responsibility, prison*) to
 escape
 **Luis se evadió de la
 responsabilidad.** Luis
 escaped responsibility.
evaluación *f.* assessment; test
evaluar *v.t.* to assess; to test
evasión *f.* escape
evitar *v.t.* to avoid
evolución *f.* evolution
evolucionar *v.i.* to evolve
exageración *f.* exaggeration
exagerar *v.t.* to exaggerate
 **No exageres el valor de las
 cosas.** Do not exaggerate the
 value of things.
examen *m.* test; exam
 examen médico physical exam
excavadora *f.* power shovel,
 excavator
excavar *v.t.* to dig, to excavate
excelente *adj.* excellent
exceso *m.* excess; too much
 en exceso in excess, too
 much

excursión *f.* hike; tour;
 excursion
 Vamos de excursión. We're
 going hiking.
excursionista *m., f.* hiker
exhibición de arte *f.* art
 exhibition
exigir (g:j) *v.t.* to demand
éxito *m.* success
 tener éxito to succeed
éxodo *m.* exodus
experiencia *f.* experience
experimentar *v.t.* to
 experiment; to try out
expiración *f.* expiration
expirar *v.t.* (*time period,
 contract*) to expire
explicar *v.t.* to explain
explorar *v.t.* to explore
 explorar un pueblo to
 explore a town
 explorar una ciudad to
 explore a city
explosivo/a *adj.* explosive
exponer *v.t. irreg.* (**yo expongo**)
 (*art*) to exhibit
exportación *f.* exportation
exportar *v.t.* to export
exposición *f.* exhibition
expresión *f.* expression
expresivo/a *adj.* expressive
exprimidor *m.* juicer
expulsar *v.t.* to expel
expulsión *m.* expulsion
extinción *f.* extinction
extinguir *v.t.* (**yo extingo**) (*fire*)
 to extinguish, to put out
 **Los bomberos extinguieron
 el incendio.** The firefighters
 put out the blaze.

extinguirse v. pron. **(yo me extingo)** to become extinct; to die out
Su entusiasmo se está extinguiendo poco a poco. Her enthusiasm is dying little by little.
extranjero/a adj. foreign; m., f. foreigner
en el extranjero abroad
extrañar (algo o a alguien) v.t. to miss
extrañarse (de) v. pron. to be surprised, to find strange
Me extraña que no te hayas quejado. I'm surprised that you haven't complained.
extraño/a adj. strange, odd
Es extraño (que…) It's strange (that…)
Es extraño que tosas tanto. It's strange that you cough so much.
extravagante adj. flamboyant
extremidades f., pl. (anatomy) extremities
extrovertido/a adj. extroverted

F

fábrica f. factory
fabricación f. manufacture
fabricación en serie mass production
fabricante m., f. manufacturer
fabricar v.t. to manufacture, to produce
fabricar en serie to mass produce
fabuloso/a adj. fabulous
fachada f. façade

fácil adj. easy
facilitar v.t. to facilitate, to make easier
faisán m. pheasant
falda f. skirt
fallecer (c:zc) v.i. to pass away
fallecido/a m., f. deceased
fallecimiento m. death
falta f. lack; (spelling) mistake
falta de recursos lack of resources
falta de ortografía spelling mistake
faltar v.t. to lack; to need
familia f. family
familiar adj. family; (known) familiar
Este lugar me resulta familiar. This place looks familiar.
familiares m., pl. relatives
famoso/a adj. famous; m., f. famous person, celebrity
fango m. mud
faringe f. pharynx
farmacia f. pharmacy
farmacia de guardia 24-hour pharmacy
faro m. (automobile) headlight
fascinar v.t. to fascinate; to love; to be fascinated by
fatigado/a adj. weary
fatigarse v. pron. to wear oneself out
favorable adj. favorable
favorito/a adj. favorite
fax m. fax (machine)
fe f. faith
febrero m. February
fecha f. date

fecha de caducidad expiration date

fecundación *f.* fertilization

fecundar *v.t.* to fertilize

felicidad *f.* happiness

¡Felicidades! Congratulations! (*for an event such as a birthday or anniversary*)

felicitar *v.t.* to congratulate

¡Felicitaciones! Congratulations! (*for an event such as an engagement or a good grade on a test*)

feliz *adj.* happy

¡Feliz cumpleaños! Happy birthday!

fenomenal *adj.* fantastic, great, phenomenal

fenómeno *m.* phenomenon

feo/a *adj.* ugly

ferrocarril *m.* railroad

fértil *adj.* fertile

fertilidad *f.* fertility

fertilizante *m.* fertilizer

festejar *v.t.* to celebrate

festejo *m.* celebration

festival *m.* festival

fiambre *m.* cold cut

fiambrera *f.* (*Spain*) lunch box

fianza *f.* bail

ficha *f.* (*game*) counter, game piece

fidelidad *f.* fidelity; faithfulness

fiebre *f.* fever

fiel *adj.* faithful; loyal

fiesta *f.* party

dar una fiesta to throw a party

fijo/a *adj.* set; fixed; permanent; steady

precio fijo fixed price

trabajo fijo permanent job

fila *f.* row

filatelia *f.* philately, stamp collecting

filmoteca *f.* film library

filología *f.* philology

filólogo/a *m., f.* philologist

filosofar *v.i.* to philosophize

filosofía *f.* philosophy

filósofo/a *m., f.* philosopher

fin *m.* end

fin de semana weekend

a fin de *conj.* in order to

a fines de at the end of

al fin *loc.* at last

al fin y al cabo *loc.* after all

por fin *adv.* at last

final *m.* end

al final at the end

a finales de at/toward the end of

finalmente *adv.* finally

financiar *v.t.* to finance

fingir (g:j) *v.t.* to pretend

Fingía no saberlo. She pretended not to know it.

firma *f.* signature

firmar *v.t.* to sign (*a document*)

física *f.* physics

físico/a *m., f.* physicist

flaco/a *adj.* skinny

flamenco/a *adj., m.* (*music*) flamenco

flan (de caramelo) *m.* baked (caramel) custard

flecha *f.* arrow

flexible *adj.* flexible

flexionar *v.t.* to flex
flor *f.* flower
florería *f.* (*L.A.*) flower shop
florero *m.* vase
florero/a *m., f.* (*L.A.*) florist
florista *m., f.* (*Spain*) florist
floristería *f.* (*Spain*) flower shop
flotar *v.i.* to float
fluir (y) *v.i.* to flow
foca *f.* seal
folklórico/a *adj.* folk; folkloric
folleto *m.* brochure
fondo *m.* (*street, corridor*) end; (*sea*) bottom
  a fondo *adv.* completely
  al fondo (de) *adv.* at the end (of)
fondos *m., pl.* (*money*) funds
fonética *f.* phonetics
fonología *f.* phonology
fontanería *f.* (*Spain*) f plumbing
fontanero/a *m., f.* (*Spain*) plumber
forense *m., f.* forensic scientist
forma *f.* shape
  estar en buena/mala forma to be in good/bad shape
formación *f.* training
  formación profesional vocational training
formal *adj.* formal
formar *v.t.* to train
formulario *m.* form
  (re)llenar el formulario fill out the form
fortaleza *f.* fortress
fortuna *f.* fortune
  por fortuna *adv.* fortunately

fósforo *m.* match
fósil *m.* fossil
fosilizarse *v. pron.* to fossilize, to become fossilized
foto(grafía) *f.* photograph
fotocopiadora *f.* photocopier
fotocopiar *v.t.* to photocopy
fotosíntesis *f.* photosynthesis
fracasado/a *adj.* failed, unsuccessful
fracasar *v.i.* to fail
fracaso *m.* failure
frambuesa *f.* raspberry
francés *m.* (*language*) French
francés, francesa *adj./m., f.* French
Francia *f.* France
frase *f.* phrase; sentence
frazada *f.* (*L.A.*) blanket
frecuencia *f.* frequency
  con (mucha) frecuencia frequently, regularly
frecuentemente *adv.* frequently
fregadero (de la cocina) *m.* (kitchen) sink
fregar *v.* (*Spain*) *trans.* to mop
fregona *f.* (*Spain*) mop
frenar *v.i.* to brake
freno *m.* brake
  freno de mano handbrake
frente *f.* (*anatomy*) forehead
fresa *f.* strawberry
fresco/a *adj.* cool, fresh
frijol *m.* bean
frío/a *adj.* cold; chilled
  Sírvase frío. Serve chilled.
fritada *f.* fried dish (*pork, fish, etc.*)
frito/a *adj.* fried
frontera *f.* border, frontier

fronterizo/a *adj.* border

fruta *f.* fruit

frutería *f.* fruit store

frutilla *f.* (*L.A.*) strawberry

fucsia *adj.* fuchsia

fuego *m.* fire
  fuegos artificiales *m., pl.* fireworks

fuente *f.* platter, serving dish; fountain
  fuente de fritada platter of fried food

fuera *adv.* outside

fuerte *adj.* strong

fuga *f.* (*prison*) escape; (*gas, water*) leak

fugarse *v. pron.* to escape, to flee, to run away

fugitivo/a *m., f.* fugitive

fumar *v.t.* to smoke
  no fumar not to smoke
  Prohibido fumar. No smoking.

función *f.* show, function

funcionar *v.i.* to work; to function
  Funciona a la perfección. It works perfectly.

funeral *m.* funeral

furioso/a *adj.* furious

fusible *m.* (*electricity*) fuse

fútbol *m.* soccer
  fútbol americano football

futbolista *m., f.* soccer player; football player

futuro/a *adj./m.* future
  en el futuro (cercano) in the (near) future
  futura mamá mother-to-be
  un trabajo sin futuro a job with no prospects

G

gacela *f.* gazelle

gafas (oscuras/de sol) *f. pl.* (sun)glasses

galardón *m.* award, prize

galardonado/a *m., f.* award-winner

galardonar *v.t.* to award

galaxia *f.* galaxy

galería *f.* gallery

galleta *f.* cookie

gallo *m.* rooster

gana *f.* desire
  de buena/mala gana *adv.* willingly/unwillingly

ganadería *f.* ranching, cattle raising

ganadero/a *m., f.* rancher, cattle farmer

ganar *v.t.* to win; (*money*) to earn
  ganarse la vida *idiom* to make a living, to earn one's living **Mario se gana la vida escribiendo guiones de telenovela.** Mario makes his living writing soap opera scripts.

ganga *f.* bargain

garaje *m.* garage

garantía *f.* guarantee, warranty

garantizar *v.t.* to guarantee

garbanzo *m.* chickpea

gardenia *f.* gardenia

garganta *f.* throat

gas *m.* gas
  gas lacrimógeno tear gas

gasolina *f.* gasoline

gasolinera *f.* gas station
gastar *v.t.* (*money*) to spend
gasto *m.* expense
gastronomía *f.* gastronomy
gatillo *m.* (*firearm*) trigger
  apretar el gatillo to pull the
  trigger
gato/a *m., f.* cat
géiser *m.* geyser
gelatina *f.* gelatine
gemelo/a *m., f.* twin
generoso/a *adj.* generous
genética *f.* genetics
genético/a *adj.* genetic
gente *f.* people
  buena gente *idiom* nice
  person, nice guy, nice gal
geografía *f.* geography
geólogo/a *m., f.* geologist
geometría *f.* geometry
geométrico/a *adj.*
  geometric(al)
geranio *m.* geranium
gerente *m., f.* manager
gimnasia *f.* gymnastics
  gimnasia rítmica rhythmic
  gymnastics
gimnasio *m.* gymnasium
gimnasta *m., f.* gymnast
ginecólogo/a *m., f.*
  gynecologist
girar *v.t./intrans.* to turn
  Gire a la izquierda en la
  próxima esquina. Turn left at
  the next corner.
  No gires la cabeza. Don't
  turn your head.
girasol *m.* sunflower
giro *m.* turn
  giro bancario bank draft

giro postal money order
globo *m.* balloon
glotón, glotona *adj.* gluttonous;
  greedy
gobernar (e:ie) *v.t.* to govern,
  to rule
gobierno *m.* government
golf *m.* golf
golfista *m., f.* golfer
golpe *m.* blow; coup; hit
  Dio unos golpes en la mesa.
  He pounded on the table
  several times.
  de golpe *adv.* suddenly
  Ocurrió de golpe. It
  happened suddenly.
goma *f.* (*pencil*) eraser
  de goma (made of) rubber
gordo/a *adj.* fat
gorra *f.* cap (*with a visor*)
  gorra de béisbol baseball cap
gorrión *m.* sparrow
gorro *m.* cap (*without a visor*)
  gorro de lana wool cap, ski
  cap
gota *f.* drop
gótico/a *adj.* Gothic
gozar (de) *v.t.* to enjoy
  Mi padre goza de una salud
  de hierro. My father has a
  strong constitution.
grabadora *f.* tape recorder
grabar *v.t.* to record
gracias *f., pl.* thank you; thanks
  Gracias por todo. Thanks for
  everything.
  Gracias una vez más. Thanks
  again.
  (Muchas) gracias. Thank you
  (very much). Thanks (a lot).

gracioso/a *adj.* funny

graduación *f.* graduation

graduar *v.t.* (*temperature, etc.*) to adjust, to regulate

graduarse (en/de) *v. pron.* (*university*) to graduate (from/in)

gran, grande *adj.* big; great; large
  Es un gran amigo. He's a great friend.

granada *f.* (*fruit*) pomegranate; (*military*) grenade

granero *m.* barn

grano *m.* grain, seed, bean; (*medical*) blemish, pimple
  ir al grano *idiom* to get to the point

grasa *f.* fat

gratis *adj.* free of charge

grave *adj.* (*illness, wound, problem*) serious

gravedad *f.* gravity

gravísimo/a *adj.* (*superlative*) extremely serious; grave

griego *m.* (*language*) Greek

griego *adj./m., f.* Greek

grifo *m.* faucet

grillo *m.* cricket

gripe *f.* flu

gris *adj./m.* gray

gritar *v.i.* to scream

grito *m.* yell, shout

grosero/a *adj.* rude, ill-mannered, impolite, rough

grúa *f.* (*machinery*) crane

grupo *m.* group

guagua *f.* bus

guantes *m., pl.* gloves

guapo/a *adj.* handsome; good-looking

guarda forestal *m., f.* ranger

guardabarros *m.* (*automobile*) fender

guardar *v.t.* to save (on a computer)

guardería *f.* nursery school, day-care center

guardia *m., f.* guard, police officer
  estar de guardia (*doctor*) to be on duty, to be on call
  guardia de seguridad security guard

guerra *f.* war

guía *m., f.* guide
  guía de teléfonos phone book
  Lo puedo usar de guía. I can use it as a guide.

guiñar (el ojo) *v.t.* to wink

guión *m.* script, screenplay

guionista *m., f.* scriptwriter, screenwriter

guisante *m.* pea

guisar *v.i.* (*Spain*) to cook

guiso *m.* stew

guitarra *f.* guitar

gusano *m.* worm

gustar *v.i.* to be pleasing to; to like
  Me gusta. I like it.
  Me gustaría. I would like it.
  ¿Te gusta(n)...? Do you like...?
  ¿Te gustaría (+ *inf.*)...? Would you like to...?

gusto *m.* pleasure; (*senses*) taste
  El gusto es mío. The pleasure is mine.
  Gusto de (+ *inf.*)... It's a pleasure to . . .

H

haber *v. impers. irreg.* **(no) hay** *sing.* there is (not); *pl.* there are (not)
  Hay (mucha) contaminación. It's (very) smoggy.
  Hay (mucha) niebla. It's (very) foggy.
  hay que it is necessary (that)
  Hay que pensar antes de hablar. Think before you speak.
  No hay de qué. You're welcome.
  No hay duda (de) que… There's no doubt that…
haber *v. aux. irreg.* (*in compound verbs*) to have
  Yo no lo he hecho. I haven't done it.
hábil *adj.* skillful
habilidad *f.* skill
habitación *f.* room
  habitación doble double room
  habitación individual single room
hablar *v.i.* to talk; to speak
hacer *v.t. irreg.* **(yo hago)** to do; to make
  hacer amigos to make friends
  hacer berrinches to throw tantrums
  hacer cola to stand in line
  hacer diligencias to do errands; to run errands
  hacer ejercicio to exercise, to work out
  hacer ejercicios aeróbicos to do aerobics
  hacer ejercicios de

  estiramiento to do stretching exercises
  hacer el papel (de) to play the role of
  hacer gimnasia to work out; to exercise,
  hacer juego (con) (*clothing*) to match (with), to go well (with)
  hacer la cama to make the bed
  hacer las maletas to pack (one's suitcases)
  hacer quehaceres domésticos to do household chores
  hacer travesuras to get into trouble
  hacer turismo to go sightseeing
  hacer un picnic to have a picnic
  hacer un viaje to go on/take a trip
  hacer una excursión to go on a hike; to go on a tour
  hacer una fiesta to throw a party
  hacer una maestría to pursue a Master's degree
hacer *v. impers.* (*weather*)
  Hace buen/mal tiempo. The weather is good/bad. It's good/bad weather.
  Hace (mucho) calor. It's (very) hot.
  Hace fresco. It's cool.
  Hace (mucho) frío. It's (very) cold.
  Hace (mucho) sol. It's (very) sunny.

Hace (mucho) viento. It's (very) windy.

hacer *v. impers.* (*time*)
hace dos semanas two weeks ago

hacerse *v. pron. irreg.* (**yo me hago**) to become
hacerse daño to hurt oneself
hacerse el sordo to pretend not to hear
hacerse rico to become rich

hacha (el) *f.* ax

hacia *prep.* toward

hada (el) *f.* fairy
hada madrina fairy godmother

hallar *v.t.* to find

hallazgo *m.* find, discovery
Aquel restaurante fue un verdadero hallazgo. That restaurant was a real find.

halterofilia *f.* (*sport*) weightlifting

hamaca *f.* hammock

hambre (el) *f.* hunger

hambriento/a *adj.* hungry

hamburguesa *f.* hamburger

harina *f.* flour
harina de otro costal *idiom* another kettle of fish

hartarse *v. pron.* to get fed up; (*food*) to fill oneself

hasta *prep.* until, toward
hasta ahora until now
Hasta la vista. See you later.
Hasta luego. See you later.
Hasta mañana. See you tomorrow.
Hasta pronto. See you soon.

hasta (que) *conj.* until

hasta que lleguen until they arrive

hebreo *m.* (*language*) Hebrew

hebreo *adj./m., f.* Hebrew

hecho *p.p. of* **hacer** done
de hecho in fact

heladería *f.* ice cream shop

helado *m.* ice cream

helado/a *adj.* iced

helicóptero *m.* helicopter

hembra *f.* female

hemisferio *m.* hemisphere

hemorragia *f.* hemorrhage

herbívoro/a *adj.* herbivorous; *m., f.* herbivore

heredar *v.t.* to inherit

heredera *f.* heiress

heredero *m.* heir

hereditario/a *adj.* hereditary

herencia *f.* inheritance

herida *f.* wound

herido/a *adj./m., f.* injured
Hubo un herido de gravedad. One person was seriously injured.

hermanastro/a *m.* stepbrother; *f.* stepsister

hermano/a *m.* brother, *f.* sister
hermano/a mayor/menor older/younger brother/sister

hermanos *m., pl.* brothers and sisters

hermético/a *adj.* airtight

hermoso/a *adj.* beautiful

héroe *m.* hero

heroína *f.* heroine

herramienta *f.* tool

hervido/a *adj.* boiled

hervir (e:ie) *v.t.* to boil

hidráulico/a *adj.* hydraulic

hiedra *f.* ivy
hielo *m.* ice
  quebrar/romper el hielo *loc.* break the ice
hierba *f.* grass
hierbas *f., pl.* herbs
hierro *m.* iron
hígado *m.* liver
higo *m.* fig
higuera *f.* fig tree
hijastro/a *m.* stepson; *f.* stepdaughter
hijo/a *m.* son; *f.* daughter
  hijo/a único/a only child
hijos *m., pl.* children
hilera *f.* row
hilo *m.* thread
  de hilo (made of) linen
  hilo dental dental floss
hindú *adj./m., f.* Hindu
hipérbole *f.* hyperbole
hípica *f.* equestrian sports
hipo *m.* hiccups
hipódromo *m.* hippodrome
hipoteca *f.* mortgage
hipotecar *v.t.* to mortgage
hipótesis *f.* hypothesis
hipotético/a *adj.* hypothetical
hispano/a *adj./m., f.* Hispanic
historia *f.* history; story
historiador(a) *m., f.* historian
hockey *m.* hockey
  hockey sobre césped (*L.A.*) field hockey
  hockey sobre hielo ice hockey
  hockey sobre hierba (*Spain*) field hockey
hoguera *f.* bonfire
hoja *f.* (*plant*) leaf; (*paper*) sheet

hoja de vida (*Colombia*) résumé
hola *interj.* hello; hi
hombre *m.* man
  hombre de negocios businessman
  hombre del tiempo weatherman
  hombre lobo werewolf
  hombre rana frogman, diver
hombrera *f.* shoulder pad
hombro *m.* shoulder
homenaje *m.* tribute, homage
homenajear *v.t.* to pay homage
honesto/a *adj.* honest
hora *f.* hour
  ¿A qué hora…? At what time…?
horario *m.* schedule
  horario fijo fixed schedule
  horario flexible flexible schedule
horizonte *m.* horizon
hormiga *f.* ant
hormigón *m.* (*Spain*) concrete
hormona *f.* hormone
hornear *v.t.* to bake
  pan recién horneado freshly baked bread
hornillo *m.* portable electric stove
horno *m.* oven
  horno de microondas microwave oven
horror *m.* horror
  …de horror horror
hortensia *f.* hydrangea
horticultor(a) *m., f.* horticulturalist
horticultura *f.* horticulture

hospedar *v.t.* to provide accommodation

hospital *m.* hospital

hospitalario/a *adj.* hospitable

hospitalidad *f.* hospitality

hostal *m.* inn; hostel

hotel *m.* hotel

hoy *adv.* today
  hoy día *adv.* nowadays
  Hoy es... Today is . . .

huelga *f.* strike

huelguista *m., f.* striker

huella *f.* footprint; mark
  huella dactilar fingerprint

huerta *f.* orchard

huerto *m.* vegetable garden

hueso *m.* bone; (*fruit*) pit

huésped *m., f.* guest

huevo *m.* egg

huida *f.* escape

huir (y) *v.i.* to flee, to escape
  Huir de la injusticia. Escape injustice.

humanidades *f., pl.* humanities

humanismo *m.* humanism

humanista *m., f.* humanist

humectante *m.* moisturizer

humedad *f.* humidity

húmedo *adj.* humid; damp

humilde *adj.* humble
  en mi humilde opinión in my humble opinion

humillado/a *adj.* humiliated

humo *m.* smoke

humor *m.* mood
  de buen/mal humor in a good/bad mood

huracán *m.* hurricane

I

iceberg *m.* iceberg

ida *f.* (*travel*) one way
  boleto/billete de ida one-way ticket

idea *f.* idea

idealista *adj.* idealist

idioma *m.* language

iglesia *f.* church

ignorancia *f.* ignorance

ignorante *adj.* ignorant

igual *adj.* equal, same, like
  dos y dos igual a cuatro two and two equals four
  Es igual que su madre. She's like her mother.
  Son las dos iguales. They are both the same.
  ¿Blanco o negro? —Me da igual. ¿Black or white? – It's all the same to me.

igualdad *f.* equality

igualmente *adv.* likewise
  ¡Que te diviertas! —Igualmente. Have fun! –Likewise.

ilegible *adj.* illegible

ilusionado/a *adj.* thrilled

ilustrar *v.t.* to illustrate

imaginar *v.t.* to imagine

imaginarse *v. pron.* to imagine

imán *m.* magnet

imitación *f.* imitation

imitar *v.t.* to imitate

impaciencia *f.* impatience

impacientarse *v. pron.* to get impatient
  Se impacientó con el retraso del autobús. She got impatient over the delay of the bus.

impaciente *adj.* impatient

impedir (e:i) *v.t.* to prevent

impensable *adj.* unthinkable
imperio *m.* empire
impermeable *adj.* waterproof
impermeable *m.* raincoat
importación *f.* importation
importante *adj.* important
  (No) Es importante que…
  It's (not) important that…
  Es importante que vengas a
  clase. It's important that you
  come to class.
importar *v.i.* to be important to;
  to matter
  No importa. It doesn't matter.
imposible *adj.* impossible
  (No) Es imposible (que…)
  It's (not) impossible (that…)
  Es imposible que tenga sed.
  It's impossible that she's
  thirsty.
impostor(a) *m., f.* impostor
imprenta *f.* print shop
impresora *f.* printer
imprimir *v.t.* to print
improbable *adj.* improbable
  (No) Es improbable (que…)
  It's (not) improbable (that…)
  Es improbable que llueva.
  It probably won't rain.
impuesto *m.* tax
inadvertido/a *adj.* unnoticed
inauguración *f.* inauguration
inaugurar *v.t.* to inaugurate
incendio *m.* fire
incertidumbre *f.* uncertainty
incógnito *adj.* unknown
  de incógnito *adv.* incognito
incomprensible *adj.*
  incomprehensible
incomprensión *f.* lack of
  understanding

inconcebible *adj.* inconceivable
inconveniente *m.* drawback
increíble *adj.* incredible
incremento *m.* increase
independiente *adj.*
  independent
independizarse *v. pron.* to
  become independent
indicar *v.t.* to indicate, to show
índice *m.* rate
  índice de mortalidad
  mortality rate
  índice de natalidad birth rate
indicio *m.* evidence
indígena *adj.* indigenous,
  native
indiscreto/a *adj.* indiscreet,
  tactless
individual *adj.* individual;
  (*room*) private; *m.* (*sport*)
  singles
individualidad *f.* individuality
inefable *adj.* indescribable
inesperado/a *adj.* unexpected
inexplicable *adj.* inexplicable
infarto *m.* heart attack
infección *f.* infection
influir (en) (y) *v.i.* to influence
  Los poemas de Darío
  influyeron en otros poetas.
  Darío's poems influenced
  other poets.
información *f.* information
informal *adj.* casual
informar *v.t.* to inform
informarse *v. pron.* to get
  information
informe *m.* report; (*written*
  work) paper
infusión (de hierbas) *f.* herbal
  tea

61

ingeniero/a *m., f.* engineer
ingerir (e:ie) *v.t.* to ingest
ingestión *f.* ingestion
Inglaterra *f.* England
ingle *f.* groin
inglés *m.* (*language*) English
inglés, inglesa *adj./m., f.*
English
ingrávido/a *adj.* weightless
injusto/a *adj.* unfair
inmaduro/a *adj.* (*person*)
immature
inmediatamente *adv.*
immediately
inmigración *f.* immigration
inmigrante *m., f.* immigrant
inmigrar *v.i.* to immigrate
**inmunizar (a alguien contra
algo)** *v.t.* to immunize
inmunológico/a *adj.*
immunological
innovación *f.* innovation
innovador(a) *adj.* innovative;
m., f. innovator
innovar *v.t.* to innovate
inodoro *m.* toilet
inolvidable *adj.* unforgettable
inquietante *adj.* worrying
inquietar(se) *v. pron.* to worry
inquieto/a *adj.* worried
inscribirse *v. pron.* to register,
to enroll
**Quiere inscribirse en la
clase de astronomía.** She
intends to register for the
astronomy class.
inscripción *f.* registration,
enrollment
insecto *m.* insect
insípido/a *adj.* (*food*) bland;

(*person, work*) insipid
insistencia *f.* insistence
insistir (en) *v.i.* to insist (on)
**(insistir en +inf.) Insistió en
invitarme.** He insisted on
inviting me.
**(insistir en que + subj.)
Insiste en que vayamos
todos.** He insists on all of us
going.
insociable *adj.* unsociable
insólito/a *adj.* unusual
insomnio *m.* insomnia
insoportable *adj.* unbearable
inspector(a) *m., f.* inspector
inspector(a) de aduanas
customs inspector
inspirar *v.t.* to inspire
instalación *f.* installation
instalaciones deportivas
sports facilities
instalar *v.t.* (*equipment*) to
install
instalarse *v. pron.* to settle,
install oneself
**Se instaló delante de la tele
y no se movió.** He settled in
front of the TV and didn't
budge.
institución *f.* institution
instrumento *m.* (*medical,
musical*) instrument
insulina *f.* insulin
inteligente *adj.* intelligent
intentar *v.* to try
intento *m.* attempt; try
intercambiar *v.t.* exchange
intercambio *m.* exchange
interés *m.* interest
interesante *adj.* interesting

interesar *v.i.* to be interesting to; to interest

interesarse (en) *v. pron.* to take an interest (in) **Siempre se interesa en los resultados.** He's always interested in the results.

intermedio *adj.* intermediate

intermitente *m.* (*automobile*) turn signal

internacional *adj.* international

Internet *m.* Internet

interpretación *f.* (*oral translation*) interpreting

interpretar *v.t.* to play (a role), to perform

intérprete *m., f.* interpreter

interrumpir *v.t.* to interrupt

intersección *f.* intersection

intervención *f.* intervention, participation
intervención quirúrgica operation

intestino *m.* intestine
intestino delgado small intestine
intestino grueso large intestine

intimar (con alguien) *v.i.* to get close (to someone)

intimidad *f.* privacy

intolerante *adj.* intolerant

intriga *f.* intrigue

intrigado/a *adj.* intrigued, in suspense

inundación *f.* flood

inundar *v.t.* to flood

inútil *adj.* useless

inválido/a *adj.* (*person*) disabled

invernadero *m.* greenhouse

inverosímil *adj.* unlikely, improbable; unrealistic

invertebrado/a *adj./m.* invertebrate

invertir (e:ie) *v.t.* to invest

investigador(a) *m., f.* researcher; investigator

investigar *v.t.* to research

invierno *m.* winter

invitado/a *m., f.* guest

invitar *v.t.* to invite

involuntario *adj.* involuntary

inyección *f.* injection

inyectar *v.t.* to inject

ir *v.i. irreg.* to go
ir a (+ inf.) to be going to (do something) **Voy a leer un rato.** I'm going to read for a while.
ir a exceso de velocidad to speed
ir a la playa to go to the beach
ir de campamento to go camping
ir de compras to go shopping
ir de excursión (a las montañas) to (go on a) hike (in the mountains)
ir de pesca to go fishing
ir de vacaciones to go on vacation
ir en auto(móvil) to go by auto(mobile); to go by car
ir en autobús to go by bus
ir en avión to go by plane
ir en barco to go by ship/boat
ir en metro to go by subway
ir en motocicleta to go by motorcycle

ir en taxi to go by taxi
ir en tren to go by train
¡Vamos! Let's go!; Come on!
ironía *f.* irony
irónico/a *adj.* ironic
irresponsable *adj.* irresponsible
irse *v. pron. irreg.* to go away; to leave **No te vayas, aún es temprano.** Don't leave; it's still early.
  irse de pinta (*idiom*) (*Mexico*) to play hooky
  irse de vacaciones to go on vacation
italiano *m.* (*language*) Italian
italiano/a *adj./m., f.* Italian
itinerario *m.* itinerary
izquierdo/a *adj.* left; *m., f.* left
  a la izquierda (de) to the left (of)

J

jabón *m.* soap
jabonera *f.* soap dish
jamás *adv.* never; not ever
jamón *m.* ham
Januká *m.* Chanukah
japonés *m.* (*language*) Japanese
japonés, japonesa *adj./m., f.* Japanese
jarabe para la tos *m.* cough syrup
jardín *m.* garden, (back) yard
jardinería *f.* gardening
jardinero/a *m., f.* gardener
jarra *f.* pitcher
jarrón *m.* vase
jeans *m., pl.* jeans

jefe/a *m., f.* boss
jerarquía *f.* hierarchy
jerárquico/a *adj.* hierarchical
jerarquizado/a *adj.* hierarchical
jerez *m.* (*wine*) sherry
jeringa *f.* syringe
jirafa *f.* giraffe
joroba *f.* hump
jorobado/a *adj.* hunchbacked
jota *f.* (*playing cards*) jack
joven *adj.* young; *m., f.* youth, young person
joyas *f.* jewels
joyería *f.* jewelry store
joyero/a *m., f.* jeweler; *m.* jewelry box
jubilado/a *m., f.* retired person
jubilarse *v. pron.* to retire (from work)
judío/a *adj.* Jewish; *m., f.* Jew
juego *m.* game
  juego limpio/sucio fair/foul play
juegos *m. pl.* games
  juegos de azar gambling
  juegos de mesa board games
  Juegos Olímpicos Olympic Games
  Juegos Paralímpicos Paralympics
jueves *m., sing.* Thursday
juez *m., f.* judge
jugador(a) *m., f.* player; gambler
jugar (u:ue) *v.t./v.i.* to play
  jugar a las cartas to play cards
jugo *m.* juice

jugo de fruta fruit juice
jugoso/a *adj.* juicy
juguete *m.* toy
juguetería *f.* toy store
juicio *m.* judgment; trial
julio *m.* July
junio *m.* June
jungla *f.* jungle
junta *f.* board, committee
  junta directiva board of directors
juntarse *v. pron.* to get together
juntos/as *adj./adv.* together
jurado *m.* jury
jurar *v.i.* to swear
justicia *f.* justice
justo/a *adj.* fair
juvenil *adj.* youthful
juventud *f.* youth
juzgar *v.t.* to judge

K

kilo(gramo) *m.* kilo(gram)
kilómetro *m.* kilometer

L

la *f., sing. art., def.* the
la *d.o. pron. f., sing.* her, it, you
labio *m.* lip
laboratorio *m.* laboratory
lacio/a *adj.* (*hair*) straight
ladera *f.* hillside, mountainside, slope
  El primer grupo subió por la ladera norte. The first group ascended the northern slope.
lado *m.* side
  al lado de beside; next to
  por un lado…, por otro

lado… on (the) one hand…, on the other hand . . .
ladrar *v.i.* to bark
ladrido *m.* bark
ladrillo *m.* brick
ladrón, ladrona *m., f.* thief; robber; burglar
lagarto *f.* lizard
lago *m.* lake
lágrima *f.* tear
lamentar *v.t.* to regret
lámpara *f.* lamp
lana *f.* wool
  de lana (made of) wool
lancha *f.* motorboat
langosta *f.* lobster
langostino *m.* prawn
lanzado *p.p. of* **lanzar** thrown
lanzado/a *adj.* (*person*) impulsive, impetuous
lanzamiento *m.* launch, throw
  lanzamiento de bala *(L. A.)* shotput
  lanzamiento de disco discus throw
  lanzamiento de jabalina javelin throw
  lanzamiento de peso *(Spain)* shotput
lanzar *v.t.* to throw; to launch
  La NASA lanzó un cohete a Saturno. NASA launched a rocket to Saturn.
lápiz *m.* pencil
  lápiz labial lipstick
largo/a *adj.* long (*in length*)
  a la larga in the long run
laringe *f.* larynx
larva *f.* larva
las *f., pl. art., def.* the

65

las *d.o. pron. f., pl.* them
lástima *f.* shame, pity
  Es una lástima (que…) It's too bad (that…); It's a shame (that…)
  Es una lástima que no te puedas quedar. It's a pity that you can't stay.
lastimar *v.t.* to hurt
lastimarse *v. pron.* to injure oneself; to get hurt
  lastimarse el pie to injure one's foot
lata *f.* (*tin*) can
  ¡Qué lata! *loc.* What a drag!
latido *m.* heartbeat
latín *m.* (*language*) Latin
latino/a *adj./m./f.* Latin
latir *v.i.* (*heart*) to beat
lavabo *m.* (bathroom) sink
lavadora *f.* washing machine
lavandería *f.* laundromat
lavaplatos *m., sing.* dishwasher
lavar (el suelo) *v.t.* to wash (the floor)
  lavar los platos to do (wash) the dishes
lavarse *v. pron.* to wash (oneself)
  lavarse la cara to wash one's face
  lavarse las manos to wash one's hands
  lavarse los dientes to brush one's teeth
lazo *m.* bow; ribbon
lazos *m., pl.* ties
  lazos familiares family ties
le *i.o. pron. sing.* to/for him, her, *form.* you

lección *f.* lesson
leche *f.* milk
lechuga *f.* lettuce
lector *m., f.* reader
leer *v.t.* to read
  leer correo electrónico to read e-mail
  leer un periódico to read a newspaper
  leer una revista to read a magazine
legado *m.* legacy
legal *adj.* legal
legalizar *v.t.* to legalize
leído *p.p. of* **leer** read
lejano/a *adj.* distant; remote; far-off
  un pariente lejano a distant relative
lejía *f.* bleach
lejos de *adv.* far from
lengua *f.* tongue; language
  lenguas extranjeras *f., pl.* foreign languages
lentamente *adv.* slowly
lenteja *f.* lentil
lentes *m., pl.* eyeglasses, lenses
  lentes de contacto contact lenses
  lentes (de sol/oscuros/ negros) (sun)glasses
lento/a *adj.* slow
leña *f.* firewood
leño *m.* log
león *m.* lion
leopardo *m.* leopard
les *i.o. pron. pl.* to/for them, *form* you

letra *f.* (*alphabet*) letter; handwriting; (*song*) lyrics
Tienes una letra ilegible. Your handwriting is illegible.
letra de imprenta printing
Escriba su nombre completo en letra de imprenta. Print your full name.

letra mayúscula capital letter
letra minúscula lowercase letter
letrero *m.* sign
levadura *f.* yeast
levantar *v.t.* to lift
levantar pesas to lift weights
levantarse *v. pron.* to get up
ley *f.* law
la ley del más fuerte the survival of the fittest
leyenda *f.* legend
liberación *f.* liberation
liberal *adj./m., f.* liberal
liberar *v.t.* to free, to release
libertad *f.* liberty, freedom
la Estatua de la Libertad the Statue of Liberty
libertad condicional parole
libertad de expresión freedom of speech
libra *f.* pound
libre *adj.* free
librería *f.* bookstore
libro *m.* book
libro de bolsillo paperback
libro de consulta reference book
licencia *f.* license
licencia de

conducir/manejar driver's license
licor *m.* liqueur, liquor
licuadora *f.* (*L.A.*) blender
licuar *v.t.* to blend
líder *m., f.* leader
liderar *v.t.* to lead
liderazgo *m.* leadership
ligar *v.i.* (*Spain*) to pick up boys/girls
ligero/a *adj.* (*weight/food*) light
lima *f.* (*tool*) file; nail file
limitar *v.t.* to limit; to restrict
límite *m.* limit
limón *m.* lemon, lime
limonada *f.* lemonade
limonero *m.* lemon tree
limosna *f.* alms, charity
vivir de limosnas to live by begging
limpiaparabrisas *m. sing.* windshield wiper
limpiar *v.t.* to clean
limpiar la casa to clean the house
limpio/a *adj.* clean
limusina *f.* limousine
lindo/a *adj.* pretty
línea *f.* line
en línea in-line
línea discontinua broken line
lingüista *m., f.* linguist
lingüística *f.* linguistics
lingüístico/a *adj.* linguistic
linterna *f.* flashlight
líquido/a *adj./m.* liquid
lirio *m.* lily
lista *f.* list
lista de espera waiting list
lista de éxitos best-seller list

pasar lista to call roll
listo/a *adj.* smart; ready
  estar listo/a to be ready
  ser listo/a to be smart
literal *adj.* literal
  Es una traducción demasiado literal; no suena natural. It's too literal a translation; it doesn't sound natural.
literario/a *adj.* literary
literatura *f.* literature
litro *m.* liter
liviano/a *adj.* light
llamada *f.* call
  llamada telefónica telephone call
llamar *v.t.* to call
  llamar a cobro revertido to call collect
  llamar la atención (a) to attract attention (to)
  llamar por teléfono to call on the phone
llamarse *v. pron.* to be called; to be named
  Me llamo… My name is…
llanta *f.* tire
llanura *f.* prairie
llave *f.* key
  llave maestra master key
llavero *m.* key chain
llegada *f.* arrival
llegar *v.i.* to arrive
  llegar a ser to become
  llegar tarde to be late
llenar *v.t.* to fill; (*form*) (*L.A.*) to fill out
  llenar el tanque to fill the tank

llenar un formulario to fill out a form
lleno/a *adj.* full
llevar *v.t.* to carry, to take (someone somewhere); (*clothes*) to wear **¿Qué es eso que llevas puesto?** What's that you're wearing?
  llevar una vida sana to lead a healthy lifestyle
llevarse *v. pron.* to take
  Puedes llevártelo. You can take it.
  llevarse bien/mal (con) to get along well/badly/poorly (with)
llorar *v.i.* to cry
lloriquear *v.i.* to whine
llorón, llorona *adj./m., f.* crybaby
llover (o:ue) *v. impers.* to rain
  llover a cántaros *idiom* to pour, to rain cats and dogs
  Llueve. It's raining.
lluvia *f.* rain
  lluvia ácida acid rain
lo *d.o. pron.* it, him, *form.* you
  Dilo. Say it.
  Díselo. Say it to him.
  lo pasamos de película we had a great time
  lo que what; that which
lobo *m.* wolf
loco/a *adj.* crazy
  loco de remate stark raving mad
locomotora *f.* locomotive
locura *f.* madness
locutor(a) *m., f.* (*TV, radio*) announcer

lograr *v.t.* to achieve
logro *m.* achievement
lombriz *f.* earthworm
lomo *m.* flank steak
  lomo a la plancha grilled flank steak
lona *f.* canvas
lonchera *f.* (*L.A.*) lunch box
longevidad *f.* longevity
loro *m.* parrot
los *m., pl. art., def.* the
los *d.o. pron. m. pl.* them, *form.* you
lucha *f.* fight, struggle
luchar (por/contra) *v.i.* to fight, to struggle (for/against)
lucir (c:zc) *v.* to look good
luego *adv.* afterwards, then; later
  desde luego *idiom* of course
  ¡Hasta luego! See you later.
  Y luego qué. And then what?
lugar *m.* place
lujo *m.* luxury
lujoso/a *adj.* luxurious
luna *f.* moon
  luna de miel honeymoon
lunar *m.* mole, beauty mark; polka dot
  una corbata de lunares a polka-dot tie
lunes *m., sing.* Monday
lupa *f.* magnifying glass
luz *f.* light, electricity
  Apaga la luz. Turn out the light.
  la luz del sol sunlight

M
maceta *f.* flower pot

macho *m.* male
madera *f.* wood
madrastra *f.* stepmother
madre *f.* mother
madrina *f.* godmother
madrugada *f.* early morning
madrugar *v.i.* to get up early
madurez *f.* maturity; middle age
maduro/a *adj.* (*person*) mature; (*fruit*) ripe
maestría *f.* (*L.A.*) Master's degree
maestro/a *m., f.* (*elementary school*) teacher
magia *f.* magic
mágico/a *adj.* magical
magma *m.* magma
magnesio *m.* magnesium
magnífico/a *adj.* magnificent
mago/a *m., f.* magician
maíz *m.* corn
mal *adv.* bad, ill
maleducado/a *adj.* rude, bad-mannered
maleta *f.* suitcase
maletero *m.* (*Spain*) (*automobile*) trunk
malgastar *v.t.* to waste
  No malgastes tu tiempo en tonterías. Don't waste your time with stupid little things.
maligno *adj.* (*tumor*) malignant
malo/a *adj.* bad; mean
  ¡Mala suerte! Unlucky!
  ¡Qué película más mala! What a terrible movie!
  (No) Es malo que... It's (not) bad that...

No es malo que lo digas. It's not bad that you say it.

mamá *f.* mom

mami *f.* mom

mamífero *m.* mammal

manantial *m.* (*water*) spring

mandar *v.t.* to order; to send; to mail

mandarina *f.* tangerine

manejar *v.i.* to drive

manera *f.* way

  de ninguna manera by no means; no way

manga *f.* sleeve

manguera *f.* hose

manicomio *m.* mental hospital

manicura *f.* manicure

manifestación *f.* demonstration

manifestante *m.*, *f.* demonstrator

manillar *m.* (*Spain*) (*bike*) handlebars

maniquí *m.* mannequin

mano *f.* hand

manta *f.* blanket

mantel *m.* tablecloth

mantener (e:ie) *v.t. irreg.* **(yo mantengo)** to maintain, to support; to keep

  Mantengan la calma. Stay calm.

  Mantener las apariencias. Keep up appearances.

  ¿Quién va a mantener a la familia? Who's going to support the family?

mantenerse en forma (e:ie) *v. pron. irreg.* **(yo me mantengo)** to stay in shape

mantequilla *f.* butter

manzana *f.* apple

mañana *f.* morning, a.m.; *adv.* tomorrow

  a las dos de la mañana at two in the morning, at two a.m.

mañanitas *f. pl.* birthday song

mapa *m.* map

  mapa de carreteras road map

maquillador(a) *m.*, *f.* makeup artist

maquillaje *m.* makeup

maquillar *v.t.* to apply makeup

maquillarse *v. pron.* to put on makeup

máquina *f.* machine

  máquina de afeitar razor

  máquina de coser sewing machine

  máquina de escribir typewriter

mar *m.* sea, ocean

  en alta mar on the high sea

maratón *m.* marathon

maravillosamente *adv.* marvelously

maravilloso/a *adj.* marvelous

marca *f.* mark; (*commerce*) brand, brand name; (*sport*) record

  Es una marca de prestigio. It's a well-known brand.

  Superó su marca. She beat her own record.

marcador *m.* (*sports*) scoreboard

marcapasos *m.*, *sing.* pacemaker

marcar *v.t.* (*telephone*) to dial; (*sports*) to score

Marca el 007. Dial 007.
¿Quién marcó el gol de la victoria? Who scored the winning goal?
marea *f.* tide
  marea alta/baja high/low tide
  marea negra oil slick
mareado/a *adj.* dizzy; nauseated
marearse *v. pron.* to get dizzy
  ¿Te mareas en barco? Do you get seasick?
maremoto *m.* seaquake; tidal wave
margarina *f.* margarine
margarita *f.* daisy
marinero *m.* sailor
mariposa *f.* butterfly
mariscada *f.* assorted seafood
mariscos *m., pl.* shellfish; seafood
mármol *m.* marble
marrón *adj./m.* brown
martes *m., sing.* Tuesday
martillo *m.* hammer
marzo *m.* March
más *adv./ pron.* more **¿Quieres más?** Would you like some more?
  más de (+ number) more than **Hay más de diez personas.** There are more than ten people.
  más o menos so so
  más… que more… than **más grande que una casa** bigger than a house
  más tarde later
masa *f.* dough

masaje *m.* massage
masajista *m.* masseur; *f.* masseuse
máscara *f.* mask
mascarilla *f.* mask
masticar *v.t.* to chew
matar *v.t.* to kill
  matar dos pájaros de un tiro *loc.* to kill two birds with one stone
matarse *v. pron.* to kill oneself
  Se mata estudiando. She studies like crazy.
matemáticas *f., pl.* mathematics
matemático/a *m., f.* mathematician
materia *f.* matter; (*school*) subject; course
  materia inorgánica inorganic matter
  ¿Qué materia enseña la Srta. López? What subject does Miss López teach?
materialista *adj.* materialistic
materno/a *adj.* (*relative*) maternal
matrícula *f.* (*education*) registration, matriculation; (*automobile*) registration number, license plate
  matrícula de honor (*grade*) distinction, magna cum laude
matricularse *v. pron.* (*education*) to register, to enroll
matrimonio *m.* marriage
máximo/a *m.* maximum, top
mayo *m.* May
mayonesa *f.* mayonnaise

mayor *adj.* older
 el/la mayor the oldest; the eldest
mayordomo *m.* butler
mayoría *f.* majority
me *pron.* me
 Dámelo. Give it to me.
mecánico/a *m., f.* mechanic
mecanismo *m.* mechanism
mecanógrafo/a *m., f.* typist
mecedora *f.* rocking chair
mecer (c:z) *v.t.* to rock
medalla *f.* medal
mediano/a *adj.* medium
medianoche *f.* midnight
medias *f., pl.* pantyhose, stockings
medicamento *m.* medication
medicina *f.* medicine
medición *f.* measurement
médico/a *m., f.* doctor; physician
 médico de cabecera family doctor
 médico de familia family doctor
 médico/a de guardia doctor on call, doctor on duty
médico/a *adj.* medical
 tratamiento médico medical treatment
medida *f.* measurement, size
medio/a *m.* half
 medio ambiente *m.* environment
 medio/a hermano/a *m.* half-brother; *f.* half-sister
mediocre *adj.* mediocre
mediodía *m.* noon, midday
medios *m., pl.* means; resources

 los medios de comunicación (the) media; means of comunication
medir (e:i) *v.t.* to measure
meditación *f.* meditation
meditar *v.i.* to meditate
médula *f.* marrow
medusa *f.* jellyfish
megáfono *m.* megaphone
mejilla *f.* cheek
mejillón *m.* mussel
mejor *adj.* better; best
 el/la mejor *m., f.* the best
 lo mejor the best (thing)
 Es mejor que… It's better that…
 Es mejor que vayas. It's better that you go.
 mejor que *adj.* better than
mejora *f.* improvement
mejorar *v.t.* to improve
mejorarse *v. pron.* to get better
mellizo/a *m., f.* twin
melocotón *m.* (*Spain*) peach
melón *m.* melon
membrana *f.* membrane
memoria *f.* memory
 de memoria *adv.* by heart
 Se sabe el poema de memoria. He knows the poem by heart.
memorizar *v.t.* to memorize
mendigo/a *m., f.* beggar
menopausia *f.* menopause
menor *adj.* younger
 el/la menor *m., f.* the youngest
menos *adv.* less
 a menos que *conj.* unless **Iré a menos que llueva.** I'll go unless it rains.

menos cuarto/quince quarter to/of **Son las dos menos cuarto/quince.** It's a quarter to/of two.
menos de (+ *number*) less/fewer than **Tengo menos de una hora.** I have less than an hour.
menos… que less… than **¿Qué es menos interesante que hablar?** What's less interesting than talking?
por lo menos at least
mensaje *m.* message
mensaje electrónico e-mail message
mensualidad *f.* (*monthly payment*) installment
menta *f.* mint
mentalidad *f.* mentality
mentir (e:ie) *v.i.* to lie
mentira *f.* lie
parecer mentira *idiom* to be hard to believe; to be incredible
Aunque parezca mentira, sólo tiene diez años. It's hard to believe, but he's only ten.
mentiroso/a *adj.* liar
menú *m.* menu
menudo/a *adj.* tiny, minute
a menudo *adv.* frequently, often
mercadillo *m.* street market
mercado *m.* market
mercado al aire libre open-air market
mercurio *m.* mercury
merecer (c:zc) *v.t.* to deserve
merendar (e:ie) *v.i.* to snack (in the afternoon); to have an afternoon snack
merienda *f.* afternoon snack
mérito *m.* merit
merluza *f.* (*fish*) hake
mermelada *f.* jam
mes *m.* month
mesa *f.* table
mesa de noche night table
mesero/a *m.* waiter; *f.* waitress
meseta *f.* plateau
mesita *f.* end table
mesita de noche night stand
meta *f.* objective, goal
metabolismo *m.* metabolism
metabolizar *v.t.* to metabolize
metáfora *f.* metaphor
metafórico/a *adj.* metaphoric
metal *m.* metal
metamorfosis *f.* metamorphosis
meteorito *m.* meteorite
meteorólogo/a *m., f.* meteorologist
meter *v.t.* to put (into)
meter la pata put one's foot in one's mouth
metereología *f.* meteorology
metódico/a *adj.* methodical
método *m.* method
metro *m.* meter; subway
mexicano/a *adj./m., f.* Mexican
México *m.* Mexico
mezclar *v.t.* to mix, to toss
mezquita *f.* mosque
mí *pron.* me
¿Para mí? For me?
mi(s) *poss.* my
micrófono *m.* microphone
microonda *f.* microwave
microondas, (el) *m.* microwave (oven)

73

microscopio *m.* microscope
miedo *m.* fear
  No tengas miedo. Don't be afraid.
miel *f.* honey
miembro *m.* member; (*body*) limb
mientras *adv.* while
  mientras tanto meanwhile
miércoles *m., sing.* Wednesday
mil *m.* one thousand
  a las mil y una very late
  Anoche llegó a las mil y una. Last night he arrived very late.
  Mil perdones. I'm extremely sorry.
milagro *m.* miracle
milla *f.* mile
millón *m.* million
  mil millones a billion (*US*)
  millones (de) millions (of)
mimbre *m.* wicker
mina *f.* mine
mineral *m.* mineral
minería *f.* mining industry
minero/a *m., f.* miner
minifalda *f.* miniskirt
mínimo/a *adj./m.* minimum
  como mínimo at least
ministro/a *m., f.* (*government*) minister
minoría *f.* minority
minúsculo/a *adj.* minute, tiny
minuto *m.* minute
mío/a(s) *poss.* my, (of) mine
miope *adj.* myopic
miopía *f.* myopia
mirar *v.t.* to watch, to see, to look at

mirar (la) televisión to watch television
misil *m.* missile
mismo/a *adj.* same
misterioso/a *adj.* mysterious
mitad *f.* half, middle
mitin *m.* political meeting
mochila *f.* backpack
moda *f.* fashion
  ir a la moda *v.* to be fashionably dressed or trendy
  de moda in fashion
módem *m.* modem
modernizar *v.t.* to modernize
moderno/a *adj.* modern, trendy
modificar *v.t.* to modify
modista *f.* dressmaker
modo *m.* way, manner; (*verb tense*) mood ¿**el modo subjuntivo o el indicativo?** the subjunctive or the indicative mood?
  de ningún modo by no means
  de todos modos anyway; in any case
moho *m.* mold
mojado/a *adj.* wet
mojar *v.t.* to wet, to get wet
mojarse *v. pron.* to get (oneself) wet
  Salí sin paraguas y me mojé toda. I went out without an umbrella and I got all wet.
molestar *v.t.* to bother, to annoy; to disturb
  No le molestes, está estudiando. Don't disturb him, he's studying.

Deja de molestarme, estoy pensando. Stop bothering me, I'm thinking.

Este ruido me molesta. This noise annoys me.

molestia *f.* inconvenience, bother

No es ninguna molestia. It's no bother at all.

molesto/a *adj.* upset

molino *m.* (*machine, factory*) mill

momento *m.* moment

monarca *m., f.* monarch

monarquía *f.* monarchy

monasterio *m.* monastery

mondadientes *m.* toothpick

moneda *f.* coin

monedero *m.* coin purse

monitor *m.* (*computer*) monitor

monitor(a) *m., f.* trainer, coach, instructor

monitor de esquí ski instructor

monja *f.* nun

monje *m.* monk

mono *m.* monkey

monólogo *m.* monologue

montacargas *m.* forklift

montaña *f.* mountain

montar *v.t.* (*bike*) to ride; (*machine, furniture*) to assemble

montar a caballo to ride a horse

¿Aún no has montado el escritorio? You still haven't assembled the desk?

monumento *m.* monument

mora *f.* blackberry

morado/a *adj.* purple

moral *f.* moral

moralidad *f.* morality

morder (o:ue) *v.t.* to bite

mordisco *m.* bite

moreno/a *adj.* brunet(te), dark-skinned, tanned

morfología *f.* morphology

moribundo/a *adj.* moribund, dying

morir (o:ue) *v.i.* to die

Me muero por ir. I'm dying to go.

Me muero por un beso. I'm dying for a kiss.

mortalidad *f.* mortality

mosca *f.* fly

mosquitero *m.* mosquito net

mostaza *f.* mustard

mostrar (o:ue) *v.t.* to show

moto *f.* motorcycle

motocicleta *f.* motorcycle

motociclismo *m.* motorcycling

motociclista *m., f.* motorcyclist

motor *m.* motor, engine

móvil *adj.* mobile

movilidad *f.* mobility

mozo/a (*L.A.*) *m.* waiter; *f.* waitress

muchacho/a *m.,* boy; *f.* girl

muchísimo/a *adj.* (*superlative*) very much

Muchísimas gracias. Thank you very much.

mucho/a(s) *adj.* many; a lot of; much; *adv.* a lot

muchas veces many times; a lot

Mucho gusto. Pleased/Nice to meet you.

mudanza *f.* move
mudar *v.t.* to move, to change
  Las serpientes mudan de piel cada año. Snakes change their skin each year.
mudarse *v. pron.* to move (from one house to another)
  ¿Cuántas veces te has mudado este año? How many times have you moved this year?
mudo/a *adj.* mute
muebles *m., pl.* furniture
muela *f.* molar, back tooth; (*generic*) tooth **Me sacaron una muela.** I had a tooth pulled.
  muela del juicio wisdom tooth
muelle *m.* spring
muerte *f.* death
muerto/a *p.p. of* **morir** died; *adj.* dead
  Estoy muerto de hambre. I'm starving.
muestra *f.* sample
mujer *f.* woman
  mujer de negocios businesswoman
  mujer policía female police officer
mujeriego *m.* womanizer
multa *f.* fine, ticket
multitud *f.* crowd
mundial *adj.* worldwide
mundo *m.* world
municipal *m.* municipal
muñeca/o *m., f.* doll; *f.* wrist
muralla *f.* wall
murciélago *m.* (*animal*) bat

muro *m.* wall
músculo *m.* muscle
musculoso/a *adj.* muscular
museo *m.* museum
música *f.* music
  poner la música muy alta to play loud music
musical *adj.* musical
músico/a *m., f.* musician
muslo *m.* thigh
musulmán, musulmana *adj./m., f.* Muslim
muy *adv.* very
  Muy amable. That's very kind of you.
  Muy bien, gracias. Very well, thank you/thanks

N

nacer (c:zc) *v.i.* to be born
nacimiento *m.* birth
nación *f.* nation
  Naciones Unidas United Nations **Ése es el edificio de las Naciones Unidas.** That's the UN building.
nacional *adj.* national
nacionalidad *f.* nationality
nacionalismo *m.* nationalism
nacionalista *adj.* nationalist
nada *pron./adv.* nothing, (not) anything
  De nada. You're welcome.
  No está nada mal. It's not bad at all.
  No me gustan nada. I don't like them at all.
  nada mal not bad at all
nadador(a) *m., f.* swimmer
nadar *v.i.* to swim

nadie *pron.* no one, nobody, not anyone, anybody
No lo sabe nadie. Nobody knows it.
naipe *m.* playing card
naranja *f.* orange
naranjo *m.* orange tree
nariz *f.* nose
narrador(a) *m., f.* narrator
nata *f.* (*Spain*) cream; (*on boiled milk*) skin
natación *f.* swimming
natación sincronizada synchronized swimming
natalidad *f.* birthrate
natural *adj.* natural
naturaleza *f.* nature
naturalmente *adv.* naturally; of course
navaja *f.* jackknife, penknife
navegar *v.i.* to sail
navegar (en Internet/la red) to surf (the Internet/Web)
Navidad *f.* Christmas
necesario/a *adj.* necessary
(No) Es necesario que… It's (not) necessary that…
No es necesario que te quedes. It's not necessary that you stay.
neceser *m.* toilet kit
necesidad *f.* necessity
necesitar (+ *inf.*) *v.t.* to need
nectarina *f.* nectarine
negación *f.* refusal
negar (e:ie) *v.t.* to deny
no negar not to deny
negarse (e:ie) *v. pron.* to refuse
negativo/a *m.* negative

negocios *m., pl.* business, commerce
negro/a *adj./m.* (*color*) black
nervio *m.* nerve
nervioso/a *adj.* nervous
neumático *m.* tire
neurona *f.* neuron
nevar (e:ie) *v. impers.* to snow
Nieva. It's snowing.
ni *conj.* nor
ni… ni *conj.* neither… nor
Ni tú ni yo. Neither you nor I.
niebla *f.* fog
nieto/a *m.* grandson; *f.* granddaughter
nieve *f.* snow
ningún, ninguno/a(s) *adj.* no; none; not any
ningún problema no problem
ninguna parte, (a) nowhere
niñero/a *m., f.* baby-sitter
niñez *f.* childhood
niño/a *m., f.* child, kid
de niño/a as a child
niño/a mimado/a spoiled child, brat
nitrógeno *m.* nitrogen
nivel *m.* level
no *adv.* no; not
No es así. That's not the way it is.
No muy bien. Not very well.
No, no vengo. No, I'm not coming.
Vienes, ¿no? You're coming, right?
¿Vienes o no? Are you coming or not?
noche *f.* night, evening
de la noche in the evening,

at night, P.M. **a las diez de la noche** at ten P.M.
por la noche at night
nogal *m.* walnut tree
nombre *m.* name
en mi nombre in my name
en nombre de on behalf of, in the name of
nombre de pila first name
nórdico/a *adj.* Nordic; *m., f.* Northern European
norte *m.* north
al norte to the north
norteamericano/a *adj./m., f.* (North) American
nos *pron.* us, ourselves, each other
Nos vemos. See you.
nosotros/as *pron.* we, us
entre nosotros/as between us; off the record
nota *f.* (*school*) grade, mark, note
notar *v.t.* to notice
noticias *f., pl.* news
noticiero *m.* newscast
novatada *f.* practical joke
hacer una novatada (a alguien) *v.* to haze (somebody)
novato/a *adj.* inexperienced, new
novecientos/as nine hundred
noveno/a *adj./m.* ninth
noventa ninety
noviembre *m.* November
novillo *m.* steer
hacer novillos *(Spain)* to play hooky
novio/a *m.,* boyfriend; *f.*

girlfriend
nube *f.* cloud
nublado/a *adj.* cloudy
Está (muy) nublado. It's (very) cloudy.
nuclear *adj.* nuclear
núcleo *m.* nucleus
nuera *f.* daughter-in-law
nuestro/a(s) *poss.* our
nueve nine
nuevo/a *adj.* new
de nuevo again
nuez *f.* walnut
número *m.* number; (*shoe*) size
nunca *adv.* never; not ever
nutrición *f.* nutrition
nutricionista *m., f.* nutritionist

Ñ
ñame *m.* yam

O
o *conj.* or
o... o *conj.* either... or
O te quedas o te vas. Either you stay or you go.
obedecer (c:zc) *v.t.* to obey
obesidad *f.* obesity
obeso/a *adj.* obese
objetivo/a *m.* objective; aim, goal
objeto *m.* object; purpose
¿Cuál es el objeto de esta discusión? What's the purpose of this argument?
obligar *v.t.* to force, to oblige; to make
(a alguien a + *inf.*)
No le obligues a estudiar. Don't force him to study.

(a alguien a que + *subj.*)
No me obligues a que lo
diga. Don't make me say it.
obra *f.* (*of art, literature, music,*
etc.) work
obra maestra masterpiece
observación *f.* observation
observador(a) *adj.* observant
observatorio *m.* observatory
observar *v.t.* to observe
obtener (e:ie) *v.t. irreg.* **(yo**
obtengo) to obtain; to get
obvio/a *adj.* obvious
Es obvio (que...) It's obvious
(that...)
océano *m.* ocean; sea
ochenta eighty
ocho eight
ochocientos/as eight hundred
ocio *m.* leisure time
ocioso/a *adj.* idle
ocre *m.* ocher
octavo/a *adj./m.* eighth
octubre *m.* October
oculista *m., f.* optician
ocupación *f.* occupation
ocupado/a *adj.* busy
ocurrir *v. impers.* to occur; to
happen
Ocurrió lo inesperado. The
unexpected happened.
odiar *v.t.* to hate
oeste *m.* west
al oeste to the west
ofender *v.t.* to offend
ofenderse *v. pron.* to take
offense
ofensa *f.* insult
oferta *f.* offer
oficina *f.* office

oficio *m.* trade
ofrecer (c:zc) *v.t.* to offer
ofrenda *f.* offering
oftalmólogo/a *m., f.*
ophthalmologist
oído *m.* (*sense of*) hearing;
inner ear
oído *p.p.* of **oír** heard
oír (y) *v.t./v.i. irreg.* **(yo oigo)** to
hear
oiga(n) *form., sing. pl.* listen
(*in conversation*)
oír decir que *idiom* to have
heard that **He oído decir que**
te casas. I've heard that you
are getting married.
oye *fam., sing.* listen (*in*
conversation)
¡Ojalá! *interj.* I hope so!
Ojalá (que) I hope (that); I
wish (that)
Ojalá que vuelva pronto.
I hope/Hopefully he comes
back soon.
Ojalá no llueva mañana.
I hope/wish it doesn't rain
tomorrow.
ojo *m.* eye
ola *f.* wave
oler (a) *v.i. irreg.* to smell (like)
Huele a humo aquí. It smells
like smoke here.
olfato *m.* (*sense*) smell
olimpiada/olimpiadas *f./f., pl.*
Olympic Games, Olympics
Olimpiadas Especiales
Special Olympics
olímpico/a *adj.* Olympic
olla *f.* cooking pot
olla a presión pressure
cooker

79

olor *m.* smell, odor
  el olor de la primavera the smell of spring
  olor corporal body odor
olvidar *v.t.* to forget
ombligo *m.* navel
omoplato *m.* scapula
once eleven
oncólogo/a *m., f.* oncologist
onda *f.* (*physics, radio*) wave
onza *f.* ounce
opaco/a *adj.* opaque
ópera *f.* opera
operación *f.* operation
opinar *v.t.* to express an opinion
opinión *f.* opinion
  en mi opinión in my opinion
oportunidad *f.* opportunity
optimista *adj./m., f.* optimist, optimistic
orden *m.* order, sequence; *f.* order, command
  A sus órdenes. At your service.
ordenado/a *adj.* orderly; well-organized
ordenador *m.* (*Spain*) computer
ordinal *adj.* ordinal
orégano *m.* oregano
oreja *f.* (*outer*) ear
organización *f.* organization; arrangement
organizar *v.t.* to organize; to arrange
órgano *m.* organ
  órganos de los sentidos sensory organs
orgullo *m.* pride
orgulloso/a *adj.* proud

original *adj.* original
originalidad *f.* originality
orilla *f.* shore, (river)bank
  La casa está a orillas del mar. The house is on the seashore.
orina *f.* urine
orinar *v.i.* to urinate
oro *m.* gold
orquesta *f.* orchestra
ortografía *f.* spelling
ortográfico/a *adj.* spelling
os *fam., pl.* you
  ¿Os gusta? Do you like it?
ositu *m.* teddy bear
oso/a *m., f.* bear
  Osa Mayor Big Dipper
  Osa Menor Little Dipper
ostra *f.* oyster
otoño *m.* autumn, fall
otro/a *adj.* other; another
  otra vez again
oveja *f.* sheep
OVNI (Objeto Volador No Identificado) *m.* UFO (Unidentified Flying Object)
oxidarse *v. pron.* to rust
óxido *m.* rust
oxígeno *m.* oxygen
oyentes *m., pl.* listeners

P

paciencia *f.* patience
paciente *adj./m., f.* patient
pacifista *adj./m., f.* pacifist
padecer de (c:zc) *v.i.* (*disease*) to suffer from
  Padece del corazón. He has heart problems.
padecimiento *m.* suffering

padrastro *m.* stepfather
padre *m.* father; priest
padres *m., pl.* parents
padrino *m.* godfather
pagar *v.t.* to pay
  pagar a plazos to pay in installments
  pagar al contado to pay in cash
  pagar en efectivo to pay in cash
  pagar la cuenta to pay the bill
página *f.* page
  página principal home page
país *m.* country
  país desarrollado developed country
  país en vías de desarrollo developing country
paisaje *m.* landscape; countryside
pájaro *m.* bird
pala *f.* shovel
palabra *f.* word
palacio *m.* palace
paladar *m.* palate
palanca *f.* lever
paleontología *f.* paleontology
paleontólogo/a *m., f.* paleontologist
pálido/a *adj.* pale, pallid
palmera *f.* palm tree
palo *m.* stick; (*golf*) club
  de tal palo, tal astilla *loc.* like father, like son
paloma *f.* dove
pan *m.* bread
  pan integral whole-wheat bread

pan tostado toasted bread; toast
panadería *f.* bakery
páncreas *m.* pancreas
pandilla *f.* gang
pandillero/a *m., f.* gang member
pantaletas *f., pl.* (*Venezuela*) panties
pantalla *f.* screen
pantalones *m., pl.* pants
  pantalones cortos shorts
pantano *m.* (*natural*) marsh, swamp; (*man-made*) reservoir
pantorrilla *f.* (anatomy) calf
pantuflas *f., pl.* slippers
pañuelo *m.* handkerchief
papa *f.* (*L.A.*) potato
  papas fritas fried potatoes; French fries
papá *m.* dad
papás *m., pl.* parents
papel *m.* paper; *m.* role
  papel de aluminio tinfoil
  papel higiénico toilet paper
  hacer un buen/mal papel *idiom* to make a good/bad impression
papelera *f.* wastebasket
papi *m.* daddy
paquete *m.* package
par *m.* pair
  un par de días a couple of days
  un par de zapatos a pair of shoes
para *prep.* for; in order to
  para que so that
parabrisas *m., sing.* windshield

paracaídas *m., sing.* parachute
paracaidismo *m.* parachuting
paracaidista *m., f.* parachutist
parachoques *m., sing.* bumper
parada *f.* (*train, bus*) stop
parador *m.* lodging
paraguas *m.* umbrella
paragüero *m.* umbrella stand
parar(se) *v.i.* to stop
pararrayos *m.* lightning rod
parásito *m.* parasite
parecer (c:zc) *v.i.* to seem; to appear
  al parecer *adv.* apparently, seemingly
parecerse (c:zc) (a alguien/a algo) *v. pron.* to look like (*somebody/something*); to be alike
  ¿A quién se parece? Who does he/she look like?
pared *f.* wall
pareja *f.* partner; (married) couple
  ¿Cuántas parejas vienen a cenar? How many couples are coming for dinner?
parientes *m., pl.* relatives
párpado *m.* eyelid
parque *m.* park
  parque acuático water park
  parque de atracciones (*Spain*) amusement park
  parque de diversiones (*L.A.*) amusement park
  parque natural nature reserve
párrafo *m.* paragraph
parrilla *f.* grill
  a la parrilla grilled, broiled

parte *f.* part
  de parte de on behalf of
participación *f.* participation
participante *m., f.* competitor
participar *v.t.* to participate
particular *adj.* private
partida *f.* departure
partido *m.* (*sports*) game, match; (*politics*) party
partir *v.t.* to cut; *v.i.* to leave
  a partir de from, starting (on)
pasa *f.* raisin
pasado *p.p. of* **pasar** passed
pasado/a *adj.* last; past
  el pasado lunes last Monday
pasaje *m.* ticket
  pasaje de ida y vuelta roundtrip ticket
pasajero/a *m., f.* passenger
pasamanos *m.* handrail, bannister
pasaporte *m.* passport
pasar *v.i.* to go by; to pass
  pasar la aspiradora to vacuum
  pasar por el banco to go by the bank
  pasar por la aduana to go through customs
  pasar tiempo to spend time
  pasarlo bien/mal to have a good/bad time
  pasarlo de película to have a great time
pasarse (el alto/el semáforo en rojo) *v. pron.* to run a red light
pasatiempo *m.* pastime; hobby
pasear *v.i.* to take a walk; to stroll

pasear en bicicleta to ride a bicycle
pasear por la ciudad/el pueblo to walk around the city/town
paseo *m.* stroll, walk
pasillo *m.* hallway
paso *m.* step; way
  paso a nivel railroad crossing
  paso de peatones (*L.A.*) crosswalk
  ceder el paso to yield (the right of way)
pasta de dientes *f.* toothpaste
pastel *m.* cake; pie
  pastel de chocolate chocolate cake
  pastel de cumpleaños birthday cake
pastelería *f.* pastry shop
pastilla *f.* pill; tablet
pacto *m.* lawn, grass
patata *f.* (*Spain*) potato
  patatas fritas fried potatoes, French fries
  tortilla de patatas potato omelet
paterno/a *adj.* (*relative*) paternal
patilla *f.* sideburn
patinaje *m.* skating
  patinaje artístico figure skating
  patinaje sobre hielo ice skating
  patinaje sobre ruedas roller skating
patinar *v.i.* to skate
  patinar en hielo to ice skate

  patinar en línea to rollerblade; to skate in-line
patio *m.* patio; yard
patrimonio *m.* heritage
patrocinador(a) *m., f.* sponsor
patrocinar *v.t.* to sponsor
patrón *m.* boss, owner
pavo *m.* turkey
payaso/a *m., f.* clown
paz *f.* peace
peatón *m.* pedestrian
peca *f.* freckle
pecho *m.* chest; breast
pechuga (de pollo) *f.* (chicken) breast
pecoso/a *adj.* freckled
pedagogía *f.* pedagogy
pedagógico/a *adj.* pedagogical
pedagogo/a *m., f.* pedagogue
pedal *m.* pedal
  pedal del acelerador gas pedal
  pedal del embrague clutch pedal
  pedal del freno brake pedal
pedante *adj.* pedantic
pedazo *m.* piece
pedicura *f.* pedicure
pedir (e:i) *v.t.* to ask (for); to request; (*food*) to order
  pedir prestado to borrow
  pedir un préstamo to apply for a loan
pegar *v.t.* to hit; to glue; to stick
peinado *m.* hairstyle; hairdo
  Su nuevo peinado le sienta bien. Her new hairdo suits her.
peinarse *v. pron.* to comb one's hair

peine *m.* comb
pelapapas *m.* peeler
pelar *v.t.* to peel
peldaño *m.* step, stair
pelea *f.* quarrel, fight
pelearse *v. pron.* to quarrel, to fight
  Siempre se pelean por lo mismo. They always quarrel over the same thing.
película *f.* movie
peligro *m.* danger
peligroso/a *adj.* dangerous
pelirrojo/a *adj.* red-headed, red-hair
pelo *m.* hair
pelota *f.* ball; baseball
peluca *f.* wig
peludo/a *adj.* hairy
peluquería *f.* beauty salon
peluquero/a *m., f.* hairdresser
pena *f.* ache, grief, pity
  No vale la pena. It's not worth the trouble.
pendiente *adj.* (*problem, matter*) unresolved
  estar pendiente to be waiting
  Estoy pendiente de que el jefe me llame. I'm waiting for the boss to call me.
  tener (un asunto) pendiente to have (an) unfinished (matter)
pendientes *m.* (*Spain*) earrings
penicilina *f.* penicillin
península *f.* peninsula
penitenciaría *f.* penitentiary
pensar (e:ie) (en) *v.t.* to think (about)
  pensar (+ *inf.*) to intend/plan

(*to do something*)
  Pienso llamarle mañana. I intend to call him tomorrow.
pensión *f.* boardinghouse; retirement pension
pensionista *m., f.* pensioner, retired person
peor *adj.* worse; worst
  el/la peor the worst
  lo peor the worst (thing)
peor que *adv.* worse than
pepino *m.* cucumber
pequeño/a *adj.* small
pera *f.* pear
percha *f.* hanger
perchero *m.* coat hanger
perder (e:ie) *v.t.* to lose; to miss
perdido *p.p. of* **perder** lost;
  perdido/a *adj.* lost
Perdón. Pardon me.; Excuse me.
perdonar *v.t.* to forgive
peregrinación *f.* pilgrimage
peregrino/a *m., f.* pilgrim
perejil *m.* parsley
pereza *f.* laziness
perezoso/a *adj.* lazy
perfecto/a *adj.* perfect
perfil *m.* profile
perforadora *f.* (*tool*) drill
perforar *v.t.* to drill; to perforate
perfume *m.* perfume
perfumería *f.* perfumery
perico *m.* parakeet
perímetro *m.* perimeter
periódico *m.* newspaper
periodismo *m.* journalism
periodista *m., f.* journalist
periquito *m.* parakeet

permanecer (c:zc) *v.i.* to remain; to stay
permiso *m.* permission
  Con permiso. Pardon me., Excuse me.
  Con su permiso, tengo que irme. If you'll excuse me, I have to leave.
  permiso de trabajo work permit
permitir *v.t.* to permit, to allow
pero *conj.* but
perro/a *m., f.* dog
perseguir (e:i) *v.t. irreg.* **(yo persigo)** to pursue; to chase
persiana *f.* blind
persistente *adj.* persistent
persistir *v.i.* to persist
persona *f.* person
personaje *m.* character
  personaje principal main character
personalidad *f.* personality
pertenecer (c:zc) (a) *v.t.* to belong to
pertenencias *f., pl.* belongings
pesa *f.* weight
pesadilla *f.* nightmare
pesado/a *adj.* heavy; annoying
pesar *m.* sorrow
  a pesar de despite, in spite of
pesar *v.t.* to weigh
pesarse *v. pron.* to weigh oneself
pesca *f.* fishing
pescadería *f.* fish market
pescado *m.* (*cooked*) fish
pescador(a) *m., f.* fisherman/fisherwoman

pescar *v.i.* to fish
pesimista *adj.* pessimist, pessimistic
peso *m.* weight
pestaña *f.* eyelash
pesticida *m.* pesticide
pétalo *m.* petal
petrificado/a *adj.* petrified
pez *m.* (*live*) fish
  pez gordo big shot
picante *adj.* spicy
pico *m.* beak
pie *m.* foot
piedra *f.* stone
piel *f.* skin
  de piel (made) of leather
pierna *f.* leg
pijama *m., f.* pajamas
píldora *f.* pill
pimienta *f.* black pepper
pimiento *m.* bell pepper
pinacoteca *f.* art gallery
pinar *m.* pine forest
pinchar *v.t.* (*tire*) to go flat
pingüino *m.* penguin
pino *m.* pine tree
pintada *f.* graffiti
  Hay pintadas de pandillas en la pared. There is gang graffiti on the wall.
pintalabios *m.* lipstick
pintar *v.t.* to paint
pintarse *v. pron.* to put on makeup
pintor(a) *m., f.* painter
pintoresco/a *adj.* picturesque
pintura *f.* painting; picture
piña *f.* pineapple
piñata *f.* container filled with candies

piragua *f.* canoe
piragüismo *m.* (*sport*) canoeing
piragüista *m.*, *f.* canoeist
pirámide *f.* pyramid
piropear *v.t.* to make flattering comments
piropo *m.* flattering comment
piscina *f.* swimming pool
  piscina climatizada indoor pool
piso *m.* (*of a building*) floor, story; (*L.A.*) floor; (*Spain*) apartment
plsta *f.* track; clue
  Dame una pista. Give me a clue.
  pista cubierta indoor track
  pista de aterrizaje landing strip
  pista de atletismo sports track
  pista de baile dance floor
  pista de esquí ski slope
  pista de hielo ice rink
  pista de hierba grass court
  pista de patinaje skating rink
  pista de tenis tennis court
  pista de tierra batida clay court
pizarra *f.* blackboard
pizarrón *m.* blackboard
pizca *f.* (*quantity*) pinch, little bit
placa (de matrícula) *f.* license plate
placer *m.* pleasure; delight
  Ha sido un placer. It's been a pleasure.
plagiar *v.t.* to plagiarize
plagio *m.* plagiarism

plancha *f.* (*appliance*) iron; griddle
  a la plancha grilled
planchar (la ropa) *v.t.* to iron (clothes)
plan *m.* plan
planeta *m.* planet
planetario *m.* planetarium
plano *m.* (*architecture*) blueprint; city map
plano/a *adj.* (*surface*) flat
planta *f.* plant; (*building*) floor
  planta baja ground floor
plantado/a: dejar plantado/a (a alguien) to stand (somebody) up
plástico *m.* plastic
  de plástico (*made*) of plastic
plata *f.* silver
plátano *m.* banana; plantain
plateado/a *adj.* silver
platillo *m.* dish
plato *m.* plate; (*meal*) dish, course
  plato principal main dish/main course
playa *f.* beach
plaza *f.* city or town square
  plaza de toros bullring
  plaza mayor town square
plazo *m.* (*time*) period, (*payments*) installment
plegable *adj.* folding
plegar *v.t.* to fold
plomería *f.* (*L.A.*) plumbing
plomero/a *m.*, *f.* (*L.A.*) plumber
plomo *m.* lead
pluma *f.* pen; feather
pluralidad *f.* plurality
pluralismo *m.* plurarism

población *f.* population
poblar (o:ue) *v.t.* to populate
pobre *adj.* poor
pobreza *f.* poverty
poco/a *adj.* little; few
poder *m.* power
poder (o:ue) *v. aux.* to be able
to; can
poderoso/a *adj.* powerful
podio *m.* podium
poema *m.* poem
poesía *f.* poetry
poeta *m., f.* poet
polémica *f.* controversy
polémico/a *adj.* controversial,
polemical
　El aborto es aún un tema
　polémico. Abortion is still a
　controversial topic.
polen *m.* pollen
policía *f.* police (force); *m., f.*
police officer
polideportivo *m.* sports center
política *f.* politics
político/a *m., f.* politician; *adj.*
political
pollo *m.* chicken
　pollo asado roast chicken
polvo *m.* dust
pomelo *m.* (*Argentina, Spain*)
grapefruit
ponchar *v.t.* to go flat
poncharse (una llanta) *v. pron.*
to have a flat tire
ponchera *f.* punchbowl
poner *v.t. irreg.* **(yo pongo)** to
put; to place; *v.i.* to turn on
(*electrical appliances*)
　poner a uno al día/al
　corriente *idiom* to bring

someone up to date
　poner el árbol to decorate
　the tree
　poner en libertad (a alguien)
　to release (*somebody*)
　poner la mesa to set the
　table
　poner una inyección to give
　an injection
ponerse *v. pron. irreg.* **(yo me**
pongo) to put on; to wear
ponerse (+ *adj.*) *v. pron. irreg.*
(yo me pongo) to become
(+ *adj.*)
　ponerse elegante to dress up
　Te has puesto muy elegante
　esta noche. You have
　dressed up tonight.
　ponerse rojo/a to blush
por *prep.* for; for the sake of;
for; by; in; through; due to; in
exchange for
　por aquí around here
　por avión by plane
　por ejemplo for example
　por eso that's why; therefore
　por favor please
　por fin finally
　por la mañana in the
　morning
　por la noche at night
　por la tarde in the afternoon;
　in the evening
　por lo menos at least
　por lo visto apparently
　¿por qué? why?
　por supuesto of course
　por teléfono by phone; on
　the phone
　por último finally

porcentaje *m.* percentage
porche *m.* porch
porción *f.* serving
porque *conj.* because
portaaviones *m., sing.* aircraft carrier
portarse *v. pron.* to behave oneself
  portarse bien/mal to behave well/badly, to behave/misbehave
portátil *adj.* portable
portavoz *m., f.* spokesperson
portero/a *m., f.* doorman, porter
porvenir *m.* future
poseer *v.t.* to own
posesión *f.* possession
posesivo/a *adj.* possessive
posible *adj.* possible
  lo antes posible as soon as possible
  (no) es posible it's (not) possible
postal *f.* postcard
postre *m.* dessert
potencia *f.* power
pozo *m.* well
práctica *f.* practice
practicar *v.i.* to practice
  practicar deportes to play sports
práctico/a *adj.* handy; useful
precaución *f.* precaution
precio *m.* price
precio fijo fixed/set price
predecir (e:i) *v.t. irreg.* **(yo predigo)** to predict, to foretell
predicción f. prediction
  predicción del tiempo weather forecast
prefabricado/a *adj.* prefabricated
prefabricar *v.t.* to prefabricate
preferir (e:ie) *v.t.* to prefer
pregunta *f.* question
preguntar *v.t.* to ask (*a question*)
premiar *v.t.* to award
premio *m.* prize; award
prenda *f.* garment
  Colgaron las prendas en el armario. They hung up the garments in the wardrobe.
prender *v.t.* to turn on
prensa *f.* press
preocupado/a (por) *adj.* worried (about)
preocuparse (por) *v. pron.* to worry (about)
  No se/te preocupe(s). Don't worry.
preparar *v.t.* to prepare
prepararse *v. pron.* to get ready
preparativos *m., pl.* preparations
  los preparativos del viaje/para la boda the travel/wedding preparations
preparatoria *f.* high school
preposición *f.* preposition
presa *f.* prey
presentación *f.* introduction
presentador(a) *m., f.* presenter
presentar *v.t.* to introduce; (*performance*) to put on; to present
  Le presento a... *form.* I would like to introduce (*name*) to you.

Te presento a... *fam.* I would like to introduce (*name*) to you.

presidiario/a *m., f.* convict

presión *f.* pressure

  las presiones de la vida diaria pressures of daily life

  presión sanguínea blood pressure

preso/a *m., f.* prisoner

prestación *f.* fringe benefits

prestado/a *adj.* borrowed

préstamo *m.* loan

prestar *v.t.* to lend; to loan

presumido/a *adj.* vain

presupuesto *m.* budget

pretencioso/a *adj.* pretentious

pretexto *m.* excuse

prevención *f.* prevention

prevenir (e:ie) *v.t. irreg.* **(yo prevengo)** to prevent

primaria *f.* grammar school

primavera *f.* spring

primer, primero/a *adj.* first

  en primer lugar *adv.* first of all

primitivo/a *adj.* primitive

primo/a *m., f.* cousin

primogénito/a *m., f.* firstborn

principal *adj.* main

príncipe *m.* prince

princesa *f.* princess

prisa *f.* haste; hurry

  a toda prisa as fast as possible

  ¡De prisa! Hurry!

  sin prisa pero sin pausa slowly but surely

prisión *f.* prison

probable *adj.* probable

(no) es probable it's (not) probable

probador *m.* dressing room

probar (o:ue) *v.t.* to taste; to try

probarse (o:ue) *v. pron.* (*clothes*) to try on

problema *m.* problem

prodigio/a *m., f.* prodigy

prodigioso/a *adj.* exceptional

productos *m., pl.* products

  productos alimenticios foodstuffs

  productos lácteos dairy (products)

profesión *f.* profession

profesor(a) *m., f.* teacher; professor

  profesor(a) particular tutor

profundidad *f.* depth

profundo/a *adj.* deep

programa *m.* program

  programa de computación software

  programa de entrevistas talk show

programador(a) *m., f.* computer programmer

prohibido *p.p. of* **prohibir** prohibited

  prohibido adelantar (*traffic sign*) no passing

  prohibido el paso (*traffic sign*) no entry

prohibir *v.t.* to prohibit; to forbid

prolífico/a *adj.* prolific

promedio *m.* average

promesa *f.* promise

prometer *v.t.* to promise

pronombre *m.* pronoun

pronto *adj.* soon
propagar *v.t.* to propagate, to spread, to disseminate
Algunos periódicos propagan rumores. Some papers disseminate rumors.
propagarse *v. pron.* to propagate, to spread
El rumor se propagaba rápidamente. The rumor was propagating rapidly.
propenso/a a *adj.* prone to
propiedad *f.* property
propietario/a *m., f.* owner, proprietor
propina *f.* tip
propio/a *adj.* own
proponer *v.t. irreg.* **(yo propongo)** to propose
propósito *m.* intention; purpose
a propósito *adv.* on purpose, deliberately
a propósito by the way
buenos propósitos good intentions
propuesta *f.* proposal
protección *f.* protection
proteger (g:j) *v.t.* to protect
proteína *f.* protein
protesta *f.* protest
protestante *adj./m., f.* Protestant
protestar *v.i.* to protest
provecho *m.* benefit
¡Buen provecho! Enjoy your meal!
provisiones *f., pl.* provisions, supplies
provocación *f.* provocation
provocado/a *adj.* induced

provocar *v.t.* to cause; to provoke
próximo/a *adj.* next
proyección *f.* projection
proyectar *v.t.* to project
proyectil *m.* missile
proyecto *m.* project
prueba *f.* test; quiz
prueba de aptitud aptitude test
prueba de la alcoholemia sobriety test
prueba de nivel placement test
(p)sicología *f* psychology
(p)sicólogo/a *m., f.* psychologist
(p)siquiatra *m., f.* psychiatrist
pubertad *f.* puberty
publicar *v.t.* to publish
público *m.* audience
pueblo *m.* town
puente *m.* bridge
puente colgante suspension bridge
puerta *f.* door
puerta principal front door
puerta trasera back door
puerto *m.* port, harbor
Puerto Rico *m.* Puerto Rico
puertorriqueño/a *adj./m., f.* Puerto Rican
pues *conj.* well; *adv.* then
puesto *m.* position; job; *p.p. of* **poner** put
puesta *f.* **de sol** sunset
pulgar *m.* thumb
pulmón *m.* lung
pulpo *m.* octopus
pulsera *f.* bracelet

punto *m.* point, period
en punto (*time*) on the dot, exactly, sharp
puntual *adj.* punctual
puñal *m.* dagger
puñalada *f.* stab
puño *m.* fist
pupila *f.* pupil
pupitre *m.* student desk
puro/a *adj.* pure; *adv.* sheer; *m.* cigar
aceite puro de oliva pure olive oil
pura casualidad sheer coincidence

Q

que *pron.* that; who; *conj.* that; (*in exclamations*) what; how
¡Qué alto eres! How tall you are!
¡Qué dolor! What pain!
¡Qué extraño! How strange!
¡Qué grande! How big!
¡Qué gusto (+ *inf.*)! What a pleasure to . . . !
¡Qué lata! *loc.* What a drag!
¡Qué ropa más bonita! What pretty clothes!
¡Qué sorpresa! What a surprise!
¿qué? *adv.* what?
¿Qué día es hoy? What day is it?
¿Qué hay de nuevo? What's new?; What's happening?
¿Qué hora es? What time is it?
¿Qué les parece? What do you (*pl.*) think?

¿Qué pasa? What's happening?; What's going on?
¿Qué pasó? What happened?; What's wrong?
¿Qué precio tiene? What is the price?
¿Qué tal? How are you?; How is it going?
¿Qué tal...? How is/are . . . ?
¿Qué talla lleva/usa? What size do you take?
¿Qué tiempo hace? What's the weather like?
quedar *v.i.* to be left over; (*clothing*) to fit; to be located; to be left behind
Ese vestido te queda muy bien. That dress fits you nicely.
¿Dónde queda la panadería? Where's the bakery (located)?
quedar embarazada to get pregnant
quedarse *v. pron.* to stay
¡Quédate! Stay!
quedarse calvo to go bald
quedarse embarazada to get pregnant
quedarse soltero/a to stay single
quedarse viudo/a to be widowed
quehaceres *m., pl.* chores
quehaceres domésticos household chores
queja *f.* complaint
quejarse (de) *v. pron.* to complain (about)

quemado/a *adj.* burned; (*figurative*) burned out

quemados *m., pl.* dodge ball

quemar *v.t.* to burn
No quemes la ropa vieja. Don't burn old clothes.

querer (e:ie) *v.t.* to want; to love
Quisiera un café. I would like a coffee.
No quiero. I don't want to.

querido/a *adj.* beloved

queso *m.* cheese

quien *pron.* who; whom
Ella es quien me lo dijo. She's the one who told me.

¿quién(es)? who?; whom?
¿Quién es...? Who is . . . ?
¿Quién habla? Who is speaking? (*telephone*)

química *f.* chemistry

químico/a *adj.* chemical; *m., f.* chemist

quince fifteen

quinceañero/a *m., f.* fifteen-year-old; teenager
(fiesta de) quinceañera young woman's fifteenth birthday celebration

quincena *f.* two weeks, fortnight

quinientos/as five hundred

quinto/a *adj./m.* fifth

quirófano *m.* operating room

quitar *v.t.* to take away
El policía me quitó los documentos. The police officer took away my documents.
quitar la mesa to clear the table

quitarse *v. pron.* (*clothes*) to take off
Quítate esos zapatos. Take those shoes off.

quizás *adv.* perhaps

R

rábano *m.* radish

rabino/a *m., f.* rabbi

racismo *m.* racism

racista *adj./m., f.* racist

radio *f.* (*medium*) radio; *m.* (*set*) radio

radiografía *f.* X-ray

radioyente *m., f.* radio listener

raíz *f.* root

rallador *m.* grater

rama *f.* branch

rana *f.* frog

rápido/a *adj.* fast
comida rápida fast food

rápido *adv.* quickly
¡Ven rápido! Come quickly!

raqueta *f.* (*sports*) racket

rascacielos *m.* skyscraper

rastrillo *m.* rake

rasuradora *f.* razor

rato *m.* while **Espera un rato, por favor.** Wait a while, please.
ratos libres *m., pl.* spare/free time

ratón *m.* mouse
ratón de biblioteca bookworm

raya *f.* stripe
de rayas striped
una camisa de rayas a striped shirt

rayo *m.* lightning bolt
raza *f.* race
razón *f.* reason
  Lo hice por dos razones.
  I did it for two reasons.
  Tienes razón. You're right.
  No tienes razón. You're
  wrong.
reacción *f.* reaction
reaccionar *v.i.* to react
real *adj.* royal
realeza *f.* royalty
realizar *v.t.* to carry out; to
  make
rebaja *f.* sale
  de rebaja reduced
rebanada *f.* slice
  una rebanada de pan a slice
  of bread
rebelde *adj.* rebellious
rebobinar *v.t.* to rewind
  Apriete el boton de
  rebobinar. Push the rewind
  button.
recado *m.* (*phone*) message
  dejar un recado to leave a
  message
recaudar (fondos) *v.t.* to raise
  (money)
receloso/a *adj.* distrustful
recepción *f.* front desk
receta *f.* prescription;
  (*cooking*) recipe
recetar *v.t.* (*medication*) to
  prescribe
rechazar *v.t.* to reject
rechazo *m.* rejection
recibir *v.t.* to receive; to get
recibirse *v. pron.* to graduate
recibo *m.* receipt; bill

el recibo del teléfono the
  phone bill
reciclaje *m.* recycling
reciclar *v.t.* to recycle
recién *adv.* just
  recién casado/a newlywed
  recién nacido/a newborn
  (baby)
  recién pintado/a wet paint
recipiente *m.* container
recital *m.* (*music, poetry*)
  recital
recoger (g:j) *v.t.* to pick up
recoger la mesa *v.t.* to clear
  the table
recomendable *adj.* advisable
recomendar (e:ie) *v.t.* to
  recommend
reconocer (c:zc) *v.t.* to
  recognize
reconocimiento *m.* recognition
récord *m.* (*sports*) record
recordar (o:ue) *v.t.* to
  remember
recorrer *v.t.* to tour around an
  area
recreo *m.* recess
rectángulo *m.* rectangle
rectificar *v.t.* to rectify
recuerdo *m.* souvenir
recuerdos *m., pl.* regards
recurso *m.* resource
  recurso natural natural
  resource
red *f.* net; network;
  Web
reducir (c:zc) *v.t.* to reduce
reemplazar *v.t.* to replace
reflexionar *v.i.* to reflect
reforma *f.* reform

reformar *v.t.* to reform
reforzar (o:ue) *v.t.* to reinforce
refrán *m.* saying
refrescante *adj.* refreshing
refresco *m.* soft drink, soda
refrigerador *m.* refrigerator
refrigerar *v.t.* to refrigerate
refuerzo *m.* reinforcement
regadera *f.* watering can
regalar *v.t.* to give (a gift)
regalo *m.* gift, present
regañar *v.t.* to scold, to reprimand
regar *v.t.* (*plants*) to water
regatear *v.i.* to bargain
régimen *m.* diet
 Está a régimen. She's on a diet.
región *f.* region; area
regla *f.* rule; ruler
regresar *v.i.* to return
regular *adj.* regular; so so; OK
regular *v.t.* to regulate
regularización *f.* regularization
reído *p.p.* of **reír** laughed
reina *f.* queen
reinar *v.i.* to reign
reino *m.* kingdom
reírse (e:i) *v.i.* **(yo río)** to laugh
reírse (e:i) (de) *v. pron.* **(yo me río)** to laugh (about)
rejuvenecer (c:zc) *v.t.* to rejuvenate
rejuvenecimiento *m.* rejuvenation
relación *f.* relationship
relajación *f.* relaxation
relajarse *v. pron.* to relax
relámpago *m.* lightning bolt
religión *f.* religion

religioso/a *adj.* religious
rellenar *v.t.* (*culinary*) to stuff; (*document*) (*Spain*) to fill out
relleno *m.* stuffing
relleno/a (de) *adj.* stuffed (with)
 Me encantan los chiles rellenos de queso rallado. I love chilies stuffed with grated cheese.
reloj *m.* clock; watch
remar *v.i.* to row
remedio *m.* remedy
remero/a *m., f.* rower
remo *m.* oar
remolacha *f.* beet
remolino *m.* whirlpool; whirlwind
remover (o:ue) *v.t.* to stir
renacentista *adj.* Renaissance
renacimiento *m.* Renaissance
rencor *m.* grudge, resentment, hard feelings
 Todavía siente rencor por lo que le hicieron. She still resents what they did to her.
rencoroso/a *adj.* resentful
renglón *m.* line
 papel con renglones lined paper
renovación *f.* renewal, updating, renovation
renovar (o:ue) *v.t.* to renew, to change, to renovate
renunciar (a) *v.t.* to resign (from)
repelente *m.* (*for insects*) repellent
repente: de repente *adv.* suddenly

repetir (e:i) *v.t.* to repeat

repollo *m.* (*L.A.*) cabbage

reportaje *m.* report

reportero/a *m., f.* reporter; journalist

reposar *v.i.* to rest
Tenía que reposar por varias semanas después de la operación. He had to rest for several weeks after the operation.

reposo *m.* rest

represa *f.* dam

representante *m., f.* representative

represión *f.* repression

reprimir *v.t.* to repress
Tuvo que reprimir la emoción. He had to repress his emotion.

reprimirse *v. pron.* (*refl.*) to control oneself

reproducir (c:zc) *v.t.* to repeat, to reproduce
Es difícil reproducir los resultados. It's difficult to reproduce the results.

reproducirse (c:zc) *v. pron.* (*biology*) to reproduce; to happen again
Es improbable que se reproduzcan tales circunstancias. It's unlikely that such circumstances will happen again.

reproductor de DVD DVD player

reptil *m.* reptile

resaca *f.* (*Spain*) hangover
tener resaca to have a hangover

rescatar *v.t.* to rescue

rescate *m.* rescue

reservación *f.* reservation
hacer una reservación to book

reservado/a *adj.* reserved

resfriado *m.* (*illness*) cold

residencia *f.* residence
residencia de ancianos home for the elderly
residencia estudiantil dormitory

residente *adj./m., f.* resident

residir *v.i.* to live, to reside

resistencia *f.* resistance

resistir *v.t.* to resist

resolución *f.* (*problem*) solution; (*conflict*) settlement

resolver (o:ue) *v.t.* to resolve; to solve

respaldar *v.t.* (*person, decision*) to back, to support

respecto: con respecto a with regard to, regarding

respetar *v.t.* to respect

respeto *m.* respect

respiración *f.* breathing, respiration
respiración boca a boca mouth-to-mouth resuscitation

respirar *v.i.* to breathe

responder *v.t.* to respond, to answer

responsable *adj.* responsible

respuesta *f.* answer

restaurante *m.* restaurant

restaurar *v.t.* to restore

restos *m., pl.* leftovers

resuelto *p.p. of* **resolver** resolved
resultado *m.* result
resumen *m.* summary
en resumen in summary
resumir *v.t.* to summarize
resumiendo summarizing
retar (a alguien a + *inf.*) *v.t.* to challenge (somebody to + *inf.*)
Me retó a imitarle. He challenged me to imitate him.
reto *m.* challenge
El gran reto de nuestro siglo es acabar con la pobreza. The great challenge of our century is to end poverty.
retórica *f.* rhetoric
retórico/a *adj.* rhetorical
retraído/a *adj.* withdrawn
retrasarse *v.i.* to be late
retraso *m.* delay
retrato *m.* portrait, photograph of people
retrovisor *m.* rearview mirror
reumatismo *m.* rheumatism
reunión *f.* meeting
revelar *v.t.* to reveal; (*photography*) to develop
revés: al revés *adv.* the other way around; backward(s)
revisar *v.t.* to check
revisar el aceite to check the oil
revisión *f.* (*Spain*) (medical) checkup
revista *f.* magazine
rey *m.* king
rezar *v.i.* to pray
riachuelo *m.* stream, brook

rico/a *adj.* rich; (*food*) tasty, delicious
ridículo/a *adj.* ridiculous
Es ridículo (que…) It's ridiculous (that…)
Es ridículo que llores. It's ridiculous that you cry.
rincón *m.* (*inside*) corner
rinoceronte *m.* rhinoceros
riñón *m.* kidney
río *m.* river
riquísimo/a *adj.* (*superlative*) extremely delicious
risa *f.* laughter
morirse/partirse de risa to die laughing
robar *v.t.* to rob; to steal
roble *m.* oak tree
robo *m.* robbery; theft
rocío *m.* dew
rodaja *f.* slice
hamburguesa con queso y rodajas de cebolla a hamburger with cheese and sliced onions
rodaje *m.* (*cinema*) filming, shooting
rodar (o:ue) *v.t.* (*cinema*) to shoot, to film
rodilla *f.* knee
rogar (o:ue) *v.t.* to beg; to plead
rojizo/a *adj.* reddish
rojo/a *adj./m.* red
al rojo vivo red-hot
La situación está al rojo vivo. The situation is at the boiling point.
románico/a *adj.* Romanesque
romano/a *adj./m., f.* Roman
romanticismo *m.* Romanticism

romántico/a *adj./m., f.* romantic

romero *m.* rosemary

rompecabezas *m., sing.* (jigsaw) puzzle

rompeolas *m.* breakwater

romper (con) *v.t./v.i.* to break; to break up (with)
  romper el hielo *loc.* break the ice
  ¿Han roto? Have they broken up?

romperse *v. pron.* to break
  Se rompió la pierna. He broke his leg.

ron *m.* rum

roncar *v.i.* to snore

ronquido *m.* snore

ropa *f.* clothing; clothes
  ropa deportiva sportswear
  ropa interior underwear

ropero *m.* wardrobe

rosa *f.* rose

rosado/a *adj./m.* pink

rosal *m.* rosebush

roto/a *adj.* broken

rubí *m.* ruby

rubio/a *m., f.* blond(e)

rueda *f.* wheel
  rueda de recambio spare tire
  rueda de repuesto spare tire

rugido *m.* roar

rugir (g:j) *v.i.* to roar

ruido *m.* noise

ruidoso/a *adj.* noisy

ruleta *f.* roulette

rumor *m.* rumor

ruta *f.* route

rutina *f.* routine
  rutina diaria daily routine

S

sábado *m.* Saturday

sábana *f.* sheet

saber *v.t. irreg.* **(yo sé)** to know; to know how (to); *m.* knowledge
  no sé I don't know
  saber (a) to taste like
  Sabe a limón. It tastes like lemon.

sabiduría *f.* wisdom

sabihondo/a *adj./m., f.* know-it-all

sabio/a *adj.* learned, wise; *m., f.* wise person

sabor *m.* flavor

sabrosísimo/a *adj.* (*superlative*) extremely delicious

sabroso/a *adj.* tasty; delicious

sacacorchos *m.* corkscrew

sacar *v.t.* to take out
  sacar buenas notas to get good grades
  sacar fotos to take pictures/photographs
  sacar la basura to take out the trash
  sacar al perro a pasear to take out (walk) the dog
  sacar(se) una muela to extract a tooth; to pull a tooth

saco *m.* bag, sack
  saco de dormir sleeping bag

sacudir *v.t.* to shake; to dust
  sacudir el polvo to dust
  sacudir los muebles to dust the furniture

saga *f.* saga

sagrado/a *adj.* sacred
sal *f.* salt
sala *f.* living room; room
  sala de emergencia
  emergency room
salado/a *adj.* salty
salario *m.* salary
salchicha *f.* sausage
salero *m.* salt shaker
salida *f.* departure; exit
  callejón sin salida dead-end
  street
  salida del sol sunrise
salir *v.i. irreg.* **(yo salgo)** to
  leave; to go out
  salir con to go out with; to
  date (*someone*)
  salir de to leave from
  salir para to leave for (*a
  place*)
salirse (en) *v. pron.* to get off
  (at)
salmón *m.* salmon
salón *m.* hall; salon; classroom
  salón de actos auditorium
  salón de belleza beauty
  salon
salsa *f.* sauce
saltar *v.i.* to jump
saltear *v.t.* to sauté
salto *m.* jump
  salto alto (*L.A.*) high jump
  salto de altura (*Spain*) high
  jump
  salto de longitud (*Spain*)
  long jump
  salto largo (*L.A.*) long jump
  salto mortal somersault
salud *f.* health
saludable *adj.* healthy

saludar *v.t.* to greet, to say
  hello
saludarse *v. pron.* to greet
  each other, to say hello to
  each other
  ¿No se saludan? They don't
  say hello to each other?
saludo *m.* greeting
  Saludos. (*in a letter*) Best
  wishes.
  saludos a… greetings to…
  Saludos a tu padre. Give my
  regards to your father.
salvaje *adj.* (*animal, flower*)
  wild
salvamento *m.* rescue
salvar *v.t.* to save
salvavidas *m., f.* lifeguard; *m.*
  life jacket
salvia *f.* sage
sandalia *f.* sandal
sandía *m.* watermelon
sándwich *m.* sandwich
sangre *f.* blood
sanguíneo/a *adj.* blood
sano/a *adj.* healthy
sapo *m.* toad
sarampión *m.* measles
sardina *f.* sardine
sartén *f.* frying pan
sastre *m.* tailor
satisfecho/a *adj.* satisfied
sauna *f.* sauna
savia *f.* (*botany*) sap
se *pron.* himself, herself, itself,
  form. yourself, themselves,
  yourselves
se one; on one; on us
  Se hizo… He/She/It
  became…

Se nos dañó el auto. The car broke down on us.

Se nos ponchó/pinchó una llanta. We got a flat tire.

Se pueden comprar boletos aquí. One can buy tickets here.

secador *m.* hairdryer

secadora *f.* clothes dryer

secar *v.t.* to dry

secarse *v. pron.* to dry (oneself)

sección *f.* section

sección de (no) fumar *f.* (non) smoking section

seco/a *adj.* dry

secretario/a *m., f.* secretary

secuencia *f.* sequence

secuestrar *v.t.* (*person*) to kidnap; (*airplane*) to hijack

secuestro *m.* kidnapping; hijack

secundaria, (escuela) *f.* high school

sed *f.* thirst

seda *f.* silk

de seda (made of) silk

sedentario/a *adj.* sedentary; related to sitting

sediento/a *adj.* thirsty

sedimentación *f.* sedimentation

sedimento *m.* sediment

seducir (c:zc) *v.t.* to seduce; to captivate

seductor(a) *adj.* seductive; *m.* seducer, *f.* seductress

seguir (e:i) *v.t.* **(yo sigo)** to follow; to continue

según *prep.* according to

segundo/a *adj./m.* second

en segundo lugar *adv.* secondly

seguro *m.* insurance; safe

seguro médico medical insurance

seguro/a *adj.* sure; safe

(No) Es seguro (que)… It's (not) sure (that)…

No es seguro que lo tenga. He may not have it.

No estoy seguro. I'm not sure

seis six

seiscientos/as six hundred

seleccionar *v.t.* to select

selecto/a *adj.* select

sello *m.* stamp

selva *f.* jungle

semáforo *m.* traffic signal; street light

semana *f.* week

semana entrante/que viene next week

la semana pasada last week

Semana Santa Holy Week

semántica *f.* semantics

semejante *adj.* similar

semestre *m.* semester

semilla *f.* seed

seminario *m.* seminar

senado *m.* senate

sencillo/a *adj.* simple; (*person*) modest

sendero *m.* trail; trailhead

sensatez *f.* good sense

sensato/a *adj.* sensible

sensibilidad *f.* sensitivity

sensible *adj.* sensitive

sentar (e:ie) *v.i.* (*clothes*) to suit

Esa chaqueta te sienta bien. That jacket suits you.

sentarse (e:ie) *v. pron.* to sit down

sentido *m.* sense

  sentido común common sense

  sentido del orden sense of order

sentimental *adj.* sentimental

sentir (e:ie) *v.t.* to feel; to be sorry; to regret

  Lo siento. I'm sorry.

sentirse (e:ie) *v. pron.* to feel

  Me siento bien/mal. I feel good/bad.

señal *f.* sign

  señal de alto stop sign

  señal de tráfico traffic sign

señor (Sr.) *m.* Mr.; sir

señora (Sra.) *f.* Mrs.; ma'am

señorita (Srta.) *f.* Miss

separado/a *adj.* separated

separar *v.t.* to separate

separarse (de) *v. pron.* to separate (from)

septiembre *m.* September

séptimo/a *adj./m.* seventh

sequía *f.* drought

ser *m.* being

  ser humano human being

  ser vivo living being

ser *v. irreg.* to be

  Es la una. It's one o'clock.

  sea lo que sea *loc.* be that as it may

  ser aficionado/a (a) to be a fan (of)

  ser alérgico/a (a) to be allergic (to)

  ser gratis to be free of charge

  Son las… It's… o'clock.

serio/a *adj.* serious

serpentina *f.* streamer

serpiente *f.* snake

  serpiente de cascabel rattlesnake

serrar *v.t.* to saw

servicio *m.* service

servilleta *f.* napkin

servir (e:i) *v.i.* to serve; to help

sesenta sixty

setecientos/as seven hundred

setenta seventy

seto *m.* hedge

seudónimo *m.* pseudonym, pen name

sexismo *m.* sexism

sexto/a *adj./m.* sixth

sí *adv.* yes

si *(conj.)* if

SIDA (síndrome de inmunodeficiencia adquirida) *m.* AIDS

sido *p.p. of* **ser** been

sidra *f.* cider

siempre *adv.* always

  siempre que (+ *subj.*) whenever **Voy siempre que puedo.** I go whenever I can.

  siempre y cuando (+ *subj.*) provided (that) **Iré siempre y cuando vengas conmigo.** I'll go provided you come with me.

sien *f.* *(anatomy)* temple

sierra *f.* saw

siesta *f.* afternoon nap

siete seven

siglo *m.* century
significar *v.t.* to mean
siguiente *adj.* next, following
silbar *v.i.* to whistle
silbato *m.* whistle
silenciador *m.* (*automobile*) muffler
silencio *m.* silence
silla *f.* seat; chair
  silla de ruedas wheel chair
sillón *m.* armchair
silvestre *adj.* (*flower, plant*) wild
simbiosis *f.* symbiosis
simbolizar *v.t.* symbolize
similar *adj.* similar
simpático/a *adj.* (*person*) nice; likeable
sin *prep.* without
  sin (+ inf.) without (+ -ing)
  sin hablar without talking
  sin que *conj.* without
  sin ton ni son *adv.* without rhyme or reason
sinagoga *f.* sinagogue
sinfín *m.* a great many, a lot
  Aún tiene un sinfín de cosas que hacer. He still has a lot of things to do.
sinfonía *f.* symphony
sinfónica *f.* symphony orchestra
sinfónico/a *adj.* symphonic
sino *conj.* but
  No una sino dos. Not one but two.
sinónimo/a *m.* synonym; *adj.* synonymous
sintaxis *f.* syntax
síntoma *m.* symptom
sinvergüenza *m., f.* shameless

person; scoundrel
sistema *m.* system
  sistema inmunológico immune system
sitio *m.* place; site
  sitio web website
situado/a *p.p. of* situar located
sobrar *v.t.* to be left over
  Sobró mucho dinero. There was a lot of money left over.
sobras *m., pl.* leftovers
sobre *m.* envelope; *prep.* on; over
sobreestimar *v.t.* overestimate
sobrehumano/a *adj.* superhuman
sobrenombre *m.* nickname
sobresaliente *adj.* outstanding; *m.* (*grade*) excellent
sobresalir *v.i. irreg.* **(yo sobresalgo)** to excel, to stand out
sobrevalorar *v.t.* to overvalue; to overrate
sobrino/a *m.* nephew; *f.* niece
sobrio/a *adj.* sober
sociable *adj.* sociable
socializar *v.i.* to socialize
sociedad *f.* society
sociología *f.* sociology
sociólogo/a *m., f.* sociologist
socorrer *v.t.* to help
socorro *m.* help; *interj.* Help!
sodio *m.* sodium
sofá *m.* couch; sofa
sofocar *v.t.* (*fire*) to suffocate, to put out; (*weather*) to be stifling
  El calor me sofoca. The heat is stifling.

sofoco *m.* suffocation
sol *m.* sun
solamente *adv.* only
solar *adj.* solar
solario *m.* solarium
soldado *m., f.* soldier
soldadura *f.* weld
soldar (o:ue) *v.t.* to weld
soleado/a *adj.* sunny
soler (o:ue) + inf. *v.i.* usually; to be accustomed to
  Suelo desayunar sólo café con leche. I usually just have coffee with milk for breakfast.
  Suelo ir los domingos. I usually go on Sundays.
solicitar (empleo) *v.t.* to apply (for a job)
solicitud (de trabajo) *f.* (job) application
sollozar *v.i.* to sob
sollozo *m.* sob
solo *adj.* alone
sólo *adv.* only
  Sólo sé que estoy solo. I only know that I'm alone.
soltar (o:ue) *v.t.* to release; to let go
soltero/a *adj.* single; unmarried
soltura *f.* ease, agility
solución *f.* solution
solucionar *v.t.* to solve
sombra *f.* shade, shadow
sombrero *m.* hat
sombrilla *f.* sunshade, beach umbrella
someterse a *v. pron.* (*test, examination*) to undergo
sonar (o:ue) *v.t.* to ring; (*alarm*)

to go off
sonreído *p.p. of* **sonreír** smiled
sonreír (e:i) *v.i.* to smile
sonrisa *f.* smile
soñar (o:ue) *v.t.* to dream; *v.i.* to dream
  soñar con algo to dream about something
  soñar despierto to daydream
sopa *f.* soup
soportar *v.t.* to support, to withstand, to endure
  No lo soporto más. I can't take it any more.
soprano *m., f.* soprano
sorbete *m.* sorbet
sorbo *m.* sip
sordo/a *adj.* deaf
sorprender *v.t.* to surprise
sorprenderse *v. pron.* to be surprised
  Se sorprendió al verme. He was surprised to see me.
sorpresa *f.* surprise
  por sorpresa *adv.* by surprise
sortija *f.* ring
soso/a *adj.* (*culinary*) bland, tasteless; (*person*) boring, dull
sospecha *f.* suspicion
sospechar (algo) *v.t.*; (**de alguien**) *v.i.* to suspect
sospechoso/a *adj.* suspicious
sostener (e:ie) *v.t. irreg.* (**yo sostengo**) support
sótano *m.* basement; cellar
soy I am
  Soy yo. It's me. That's me.
  soy de… I'm from…
su(s) *poss.* his; her; *form.* your; their

suave *adj.* (*to the touch*) soft; (*taste*) mild

subir *v.t.* to go up

subir(se) a *v.t.* to get on/into (a vehicle)

  subirse a los árboles *v.* to climb trees

  subirse a los columpios *v.* to go on the swings

  subirse a los juegos *v.* to go on rides

subjetivo/a *adj.* subjective

submarino *m.* submarine

subrayado *adj.* underlined

subrayar *v.t.* to underline

subterráneo/a *adj.* underground, subterranean

sucesivamente *adv.* successively

  y así sucesivamente and so forth

sucio/a *adj.* dirty

sucre *m.* Ecuadorian currency

sudado/a *adj.* sweaty

sudamericano/a *adj./m., f.* South American

sudar *v.i.* to sweat

suegro/a *m.* father-in-law; *f.* mother-in-law

sueldo *m.* salary, wage

suelo *m.* floor

sueño *m.* sleep

suerte *f.* luck

suéter *m.* sweater

sufrir *v.t.* to suffer **Sufre muchas presiones.** He's under a lot of pressure. **sufrir una enfermedad** to suffer an illness **Sufre una grave enfermedad.** He has a serious illness.

sugerencia *f.* suggestion

sugerir (e:ie) *v.t.* to suggest

suicidarse *v. pron.* to commit suicide

suicidio *m.* suicide

sujetador *m.* (*Spain*) *m.* bra

sumamente *adv.* extremely

suministrador(a) *m., f.* supplier

suministrar *v.t.* to supply

suministro *m.* supply; *m., pl.* supplies

suntuoso/a *adj.* sumptuous

superar *v.t.* to exceed, to go beyond; to overcome **La realidad supera la ficción.** Truth is stranger than fiction.

superarse *v. pron.* to better oneself

supermercado *m.* (super)market

superstición *f.* superstition

supersticioso/a *adj.* superstitious

supervisar *v.t.* to supervise

supervivencia *f.* survival

superviviente *m., f.* survivor

suponer *v.t. irreg.* **(yo supongo)** to suppose; to assume

sur *m.* south

  al sur to the south

surtido *m.* assortment; variety

suspender *v.t.* (*examination*) to fail; (*performance*) to cancel

suspenso *m.* (*grade*) fail, F

sustancia *f.* substance

sustantivo *m.* noun

sustituir (y) *v.t.* to replace **Sustituyeron el azúcar por la miel.** They replaced the sugar with honey.

sustituto/a *m., f.* substitute

suyo/a(s) *adj./pron. poss.* (of) his; her; (of) hers; (of) its; *form.* your, (of) yours; their (of)

T

tabaco *m.* tobacco
tablero *m.* blackboard; board
  tablero de anuncios bulletin board
  tablero de control control panel
taburete *m.* stool
tacaño/a *adj.* stingy
tachadura *f.* crossing out, correction
tachar *v.t.* to cross out, to delete
tacto *m.* (*sense*) touch
tal *adv.* such **Nunca te dije tal cosa.** I never told you any such thing.
  Son tal para cual. They are two of a kind.
  tal vez *adv.* maybe
  tales como such as
talentoso/a *adj.* talented
talla *f.* size
  talla grande large
tallar *v.t.* (*wood, stone*) to carve
taller *m.* workshop
  taller de mecánica mechanic's workshop
  taller mecánico mechanic's repairshop
talón *m.* heel
tamaño *m.* size
también *adv.* also; too
tampoco *adv.* neither; not either

tan *adv.* so
  tan pronto como as soon as
  tan… como as … as
tanque *m.* tank
tanto *adv.* so much
  No es para tanto. It's no big deal.
  por lo tanto therefore
  tanto… como as much … as
tantos/as… como as many … as
tapa *f.* lid; (*Spain*) bar snack
  ir de tapas (*Spain*) to go out and have a snack in a bar
tapar *v.t.* to cover
tapete (verde) *m.* (*games*) card table
tapiz *m.* tapestry
taquilla *f.* box office, ticket office
tardar (en) *v.i.* to be late (in) **El autobús tardó en llegar.** The bus was late (in arriving).
  a más tardar at the very latest **Llévamelo el jueves a más tardar.** Bring it to me on Thursday at the very latest.
tarde *adv.* late
tarde *f.* afternoon; evening; p.m.
  a las tres de la tarde at three in the afternoon, at three p.m.
tarea *f.* homework
tarjeta *f.* (post)card
  tarjeta de crédito credit card
  tarjeta de invitación invitation
  tarjeta de Navidad Christmas card

tarjeta postal postcard
tartamudear *v.i.* to stutter, to stammer
tatarabuelo/a *m.* great-great grandfather; *f.* great-great grandmother
tauromaquia *f.* bullfighting
taxi *m.* taxi(cab)
taza *f.* cup; mug
tazón *m.* bowl
te *pron. fam.* you
  Te presento a... Let me/I would like to introduce you to . . .
té *m.* tea
  té helado iced tea
teatro *m.* theater
techo *m.* (*L.A.*) roof, ceiling; (*Spain*) ceiling
teclado *m.* keyboard
técnico/a *m., f.* technician
teja *f.* (*roof*) tile
tejado *m.* (*Spain*) roof
tejido *m.* weaving; (*anatomy*) tissue
tela *f.* fabric
  tela metálica wire netting
telaraña *f.* spiderweb
teleadicto/a *m., f.* couch potato
teléfono (celular) *m.* (cellular) telephone
telenovela *f.* soap opera
telescopio *m.* telescope
teletrabajo *m.* telecommuting
televisión *f.* television
  televisión por cable cable television
televisor *m.* television set
tema *m.* subject; theme

temática *f.* subject matter
temático/a *adj.* thematic, according to subject
temer *v.t.* to fear
temperamento *m.* temperament
temperatura *f.* temperature
templo *m.* temple
temporada *f.* season
temprano *adj.* early
tenazas *f., pl.* tongs
tendedero *m.* clothesline
  colgar la ropa en el tendedero to hang clothes on the line
tendencia *f.* tendency
tender (e:ie) *v.t.* (*clothes*) to hang out
tendón *m.* tendon
tenedor *m.* fork
tener (e:ie) *v.t. irreg.* (*yo tengo*) to have
  tener algo en la punta de la lengua *loc.* to have something on the tip of one's tongue
  tener calor to be hot
  tener cuidado to be careful
  tener dolor to have a pain
  tener dolor de... to have a(n) ...ache
  tener en cuenta to keep in mind
  tener éxito to be successful
  tener fama de to be well-known for, to have a reputation for
  tener buena/mala fama to have a good/bad reputation
  tener fiebre to have a fever

tener frío to be cold
tener ganas de (+ *inf.*) to feel like (*doing something*); would like to **Tengo ganas de visitar Diamantina.** I would like to visit Diamantina.
tener hambre to be hungry
tener malas pulgas *idiom* to be bad tempered
tener miedo de to be afraid of, to be scared of
tener miedo (de) que to be afraid that
tener planes to have plans
tener prisa to be in a hurry
tener razón to be right
tener sed to be thirsty
tener sueño to be sleepy
tener suerte to be lucky
tener tiempo to have time
tener una cita to have a date; to have an appointment
tener… años to be . . . years old
Tengo… años. I'm . . . years old.
tener (e:ie) *v.aux. irreg.* **(yo tengo)** to have
tener que (+ *inf.*) to have to (*do something*) **Tengo que irme.** I have to go.
tener que ver con *loc.* to have to do with **La carta no tiene nada que ver con el problema.** The letter doesn't have anything to do with the problem.
tenis *m.* tennis(sport); tennis(sneakers)
tenista *m., f.* tennis player

tenor *m.* tenor
tensión *f.* tension
tentáculo *m.* tentacle
teñir (e:i) *v.t.* to dye
teoría *f.* theory
teorizar (sobre algo) *v.i.* to theorize (about something)
terapeútico/a *adj.* therapeutic
terapia *f.* therapy
tercer, tercero/a *adj.* third
en tercer lugar *adv.* thirdly
tercio *m.* third
terciopelo *m.* velvet
terminar *v.t.* to end; to finish
terminar de (+*inf.*) *v.i.* to finish (*doing something*)
¿Has terminado de leer el libro? Have you finished reading the book?
termostato *m.* thermostat
ternera *f.* veal
terraza *f.* terrace
terremoto *m.* earthquake
terreno *m.* plot of land, lot; terrain
terrible *adj.* terrible
Es terrible (que…) It's terrible (that…)
Es terrible que diga eso. It's terrible that he says that.
terrorista *adj./m., f.* terrorist
tertulia *f.* gathering (*to discuss literature, politics, etc.*)
tesis *f.* thesis
tesoro *m.* treasure
testarudo/a *adj.* stubborn
testigo *m., f.* witness; *m.* (*relay race*) baton
tetera *f.* teapot
ti *obj. of prep., fam.* you

tiburón *m.* shark
tiempo *m.* time; weather; occasion
  a tiempo on time
  tiempo completo/parcial full-time, part-time
  tiempo libre free/spare time
tienda *f.* shop, store
  tienda de campaña tent
tierno/a *adj.* tender; (*person*) affectionate
tierra *f.* land; ground; soil; Earth
tigre *m.* tiger
tijeras *f., pl.* scissors
timbre *m.* doorbell
tímido/a *adj.* timid, shy
timón *m.* (*ship*) rudder
tina *f.* (*L.A.*) bathtub
tinta *f.* ink
tinto *m.* red (wine)
tío/a *m.* uncle; *f.* aunt
  tíos *m. pl.* aunts and uncles
típico/a *adj.* typical, traditional
tipo *m.* type, kind, sort; (*person*) figure
  No es mi tipo. He's not my type.
  ¿Qué tipo de música te gusta? What kind of music do you like?
  Tiene muy buen tipo. She has a lovely figure.
tirantes *m., pl.* suspenders
tirar *v.t.* to throw
tiro *m.* shot
  tiro al blanco target shooting
  tiro al plato trapshooting
  tiro con arco archery
título *m.* title
tiza *f.* chalk

toalla *f.* towel
toallero *m.* towel bar
tobillo *m.* ankle
tobogán *m.* (*child's toy*) slide
tocadiscos compacto *m., sing.* compact disc player
tocar *v.t.* to touch
  tocar (un instrumento musical) to play (a musical instrument)
todavía *adv.* yet; still; already
todo *m.* everything
  Todo está bajo control. Everything is under control.
todo/a *adj.* whole, entire; all
  del todo *adv.* entirely **No está del todo equivocada.** She is not entirely mistaken.
  por todo el mundo all over the world
  todo el mundo the whole world
  todos los días every day
todos *m., pl.* all of us; everybody; everyone
tolerancia *f.* tolerance
tolerante *adj.* tolerant
tolerar *v.t.* to tolerate
tomar *v.t.* to take; to drink
  algo de tomar something to drink
  tomar clases to take classes
  tomar el sol to sunbathe
  tomar en cuenta take into account
  tomar fotos to take photos
  tomar la temperatura to take someone's temperature
  tomarle el pelo a alguien *idiom* to pull someone's leg, to kid someone

tomate *m.* tomato
tomillo *m.* thyme
tonto/a *adj.* silly; foolish; dumb
torcer (o:ue) (c:z) *v.t.* to twist
torcerse (o:ue) (c:z) (el tobillo)
  v. pron. to sprain (one's
  ankle)
torcido/a *adj.* twisted; sprained
torero/a *m., f.* bullfighter
tormenta *f.* storm
tornado *m.* tornado
tornillo *m.* screw
toro *m.* bull
toronja *f.* (*L.A.*) grapefruit
torpe *adj.* clumsy, awkward
torre *f.* tower
  torre de control control
  tower
tortilla *f.* (*egg*) omelet; (*corn*)
  kind of flat bread
  tortilla de maíz flat bread
  made of corn flour
  tortilla de patatas potato
  omelet
tortuga *f.* turtle
tos *f., sing.* cough
toser *v.i.* to cough
tostado/a *adj.* toasted
tostadora *f.* toaster
trabajador(a) *m., f.* hard-
  working person
trabajar *v.i.* to work
trabajo *m.* job; work; (*paper*)
  written work
tradición *f.* tradition
traducción *f.* translation
traducir (c:zc) *v.t.* to translate
traductor(a) *m., f.* translator
traer *v.t. irreg.* **(yo traigo)** to
  bring; to take

traficante *m., f.* (*arms, drugs*)
  dealer
traficar (en/con) *v.i.* to traffic in
tráfico *m.* traffic
tragaluz *m.* skylight
tragaperras *f., sing.* slot
  machine
tragar *v.t.* to swallow
tragedia *f.* tragedy
trágico/a *adj.* tragic
traición *f.* treason, betrayal,
  treachery
traicionar (algo o a alguien)
  v.t. to betray (something or
  someone)
traicionero/a adj. treacherous
traído *p.p. of* **traer** brought
traje *m.* suit
  traje de baño
  bathing/swimming suit
traidor(a) *m., f.* traitor; *adj.*
  treacherous
tramar *v.t.* to plot, to scheme
trampa *f.* trap; trick; catch
  ¿Cuál es la trampa? What's
  the catch?
  hacer trampa(s) to cheat
trampolín *m.* diving board
tranquilidad *f.* calm, tranquility
tranquilizar *v.t.* to calm down
tranquilizarse *v. pron.* to calm
  down
tranquilo/a *adj.* (*person*)
  easygoing; quiet; calm
  ¡Tranquilo! Stay calm!
transatlántico *m.* ocean liner
transbordador *m.* ferry; (*space*)
  shuttle
transeúnte *m., f.* passer-by;
  non-resident

transferencia *f.* transfer
transfusión *f.* transfusion
transmitir *v.t.* to broadcast
transparente *adj.* transparent;
see-through
transpiración *f.* perspiration
transpirar *v.i.* to perspire
transplante *m.* transplant
transportar *v.t.* to transport; to
carry
transporte *m.* transportation
trapeador *m.* (*L.A.*) mop
trapear *v.t.* (*L.A.*) to mop
trapo *m.* dishcloth
trasnochar *v.i.* to stay up all
night
trastorno *m.* (*medicine*)
disorder
  trastorno estomacal
  stomach disorder
  trastorno mental mental
  disorder
trasvasar *v.t.* (*computer*) to
download
tratar *v.i.* to try
  tratar de (+ inf.) to try (*to do
  something*)
  Trata de resolverlo. Try to
  solve it.
trato *m.* deal
  Trato hecho. It's a deal.
travesura *f.* prank; mischief
travieso/a *adj.* naughty,
mischievous
trayectoria *f.* (*rocket, ball*)
path, trajectory
trece thirteen
treinta thirty
tren *m.* train
  tren de alta velocidad high-

speed train
trenza *f.* braid
tres three
trescientos/as three hundred
triángulo *m.* triangle
tribunal *m.* (*Spain*) court
  Tribunal Supremo (*Spain*)
  Supreme Court
triciclo *m.* tricycle
trigo *m.* wheat
trigonometría *f.* trigonometry
trimestre *m.* trimester; quarter
  **El año tiene cuatro
  trimestres.** The year has four
  quarters.
trípode *m.* tripod
triste *adj.* sad
  Es triste (que…) It's sad
  (that…)
  **Es triste que esté tan
  enfermo.** It's sad that he's so
  sick.
tristeza *f.* sadness
triturar *v.t.* to crush
  triturador de basura garbage
  disposal
triunfar *v.t.* to succeed; to win
trivialidad *f.* triviality
trivializar *v.t.* to trivialize
tronco *m.* (*living tree*) trunk;
(*lumber*) log
  dormir como un tronco
  idiom. to sleep like a log
tropezar (e:ie) *v.i.* to stumble
tropezarse (e:ie) (con alguien)
v. pron. to run/bump into
(*somebody*)
trozo *m.* piece, bit, slice
trucha *f.* trout
trueno *m.* thunder

109

tú *pron. fam.* you
  Tú eres... You are . . .
tu(s) *poss. fam.* your
tuberculosis *f.* tuberculosis
tubería *f.* pipe
tubo *m.* tube
  tubo de ensayo test tube
  tubo de escape exhaust pipe
tulipán *m.* tulip
tumbarse *v. pron.* to lie down
  tumbarse al sol lie down in the sun, sunbathe
tumbona *f.* lounge chair, deck chair
túnel *m.* tunnel
turbina *f.* turbine
turismo *m.* tourism
turista *m., f.* tourist
turístico/a *adj.* touristic
turno *m.* turn; (*work*) shift
turquesa *f.* turquoise
tuyo/a(s) *poss. fam.* your; (of) yours

U

Ud. *pron. form. sing.* you
Uds. *pron. form. pl.* you
últimamente *adv.* lately
último/a *adj.* last
  por último *adv.* finally
un, uno/a *indef. art.* a; one
  uno/a *m., f., sing. pron.* one
  a la una at one o'clock
único/a *adj.* only
  ...y ese es el único problema ...and that's the only problem
unido/a *adj.* close
  una familia muy unida a close family

universidad *f.* university; college
universo *m.* universe
unos/as *m., f., pl., indef. art.* some
  unos/as *pron.* some
untar *v.t.* to spread (*butter, honey*)
  untar pan con mantequilla to butter a piece of bread
uña *f.* (*finger, toe*) nail
urbanización *f.* (*housing*) development
urgente *adj.* urgent
  (No) Es urgente (que...) It's (not) urgent (that...)
  Es urgente que termines. It's urgent that you finish.
usar *v.t.* to use; to wear
  Esta camisa está sin usar. This shirt hasn't been worn.
usted *pron. form. sing.* you
ustedes *pron. form. pl.* you
utensilio *m.* utensil
útero *m.* womb, uterus
útil *adj.* useful
uva *f.* grape

V

vaca *f.* cow
vacaciones *f., pl.* vacation
  de vacaciones on vacation
vacío/a *adj.* empty
vainilla *f.* vanilla
vajilla *f.* dishes, crockery, china
vale *interj.* (*Spain*) okay
  Ven a la una, ¿vale? Come at one o'clock, okay?
  ¡Sí, vale! Yes, sure!

valentía *f.* bravery, courage
valer *v.t. irreg.* **(yo valgo)** to be
worth, to cost
   No vale la pena. It's not
   worth the trouble.
valiente *adj.* brave
valla *f.* fence
vallas *f., pl.* (*sport*) hurdles
valle *m.* valley
valor *m.* value; courage
valorar *v.t.* to value
vapor *m.* vapor, steam
vaquero/a *m.* cowboy;
   f. cowgirl
   (una película) de vaqueros
   a western (movie)
variación *f.* variation
variado/a *adj.* varied, diverse
variar *v.t./v.i.* **(yo varío)** to vary
varios/as *pron.* several;
   various
   Irán varios de ustedes.
   Several of you will go.
vaso *m.* glass
veces *f., pl.* times
   a veces *adv.* sometimes
vecino/a *m., f.* neighbor
vegetación *f.* vegetation
vehículo *m.* vehicle
   vehículos pesados heavy
   vehicles
veinte twenty
veinticinco twenty-five
veinticuatro twenty-four
veintidós twenty-two
veintinueve twenty-nine
veintiocho twenty-eight
veintiséis twenty-six
veintisiete twenty-seven
veintitrés twenty-three

veintiún, veintiuno/a twenty-
one
vejez *f.* old age
vejiga *f.* bladder
vela *f.* (*ship*) sail; (*sport*)
   sailing; candle
velero *m.* sailboat
velocidad *f.* speed
   velocidad máxima speed
   limit
velódromo *m.* velodrome
vena *f.* vein
venda *f.* bandage
vendaje *m.* dressing
vendar *v.t.* to bandage
vendedor(a) *m., f.* salesperson
vender *v.t.* to sell
venido *p.p. of* **venir** come;
   arrived
venir (e:ie) *v.i. irreg.* **(yo vengo)**
to come
   venir al mundo to be born; to
   come into the world
ventaja *f.* advantage
ventana *f.* window
ventilador *m.* fan
ver *v.t./v.i. irreg.* **(yo veo)** to
see; to watch
   ¡A ver! Let's see!
   ver películas to see movies
veraneante *m., f.* summer
vacationer
veranear *v.i.* to spend the
summer
   Veraneo en las montañas.
   I summer in the mountains.
verano *m.* summer
veras: de veras *loc.* really
verbena *f.* festival; open-air
dance

verbo *m.* verb
verdad *f.* truth
  Es cierto, ¿verdad? It's true, right?
  (No) Es verdad que (+ *ind.*) It's (not) true that… **¿Es verdad que eres millonario?** Is it true that you're a millionaire?
verdadero/a *adj.* true
verde *adj./m.* green
  verde claro light green
  verde oscuro dark green
verduras *f., pl.* vegetables
vergonzoso/a *adj.* disgraceful; shameful
vergüenza *f.* embarrassment; shame
verosímil *adj.* credible; realistic, true-to-life
  Sus personajes no son verosímiles. His characters aren't realistic.
verruga *f.* wart
versátil *adj.* versatile
vértebra *f.* vertebra
vertebrado/a *adj./m.* vertebrate
vertedero *m.* garbage dump
vesícula (biliar) *f.* gall bladder
vestido *m.* dress
vestirse (e:i) *v. pron.* to get dressed
vestuario *m.* locker room
veterinaria *f.* veterinary science
veterinario/a *m., f.* veterinarian
vez *f.* time
  a veces sometimes
  dos veces twice
  en vez de instead of

  tres veces three times
  una vez once; one time
  una vez más one more time
vía *f.* (railroad) track
  Vía Láctea Milky Way
viajar *v.i.* to travel
viaje *m.* trip
viajero/a *m., f.* traveler
vibración *f.* vibration
vibrar *v.i.* to vibrate
vicio *m.* vice
  El trabajo es su único vicio. Work is his only vice.
vicioso/a *m., f.* dissolute person
vid *f.* (grape) vine
vida *f.* life
  de mi vida of my life
video(casete) *m.* video (cassette)
videocasetera *f.* VCR
videoconferencia *f.* videoconference; teleconference
vidrio *m.* glass
  de vidrio (*made*) of glass
vieira *f.* scallop
viejo/a *adj.* old
viento *m.* wind
viernes *m., sing.* Friday
villancicos *m., pl.* carols
vinagre *m.* vinegar
vínculo *m.* tie, bond
vino *m.* wine
  vino blanco white wine
  vino tinto red wine
violencia *f.* violence
viruela *f.* smallpox
visera *f.* eyeshade
visitante *m., f.* visitor

visitar *v.t.* to visit
 visitar monumentos to visit monuments
vista *f.* (*senses*) sight; view
 amor a primera vista love at first sight
 habitación con vistas a room with a view
 Hasta la vista. See you.
 Tener vista de águila. To have eyes like a hawk.
 Tierra a la vista. Land ho!
visto/a *p.p.* of **ver** seen
 por lo visto *adv.* apparently
vitamina *f.* vitamin
vitrina *f.* (*L.A.*) shop window
viudo/a *m.* widower; *f.* widow; widowed
víveres *m., pl.* provisions, supplies
vivienda *f.* housing
vivir *v.i.* to live
vivo/a *adj.* bright; lively; living
volante *m.* steering wheel
volar (o:ue) *v.i.* to fly
volcán *m.* volcano
vóleibol *m.* volleyball
voltear *v.t.* (*L.A.*) to turn (over)
volumen *m.* volume
voluntario *adj.* voluntary; *m., f.* volunteer
volver (o:ue) *v.i.* to return; to come back
 volver a ver(te, lo, la) to see (you/him/her) again
 ¿Cuándo te volveré a ver? When will I see you again?
vomitar *v.t./v.i.* to vomit
vos (*Argentina*) *pron.* you
vosotros/as *pron. fam. pl.* you

votar *v.t./v.i.* to vote
voto *m.* vote
voz *f.* voice
vuelta *f.* lap
vuelta *f.* return trip; (*sports*) lap; turn
 de vuelta back
 Estará de vuelta a la una. She will be back at one.
vuelto *p.p.* of **volver** returned
vuestro/a(s) *poss. fam.* your

W

walkman *m.* Walkman

X

xenofobia *f.* xenophobia
xenófobo/a *adj.* xenophobic; *m., f.* xenophobe

Y

y *conj.* and
 y cuarto quarter after/past (time)
 y media half-past (time)
 y quince quarter after/past (time)
 y treinta thirty (minutes past the hour)
 ¿Y Ud.? *form.* And you?
 ¿Y tú? *fam.* And you?
ya *adv.* already; still
 Ya fui. I already went.
yerno *m.* son-in-law
yeso *f.* (*L.A.*) plaster cast
yo *pron.* I
 Yo soy... I'm . . .
yoga *m.* yoga
yogur *m.* yogurt

113

Z

zanahoria *f.* carrot
zapatería *f.* shoe store
zapatilla *f.* slipper
  zapatillas de deporte tennis
  shoes; sneakers
zapato *m.* shoe
  zapato de tacón alto high-
  heeled shoe
  zapatos de tenis tennis
  shoes; sneakers
zona *f.* area
  zona verde green space
zoológico *m.* zoo
zoólogo/a *m., f.* zoologist
zorro *m.* fox
zueco *m.* clog
zumo *m.* (*Spain*) juice

English-Spanish
Inglés-Español

A

@ (symbol) arroba *f.*

a un, uno/a *m., f., sing., indef. art.*

A.M. en la mañana, de la mañana

abbey *n.* abadía *f.*

abbreviate *v.t.* abreviar

abbreviation *n.* abreviatura *f.*

able: be able to poder (o:ue)

abnormal *adj.* anormal

aboard *adv.* a bordo

   All aboard! ¡Todos a bordo!

abortion *n.* aborto *m.* provocado

   have an abortion abortar de manera provocada

abroad *adv.* en el extranjero

absence *n.* ausencia *f.*

absent *adj.* ausente

absorb *v.t.* absorber

absorbent *adj.* absorbente

absurd *adj.* absurdo/a

accelerate *v.t.* acelerar

accelerator (pedal) *n.* acelerador *m.*

accept *v.t.* aceptar

accessory *n.* accesorio *m.*

accident *n.* accidente *m.*

   industrial accident accidente laboral

accommodation: provide accommodation hospedar

accompany *v.t.* acompañar

according to *prep.* de acuerdo a; según

account *n.* cuenta *f.*

checking account cuenta corriente

take into account tomar en cuenta

accountant *n.* contador(a) *m., f.*

accounting *n.* contabilidad *f.*

accustomed *adj.* acostumbrado/a

   be accustomed to acostumbrarse (a)

ache *n.* dolor *m.*

achieve *v.t.* lograr

achievement *n.* logro *m.*

acid *n.* ácido *m.;* ácido/a *adj.*

   acid rain lluvia *f.* ácida

acquainted: be acquainted with conocer

acquire *v.t.* adquirir

acquisition *n.* adquisición *f.*

acrobat *n.* acróbata *m., f.*

acrobatics *n.* acrobacia *f.*

across from *prep.* enfrente

action *n.* acción *f.;* ...de acción

activate *v.t.* activar

active *adj.* activo/a

activity *n.* actividad *f.*

actor *n.* actor *m.,* actriz *f.*

adapt *v.i.* adaptarse

adaptation *n.* adaptación *f.*

addict *n.* adicto/a *m., f.*

   drug addict drogadicto/a

addicted *adj.* adicto/a

   drug-addicted drogadicto/a

addiction *n.* adicción *f.*

additional *adj.* adicional

additive *n.* aditivo *m.*

address *n.* dirección *f.*

adhesive bandage *n.* curita *f.*

adjective *n.* adjetivo *m.*
adjust *v.t. (temperature, etc.)* graduar; *v.i.* adaptarse
administration *n.* administración *f.*
adolescence *n.* adolescencia *f.*
adolescent *n.* adolescente *m., f.*
advance *n.* avance *m.*
advance *v.i.* avanzar
advanced *adj.* avanzado/a
advantage *n.* ventaja *f.*
adventure *n.* aventura *f.;* ...de aventuras
adventurer *n.* aventurero/a *m., f.*
adventurous *adj.* aventurero/a
advertise *v.t.* anunciar
advertisement *n.* anuncio *m.*
advice *n.* consejo *m.*
  give advice dar un consejo
advisable *adj.* aconsejable, recomendable
advise *v.t.* aconsejar; recomendar
advisor *n.* consejero/a *m., f.*
aerobic *adj.* aeróbico/a
  aerobic exercise *n.,* ejercicios *m., pl.* aeróbicos
  do aerobics hacer ejercicios aeróbicos
  aerobics class *n.* clase *f.* de ejercicios aeróbicos
affected *adj.* afectado/a
  be affected (by) estar afectado/a (por)
affectionate *adj.* cariñoso/a, tierno/a
affirmative *adj.* afirmativo/a

afraid: be afraid (of) tener miedo (de); **be afraid that** tener miedo (de) que
African *n., adj.* africano/a *m., f.*
after *prep.* después de; después de que
afternoon *n.* tarde *f.*
  in the afternoon de la tarde; por la tarde
afterwards *adv.* después (de); luego
again *adv.* otra vez
age *n.* edad *f.*
age *v.i.* envejecer
agility *n.* soltura *f.*
aging *n.* envejecimiento *m.*
agree (about) *v.* concordar (con), estar de acuerdo (sobre)
agreement *n.* acuerdo *m.*
  be in agreement with estar de acuerdo (con)
  reach an agreement llegar a un acuerdo
agricultural *adj.* agrícola
agriculture *n.* agricultura *f.*
AIDS (Acquired Immune Deficiency Syndrome) *n.* SIDA *m.* (Síndrome de Inmunodeficiencia Adquirida)
aim *n.* objetivo *m.*, meta *f.*
air *n.* aire *m.*
air-conditioned *adj.* climatizado/a
air conditioning *n.* aire acondicionado
air freshener *n.* ambientador *m.*
aircraft carrier *n.* portaaviones *m., sing.*

airline *n.* aerolínea *f.*
airplane *n.* aeroplano *m.*;
avión *m.*
  by plane en avión
  go by plane ir en avión
airport *n.* aeropuerto *m.*
airtight *adj.* hermético/a
alarm *n.* alarma *f.*
alarming *adj.* alarmante
alcohol *n.* alcohol *m.*
alcoholic *adj.* alcohólico/a
  alcoholic beverage bebida *f.*
  alcohólica
all *adj.* todo/a
  all of a sudden de repente
  all of us *n.* todos *m.*, *pl.*
  all over the world en todo el
  mundo
  all-boys/girls school *n.*
  escuela *f.* de niños/as
allergic *adj.* alérgico/a
  be allergic (to) ser alérgico/a
  (a)
alleviate *v.t.* aliviar
alley *n.* callejón *m.*
allow *v.* dejar
almond *n.* almendra *f.*
almond tree *n.* almendro *m.*
almost *adv.* casi
alms *n.* limosna *f.*
alone *adj.* solo/a
along *prep.* por
alphabet *n.* alfabeto *m.*,
abecedario *m.*
already *adv.* ya; todavía
also *adv.* también
alternating current: AC
corriente *f.* alterna
alternative *n.* alternativa *f.*
alternator *n.* alternador *m.*

although *conj.* aunque
aluminum *n.* aluminio *m.*
  made of aluminum de
  aluminio
always *adv.* siempre
amazing *adj.* asombroso/a
ambition *n.* ambición *f.*
ambitious *adj.* ambicioso/a
ambulance *n.* ambulancia *f.*
American *n., adj.*
norteamericano/a, *m., f.*;
estadounidense *m., f.*
among *prep.* entre
amount *n.* cantidad *f.*
amuse oneself *v.* entretenerse
amusement *n.* diversión *f.*
  amusement park *n.* parque
  m. de atracciones *(Spain)*;
  parque de diversiones *(L.A.)*
amusing *adj.* chistoso/a,
gracioso/a, divertido/a
analyst *n.* analista *m., f.*
anarchic *adj.* anárquico/a
anarchy *n.* anarquía *f.*
anatomy *n.* anatomía *f.*
ancestor *n.* antepasado/a *m., f.*
anchovy *n.* anchoa *f.*
and *conj.* y (e *before words*
beginning with i *or* hi)
  and so forth y así
  sucesivamente
  And you? ¿Y tú? *fam.*; ¿Y
  usted? *form.*
anesthesia *n.* anestesia *f.*
anesthesiologist *n.*
anestesiólogo/a *m., f.*
anesthetize *v.t.* anestesiar
angle *n.* ángulo *m.*
Anglo-Saxon *n,. adj.*
anglosajón *m.*, anglosajona *f.*

angry *adj.* enojado/a
  get angry (with) enojarse
  (con)
animal *n.* animal *m.*
ankle *n.* tobillo *m.*
anniversary *n.* aniversario *m.;*
  (wedding) aniversario de
  bodas
announce *v.t.* anunciar
announcer *n. (TV/radio)*
  locutor(a) *m., f.*
annoy *v.t.* molestar
  The noise is annoying me.
  Me molesta el ruido.
another *adj.* otro/a
answer *n.* respuesta *f.*
answer *v.t.* contestar
ant *n.* hormiga *f.*
anthology *n.* antología *f.*
antibiotic *n.* antibiótico *m.*
anticipation *n.* expectativa *f.*
antidote *n.* antídoto *m.*
antiques *n., pl.* antigüedades
  f., pl.
antiquities *n., pl.* antigüedades
  f., pl.
any *adj.* algún, alguno/a(s)
anybody *pron.* nadie
anyone *pron.* alguien
anything *pron.* algo; *n.* nada *f.*
apartment *n.* apartamento *m.*
apartment building *n.* edificio
  m. de apartamentos
apologize *v.i.* disculparse
apology *n.* disculpa *f.*
apparently *adv.* por lo visto
appear *v.i. (come into view)*
  aparecer; *(seem)* parecer
appearance *n. (looks)* aspecto
  m.

appetizers *n., pl.* aperitivos
  m., pl.; entremeses *(Spain)*
  m., pl.
applaud *v.t./v.i.* aplaudir
applause *n.* aplauso *m.*
apple *n.* manzana *f.*
appliance *n.* aparato *m.*
  electric appliance *n.*
  electrodoméstico *m.*
  household appliance
  aparato doméstico
applicant *n.* aspirante *m., f.*
application *n.* solicitud *f.*
  job application solicitud de
  trabajo
apply *v.t. (for a job)* solicitar
  (empleo); (for a loan) pedir
  un préstamo; *(oneself)*
  aplicarse
appointment *n.* cita *f.*
  have an appointment tener
  una cita
appreciate *v.t.* apreciar
approach *n.* enfoque *m.*
apricot *n.* albaricoque *m.*
April *n.* abril *m.*
apron *n.* delantal *m.*
aptitude test *n.* prueba *f.* de
  aptitud
aquarium *n.* acuario *m.*
aquatic *adj.* acuático/a
Arab *n.* árabe *m., f.; (language)*
  árabe
Arabic *adj.* árabe
archaeologist *n.* arqueólogo/a
  m., f.
archery *n.* tiro *m.* con arco
archipelago *n.* archipiélago *m.*
architect *n.* arquitecto/a *m., f.*
area *n.* región *f.;* zona *f.*

argue *v.t.* discutir; argumentar

argument *n.* *(reasoning)* argumento *m.*; *(dispute)* discusión *f.*

aristocracy *n.* aristocracia *f.*

aristocrat *n.* aristócrata *m., f.*

arm *n.* *(limb)* brazo *m.*; *(weapon)* arma (el) *f.*

armchair *n.* sillón *m.*

armpit *n.* axila *f.*

army *n.* ejército *m.*

around *prep.* alrededor (de) **There is a wall around the old city.** Hay una muralla alrededor de la ciudad vieja. *adv.* alrededor **a table with four chairs around it** una mesa con cuatro sillas alrededor **around here** por aquí

arrange *v.t.* colocar; organizar; arreglar **arranged marriage** *n.* boda *f.* concertada

arrangement *n.* *(position)* colocación *f.*

arrest *n.* detención *f.*, arresto *m.*

arrest *v.t.* arrestar **under arrest** detenido/a; arrestado/a **be under arrest** estar arrestado; estar detenido

arrested *p.p.* arrestado *(of arrestar)*

arrival *n.* llegada *f.*

arrive *v.i.* llegar

arrogant *adj.* arrogante

arrow *n.* flecha *f.*

art *n.* arte *m.*; las artes *f., pl.*

art exhibition *n.* exhibición *f.* de arte

artery *n.* arteria *f.*

artichoke *n.* alcachofa *f.*

article *n.* artículo *m.*

artist *n.* artista *m., f.*

artistic *adj.* artístico/a

arts *n., pl.* artes *f., pl.*

as como **as . . . as** tan… como **as a child** de niño/a **as many . . . as** tantos/as… como **as much . . . as** tanto… como **as soon as** en cuanto; tan pronto como

ascent *n.* *(hill, mountain)* escalada *f.*

ash *n.* ceniza *f.*

ashamed: be ashamed avergonzarse

ashtray *n.* cenicero *m.*

Asian *n., adj.* asiático/a *m., f.*

ask *v.t.* *(a question)* preguntar **ask (for)** pedir (e:i)

ask oneself *v.ref.* preguntarse; cuestionarse; **We have to ask ourselves if the conclusion is valid.** Tenemos que cuestionarnos si es válida la conclusión.

asparagus *n.* espárrago *m.*

asphalt *n.* asfalto *m.*

aspire (to) *v.i.* ambicionar

aspirin *n.* aspirina *f.*

assassin *n.* asesino/a *m., f.*

assassination *n.* asesinato *m.*

assemble (a puzzle) *v.t.* armar (un rompecabezas)

assess *v.t.* evaluar

assessment *n.* evaluación *f.*

assistance *n.* asistencia *f.*

association n. asociación f.
assortment n. surtido m.
assume v.t. asumir; suponer
assure v.t. asegurar
astonishing adj. asombroso/a
astrologist n. astrólogo/a m., f.
astrology n. astrología f.
astronaut n. astronauta m., f.
astronomer n. astrónomo/a m., f.
astronomy n. astronomía f.
at prep. a
   at + time a la(s) + time
   At what time . . . ? ¿A qué
   hora…?
   At your service. A sus
   órdenes.
atheism n. ateísmo m.
atheist n. ateo/a m., f.
atheistic adj. ateo/a
athlete n. atleta m., f.
athletic adj. atlético/a
ATM n. cajero m. automático
atmosphere n. (created by
   people, decoration) ambiente
   m. (metheorology) atmósfera f.
atrocious adj. atroz
attack n. ataque m.
attack v.t. atacar
attempt n. intento m.
   assassination attempt
   atentado m. terrorista
attempt to assassinate v.t.
   atentar (contra)
attend v.t. asistir (a)
attention n. atención f.
attic n. altillo m.
attract v.t. atraer
attraction n. atracción f.
attractive adj. atractivo/a
audience n. público m.

audiotape n. cinta f.
audition n. (try-out) audición f.
auditorium n. auditorio m.;
   salón m. de actos
August n. agosto m.
aunt n. tía f.
aunts and uncles n., pl. tíos
   m., pl.
Australian n., adj.
   australiano/a m., f.
author n. autor(a) m., f.
authoritarian adj. autoritario/a
authoritarianism n.
   autoritarismo m.
autograph n. autógrafo m.
automatic adj. automático/a
   automatic teller machine n.
   (ATM) cajero m. automático
automobile n. automóvil m.;
   carro m.; coche m.
   auto racing n. automovilismo
   m.
autonomous adj. autónomo/a
autonomy n. autonomía f.
autumn n. otoño m.
availability n. disponibilidad f.
available adj. disponible
avarice n. avaricia f.
avaricious adj. avaricioso/a
avenue n. avenida f.
average n. promedio m.
aversion n. aversión f.
avocado n. aguacate m.
avoid v.t. evitar; (danger,
   problem) evadir
award n. premio m.; galardón
   m.
award v.t. galardonar; premiar
award-winner n.
   galardonado/a m., f.

aware: become aware of
darse cuenta de
awful *adj.* atroz, horrible
awkward *adj.* torpe
ax *n.* hacha (el) *f.*

B

baby *n.* bebé *m., f.*
baby-sitter *n.* niñero/a *m., f.*
back *n.* espalda *f.*
back *v.t.* respaldar
  be back estar de vuelta
backpack *n.* mochila *f.*
backseat *n.* asiento *m.* trasero
backstroke *n.* estilo *m.* espalda
backyard *n.* jardín *m.*
bad *adj. adv.* mal, malo/a
  It's (not) bad that… (No) Es
  malo que…
  It's not at all bad. No está
  nada mal.
bad-mannered *adj.*
  maleducado/a
bad-tempered: be bad-
  tempered *idiom* tener malas
  pulgas
bag *n.* bolsa *f.*
bail *n.* fianza *f.*
bake *v.t.* hornear
bakery *n.* panadería *f.*
baking soda *n.* bicarbonato *m.*
balanced *adj.* equilibrado/a
balcony *n.* balcón *m.*
bald *adj.* calvo/a
ball *n.* pelota *f.;* bola *f.*
ballet *n.* ballet *m.*
balloon *n.* globo *m.*
banana *n.* banana *f.;* plátano *m.*
band *n.* banda *f.*
bandage *n.* venda *f.*

bandage *v.t.* vendar
bank *n.* banco *m.*
  bank draft *n.* giro *m.*
  bancario
banker *n.* banquero/a *m., f.*
banister *n.* pasamanos *m.,*
  sing.
baptism *n.* bautizo *m.*
baptize *v.t.* bautizar
barbecue *n.* asador *m.*
barber *n.* barbero *m.*
bargain *n.* ganga *f.*
bargain *v.i.* regatear
bark *n.* ladrido *m.*
bark *v.i.* ladrar
barn *n.* granero *m.*
baroque *adj.* barroco/a
baseball *n. (sport)* béisbol *m.;*
  (ball) pelota *f.*
basement *n.* sótano *m.*
basil *n.* albahaca *f.*
basketball *n. (sport)*
  baloncesto *m.*
bat *n. (sport)* bate *m.; (animal)*
  murciélago *m.*
bath *n.* baño *m.*
  take a bath bañarse
bathe *v.i.* bañarse
bathing suit *n.* traje *m.* de baño
bathrobe *n.* bata *f.* de baño
bathroom *n.* baño *m.;* cuarto *m.*
  de baño
bathtub *n.* bañera *f.;* tina *(L.A.)*
  f.
baton *n. (sport)* testigo *m.*
bay *n.* bahía *f.*
be *v.* ser; estar
  be at/in/on estar en
  be that as it may *loc.* sea lo
  que sea

He/She/It is from . . . Es de…
I'm from… Soy de…
beach *n.* playa *f.*
beach umbrella *n.* sombrilla *f.*
beak *n.* pico *m.*
bean *n. (coffee)* grano *m.;*
frijol *m.*
bear *n.* oso/a *m., f.*
beard *n.* barba *f.*
bearded *adj.* barbudo/a
beat *n. (music)* compás *m.*
beat *v.t.* batir; *(an opponent)*
derrotar; *(heart)* latir
beautician *n.* esteticista *m., f.*
beautiful *adj.* hermoso/a
beauty *n.* belleza *f.*
beauty salon *n.* peluquería *f.;*
salón *m.* de belleza
because *conj.* porque
because of *prep.* debido a
become *v.i.* hacerse **He
became famous.** Se hizo
famoso.; llegar a ser **She
wants to become president.**
Ella quiere llegar a ser
presidente.; ponerse (+ *adj.*)
He becomes sad sometimes.
A veces él se pone triste.;
convertirse (en) **The church
became a museum.** La
iglesia se convirtió en
museo.
bed *n.* cama *f.*
go to bed acostarse (o:ue)
make the bed hacer la cama
bedroom *n.* alcoba *f.;*
recámara *f.;* cuarto *m.;*
dormitorio
bee *n.* abeja *f.*
beef *n.* carne *f.* de res

been *p.p.* sido *(of* ser)
beer *n.* cerveza *f.*
beet *n.* remolacha *f.;* betabel
(Mexico.) f.
before *adv., conj., prep.* antes;
antes (de) que; antes de
beg *v.t.* rogar (o:ue)
beggar *n.* mendigo/a *m., f.*
begin *v.t.* comenzar (e:ie);
empezar (e:ie)
behalf: on behalf of de parte
de; en nombre de
behave (oneself) *v.* portarse
(bien), comportarse
behave well/badly portarse
bien/mal
behavior *n.* comportamiento
m., conducta *f.*
behind *prep.* detrás de; atrás
being *n.* ser *m.*
belch *v.i.* eructar
belch *n.* eructo *m.*
believe (in) *v.t.* creer (en)
be hard to believe parecer
mentira **It's hard to believe,
but he's only ten.** Aunque
parezca mentira, tiene sólo
diez años.
not to believe no creer
bellhop *n.* botones *m., sing.*
belly *n.* barriga *f.,* vientre *m.*
belong to *v.t.* pertenecer (a)
belongings *n., pl.* pertenencias
f., pl.
beloved *adj.* querido/a;
enamorado/a
below *adv., prep.* abajo;
debajo de
belt *n.* correa *f.;* cinturón *m.*
bench *n.* banco *m.*

bend *n.* curva *f.*
beneficial *adj.* beneficioso/a
benefit *n.* beneficio *m.*
fringe benefits *n.* prestaciones *f., pl*
benefit *v.i.* beneficiarse
benign *adj.* benigno
beret *n.* boina *f.*
beside *prep.* al lado de
besides *adv.* además (de)
best *adj.* mejor
  the best *n.* el/la mejor *m., f.; (neuter)* lo mejor
betray *v.t.* traicionar
betrayal *n.* traición *f.*
better *adj.* mejor
  better than *adj.* mejor que
  It's better that . . . Es mejor que…
  get better mejorarse; *(health)* aliviarse
better (oneself) *v t* superaroc
  Better late than never. *loc.* Más vale tarde que nunca.
between *prep.* entre
bib *n.* babero *m.*
bicycle *n.* bicicleta *f.*
  ride a bicycle pasear/montar en bicicleta
big *adj.* gran, grande
Big Dipper *n.* Osa *f.* Mayor
big shot *n.* pez *m.* gordo
bikini *n.* bikini *m.*
bill *n.* cuenta *f.;* factura *f.*
billion *n.* mil *m.* millones (de)
biodiversity *n.* biodiversidad *f.*
biographical *adj.* biográfico/a
biography *n.* biografía *f.*
biologist *n.* biólogo/a *m., f.*
biology *n.* biología *f.*

biosphere *n.* biosfera *f.*
bird *n.* ave (el) *f.,* pájaro *m.*
birth *n.* nacimiento *m.*
birth control *n.* control *m.* de natalidad
birthday *n.* cumpleaños *m., sing.*
  birthday cake pastel *m.* de cumpleaños
  birthday song *n.* mañanitas *f., pl.*
  Happy birthday! ¡Feliz cumpleaños!
  have a birthday cumplir años
birthrate *n.* (índice *m.* de) natalidad *f.*
bite *n.* mordisco *m.*
bite *v.t.* morder
bitter *adj.* amargo/a
bittersweet *adj.* agridulce
black *n., adj.* negro/a
blackberry *n.* mora *f.*
blackboard *n.* pizarra *f.; m.* pizarrón
blackout *n.* apagón *m.*
bladder *n.* vejiga *f.*
bland *adj.* insípido/a; soso/a
blanket *n.* cobija *(L.A.) f.;* frazada *(L.A.) f.;* manta *f.*
bleach *n.* lejía *f.*
blend *v.t.* licuar
blender *n.* licuadora *(L.A.) f.;* batidora *(Spain) f.*
bless *v.t.* bendecir
blind *adj.* ciego/a
blind *n.* persiana *f.*
block *n. (city)* cuadra *(L.A.) f.;* manzana *(Spain)*
blond(e) *adj.* rubio/a
blood *n.* sangre *f.*

blood circulation *n.* circulación *f.* (sanguínea)
blood pressure *n.* presión *f.* sanguínea
blouse *n.* blusa *f.*
blue *n., adj.* azul
blueprint *n.* plano *m.*
bluish *adj.* azulado/a
blush *v.i.* ponerse rojo/a, sonrojarse
board *n. (organizational)* junta *f.;* tablero *m.*
board *v.i. (ship)* embarcar
board games *n., pl.* juegos *m., pl.* de mesa
board of directors *n.* junta *f.* directiva
boardinghouse *n.* pensión *f.*
boast (about) *v.t.* alardear (de) *(Spain)*
   He was boasting about having won. Alardeaba de haber ganado.
boat *n.* barco *m.*
   go by boat ir en barco
body *n.* cuerpo *m.*
boil *v.t.* hervir
boiled *adj.* hervido/a
bolt *n. (lock)* cerrojo *m.*
bolt (the door) *v.t.* correr el cerrojo
bomb *n.* bomba *f.*
bond *n.* vínculo *m.*
bone *n.* hueso *m.; (fish)* espina *f.*
bonfire *n.* hoguera *f.*
book *n.* libro *m.*
book *v.t.* hacer una reservación
bookcase *n.* estantería *f.;* estante *m.*

bookshelf, bookshelves *n.* estante *m.*
bookstore *n.* librería *f.*
bookworm *n.* ratón *m.* de biblioteca
boot *n.* bota *f.*
   rubber boot bota de agua
bore *v.t.* aburrir
bored *adj.* aburrido/a
   be bored estar aburrido/a
   get bored aburrirse
boring *adj.* aburrido/a; soso/a
born: be born nacer
borrow *v.t.* pedir prestado
borrowed *adj.* prestado/a
boss *n.* jefe *m.,* jefa *f.*
botanical *adj.* botánico/a
botanist *n.* botánico/a *m., f.*
botany *n.* botánica *f.*
bother *v.t.* molestar **Does the music bother you?** ¿Te molesta la música?
bottle *n.* botella *f.*
bottle opener *n.* abrebotellas *m., sing.*
bottom *n.* fondo *m.*
boulevard *n.* bulevar *m.*
bow *n.* lazo *m.; (sport)* arco *m.*
bowl *n.* tazón *m.*
bowling *n.* boliche *m.*
box *v.i.* boxear
boxer *n.* boxeador(a) *m., f.*
boxer shorts *n., pl.* calzoncillos *m., pl.*
boxing *n.* boxeo *m.*
boy *n.* chico *m.;* muchacho *m.;* niño *m.*
boyfriend *n.* novio *m.*
bra *n.* sostén *m.;* sujetador *(Spain) m.;* brasier *(L.A.) m.*

braid *n.* trenza *f.*
brain *n.* cerebro *m.*
brake *v.i.* frenar
brake *n.* freno *m.*
  brake pedal *n.* pedal *m.* del freno
branch *n.* rama *f.*
brand (name) *n.* marca *f.*
  It's a well-known brand. Es una marca de prestigio.
brat *n.* niño/a *m., f.* mimado/a
brave *adj.* valiente
bravery *n.* valentía *f.*
bread *n.* pan *m.*
  freshly-baked bread pan recién horneado
break *v.t.* romper **She breaks the glass.** Ella rompe el vaso.; romperse **He broke his leg.** Se rompió la pierna.
  break a world record batir un récord mundial
break down *v.i. (auto)* descomponerse *(L.A.),* dañarse *(L.A.);* averiarse *(Spain);* estropearse, sufrir una avería
  The . . . broke down on us. Se nos dañó el/la…
  break the ice *loc.* romper el hielo
break up (with) *v.i.* romper (con)
breakdown *n. (mechanical)* avería *(Spain) f.*
breakfast *n.* desayuno *m.*
  have breakfast desayunar
breakwater *n.* rompeolas *m., sing.*
breast *n.* pecho *m.*

chicken breast pechuga *f.* (de pollo)
breaststroke *n.* estilo *m.* braza *(Spain);* estilo *m.* pecho *(L.A.)*
breath *n.* aliento *m.*
breathe *v.i.* respirar
breathing *n.* respiración *f.*
breeze *n.* brisa *f.*
brick *n.* ladrillo *m.*
bricklayer *n.* albañil *m.*
bricklaying *n.* albañilería *f.*
bridge *n.* puente *m.*
bright *adj. (color)* vivo/a
bring *v.t.* traer
bring up *v.t. (children)* criar
broadcast *v.t.* transmitir; emitir
broccoli *n.* brócoli *m.*
brochure *n.* folleto *m.*
broiled *adj.* a la parrilla
broken *adj.* roto/a
  be broken estar roto/a
broken down *adj.* averiado/a *(Spain)*
bronze *n.* bronce *m.*
brook *n.* riachuelo *m.*
broom *n.* escoba *f.*
broth *n.* caldo *m.*
brother *n.* hermano *m*
  brothers and sisters *n., pl.* hermanos *m., pl.*
  younger brother *n.* hermano *m.* menor
brother-in-law *n.* cuñado *m.*
brought *p.p.* traído *(of* traer)
brown *n., adj. (color)* café; marrón; *(eyes, hair)* castaño/a
brunet(te) *adj.* moreno/a
brush *n.* cepillo *m.*
brush *v.t.* cepillar

125

brush one's hair cepillarse el pelo

brush one's teeth cepillarse/lavarse los dientes

bubble *n.* burbuja *f.*

Buddhist *n., adj.* budista *m., f.*

build *v.t.* construir

builder *n.* albañil *m.*; constructor(a) *m., f.* (de obras)

building *n.* edificio *m.*; (*profession*) albañilería *f.*

 apartment building casa *f.* de apartamentos/edificio *m.* de apartamentos

 building contractor *n.* constructor(a) *m., f.* (de obras)

bull *n.* toro *m.*

bulletin *n.* boletín *m.*

bulletin board *n.* tablero *m.* de anuncios

bullfight *n.* corrida *f.* de toros

bullfighter *n.* torero/a *m., f.*

bullfighting *n.* tauromaquia *f.*

bullring *n.* plaza *f.* de toros

bump into *v.* (*meet accidentally*) darse con

bumper *n.* parachoques *m., sing.*

burglar *n.* ladrón *m.*, ladrona *f.*

burial *n.* entierro *m.*

burn *v.t.* quemar

burned (out) *adj.* quemado/a

burp *n.* eructo *m.*

burp *v.i.* eructar

bus *n.* autobús *m.*; camión *m.* (*Mexico*)

 go by bus ir en autobús

bus station *n.* estación *f.* de autobuses

bush *n.* arbusto *m.*

business *n.* negocios *m., pl.*; empresa *f.*

business administration *n.* administración *f.* de empresas

businessman *n.* hombre *m.* de negocios

business-related *adj.* comercial

businesswoman *n.* mujer *f.* de negocios

busy *adj.* ocupado/a

but *conj.* pero; (*in negative sentences*) sino

butcher shop *n.* carnicería *f.*

butler *n.* mayordomo *m.*

butter *n.* mantequilla *f.*

 butter a piece of toast untar una tostada con mantequilla

butterfly *n.* mariposa *f.*

butterfly stroke *n.* estilo *m.* mariposa

button *n.* botón *m.*

buy *v.t.* comprar

by *prep.* por

 by the way a propósito, por cierto

bye *fam.* chau; adiós

C

cabbage *n.* col (*Spain*) *f.*; repollo (*L.A.*) *m.*

cabin *n.* cabaña *f.*

cable *n.* cable *m.*

 cable television *n.* televisión *f.* por cable

café *n.* café *m.*

cafeteria *n.* cafetería *f.*

caffeine *n.* cafeína *f.*
cake *n.* pastel *m.*
calculate *v.t.* calcular
calculation *n.* cálculo *m.*
calculator *n.* calculadora *f.*
calendar *n.* calendario *m.*
calf *n.* *(anat.)* pantorrilla *f.*
call *v.t.* llamar
  be called llamarse
  be on call estar de guardia
  call on the phone llamar por teléfono
calm *n., adj.* tranquilidad *f.;* tranquilo/a
  Stay calm! ¡Tranquilo/a!
calm down *v.* tranquilizarse
calorie *n.* caloría *f.*
camaraderie *n.* compañerismo *m.*
camel *n.* camello *m.*
camera *n.* cámara *f.*
camp *n.* acampada *f.*
camp *v.i.* acampar
  go camping ir de acampada/campamento
can *n.* *(tin)* lata *f.*
  can opener *n.* abrelatas *m., sing.*
can *v.aux.* poder (o:ue)
  I can't take it any more! *loc.* ¡No puedo más!/¡No soporto más!
Canadian *n., adj.* canadiense *m., f.*
canary *n.* canario *m.*
cancel *v.t.* cancelar; anular; *(performance)* suspender
candidate *n.* aspirante *m., f.;* candidato/a *m., f.*
candle *n.* vela *f.*

candy *n.* dulces *m., pl.*
cane *n.* caña *f.*
canoe *n.* piragua *f.*
canoeing *n.* piragüismo *m.*
canoeist *n.* piragüista *m., f.*
canvas *n.* lona *f.*
cap *n.* *(with a visor)* gorra *f.;* *(without a visor)* gorro *m.*
capital *n.* capital *f.*
  capital letter *n.* mayúscula *f.*
capsule *n.* cápsula *f.*
capture *v.t.* capturar
car *n.* carro *(L.A.)* *m.;* coche *(Spain)* *m.;* automóvil *m.*
  go by car ir en auto(móvil)
car accident *n.* *(crash)* choque *m.*
carbohydrate *n.* carbohidrato *m.*
carburator *n.* carburador *m.*
card *n.* tarjeta *f.;* *(playing)* carta *f.,* naipe *m.*
card table *n.* tapete (verde) *m.*
cardiology *n.* cardiología *f.*
care *n.* cuidado *m.,* atención *f.*
  take care of cuidar
  take care of oneself cuidarse
careful: be careful tener cuidado; ¡Cuidado!
career *n.* carrera *f.*
caretaker *n.* el ama *(m., f.)* de casa
Caribbean *adj.* caribeño/a
carnation *n.* clavel *m.*
carnivore *n.* carnívoro/a *m., f.*
carnivorous *adj.* carnívoro/a
carols *n.* villancicos *m., pl.*
carpenter *n.* carpintero/a *m., f.*
carpet *n.* alfombra *f.*

carrot *n.* zanahoria *f.*
carry *v.t.* llevar; transportar
cart *n.* carro *(Spain) m.*
cartoons *n., pl. (animated)* dibujos *m., pl.* animados; *(political)* caricaturas *f., pl.* (políticas)
carve *v.t.* tallar
case *n.* caso *m.*
  in case of en caso de que
  in case (that) en caso (de) que
cash *n.* (en) efectivo *m.*
cash (a check) *v.t.* cobrar
cash register *n.* caja *f.*
cashier *n.* cajero/a *m., f.*
casserole *n.* cazuela *f.*
cast *n.* yeso *(L.A.) m.;* escayola *(Spain) f.*
castle *n.* castillo *m.*
casual *adj.* informal
cat *n.* gato/a *m., f.*
catastrophe *n.* catástrofe *f.*
catastrophic *adj.* catastrófico/a
catch *v.t. (illness)* pegar
category *n.* categoría *f.*
cathedral *n.* catedral *f.*
Catholic *n., adj.* católico/a *m., f.*
cattle *n.* ganado *m.*
cattle farmer *n.* ganadero/a *m., f.*
cattle raising *n.* ganadería *f.*
cause *v.t.* causar; provocar
cavern *n.* caverna *f.*
CD-ROM *n.* cederrón *m.*
cedar *n.* cedro *m.*
celebrate *v.t.* celebrar; festejar
celebration *n.* festejo *m.*
celery *n.* apio *m.*
cell *n.* célula *f.*

cellar *n.* sótano *m.; (wine)* bodega *f.*
cellular *adj.* celular
cement *n.* cemento *m.*
cemetery *n.* cementerio *m.*
censor *v.t.* censurar
censorship *n.* censura *f.*
censure *n.* censura *f.*
censure *v.t.* censurar
census *n.* censo *m.*
century *n.* siglo *m.*
cereal *n.* cereales *m., pl.*
certain *adj.* cierto/a; seguro/a
  it's (not) certain (no) es cierto/seguro
certainty *n.* certeza *f.*
chain *n.* cadena *f.*
chair *n.* silla *f.*
chalk *n.* tiza *f.*
challenge *n.* reto *m.;* desafío *m.*
challenge *v.t.* desafiar; retar
champagne *n.* champán *m.*
champion *n.* campeón *m.,* campeona *f.*
championship *n.* campeonato *m.*
chance *n.* azar *m.*
chandelier *n.* araña *f.* (de luces)
change *v.t.* cambiar (de/en); renovar
change *n.* cambio *m.*
change purse *n.* monedero *m.*
channel *n. (TV, radio)* canal *m.;* cadena *f.*
Chanukah *n.* Januká *m.*
chapel *n.* capilla *f.;* ermita *f.*
character *n.* carácter *m.; (fictional)* personaje *m.*

main character personaje principal
charisma *n.* carisma *m.*
charity *n.* caridad *f.; (money)* limosna *f.; (organization)* sociedad *f.* benéfica
charm *n.* encanto *m.*
charming *adj.* encantador(a)
chase *v.t.* perseguir
chat *v.* conversar
chatterbox *n.* charlatán *m.,* charlatana *f.*
chauffeur *n.* conductor(a) *m., f.*
cheap *adj.* barato/a
cheat *v.i.* hacer trampa(s); *(money)* engañar
cheat on *v.t. (relationship)* engañar
check *n. (bank)* cheque *m.*
check *v.t.* comprobar; revisar; averiguar
  check the oil revisar el aceite
checkers *n., pl. (game)* damas (chinas) *f., pl.*
checkup *n.* revisión *(Spain) f.;* chequeo *(médico) (L.A.) m.*
cheek *n.* mejilla *f.*
cheeky *adj.* caradura
cheeky person *n.* caradura *m., f.*
cheer up *v.* animar(se)
cheese *n.* queso *m.*
chef *n.* cocinero/a *m., f.*
chemical *adj.* químico/a
chemist *n.* químico/a *m., f.*
chemistry *n.* química *f.*
cherry *n.* cereza *f.*
cherry tree *n.* cerezo *m.*
chess *n.* ajedrez *m.*

chess player *n.* ajedrecista *m., f.*
chest *n. (anatomy)* pecho
chest of drawers *n.* cómoda *f.*
chew *v.t.* masticar
chicken *n.* pollo *m.*
chickpea *n.* garbanzo *m.*
child *n.* niño/a *m., f. (son, daughter)* hijo/a *m., f.*
  only child hijo/a único/a
childhood *n.* niñez *f.*
children *n., pl. (sons and daughters)* hijos *m., pl.*
chill *v.t.* enfriar
chilled *adj.* frío/a
chimney *n.* chimenea *f.*
china *n. (fine)* porcelana *f.*
Chinese *n., adj.* chino/a *m., f.; (language)* chino
chlorine *n.* cloro *m.*
chlorophyll *n.* clorofila *f.*
chocolate *n.* chocolate *m.*
chocolate cake *n.* pastel *m.* de chocolate
choir *n.* coro *m.*
choke *v.i.* atragantarse
cholesterol *n.* colesterol *m.*
choose *v.t.* escoger
chop *n. (meat)* chuleta *f.*
chop *v.t.* cortar
chores *n., pl.* quehaceres *m., pl.*
  household chores quehaceres domésticos
  do household chores hacer quehaceres domésticos
chorus *n.* coro *m.*
Christian *n., adj.* cristiano/a *m., f.*
Christmas *n.* Navidad *f.*

Christmas card *n.* tarjeta *f.* de Navidad

church *n.* iglesia *f.*

cider *n.* sidra *f.*

cinnamon *n.* canela *f.*

circle *n.* círculo *m.*

circuit *n. (electric)* circuito *m.*

circus *n.* circo *m.*

citizen *n.* ciudadano/a *m., f.*

citrus *adj.* cítrico/a

city *n.* ciudad *f.*

city hall *n.* ayuntamiento *m.*

clam *n.* almeja *f.*

clap *v.t./v.i.* aplaudir

clash *n.* enfrentamiento *m.*

class *n.* clase *f.*

take classes tomar clases

classical *adj.* clásico/a

classmate *n.* compañero/a *m., f.* de clase

classroom *n.* aula *f.;* salón *m.*

clavicle *n.* clavícula *f.*

clay *n.* arcilla *f.*

clean *adj.* limpio/a

clean *v.t.* limpiar

clean the house limpiar la casa

clear *adj.* claro/a; *(weather)* despejado/a

It's (very) clear. *(weather)* Está (muy) despejado.

clear *v.t. (pipes)* desatascar

clear the table quitar/recoger la mesa

clerk *n.* dependiente/a *m., f.*

cliff *n.* acantilado *m.*

climate *n.* clima *m.*

climatology *n.* climatología *f.*

climb *n. (mountain)* escalada *f.*

climb *v.t.* escalar

climb mountains escalar montañas

climb trees *v.* subirse a los árboles

climber *n. (mountain)* alpinista *m., f.,* escalador(a) *m., f.*

climbing *n. (mountain)* alpinismo *m.*

clinic *n.* clínica *f.*

clock *n.* reloj *m.*

alarm clock despertador *m.*

clog *n.* zueco *m.*

close *adj. (relative)* cercano/a; *(people)* unido/a

get close (to someone) intimar (con alguien)

close *v.t.* cerrar (e:ie)

closed *adj.* cerrado/a

closet *n.* armario *m.;* clóset *m.*

closing *n.* clausura *f.*

clothes *n., pl.* ropa *f.*

What pretty clothes! ¡Qué ropa más bonita!

clothes dryer *n.* secadora *f.*

clothesline *n.* tendedero *m.*

clothing *n.* ropa *f.*

cloud *n.* nube *f.*

have one's head in the clouds estar en las nubes

cloudy *adj.* nublado/a

It's (very) cloudy. Está (muy) nublado.

clown *n.* payaso/a *m., f.*

clue *n.* pista *f.*

Give me a clue. Dame una pista.

clumsy *adj.* torpe

clutch *n.* embrague *m.*

clutch pedal *n.* pedal *m.* del embrague

coach *n.* entrenador(a) *m., f.*
coaching *n.* entrenamiento *m.*
coal *n.* carbón *m.*
coast *n.* costa *f.*
coastal *adj.* costero/a
coastline *n.* costa *f.*
coat *n.* abrigo *m.*
  coat hanger *n.* perchero *m.*
cockroach *n.* cucaracha *f.*
coconut *n.* coco *m.*
cod *n.* bacalao *m.*
coffee *n.* café *m.*
  coffee maker *n.* cafetera *f.*
coffin *n.* ataúd *m.*
coincide *v.i.* coincidir
coincidence *n.* azar *m.;*
  coincidencia *f.*
colander *n.* colador *m.*
cold *n. (temperature)* frío *m.;*
  (illness) catarro *m.,* resfriado
  m.
  be cold *(thing)* estar frío/a
  be (feel) cold tener frío
  It's (very) cold. *(weather)*
  Hace (mucho) frío.
collaborate *v.i.* colaborar
  collaborate (with) *v. pron.*
  asociarse (con)
collaboration *n.* colaboración
  f.
collect *v.t.* coleccionar
collecting *n.* coleccionismo *m.*
collector *n.* coleccionista *m., f.*
college *n.* universidad *f.*
collision *n.* choque *m.*
cologne *n.* colonia *f.*
colonist *n.* colono *m.*
colonization *n.* colonización *f.*
colonize *v.t.* colonizar
colony *n.* colonia *f.*

color *n.* color *m.*
color *v.t.* colorear
column *n.* columna *f.*
comb *n.* peine *m.*
comb one's hair *v. refl.*
  peinarse
come *v.i.* venir
come back *v.* volver; regresar
comedy *n.* comedia *f.*
comfort *n.* confort *m.*
comfortable *adj.* confortable;
  cómodo/a
comic strip *n.* tira *f.* cómica,
  historieta *f.*
commemorate *v.t.* conmemorar
commemoration *n.*
  conmemoración *f.*
commerce *n.* negocios *m., pl.*
commercial *adj.* comercial
committee *n.* junta *f.*
common *adj.* común
communicate *v.t.* comunicar;
  (speak with) comunicarse
  (con)
communication *n.*
  comunicación *f.*
community *n.* comunidad *f.*
compact disc (CD) *n.* disco *m.*
  compacto
compact disc player *n.*
  tocadiscos *m., sing.*
  compacto
companion *n.* compañero/a
  m., f.
company *n.* compañía *f.;*
  empresa *f.*
comparison *n.* comparación *f.*
compete *v.i.* competir
competence *n.* aptitud *f.*
competent *adj.* competente

competition *n.* competencia *(L.A.) f.;* competición *(Spain) f.*

competitive *adj.* competitivo/a

competitor *n.* competidor(a) *m., f.;* participante *m., f.*

complain *v.i.* quejarse

complaint *n.* queja *f.*

completely *adv.* completamente; a fondo

complex *adj.* complejo

complexion *n.* cutis *m.*

complicate *v.t.* complicar

composer *n.* compositor(a) *m., f.*

computer *n.* computadora *f.*

computer disk *n.* disco *m.*

computer monitor *n.* monitor *m.*

computer programmer *n.* programador(a) *m., f.*

computer science *n.* computación *f.*

con artist *n.* estafador(a) *m., f.*

conceal *v.t.* disimular

conceited *adj.* engreído/a

concert *n.* concierto *m.*

concrete *n.* concreto *(L.A.) m.;* hormigón *(Spain) m.*

condense *v.t.* condensar

conditioned *adj.* acondicionado/a

conduct *n.* conducta *f.*

conductor *n. (musical)* director(a) *m., f.*

conference *n.* congreso *m.*

confirm *v.t.* confirmar

   confirm a reservation confirmar una reservación

confirmation *n.* confirmación *f.*

confront *v.t.* enfrentar; enfrentarse (con)

   The army will confront the enemy. El ejército se enfrentará con el enemigo.

confuse *v.t.* confundir

confused *adj.* confundido/a

confusion *n.* confusión *f.*

congested *adj.* congestionado/a

congratulate *v.t.* felicitar

Congratulations! *(for an event such as a birthday or anniversary)* ¡Felicidades! *f., pl.; (for an event such as an engagement or a good grade on a test)* ¡Felicitaciones! *f., pl.*

conquer *v.t.* conquistar

conqueror *n.* conquistador(a) *m., f.*

conquest *n.* conquista *f.*

conscience *n.* conciencia *f.*

consensus *n.* consenso *m.*

consent *n.* consentimiento *m.*

consent to *v.* consentir

conservation *n.* conservación *f.*

conservative *n., adj.* conservador(a) *m., f.*

conserve *v.t.* conservar

considerate *adj.* considerado/a

constellation *n.* constelación *f.*

constipated *adj.* estreñido/a

constipation *n.* estreñimiento *m.*

constitution *n.* constitución *f.*

consume *v.t.* consumir

consume alcohol consumir alcohol

consumer *n.* consumidor(a) *m., f.*
consumption *n.* consumo *m.*
contact lenses *n., pl.* lentes *m., pl.* de contacto
contagion *n.* contagio *m.*
contagious *adj.* contagioso/a
container *n.* recipiente *m.;* envase *m.*
contamination *n.* contaminación *f.*
content *adj.* contento/a
contest *n.* competencia *(L.A.) f.;* concurso *m.*
continue *v.t.* seguir (e:i)
contraceptive *n.* anticonceptivo *m.*
contract *n.* contrato *m.*
contradict *v.t.* contradecir
contradiction *n.* contradicción *f.*
contrast *v.t.* contraponer
control *n.* control *m.*
  control panel *n.* tablero *m.* de control
  control tower *n.* torre *f.* de control
control *v.t.* controlar
  be under control estar bajo control
control oneself *v.* dominarse
controversial *adj.* polémico/a
controversy *n.* polémica *f.*
convent *n.* convento *m.*
conversation *n.* conversación *f.*
converse *v.* conversar
convertible *n., adj. (car)* descapotable *m.*
convict *n.* presidiario/a *m., f.*
conviction *n.* convicción *f.*

convince *v.t.* convencer
convincing *adj.* convincente
cook *n.* cocinero/a *m., f.*
cook *v.t./v.i.* cocinar
cookie *n.* galleta *f.*
cool *adj.* fresco/a; *(slang)* chévere
  It's cool. *(weather)* Hace fresco.
copper *n.* cobre *m.*
copy *v.t.* copiar
cork *n.* corcho *m.*
corkscrew *n.* sacacorchos *m, sing.*
corn *n.* maíz *m.*
corner *n.* esquina *m.*
corpse *n.* cadáver *m.*
correct *v.t.* corregir
correction *n.* corrección *f.*
correctness *n.* corrección *f.*
cost *v.t.* costar (o:ue)
  cost an arm and a leg *idiom.* costar un ojo de la cara
costume *n.* disfraz *m.*
cotton *n.* algodón *m.*
  made of cotton de algoldón
couch *n.* sofá *m.*
  couch potato *n.* teleadicto/a *m., f.*
cough *n.* tos *f.*
cough syrup *n.* jarabe *m.* para la tos
cough *v.i.* toser
counselor *n.* consejero/a *m., f.*
count (o:ue) *v.t.* contar
counter *n. (game)* ficha *f.*
country *n. (nation)* país *m.;* *(rural)* campo *m.*
  developed country país desarrollado

developing country país en vías de desarrollo

countryside *n.* campo *m.*; paisaje *m.*

couple, (married) *n.* pareja *f.*

a couple of days un par de días

courage *n.* valentía *f.;* valor *m.*

course *n.* curso *m.*; materia *f.*

court *n. (of law)* corte *(L.A.) f.*, tribunal *(Spain) m.; (sport)* cancha *f.*

clay court pista *f.* de tierra batida

grass court pista *f.* de hierba

courtesy *n.* cortesía *f.*

cousin *n.* primo/a *m., f.*

cover *v.t.* cubrir; *(container, pan)* tapar

covered *p.p.* cubierto *(of* cubrir)

cow *n.* vaca *f.*

coward *adj.* cobarde

cowardice *n.* cobardía *f.*

cowboy *n.* vaquero *m.*

cowgirl *n.* vaquera *f.*

cozy *adj.* acogedor(a)

crab *n.* cangrejo *m.*

cracker *n.* galleta *f.* (salada)

cradle *n.* cuna *f.*

crafts *n.* artesanía *f.*

craftsmanship *n.* artesanía *f.*

crane *n. (machinery)* grúa *f.*

crash (into sthg.) *v.i.* chocar (contra algo)

crash a party colarse en una fiesta

crater *n.* cráter *m.*

crave *v.t.* ansiar

crawl *v.i.* arrastrarse (por el

suelo)

crazy *adj.* loco/a

cream *n.* crema *f.; (dairy)* nata *f.*

anti-wrinkle cream crema antiarrugas

creamy *adj.* cremoso/a

create *v.t.* crear

creative *adj.* creativo/a

creator *n.* creador(a) *m., f.*

credible *adj.* verosímil

credit *n.* crédito *m.*

credit card *n.* tarjeta *f.* de crédito

cricket *n.* grillo *m.*

crime *n.* crimen *m.;* delincuencia *f.*

criminal *n.* delincuente *m., f.*

crisis *n.* crisis *f.*

mid-life crisis crisis de los cuarenta

critic *n.* detractor(a) *m., f.*

crockery *n.* vajilla *f.*

cross *v.t.* cruzar; atravesar

cross section *n. (Tech.)* corte *m.* transversal

crossroads *n., pl.* cruce *m.*

crosswalk *n.* paso *m.* de peatones

crossword (puzzle) *n.* crucigrama *m.*

cruise *n.* crucero *m.*

crunchy *adj.* crujiente

crusty *adj. (bread)* crujiente

cry *v.i.* llorar

crybaby *n.* llorón *m.*, llorona *f.*

crystal *n.* cristal *m.*

cucumber *n.* pepino *m.*

culture *n.* cultura *f.*

cup *n.* taza *f.*

cure *n.* cura *f.*
cure *v.t.* curar
currency exchange *n.* cambio *m.* de moneda
current *n.* corriente *f.*
  alternating current (AC) corriente alterna
  direct current (CD) corriente continua
  current events *n., pl.* actualidades *f., pl.*
curriculum vitae *n.* currículum *m.*
curtain *n.* cortina *f.*
curve *n.* curva *f.*
cushion *n.* cojín *m.*
custard *n. (baked)* flan *m.;* natillas *f., pl.*
  baked caramel custard flan de caramelo
custom *n.* costumbre *f.*
customer *n.* cliente/a *m., f.*
customs *n.* aduana *f.*
  go through customs pasar por la aduana
  customs inspector *n.* inspector(a) *m., f.* de aduanas
cut *n.* corte *f.*
cut *v.t.* cortar; partir (un pastel)
  cut class *idiom* irse de pinta *(Mexico)*; hacer novillos *(Spain)*
cutlery *n.* cubertería *f.*
cybercafé *n.* cibercafé *m.*
cycling *n.* ciclismo *m.*
cycling race *n.* carrera *f.* ciclista
cyclist *n.* ciclista *m., f.*
cylinder *n.* cilindro *m.*

cypress *n.* ciprés *m.*

D

dad *n.* papá *m.*
daily *adj.* diario/a
daily routine *n.* rutina *f.* diaria
dairy *n.* productos *m., pl.* lácteos
daisy *n.* margarita *f.*
dam *n.* represa *f.*
damage *v.t.* dañar; estropear
damp *adj.* húmedo/a
dance *n.* baile *m.;* danza *f.*
dance *v.t.* bailar
dance floor *n.* pista *f.* de baile
dancer *n.* bailarín *m.,* bailarina *f.*
danger *n.* peligro *m.*
dangerous *adj.* peligroso/a
dare (to + *inf.*) *v.t.* atreverse (a + *inf.*)
daring *adj.* atrevido/a
dark-skinned *adj.* moreno/a
darken *v.t. (sky, clouds)* ennegrecerse
darts *n., pl. (game)* dardos *m., pl.*
date (someone) *v.t.* salir con (alguien)
date *n. (appointment)* cita *f.; (calendar)* fecha *f.*
  have a date tener una cita
  What is the date (today)? ¿Cuál es la fecha (de hoy)?
  What is today's date? ¿Cuál es la fecha de hoy?
daughter *n.* hija *f.*
daughter-in-law *n.* nuera *f.*
dawn *n.* amanecer *m.*
dawn *v.i.* amanecer

day *n.* día *m.*
 What day is it? ¿Qué día es hoy?
day before yesterday *adv.* anteayer
day-care center *n.* guardería *f.*
daydream *v.i.* soñar despierto
dazed *adj.* atontado/a
dead-end street *n.* callejón *m.* sin salida
deaf *adj.* sordo/a
deal *n.* trato *m.*
 It's a deal. Trato hecho.
 It's no big deal. No es para tanto.
dealer *n. (arms, drugs)* traficante *m., f.*
dean *n. (university)* decano/a *m., f.*
death *n.* muerte *f.;* defunción *f.;* fallecimiento *m.*
debate *n.* debate *m.*
debate *v.t.* debatir
debut *v.t. (movie, play)* estrenar
decadence *n.* decadencia *f.*
decaffeinated *adj.* descafeinado/a
deceased *n., adj.* fallecido/a *m., f.,* difunto/a *m., f.*
deceive *v.t.* engañar
December *n.* diciembre *m.*
deception *n.* engaño *m.*
decide *v.t.* decidir (+ inf.)
decided *adj.* decidido/a
decipher *v.t.* descifrar
decision *n.* decisión *f.*
 make a decision tomar una decisión
deck (of cards) *n.* baraja *f.* (de cartas/naipes)
deck chair *n.* tumbona *f.*
declare *v.t.* declarar
decline *n.* descenso *m.;* decadencia *f.*
decode *v.t.* descifrar
decorate *v.t.* decorar; adornar
 decorate the tree poner el árbol
decrease *n.* descenso *m.;* disminución *f.*
decrease *v.t.* disminuir
dedicate *v.t.* dedicar
dedication *n.* dedicación; dedicatoria *f.*
deer *n.* ciervo *m.*
defeat *n.* derrota *f.*
defeat *v.t.* derrotar
deficiency *n.* deficiencia *f.*
deficit *n.* déficit *m.*
define *v.t.* definir
definition *n.* definición *f.*
deforestation *n.* deforestación *f.*
defraud *v.t.* estafar
defuse *v.t.* desactivar
dejected *adj.* abatido/a
delay *n.* retraso *m.,* atraso *m.*
delicious *adj.* delicioso/a, rico/a, sabroso/a
 be delicious *loc.* estar para chuparse los dedos
delight *n.* deleite *m.,* placer *m.*
delighted *adj.* encantado/a
delineate *v.t.* delinear
delinquency *n.* delincuencia *f.*
democracy *n.* democracia *f.*
democrat *n.* demócrata *m., f.*
democratic *adj.* democrático/a
demonstrate *v.i.* manifestarse

demonstration *n.* manifestación *f.*

demonstrator *n.* manifestante *m., f.*

density *n.* densidad *f.*

dental floss *n.* hilo *m.* dental

dentist *n.* dentista *m., f.*

deny *v.t.* negar (e:ie)
  not to deny no negar

deodorant *n.* desodorante *m.*

department *n.* departamento *m.*

department head *n.* catedrático/a *m., f.*

department store *n.* almacén *m.*

departure *n.* partida *f.*; salida *f.*

deposit *v.t.* depositar

depressed *adj.* deprimido/a

depression *n.* depresión *f.*

depth *n.* profundidad *f.*

derail *v.t.* descarrilar

derailment *n.* descarrilamiento *m.*

dermatologist *n.* dermatólogo/a *m., f.*

descend *v.i.* descender

descendant *n.* descendiente *m., f.*

descent *n.* descenso *m.*

describe *v.t.* describir

described *pp.* descrito (*of describir*)

desert *n., adj.* desierto *m.*; desértico/a

deserve *v.t.* merecer

design *n.* diseño *m.*

designer *n.* diseñador(a) *m., f.*

desire *n.* deseo *m.*

desire *v.t.* desear

desk *n.* escritorio *m.*

despair *n.* desesperanza *f.*

despair *v.i.* desesperar(se); perder las esperanzas

desperate *adj.* desesperado/a

desperation *n.* desesperación *f.*

dessert *n.* postre *m.*

destroy *v.t.* destruir

destruction *n.* destrucción *f.*

detail *n.* detalle *m.*

detained *adj.* detenido/a

deteriorate *v.* decaer

determined *adj.* condicionado/a

detoxification *n.* desintoxicación *f.*

detoxify *v.t.* desintoxicar

detractor *n.* detractor(a) *m., f.*

develop *v.t.* desarrollar

development *n.* desarrollo *m.*, (*housing*) urbanización *f.*

dew *n.* rocío *m.*

diabetes *n.* diabetes *f.*

diabetic *n., adj.* diabético/a *m., f.*

diagnose *v.t.* diagnosticar

diagnostic *n.* diagnóstico *m.*

dial (the number) *v.t.* marcar (el número)

dialogue *n.* diálogo *m.*

diamond *n.* diamante *m.*

diarrhea *n.* diarrea *f.*

diary *n.* diario *m.*

dice *n., pl.* dados *m., pl.*

dictator *n.* dictador(a) *m., f.*

dictatorship *n.* dictadura *f.*

dictionary *n.* diccionario *m.*

die out *v.t.* extinguirse

die *v.i.* morir (o:ue)

137

died *p.p.* muerto (*of* morir)
diet *n.* dieta *f.*; alimentación *f.*
  eat a balanced diet comer
  una dieta equilibrada
  be on a diet estar a dieta
differ *v.i.* divergir
difference *n.* diferencia *f.*,
  divergencia *f.*
different *adj.* diferente
differing *adj.* (*opinions*)
  divergente
difficult *adj.* difícil
  make difficult dificultar;
  complicar
difficulty *n.* dificultad *f.*
dig *v.t.* excavar
digital camera cámara digital
dine *v.i.* cenar
dining room *n.* comedor *m.*
dinner *n.* cena *f.*
  have dinner cenar
dinosaur *n.* dinosaurio *m.*
diplomat *n.* diplomático/a *m., f.*
diplomatic *adj.* diplomático/a
direct *v.t.* dirigir
directions *n., pl.* direcciones *f.,*
  pl. indicaciones (*Spain*) *f., pl.*
  give directions dar
  direcciones
director *n.* director(a) *m., f.*
dirty *adj.* sucio/a
dirty *v.t.* ensuciar
  get (something) dirty
  ensuciar
disabled *adj.* (*person*)
  inválido/a
disadvantage *n.* desventaja *f.*
disagree *v.i.* no estar de
  acuerdo
disappear *v.i.* desaparecer

disappearance *n.* desaparición
  f.
disappointed *adj.*
  decepcionado/a;
  desilusionado/a
  be disappointed
  decepcionarse
disaster *n.* desastre *m.*
  natural disaster desastre
  natural
disastrous *adj.* desastroso/a
discipline *n.* disciplina *f.*
discoteque *n.* discoteca *f.*
discount *n.* descuento *m.*
discount *v.t.* descontar
  give a discount descontar
discover *v.t.* descubrir
discovered *p.p.* descubierto
  (*of* descubrir)
discovery *n.* descubrimiento
  m.; hallazgo *m.*
discreet *adj.* discreto/a
discrete *adj.* discreto/a
discrimination *n.*
  discriminación *f.*
discuss *v.t.* discutir
discus throw *n.* lanzamiento *m.*
  de disco
disgraceful *adj.* vergonzoso/a
disgusting *adj.* asqueroso/a
dish *n.* plato *m.*; platillo
  main dish plato principal
  serving dish fuente *f.*
dishcloth *n.* trapo *m.*
dishes (set) *n., pl.* vajilla *f.*
disheveled *adj.* despeinado/a
dishonest *adj.* deshonesto/a
dishwasher *n.* lavaplatos *m.,*
  sing.
disinfect *v.t.* desinfectar

disinfectant n., adj. desinfectante
disk n. disco m.
dislike n. antipatía f.; aversión f.
dislike v.i. chocar
disobey v.t. desobedecer
disorder n. desorden m.; (medical) trastorno m.
disorderly adj. desordenado/a
disposable adj. desechable
disqualification n. (sport) descalificación f.
disqualify v.t. (sports) descalificar
disseminate v.t. propagar
distant adj. lejano/a
distinction n. (grade) matrícula f. de honor
distinguish v.t. distinguir
distinguished adj. distinguido/a
distribute v.t. distribuir
distribution n. distribución f.
distrustful adj. receloso/a
dive n. salto m.; clavado (L.A.) m.
dive, (scuba) v.i. (underwater) bucear
diving board n. trampolín m.
diver n. (scuba) buceador(a) m., f.
diverse adj. variado/a
divorce n. divorcio m.
divorced adj. divorciado/a
get divorced (from) divorciarse (de)
dizzy adj. mareado/a
feel dizzy marearse
do v.t. hacer

do the dishes lavar los platos
do oneself up v. arreglarse
doctor n. doctor(a) m., f.; médico/a m., f.
doctor on call/duty médico/a de guardia
doctorate n. doctorado m.
document n. documento m.
document v.t. documentar
documentary n. documental m.
dodge ball n. quemados m., pl.
dog n. perro/a m., f.
doll n. muñeco/a m., f.
dolphin n. delfín m.
domestic adj. doméstico/a
domestic appliance electrodoméstico m.
dominate v.t. dominar
domino n. dominó m.
done p.p. hecho (of hacer)
donor n. donante m., f.
donut n. dona f.
door n. puerta f.
back door puerta trasera
front door puerta principal
doorbell n. timbre m.
doorman n. portero/a m., f.
dormitory n. residencia f. estudiantil
double adj. doble
doubt n. duda f.
There is no doubt that . . . No cabe duda (de) que… ; No hay duda (de) que…
without a doubt sin duda
doubt v.t. dudar
not to doubt no dudar
dough n. masa f.
dove n. paloma f.
down adv. abajo, debajo (de)

Down with...! ¡Abajo el/la...!
downhearted *adj.* desanimado/a
download *v.t. (computer)* descargar
downtown *n.* centro *m.*
draftsman *n.* delineante *m.*
draftswoman *n.* delineante *f.*
drag *v.t.* arrastrar
drain *v.t.* colar *(L.A.); (the dishes)* escurrir (los platos)
drainpipe *n.* desagüe *m.*
drama *n.* drama *m.*
dramatic *adj.* dramático/a
draw *v.t.* dibujar
drawback *n.* inconveniente *m.*
drawing *n.* dibujo *m.*
dream *v.i.* soñar
dress *n.* vestido *m.*
dress *v.t.* vestirse (e:i); *(salad)* aderezar; aliñar
get dressed vestirse (e:i)
dress up *v.* ponerse elegante
You have dressed up tonight. Te has puesto muy elegante esta noche.
dresser *n.* cómoda *f.*
dressing *n. (culinary)* aderezo *m.,* aliño *m.; (medical)* vendaje *m.*
dressing room *n.* probador *m.*
dressmaker *n.* modista *f.*
drill *n. (tool)* perforadora *f.*
drill *v.t.* perforar
drink *n.* bebida *f.*
drink *v.t.* beber; tomar
Do you want something to drink? ¿Quieres algo de tomar?
drive *v.t.* conducir *(Spain);*

manejar *(L.A.)*
driver *n.* conductor(a) *m., f.*
driveway *n.* entrada *f.*
drop *n.* gota *f.; (temperature, price)* descenso *m.*
drop off *v.t.* dejar
drought *n.* sequía *f.*
drown *v.t.* ahogar **Ahoga sus penas cantando.** She drowns her sorrows by singing. *v.i.* ahogarse **Te ahogas en un vaso de agua.** You get worked up about nothing.
drowned *adj.* ahogado/a
drug *n.* droga *f.*
drug addict *n., adj.* drogadicto/a *m., f.*
drunk *adj.* borracho/a; ebrio/a; embriagado/a
dry *adj.* seco/a
dry (oneself) *v. pron.* secarse
due to *prep.* debido a; por
due to the fact that debido a
dull *adj.* sin brillo; *(person)* aburrido/a, soso/a
dumb *adj.* tonto/a
dune *n.* duna *f.*
during *prep.* durante; por
dusk *n.* atardecer *m.*
dust *n.* polvo *m.*
dust *v.t.* sacudir
dust the furniture sacudir los muebles
duty: be on duty estar de guardia
DVD player reproductor de DVD
dye *v.t.* teñir
dying *adj.* moribundo/a
I'm dying to/for . . . Me muero por (+ *inf.*)/n. . . .

dynamite *n.* dinamita *f.*
dynamite *v.t.* dinamitar
dynasty *n.* dinastía *f.*
dysfunction *n.* disfunción *f.*

E
each *adj.* cada
eagle *n.* águila (el) *f.*
ear, (outer) *n.* oreja *f.*
  inner ear *n.* oído *m.*
early *adj., adv.* temprano/a
  early morning *n.* madrugada
  f.
earn *v.t.* ganar
  earn one's living *idiom*
  ganarse la vida
earring *n.* arete *(L.A)* m.;
  pendiente *m. (Spain)*
earth *n.* tierra *f.*
earthquake *n.* terremoto *m.*
earthworm *n.* lombriz *f.*
eaco *n.* ooltura *f.*
ease *v.t.* aliviar
east *n.* este *m.*
  to the east al este
easy *adj.* fácil
  make easier facilitar
  Easier said than done. *idiom*
  Del dicho al hecho hay gran
  trecho.
easygoing *adj.* tranquilo/a
eat *v.t.* comer
eclipse *n.* eclipse *m.*
ecological *adj.* ecológico/a
ecologist *n.* ecologista *m., f.*
ecology *n.* ecología *f.*
economics *n.* economía *f.*
ecosystem *n.* ecosistema *m.*
ecotourism *n.* ecoturismo *m.*
Ecuadorian *n., adj.*

ecuatoriano/a *m., f.*
edible *adj.* comestible
educator *n.* educador(a) m., f.
eel *n.* anguila *f.*
effective *adj.* eficaz
effectiveness *n.* eficacia *f.*
efficiency *n.* eficiencia *f.*
efficient *adj.* eficiente, eficaz
effort *n.* esfuerzo *m.*
egg *n.* huevo *m.*
eggplant *n.* berenjena *f.*
eight ocho
eight hundred ochocientos/as
eighteen dieciocho
eighth octavo *m.; adj.* octavo/a
eighty ochenta
either . . . or *conj.* o… o
elastic *adj.* elástico/a
elbow *n.* codo *m.*
elderly *adj.* anciano/a
eldest el/la mayor
elect *v.t.* elegir
election *n.* elección *f.*,
  elecciones *f., pl.*
electorate *n.* electorado *m.*
electric *adj.* eléctrico/a
electric current *n.* corriente *f.*
  eléctrica
electric shock *n.* descarga *f.*
  eléctrica
electrician *n.* electricista *m., f.*
electricity *n.* electricidad *f.; luz
  f.*
electrocuted: be electrocuted
  electrocutarse
electrolysis *n.* electrólisis *f.*
electronics *n.* electrónica *f.*
elegant *adj.* elegante
elementary *adj.* elemental;
  (school) primario/a

elephant n. elefante m.
elevator n. ascensor m.
eleven once
eliminate v.t. eliminar
elimination n. eliminación f.
eloquence n. elocuencia f.
eloquent adj. elocuente
e-mail n. correo m. electrónico
  e-mail address dirección
  electrónica
  e-mail message n. mensaje
  m. electrónico
embarrass v.t. avergonzar
embarrassed adj.
  avergonzado/a
embarrassment n. vergüenza f.
embrace v.t. abrazar; (each
  other) abrazarse
embroider v.t. bordar
emerald n. esmeralda f.
emergency n. emergencia f.
emergency room n. sala f. de
  emergencia
emigrant n. emigrante m., f.
emigrate v.i. emigrar
emigration n. emigración f.
emphasis n. énfasis m.
emphasize v.t. destacar;
  enfatizar
empire n. imperio m.
employee n. empleado/a m., f.
employment n. empleo m.
enchant v.t. encantar
encourage v.t. dar aliento;
  animar
end n. fin m.
  at the end (of) (physical
  location) al fondo (de);
  (month, century) a fines de
end v.t. terminar

end table n. mesita f.
endangered species n., pl.
  especie(s) f. (pl.) en peligro
  de extinción
endurance n. resistencia f.;
  aguante m.;
endure v.t. soportar; aguantar
energy n. energía f.
  (nuclear/solar) energy
  energía (nuclear/solar)
engaged: get engaged (to)
  comprometerse (con)
engagement n. compromiso
  m., noviazgo m.
engagement ring n. anillo m.
  de compromiso
engineer n. ingeniero/a m., f.
English adj., n. inglés m.,
  inglesa f.; (language) inglés
enigma n. enigma m.
enigmatic adj. enigmático/a
enjoy v.t. disfrutar (de)
enjoyable adj. agradable;
  divertido/a
enough adj. bastante
enrich v.t. enriquecer
enroll v.i. matricularse;
  inscribirse
enrollment n. inscripción f.
enter v. entrar
entertaining adj. entretenido/a
entertainment n. diversión f.
enthusiasm n. entusiasmo m.
enthusiastic adj.
  entusiasmado/a
entirely adv. totalmente; del
  todo **He is not entirely
  mistaken.** No está del todo
  equivocado.
entrance n. entrada f.

entrance hall *n. (residence)* recibidor *m.*
entrepreneur *n.* empresario/a *m., f.*
envelope *n.* sobre *m.*
envious *adj.* envidioso/a
environment *n.* medio ambiente *m.; (natural)* ambiente *m.*
environmentalist *n.* ecologista *m., f.*
equality *n.* igualdad *f.*
equestrian sports *n., pl.* hípica *f.*
equipped *adj.* equipado/a
equivalence *n.* equivalencia *f.*
equivalent: be equivalent to equivaler
erase *v.t.* borrar
eraser *n.* borrador *m.; (pencil)* goma *f.*
errand *n.* diligencia *f.*
do/run errands hacer diligencias
erupt *v.i. (volcano)* hacer erupción
eruption *n.* erupción *f.*
escalator *n.* escalera *f.* mecánica
escape *n.* evasión *f.;* huida *f.; (prison)* fuga *f.*
escape *v.i.* huir; fugarse; evadirse **Luis escaped responsibility.** Luis se evadió de la responsabilidad.
esophagus *n.* esófago *m.*
establish *v.t.* establecer
esteem *n.* aprecio *m.*
estimate *n.* cálculo *m.*
ethical *adj.* ético/a

ethics *n.* ética *f.*
euphoria *n.* euforia *f.*
euphoric *adj.* eufórico/a
European *n., adj.* europeo/a *m., f.*
evade *v.t.* evadir
evening *n.* tarde *f.;* noche *f.*
in the evening de la noche; por la noche
event *n.* acontecimiento *m.*
ever alguna vez
every *adj.* cada
every day cada día, todos los días
everybody *n.* todos *m., pl.*
everything *n.* todo *m.*
Everything is under control. Todo está bajo control.
evidence *n.* indicio *m.;* pruebas *f., pl.*
lack of evidence falta *f.* de pruebas
evolution *n.* evolución *f.*
evolve *v.i.* evolucionar
exactly *adv.* exactamente; *(time)* en punto
exaggerate *v.t.* exagerar
exaggeration *n.* exageración *f.*
exam *n.* examen *m.*
example: for example por ejemplo
exasperate *v.t.* desesperar
The slowness of the train exasperated him. La lentitud del tren le desesperó.
excavate *v.t.* excavar
excavator *n.* excavadora *f.*
exceed *v.t.* superar
excel *v.i.* sobresalir

excellent *adj.* excelente; *(grade)* sobresaliente
exceptional *adj.* prodigioso/a
excess *n.* exceso *m.*
  in excess en exceso
exchange *n.* intercambio *m.*
  in exchange for a cambio de; por
exchange *v.t.* intercambiar
excited *adj.* emocionado/a
exciting *adj.* emocionante
excursion *n.* excursión *f.*
excuse *v.t.* disculpar
  Excuse me. *(May I?)* Con permiso.; *(Pardon me.)* Perdón.; *(interrupting)* Disculpe. **Excuse me, can you tell me…** Disculpe, puede decirme…
exercise *n.* ejercicio *m.*
exercise *v.i.* hacer ejercicio
  do stretching exercises hacer ejercicios de estiramiento
exhaust pipe *n.* tubo *m.* de escape
exhausted *adj.* agotado/a
exhaustion *n.* agotamiento *m.*
exhibit *v.t. (paintings, goods)* exponer; *(skill)* demostrar
exhibition *n.* exposición *f.*
exit *n.* salida *f.*
exodus *n.* éxodo *m.*
expect *v.t.* esperar
expel *v.t.* expulsar
expense *n.* gasto *m.*
expensive *adj.* caro/a
experience *n.* experiencia *f.*
experiment *v.i.* experimentar
expiration *n.* expiración *f.*

expiration date *n.* fecha *f.* de caducidad
expire *v.i.* expirar
explain *v.t.* explicar
explore *v.t.* explorar
  explore a city/town explorar una ciudad/un pueblo
explosive *adj.* explosivo/a
export *v.t.* exportar
exportation *n.* exportación *f.*
expression *n.* expresión *f.*
expressive *adj.* expresivo/a
expressway *n.* autopista *f.*
expulsion *n.* expulsión *m.*
extinction *n.* extinción *f.*
  become extinct extinguirse
extinguish *v.t.* extinguir
extremely *adv.* sumamente
extremities *n., pl.* extremidades *f., pl.*
extroverted *adj.* extrovertido/a
eye *n.* ojo *m.*
eyebrow *n.* ceja *f.*
eyelash *n.* pestaña *f.*
eyelid *n.* párpado *m.*

F

fabric *n.* tela *f.*
fabulous *adj.* fabuloso/a
façade *n.* fachada *f.*
face *n.* cara *f.*
face *v.t.* enfrentar **It's necessary to face the problem immediately.** Hay que enfrentar el problema en seguida.
facedown *adv.* boca abajo
faceup *adv.* boca arriba
facilitate *v.t.* facilitar
facing *prep.* enfrente de

fact *n.* hecho *m.*
  in fact de hecho; en efecto
factory *n.* fábrica *f.*
fail *v.t. (exam)* suspender; fracasar
fail *n. (grade)* suspenso *m.*
failed *adj.* fracasado/a
failure *n.* fracaso *m.*
fair *adj.* justo/a
fairy *n.* hada (el) *f.*
fairy godmother *n.* hada madrina
faithful *adj.* fiel
fall *n.* **(season)** otoño *m.*
faithfulness *n.* fidelidad *f.*
fall *v.i.* caer; *(down)* caerse
  fall asleep *v.* dormirse (o:ue)
fallen *p.p.* caído *(of* caer*)*
familiar *adj.* conocido/a
family *n., adj.* familia *f.;* familiar
family doctor *n.* médico/a *m., f.* de cabecera; médico/a de familia
family tree *n.* árbol *m.* genealógico
famine *n.* hambre *m.*
famous *adj.* famoso/a
fan *n., adj.* aficionado/a *m., f.;* ventilador *m.*
  be a fan of ser aficionado/a a
fang *n.* colmillo *m.*
far from *adv.* lejos de
farewell *n.* despedida *f.*
farmer *n.* agricultor(a) *m., f.*
farming *n.* agricultura *f.*
far-off *adj.* lejano/a
fascinate *v.t.* fascinar
  be fascinated by fascinar
fashion *n.* moda *f.*
  be in fashion estar de moda

  be fashionably dressed ir a la moda
fast *adj.* rápido/a
fast *n.* ayuno *m.*
fast *v.i.* ayunar
fast *adj.* rápido/a, veloz
  fast food *n.* comida *f.* rápida
fat *adj.* gordo/a
fat *n.* grasa *f.*
father *n.* padre *m.*
father-in-law *n.* suegro *m.*
fatigue *n.* cansancio *m.*
fatten *v.t.* engordar
faucet *n.* grifo *m.*
fault *n.* culpa *f.*
favorable *adj.* favorable
favorite *adj.* favorito/a
fax (machine) *n.* fax *m.*
fear *n.* miedo *m.*
fear *v.t.* temer
February *n.* febrero *m.*
food *v.t.* alimentar, dar de comer
  get fed up hartarse
feel *v.t.* sentir, sentirse
  feel like (doing something) tener ganas de (+ *inf.*)
feeling sorry *adj.* arrepentido/a
female *n.* hembra *f.*
fence *n.* valla *f.*
fencer *n.* esgrimidor(a) *m., f.*
fencing *n. (sport)* esgrima *f.*
fender *n.* guardabarros *m., sing.*
ferry *n.* transbordador *m.*
fertile *adj.* fértil
fertility *n.* fertilidad *f.*
fertilization *n.* fecundación *f.*
fertilize *v.t.* fecundar; *(the soil)* abonar (la tierra)

fertilizer *n.* abono *m.;* fertilizante *m.*

festival *n.* festival *m.;* verbena *f.*

fever *n.* fiebre *f.*
  have a fever tener fiebre

few *adj.* pocos/as
  fewer than menos de (+ *number*)

fidelity *n.* fidelidad *f.*

field *n.* campo *m.; (sport)* cancha *f.*
  major field of study *n.* especialización *f.*

field hockey *n.* hockey *m.* sobre césped *(L.A.);* hockey sobre hierba *(Spain)*

fifteen quince

fifth quinto *m.; adj.* quinto/a

fifty cincuenta

fig *n.* higo *m.*

fig tree *n.* higuera *f.*

fight *n.* pelea *f.;* lucha *f.*

fight *v.i.* luchar (por/contra); pelear; pelearse

figure *n.* figura *f.; (number) n.* cifra *f.*

figure skating *n.* patinaje *m.* artístico

file *n.* archivo *m.; (tool)* lima *f.*

file *v.t.* archivar

fill *v.t.* llenar
  fill the tank llenar el tanque

fill out *v.t. (document)* rellenar *(Spain);* llenar *(L.A.)*
  fill out a form llenar un formulario

film *v.t.* rodar

film *n.* película

film library *n.* filmoteca *f.*

filming *n.* rodaje *m.*

filmmaker *n.* cineasta *m., f.*

fin *n.* aleta *f.*

finally *adv.* finalmente; por último; por fin

finance *v.t.* financiar

find *n.* hallazgo *m.* **That restaurant was a real find.** Ese restaurante fue un verdadero hallazgo.

find *v.t.* encontrar (o:ue); *(each other)* encontrarse
  I can't find my shoe. No encuentro el zapato.
  Finally, they found each other. Al fin se encontraron.

find out *v.t.* averiguar

fine *n.* multa *f.*

fine *adj.* bien
  That's fine. Está bien.

fine arts *n., pl.* bellas artes *f., pl.*

finger *n.* dedo *m.* (de la mano)

fingerprint *n.* huella *f.* dactilar

finish *v.t.* terminar; *(doing something)* terminar de (+ *inf.)*

fir tree *n.* abeto *m.*

fire *n.* fuego *m.;* incendio *m.*
  fire engine *n.* carro *m.* de bomberos
  fire escape *n.* escalera *f.* de incendios

fire *v.* despedir (e:i)

firefighter *n.* bombero/a *m., f.*

fireplace *n.* chimenea *f.*

firewood *n.* leña *f.*

fireworks *n., pl.* fuegos *m., pl.* artificiales

firm *n.* compañía *f.;* empresa *f.*

first *adj.* primer, primero/a
　first of all *adv.* en primer
　lugar
first name *n.* nombre *m.* de pila
first-aid kit *n.* botiquín *m.* de
　primeros auxilios
firstborn *n.* primogénito/a *m., f.*
fish *n. (food)* pescado *m.; (live)*
　pez *m.*
　marinated fish *n.* ceviche *m.*
fish *v.t.* pescar
fish market *n.* pescadería *f.*
fisherman *n.* pescador *m.*
fisherwoman *n.* pescadora *f.*
fishing *n.* pesca *f.*
　go fishing ir de pesca
fit *adj. (suitable)* apto/a **He's**
　not fit to practice
　psychology. No es apto para
　ejercer la psicología.;
　(physically) en forma
fit *v.i. (clothing)* quedar
　Does it fit me? ¿Me queda
　bien?
five cinco
five hundred quinientos/as
fix *v.t. (put in working order)*
　arreglar
fixed *adj. (set)* fijo/a
　fixed price *n.* precio *m.* fijo
　fixed schedule horario fijo
flag *n.* bandera *f.*
flamboyant *adj.* extravagante
flank steak *n.* lomo *m.*
flashlight *n.* linterna *f.;* foco *m.*
flat: go flat *v.t.* ponchar
　(Mexico); pinchar **We got a**
　flat tire. Se nos ponchó/
　pinchó una llanta.
flatter *v.t.* adular

flatter someone *idiom*
　echarle flores a alguien
flatterer *n.* adulador(a) *m., f.*
flattery *n.* adulación *f.*
flavor *n.* sabor *m.*
flee *v.i.* fugarse; huir
flex *v.t.* flexionar
flexible *adj.* flexible
　flexible schedule horario
　flexible
flight *n.* vuelo *m.; (escape)*
　huida *f.*
flipper *n.* aleta *f.*
flirt *n.* coqueta *f.*
flirt *v.i.* coquetear
float *n.* carroza *f.*
float *v.i.* flotar
flood *n.* inundación *f.*
flood *v.t.* inundar
floor *n. (story in a building)*
　piso *m.; (ground)* suelo
　(Spain) m., piso *(L.A.) m.*
　ground floor planta *f.* baja
　top floor planta alta
florist *n.* florista *(Spain) m., f.;*
　florero/a *(L.A.) m., f.*
flour *n.* harina *f.*
flow *v.i.* fluir
flower *n.* flor *f.*
flower pot *n.* maceta *f.*
flower shop *n.* florería *(L.A.) f.;*
　floristería *(Spain) f.*
flu *n.* gripe *f.*
fluffy *adj. (fabric, baked goods)*
　esponjoso/a
fly *n.* mosca *f.*
foam *n.* espuma *f.*
focus on *v.t.* enfocar
fog *n.* niebla *f.*

147

It's (very) foggy. Hay (mucha) niebla.
fold *v.t.* plegar
folder *n.* carpeta *f.*
folding *adj.* plegable
folic acid *n.* ácido *m.* fólico
folk *adj.* folklórico/a
follow *v.t.* seguir (e:i)
food *n.* comida *f.;* alimento *m.*
foolish *adj.* tonto/a
foot *n.* pie *m.*
football *n.* fútbol *m.* americano
footprint *n.* huella *f.*
foot race *n.* carrera *f.* pedestre
for *prep.* para; por
  for me para mí
forbid *v.t.* prohibir
forehead *n.* frente *f.*
foreign *adj.* extranjero/a
forensic scientist *n.* forense *m., f.*
forest *n.* bosque *m.*
  tropical forest bosque tropical
forget *v.t.* olvidar
forgive *v.t.* perdonar
forgiveness *n.* perdón *m.*
fork *n.* tenedor *m.*
forklift *n.* montacargas *m., sing.*
form *n. (shape)* forma *f.; (document)* formulario *m.*
formal *adj.* formal
fortnight *n.* quincena *f.*
fortress *n.* fortaleza *f.*
forty cuarenta
forward *adv.* hacia adelante; en marcha
fossil *n.* fósil *m.*
fossilize *v.i.* fosilizarse

become fossilized fosilizarse
foundation *n. (building)* cimientos *m., pl.*
fountain *n.* fuente *f.*
four cuatro
four hundred cuatrocientos/as
fourteen catorce
fourth cuarto *m.; adj.* cuarto/a
fox *n.* zorro *m.*
fraud *n.* estafador(a) *m., f.*
freckle *n.* peca *f.*
freckled *adj.* pecoso/a
free *adj.* libre; *(price)* gratis
  be free of charge ser gratis
  free fall *n.* caída *f.* libre
  free time *n.* tiempo *m.* libre; ratos *m., pl.* libres
free *v.t.* liberar
freedom *n.* libertad *f.*
freedom of speech *n.* libertad de expresión
freelancer *n.* [trabajador(a)] autónomo/a *m., f.*
freestyle *n.* estilo *m.* libre
freeway *n.* autopista *f.*
freezer *n.* congelador *m.*
French *n., adj.* francés *m.,* francesa *f.; (language)* francés
French fries *n., pl.* papas *f., pl.* fritas; patatas *f., pl.* fritas
frequently *adv.* frecuentemente; con frecuencia; a menudo
fresh *adj.* fresco/a
Friday *n.* viernes *m., sing.*
fried *adj.* frito/a
fried food *n.* fritada *f.*
fried potatoes *n., pl.* papas (L.A.) *f., pl.* fritas; patatas

(Spain) f., pl. fritas
friend *n.* amigo/a *m., f.*
  make friends hacer amigos
friendly *adj.* amable;
  amistoso/a
friendship *n.* amistad *f.*
frog *n.* rana *f.*
from *prep.* de; desde
  from the United States
  estadounidense
  from time to time *adv.* de vez
  en cuando
front desk *n.* recepción *f.*
front door *n.* puerta *f.* principal
front seat *n.* asiento *m.*
  delantero
frost *n.* escarcha *f.*
frugal *adj.* ahorrador(a)
fruit *n.* fruta *f.*
fruit juice jugo *m.* de fruta
fruit store *n.* frutería *f.*
fruit tree *n.* árbol *m.* frutal
fuchsia *adj.* fucsia
fuel *n.* combustible *m.*
fugitive *n.* fugitivo/a *m., f.*
full *adj.* lleno/a
fun *adj.* divertido/a
  have fun divertirse (e:ie)
fun activity *n.* diversión *f.*
function *v.i.* funcionar
funds *n., pl. (money)* fondos *m.,
  pl.*
funeral *n.* funeral *m.*
funnel *n.* embudo *m.*
funny *adj.* chistoso/a;
  gracioso/a
furious *adj.* furioso/a
furnish *v.t.* amueblar
furnished *adj.* amueblado/a
furniture *n.* muebles *m., pl.*

furthermore *adv.* además (de)
fuse *n.* fusible *m.*
future *n., adj.* futuro/a; futuro
  m.; porvenir *m.*
  in the (near) future en el
  futuro (cercano)

G

gain *v.t.* ganar; obtener
  gain weight aumentar de
  peso; engordar
galaxy *n.* galaxia *f.*
gallbladder *n.* vesícula *f.*
  (biliar)
gallery *n.* galería *f.*
  art gallery pinacoteca *f.*
gambler *n.* jugador(a) *m., f.*
gambling *n.* juegos *m., pl.* de
  azar
game *n.* juego *m.; (match)*
  partido *m.*
game piece *n.* ficha *f.*
game show *n.* concurso *m.*
gang *n.* pandilla *f.*
gang member *n.* pandillero/a
  m., f.
garage *n.* garaje *m.*
garbage *n.* basura *f.*
garbage can *n.* basurero *m.*
garbage collector *n.*
  basurero/a *m., f.*
garbage disposal *n.* triturador
  m. de basura
garbage dump *n.* basurero *m.;*
  vertedero *m.*
garden *n.* jardín *m.;* huerto *m.*
  large garden *n.* huerta *f.*
gardener *n.* jardinero/a *m., f.*
gardenia *n.* gardenia *f.*
gardening *n.* jardinería *f.*

garlic *n.* ajo *m.*
garment *n.* prenda *f.*
garnish *v.t.* decorar; adornar
gas pedal *n.* pedal *m.* del acelerador
gas station *n.* gasolinera *f.*
gas tank *n.* depósito *m.* de gasolina
gasoline *n.* gasolina *f.*
gastronomy *n.* gastronomía *f.*
gathering *n. (to discuss politics, literature, etc.)* tertulia *f.*
gaze at *v.* contemplar
gazelle *n.* gacela *f.*
gearshift *n. (car)* cambio *m.* de marchas/velocidades
gelatin *n.* gelatina *f.*
generous *adj.* generoso/a
genetic *adj.* genético/a
genetic engineering *n.* biogenética *f.*
genetics *n.* genética *f.*
geography *n.* geografía *f.*
geologist *n.* geólogo/a *m., f.*
geometric(al) *adj.* geométrico/a
geometry *n.* geometría *f.*
geranium *n.* geranio *m.*
German *n., adj.* alemán *m.,* alemana *f.; (language)* alemán
get *v.t.* conseguir (e:i); obtener
　get along well/badly with llevarse bien/mal con
　get good grades *v.* sacar buenas notas
　get hurt *v. pron.* lastimarse
　get into trouble *v.* hacer travesuras

　get pregnant *v.* quedar embarazada
　get together *v. pron.* juntarse
get off (at) *v.* salirse (en)
get off of (a vehicle) *v.* bajar(se) de
get on/in to (a vehicle) *v.* subir(se) a
get up *v.* levantarse
　get up early madrugar
getaway *n.* escapada *f.*
geyser *n.* géiser *m.*
gift *n.* regalo *m.*
giraffe *n.* jirafa *f.*
girl *n.* chica *f.;* muchacha *f.;* niña
girlfriend *n.* novia *f.*
give *v.t.* dar; *(gift)* regalar
give in *v.* ceder
give up (doing something) *v.* dejar de (+ *inf.*)
give up hope *v.* desesperarse
give way *v.* ceder (el paso)
glass *n. (drinking)* vaso *m., (material)* vidrio *m.,* cristal *m.*
　made of glass de vidrio
glasses *n., pl.* gafas *f., pl.*
glassware *n.* cristalería *f.*
gloves *n.* guantes *m.*
glue *v.t.* pegar
gluttonous *adj.* glotón *m.,* glotona *f.*
go *v.i.* ir
　go on rides *v.* subirse a los juegos
　go on the swings *v.* subirse a los columpios
　go shopping ir de compras
　Let's go. Vamos.
go away *v.* irse; ausentarse

go beyond v. superar
go by v. pasar por
  go by the bank pasar por el banco
go down v. bajar(se)
go off v. *(alarm)* sonar
go out (with) v. salir (con)
  go out and have a snack in a bar ir de tapas *(Spain)*
go overboard *loc.* echar la casa por la ventana
go up v. subir
go with v. acompañar
goal n. meta f.; objetivo m.
goblet n. copa f.
God n. Dios m.
god n. *(deity)* dios
goddaughter n. ahijada f.
godfather n. padrino m.
godmother n. madrina f.
godson n. ahijado m.
going to: be going to *(do something)* ir a (+ *inf.*)
gold adj. dorado/a
gold n. oro m.
golden adj. dorado/a
golf n. golf m.
golf club n. palo m. de golf
golf course n. campo m. de golf
golfer n. golfista m., f.
good adj. buen, bueno/a
  Good afternoon. Buenas tardes.
  Good evening. Buenas noches.
  Good morning. Buenos días.
  Good night. Buenas noches.
  I'm good, thanks. Bien, gracias.

  in good spirits adj. animado/a
  It's good that… Es bueno que…
good sense n. sensatez f.
good-bye n. adiós m.; despedida f.
  say good-bye despedirse
good-looking adj. guapo/a
goods n. artículos m., pl.
gossip n. chismes m., pl.; cotilleo *(Spain)* m.
gossip v.i. cotillear *(Spain)*; chismear
Gothic adj. gótico/a
govern v.t. gobernar
government n. gobierno m.
grade n. calificación f.; nota f.
grade v.t. calificar
graduate (from, in) v.i. graduarse (de), recibirse
graduation n. graduación f.
graffiti n. pintada f.
  There was gang graffiti on the wall. Había pintadas de pandillas en la pared.
grain n. grano m.
grains n., pl. cereales m., pl.
grammar school n. primaria f.
grandchildren n., pl. nietos m., pl.
granddaughter n. nieta f.
grandfather n. abuelo m.
grandmother n. abuela f.
grandparents n., pl. abuelos m., pl.
grandson n. nieto m.
grant n. beca f.
grape n. uva f.
grapefruit n. pomelo

(Argentina, Spain) m.; toronja (L.A.) f.

grass n. césped m.; hierba f.; pasto (L.A.) m.

grateful adj. agradecido/a

grater n. rallador m.

grave n. tumba f.

grave adj. grave

gravity n. gravedad f.

gray n., adj. gris m.

gray hair n. cana f.

great adj. fenomenal

great-grandchildren n., pl. bisnietos m., pl.

great-granddaughter n. bisnieta f.

great-grandfather n. bisabuelo m.

great-grandmother n. bisabuela f.

great-grandparents n., pl. bisabuelos m., pl.

great-grandson n. bisnieto m.

great-great-grandfather n. tatarabuelo m.

great-great-grandmother n. tatarabuela f.

great-great-grandparents n., pl. tatarabuelos m., pl.

greedy adj. avaricioso/a

Greek n., adj. griego/a m., f.; (language) griego

green n., adj. verde m.
  dark green verde oscuro

green space n. zona f. verde

greet v.t. saludar **He greets his friend.** Él saluda a su amigo.; (each other) saludarse **They greet each other.** Ellos se saludan.

greeting n. saludo m.
  Greetings to . . . Saludos a…

grenade n. (military) granada f.

grill n. parrilla f.; plancha f.

grilled adj. (food) a la plancha; a la parrilla **grilled flank steak** lomo a la plancha

groceries n., pl. comestibles m., pl.

group n. grupo m.

group v.t. agrupar
  get into groups agruparse

grove n. arboleda f.

grow v.t. cultivar; v.i. crecer

growing adj. creciente

growth n. crecimiento m.

grudge n. rencor m.

guarantee n. garantía f.

guarantee v.t. garantizar; asegurar

guard v.t. custodiar

guess v.t. adivinar

guest n. (at a house/hotel) huésped m., f.; (at a function) invitado/a m., f.

guide n. guía m., f.

guitar n. guitarra f.

gum n. (chewing) chicle m.; (anat.) encía f.

gunshot n. disparo m.

gymnasium n. gimnasio m.

gymnast n. gimnasta m., f.

gymnastics n. gimnasia f.
  rhythmic gymnastics gimnasia rítmica

gynecologist n. ginecólogo/a m., f.

H

hair n. pelo m.; cabello m.

hairbrush n. cepillo m. de pelo
hairdo n. peinado m. **Her new hairdo suits/suited her.** Su nuevo peinado le sienta/le sentaba bien.
hairdresser n. peluquero/a m., f.
hairdryer n. secador m.
hairstyle n. peinado m.
hairy adj. peludo/a
hake n. merluza f.
half n., adj. medio m.; medio/a
half-brother n. medio hermano m.
half-past . . . . . .y media
half-sister n. media hermana f.
hall n. salón m.
hallway n. pasillo m.
ham n. jamón m.
hamburger n. hamburguesa f.
hammer n. martillo m.
hammock n. hamaca f.
hand n. mano f.
   Hands up! ¡Manos arriba!
handball n. balonmano m.
handbrake n. freno m. de mano
handkerchief n. pañuelo m.
handle n. asa m.
handlebars n., pl. manillar (Spain) m.; manubrio (L.A.) m.
handrail n. pasamanos m., sing.
handsome adj. guapo/a
handy adj. práctico/a
hang v.t. colgar
   hang clothes on the line colgar la ropa en el tendedero
hang glider n. ala (el) f. delta
hang gliding v. practicar el ala

delta
hang out (clothes) v. tender (ropa)
hanger n. percha f.
hangover n. resaca (Spain) f.; cruda (Mexico) f.
   have a hangover tener cruda; tener resaca
happen v.t. ocurrir
   What happened? ¿Qué pasó?
   What's happening? ¿Qué pasa?
happiness n. alegría f.
happy adj. alegre; contento/a; feliz
   be happy alegrarse (de)
   be happy (with) contentarse (con)
harbor n. puerto m.
hard adj. difícil; duro/a
   hard to believe idiom parece mentira
hard feelings n., pl. rencor m.
hardly adv. apenas
hardship n. dificultad f.
hard-working adj. trabajador(a)
harmful adj. dañino/a
harvest n. cosecha f.
harvest v.t. cosechar
haste n. prisa f.
hat n. sombrero m.
hate v.i. odiar
have v.t. tener
   have a(n) . . .ache tener dolor de. . .
   have a good/bad time pasarlo bien/mal
   have a flat tire poncharse una llanta

have a picnic hacer un picnic

have an unfinished (matter) tener (un asunto) pendiente

have just done something acabar de (+ inf.)

have something on the tip of one's tongue loc. tener algo en la punta de la lengua

have to (do something) tener que (+ inf.); deber (+ inf.)

have to do with loc. tener que ver con **The letter doesn't have anything to do with the problem.** La carta no tiene nada que ver con el problema.

haze (someone) v.t. hacer una novatada (a alguien)

hazel tree n. avellano m.

hazelnut n. avellana f.

head n. cabeza f.

headache n. dolor m. de cabeza

headlight n. faro m.

headphone n. auricular m.

health n. salud f.

health care n. asistencia f. médica

health center n. enfermería f.

healthful adj. saludable

healthy adj. sano/a, saludable

hear v.t. oír

heard p.p. oído (of oír)

have heard idiom oír decir que

I've heard that Mapi and Kiko are getting married. He oído decir que Mapi y Kiko se van a casar.

hearing: (sense of) hearing n. oído m.

heart n. corazón m.

by heart de memoria **He knows the poem by heart.** Se sabe el poema de memoria.

heart attack n. infarto m.; ataque m. al corazón; ataque cardíaco

heartbeat n. latido m.

heat n. calor m.

heat v.t. calentar

heater n. calentador m.

heating n. calefacción f.

heaven n. cielo m.

Heaven forbid! loc. ¡Dios me libre!

heavy vehicles n., pl. vehículos m., pl. pesados

Hebrew n., adj. hebreo/a m., f; (language) hebreo

hedge n. seto m.

heel n. talón m.

hefty adj. corpulento/a

height n. altura f.

heir n. heredero m.

heiress n. heredera f.

helicopter n. helicóptero m.

hello interj. hola; (on the telephone) ¿Aló?, ¿Bueno?, ¿Diga?

helmet n. casco m.

help (to) v.t. ayudar (a); servir (e:i); (each other) ayudarse (a)

Help! interj. ¡Auxilio!; ¡Socorro!

hemisphere n. hemisferio m.

hemorrhage n. hemorragia f.

her poss. adj. su(s)

herbivore *n.* herbívoro/a *m., f.*
herbivorous *adj.* herbívoro/a
herbs *n., pl.* hierbas *f., pl.*
here *adv.* aquí
  Here it is. Aquí está.
  Here we are in . . . Aquí
  estamos en…
hereditary *adj.* hereditario/a
heritage *n.* patrimonio *m.*
hermit *n.* ermitaño/a *m., f.*
hero *n.* héroe *m.*
heroine *n.* heroína *f.*
hers *poss. pron.*
  suyo(s)/suya(s)
hi *interj.* hola
hiccups *n., pl.* hipo *m.*
hide *v.t.* esconder; disimular
hide-and-seek *n.* escondidillas
  f.; al escondite *m.*
hierarchical *adj.* jerárquico/a;
  jerarquizado/a
hierarchy *n.* jerarquía *f.*
high *adj.* alto/a
high jump *n.* salto *m.* alto
  (L.A.); salto *m.* de altura
  (Spain)
high school *n.* escuela *f.*
  secundaria; preparatoria *f.*
highway *n.* autopista *f.;*
  carretera *f.*
hijack *n.* secuestro *m.*
hijack *v.t (aircraft)* secuestrar
hike *n.* excursión *f.*
  **go for a hike (in the
  mountains)** ir de excursión (a
  las montañas)
  go hiking ir de excursión
  go on a hike hacer una
  excursión
hiker *n.* excursionista *m., f.*

hillside *n.* ladera *f.*
Hindu *n., adj.* hindú *m., f*
hint *n.* consejo *m.;* indicación *f.*
hip *n.* cadera *f.*
hippodrome *n.* hipódromo *m.*
hire *v.* contratar
his su(s) *poss. adj.;*
  suyo(s)/suya(s) *poss. pron.*
Hispanic *n., adj.* hispano/a *m.,
  f.*
historian *n.* historiador(a) *m., f.*
history *n.* historia *f.*
hit *n.* golpe *m.*
hit *v.i.* pegar
  hit (a car) *v.i.* chocar
hitchhike *v.i.* hacer auto(e)stop
hitchhiker *n.* auto(e)stopista
  m., f.
hobby *n.* afición *f.;* pasatiempo
  m.
hockey *n.* hockey *m.*
hold *v.t.* aguantar *(Spain)*
hold up *v.t. (bank)* atracar
holdup *n.* atraco *m.*
hole *n.* agujero *m.;* hueco *m.;
  (in the ground)* hoyo
  make holes in agujerear
holiday *n.* día *m.* de fiesta
Holy Week *n.* Semana *f.* Santa
homage *n.* homenaje *m.*
  pay homage to homenajear
home *n.* casa *f.;* hogar *m.*
  at home en casa
  home for the elderly *n.*
  residencia *f.* de ancianos
homemade *adj.* casero/a
home-maker *n.* el ama *(m., f.)*
  de casa
home page *n.* página *f.*
  principal

155

home run *n.* cuadrilátero *m.*

home style *adj.* casero/a

home team *n. (sports)* equipo *m.* local

hometown *n.* ciudad *f.* natal; *(my…)* mi pueblo *m.,* mi ciudad *f.*

homework *n.* deberes *m., pl.;* asignación *f.;* tarea *f.*

honest *adj.* honesto/a

honey *n.* miel *f.*

honeymoon *n.* luna *f.* de miel

hood *n. (car)* capó *m.,* cofre *m. (jacket)* capucha *f.*

hope *n.* esperanza *f.*

hope *v.t.* esperar
I hope (that) *interj.* Ojalá (que)

hopefully ojalá que…

horizon *n.* horizonte *m.*

hormone *n.* hormona *f.*

horn *n.* cuerno *m.; (car)* bocina *f.*

horror *n.* horror *m.;* …de horror

hors d'oeuvres *n., pl.* entremeses *m., pl.*

horse *n.* caballo *m.*
ride a horse montar a caballo

horse race *n.* carrera *f.* de caballos

horseback riding *n.* equitación *f.*

horticulturalist *n.* horticultor(a) *m., f.*

horticulture *n.* horticultura *f.*

hose *n.* manguera *f.*

hospitable *adj.* hospitalario/a

hospital *n.* hospital *m.*

hospitality *n.* hospitalidad *f.*

host *n.* anfitrión *m.*

hostel *n.* albergue *m.;* hostal *m.*

hostess *n.* anfitriona *f.*

hot *adj.* caliente
be hot *(weather)* hacer calor; *(feel)* tener calor; *(thing)* estar caliente
It's (very) hot. *(weather)* Hace (mucho) calor.

hotel *n.* hotel *m.*

hour *n.* hora *f.*

house *n.* casa *f.*

housekeeper *n.* el ama *(m., f.)* de casa

housewife *n.* ama *f.* de casa

housing *n.* vivienda *f.*

how? *adv.* ¿cómo?
How are you? *fam.* ¿Cómo estás?; ¿Qué tal? *form.* ¿Cómo está usted?
How did it go for you . . .? ¿Cómo le/les fue…?
How is it going? ¿Qué tal?
How is/are . . . ? ¿Qué tal…?
How many? ¿Cuánto/a(s)?
How may I help you? ¿En qué puedo servirle(s)?

how much? *adv.* ¿cuanto/a?
How much does it cost? ¿Cuánto cuesta…?
How…! ¡Qué…!
How big! ¡Qué grande!
How nice to see you. *loc.* Dichosos los ojos (que te ven).

however *conj.* sin embargo

hug *v.t.* abrazar; *(each other)* abrazarse

human *adj.* humano/a
human being *n.* ser *m.* humano
humanism *n.* humanismo *m.*
humanist *n.* humanista *m., f.*
humanities *n., pl.* humanidades *f., pl.*
humble *adj.* humilde
humid *adj.* húmedo/a
humidity *n.* humedad *f.*
humiliated *adj.* humillado/a
humming bird *n.* colibrí *m.*
hump *n.* joroba *f.*
hunchbacked *adj.* jorobado/a
hunger *n.* hambre *f.*
  be hungry tener hambre
hungry *adj.* hambriento/a
hunt *v.t.* cazar
hunter *n.* cazador(a) *m., f.*
hunting *n.* caza *f.*
hurdles *n., pl. (sport)* vallas *f., pl.*
hurricane *n.* huracán *m.*
hurry *v.i.* apurarse; darse prisa; apresurarse
  be in a hurry tener prisa
hurt *v.t.* doler (o:ue); lastimar
  hurt oneself hacerse daño
  It hurts me a lot . Me duele mucho.
husband *n.* esposo *m.;* marido *m.*
hydrangea *n.* hortensia *f.*
hydraulic *adj.* hidráulico/a
hyperbole *n.* hipérbole *f.*
hypothesis *n.* hipótesis *f.*
hypothetical *adj.* hipotético/a

I

I am… Yo soy…
ice *n.* hielo *m.*

ice cream *n.* helado *m.*
ice cream shop *n.* heladería *f.*
ice hockey *n.* hockey *m.* sobre hielo
ice rink *n.* pista *f.* de hielo
ice skate patinar en hielo
ice skating *n.* patinaje *m.* sobre hielo
iceberg *n.* iceberg *m.*
iced *adj.* helado/a
iced tea *n.* té *m.* helado
idea *n.* idea *f.*
idealist *adj.* idealista
idle *adj.* ocioso/a
if *conj.* si
ignorance *n.* ignorancia *f.*
ignorant *adj.* ignorante
ill *adv.* mal
illiterate (person) *n., adj.* analfabeto/a *m., f.*
ill-mannered *adj.* grosero/a; maleducado/a
illness *n.* enfermedad *f.*
imagine *v.t.* imaginar
imitate *v.t.* imitar
imitation *n.* imitación *f.*
immediately *adv.* inmediatamente; en el acto
immigrant *n., adj.* inmigrante *m., f.*
immigrate *v.i.* inmigrar
immigration *n.* inmigración *f.*
immune system *n.* sistema *m.* inmunológico
immunize *v.t.* inmunizar
immunological *adj.* inmunológico/a
impatience *n.* impaciencia *f.*
impatient *adj.* impaciente
  get impatient impacientarse

She got impatient over the delay. Se impacientó con el atraso.
impetuous *adj. (person)* lanzado/a, impulsivo/a
impolite *adj.* grosero/a
import *v.t.* importar
important *adj.* importante
  be important (to) *v.i.* importar
  It's (not) important that… (No) Es importante que…
importation *n.* importación *f.*
impossible *adj.* imposible
  it's impossible es imposible
impostor *n.* impostor(a) *m., f.*
impoverish *v.t.* empobrecer
impression *n.* impresión *f.*
  make a good/bad impression causar una buena/mala impresión
imprison *v.t.* encarcelar
improbable *adj.* improbable; inverosímil
  it's improbable es improbable
improve *v.t.* mejorar
improvement *n.* mejora *f.*
impulsive *adj.* lanzado/a
in *prep.* en
  in a jiffy *idiom* en un dos por tres; en un santiamén
in front of *prep.* delante de; enfrente
inaugurate *v.t.* inaugurar
inauguration *n.* inauguración *f.*
incomprehensible *adj.* incomprensible
inconceivable *adj.* inconcebible
inconvenience *n.* molestia *f.*

increase *n.* aumento *m.*; incremento *m.*
  be on the increase estar en auge
increasing *adj.* creciente
incredible *adj.* increíble
independent *adj.* independiente
  become independent independizarse
indescribable *adj.* inefable
indigenous *adj.* indígena
indigo *n., adj.* añil *m.*
individual *n., adj.* individuo *m. (may be pejorative:* **Who's that guy?** ¿Quién es ese individuo?); individual
individuality *n.* individualidad *f.*
inebriated *adj.* ebrio/a; embriagado/a
inequality *n.* desigualdad *f.*
inexperienced *adj.* novato/a
inexplicable *adj.* inexplicable
infection *n.* infección *f.*
influence *v.t.* influir en; influenciar
  Darío's poems influenced other poets. Los poemas de Darío influyeron en otros poetas.
inform *v.t.* informar
  inform oneself informarse
information *n.* información *f.*
ingest *v.t.* ingerir
ingestion *n.* ingestión *f.*
inherit *v.t.* heredar
inheritance *n.* herencia *f.*
inject *v.t.* inyectar
injection *n.* inyección *f.*

give an injection poner una inyección
injure v.t. (oneself) lastimarse
injure one's (foot) lastimarse el (pie)
injured n., adj. herido/a m., f.
inn n. hostal m.
innovate v.i. innovar
innovation n. innovación f.
innovative adj. innovador(a)
innovator n. innovador(a) m., f.
insect n. insecto m.
inside adv. (a)dentro
insipid adj. insípido/a
insist (on + gerund) insistir (en + inf.)
He insists on going. Insiste en ir.
insistence n. insistencia f.
insomnia n. insomnio m.
inspire v.t. inspirar
install v.t. (equipment) instalar
install oneself instalarse
installment n. (payment) plazo m. (monthly payment) mensualidad f.
pay in installments pagar a plazos
institution n. institución f.
instrument n. instrumento m.
insulate v.t. aislar
insulation n. aislante m.
insulin n. insulina f.
insult n. insulto m.; ofensa f.
insurance n. seguro m.
intake n. consumo m.
intelligent adj. inteligente
intend (to do something) v. pensar (+ inf.)
intentionally adv.

intencionalmente, adrede, a propósito
interest n. interés m.
interest v.t. interesar
take an interest (in) interesarse (en) **He's only interested in the results.** Sólo se interesa en los resultados.
be interested interesar
interesting adj. interesante
be interesting to interesar
intermediate adj. intermedio/a
international adj. internacional
Internet n. Internet m.; red f.
interpreter n. intérprete m., f.
interpreting n. interpretación f.
interrupt v.t. interrumpir
intersection n. intersección f.
intervention n. intervención f.
interview n. entrevista f.
interview v.t. entrevistar
interviewer n. entrevistador(a) m., f.
intestine n. intestino m.
intolerant adj. intolerante
intrigue n. intriga f.
intrigued adj. intrigado/a
introduction n. presentación f.
invertebrate n., adj. invertebrado m.; invertebrado/a
invest v.t. invertir (e:ie)
investigator n. investigador(a) m., f.
invitation n. invitación f.
invite v.t. invitar
involuntary adj. involuntario/a
iron n. (metal) hierro m.; (clothes) plancha f.

iron *v.t.* planchar (la ropa)
ironic *adj.* irónico/a
irony *n.* ironía *f.*
irresponsible *adj.* irresponsable
irritating *adj.* antipático/a
isolate *v.t.* aislar
  isolate oneself aislarse
issue *n.* cuestión *f.*
Italian *n., adj.* italiano/a *m., f.; (language)* italiano
item *n.* artículo *m.*
itinerary *n.* itinerario *m.*
its su(s) *poss. adj.;* suyo(s)/suya(s) *poss. pron.*
ivy *n.* hiedra *f.*

J

jack *n. (playing cards)* jota *f.*
jacket *n.* chaqueta *f.;* abrigo; saco
jackknife *n.* navaja *f.*
jail *n.* cárcel *f.*
jail *v.t.* encarcelar
jam *n.* mermelada *f.*
January *n.* enero *m.*
Japanese *n., adj.* japonés *m.,* japonesa *f.; (language)* japonés
javelin throw *n.* lanzamiento *m.* de jabalina
jealous *adj.* celoso/a; envidioso/a
jealousy *n.* celos *m., pl.*
jeans *n.* (blue)jeans *(L.A.) m., pl.;* vaqueros, tejanos *(Spain) m., pl.*
jellyfish *n.* medusa *f.*
jest: in jest en broma
jetty *n.* embarcadero *m.*

Jew *n.* judío/a *m., f.*
jeweler *n.* joyero/a *m., f.*
jewelry box *n.* joyero *m.*
jewelry store *n.* joyería *f.*
jewel *n.* joya *f.*
Jewish *adj.* judío/a
job *n.* empleo *m.;* puesto *m.;* trabajo *m.*
job application *n.* solicitud *f.* de trabajo
jog *v.i.* correr
joint *n. (anatomy)* articulación *f.*
joke *n.* broma *f.*
  as a joke en broma
  make jokes hacer bromas
  practical joke broma pesada; novatada *f.*
joker *n.* bromista *m., f.*
journalism *n.* periodismo *m.*
journalist *n.* periodista *m., f.;* reportero/a *m., f.*
joy *n.* alegría *f.*
  give joy dar alegría
joyful *adj.* alegre
jubilation *n.* algarabía *f.*
judge *n.* juez *m., f.*
judge *v.t.* juzgar
judgment *n.* juicio *m.*
juice *n.* jugo *(L.A.) m.;* zumo *(Spain) m.*
  fruit juice jugo/zumo de fruta
juicer *n.* exprimidor *m.*
juicy *adj.* jugoso/a
July *n.* julio *m.*
jump *n.* salto *m.*
jump *v.i.* saltar, brincar
June *n.* junio *m.*
jungle *n.* selva *f.,* jungla *f.*
jury *n.* jurado *m.*

just *adv.* apenas
justice *n.* justicia *f.*

K

kangaroo *n.* canguro *m.*
key *n.* llave *f.*
key chain *n.* llavero *m.*
keyboard *n.* teclado *m.*
kid *n.* niño/a *m., f.*
kid *v.i.* bromear
  kid someone *idiom* tomarle
  el pelo a alguien
kidnap *v.t. (people)* secuestrar
kidnapping *n.* secuestro *m.*
kidney *n.* riñón *m.*
kill *v.t.* matar (a alguien)
  kill two birds with one stone
  loc. matar dos pájaros de un
  tiro
kilometer *n.* kilómetro *m.*
kind *adj.* amable
  That's very kind of you.
  (Eres/Es usted) Muy amable.
kingdom *n.* reino *m.*
kiss *n.* beso *m.*
  give a kiss dar un beso
kiss *v.t.* besar; *(each other)*
  besarse
kitchen *n.* cocina *f.*
kitchenware *n.* artículos *m., pl.*
  de cocina
knee *n.* rodilla *f.*
knife *n.* cuchillo *m.*
knit *v.i.* hacer punto
knitted *adj.* de punto
knitwear *n.* artículos *m., pl.* de
  punto
know *v.t.* saber; conocer
  know how (to) saber
know-it-all *n., adj.*

sabihondo/a *m., f.*
known *adj.* conocido/a

L

laboratory *n.* laboratorio *m.*
lack *n.* falta *f.;* carencia *f.*
lack *v.t.* faltar
lack of understanding *n.*
  incomprensión *f.*
ladle *n.* cucharón *m.*
lake *n.* lago *m.*
lamb *n.* cordero *m.*
lame *adj.* cojo/a
lamp *n.* lámpara *f.*
land *n.* tierra *f.; (parcel)*
  terreno *m.*
land *v.t.* aterrizar
landing *n.* aterrizaje *m.*
landing strip *n.* pista *f.* de
  aterrizaje
landlord *n.* dueño/a *m., f.*
landscape *n.* paisaje *m.*
lane *n. (highway)* carril *m.*
language *n.* lengua *f.;* idioma
  m.
  foreign languages *n., pl.*
  lenguas *f., pl.* extranjeras
lap *n. (sports)* vuelta *f.*
laptop (computer) *n.*
  computadora *f.* portátil
large *n., adj. (clothing size)*
  talla *m.* grande; grande,
  (quantity) elevado/a **You
  notice a large quantity of fat
  in the food.** Se nota una
  cantidad elevada de grasa
  en la comida.
large intestine *n.* intestino *m.*
  grueso
larva *n.* larva *f.*

larynx n. laringe f.
last adj. pasado/a; último/a
last v.i. durar
  last week la semana pasada
  last year el año pasado
last night adv. anoche
lasting adj. duradero/a
late adv. tarde
  be late llegar tarde;
  retrasarse **be late (in)** tardar
  en **The bus was late (in
  arriving).** El autobús tardó en
  llegar.
lately adv. últimamente
later adv. más tarde
  at the very latest a más
  tardar **Bring it to me on
  Thursday at the very latest.**
  Tráemelo el jueves a más
  tardar.
Latin n., adj. latino/a m., f.;
  (language) latín m.
laugh v.i. reír, reírse (e:i)
laughed p.p. reído (of reír)
launch n. lanzamiento m.
launch v.t. lanzar **NASA
  launched a rocket to Saturn.**
  La NASA lanzó un cohete a
  Saturno.
laundromat n. lavandería f.
law n. ley f.
lawn n. pasto m.
lawn mower n. cortacésped f.
lawyer n. abogado/a m., f.
laziness n. pereza f.
lazy adj. perezoso/a; flojo/a
lead n. plomo m. **a lead pipe**
  un tubo de plomo
lead v.t. liderar
leader n. líder m., f.

leadership n. liderazgo m.
leaf n. hoja f.
leak n. (gas, water) fuga f.
learn v.t. aprender (a + inf.)
learned adj. sabio/a
learning n. enseñanza f.
lease n. contrato m.
least: at least por lo menos
leather n. piel
  made of leather de piel
leather goods n., pl. artículos
  m., pl. de piel
leave v.i. salir; irse; partir;
  dejar
  leave a message dejar un
  mensaje/recado
  leave alone dejar
  leave (behind) dejar
  leave for (a place) salir
  para…
  leave from salir de
lecture n. conferencia f.
lecture hall n. aula (el) f.
  main lecture hall aula
  magna
left adj., n. izquierdo/a m., f.
  be left over quedar, sobrar
  to the left (of) a la izquierda
  (de)
leftovers n., pl. restos m., pl.;
  sobras f., pl.
leg n. pierna f.
legacy n. legado m.
legal adj. legal
legalize v.t. legalizar
legend n. leyenda f.
leisure time n. ocio m.
lemon n. limón m.
lemon tree n. limonero m.
lemonade n. limonada f.

lend *v.t.* prestar
lengthwise section *n. (Tech.)* corte *m.* longitudinal
lentil *n.* lenteja *f.*
leopard *n.* leopardo *m.*
less *adv.* menos
  less . . . than menos… que
  less than + *(number)* menos de + *(number)*
lesson *n.* lección *f.*
let *v.t.* dejar
  let go soltar
  let up *(pain)* aliviarse
letter *n.* carta *f.; (alphabet)* letra *f.*
  put a letter in the mailbox echar una carta al buzón
lettuce *n.* lechuga *f.*
level *n.* nivel *m.*
lever *n.* palanca *f.*
liar *n.* mentiroso/a *m., f.*
liberal *n., adj.* liberal *m., f*
liberation *n.* liberación *f.*
liberty *n.* libertad *f.*
librarian *n.* bibliotecario/a *m., f.*
library *n.* biblioteca *f.*
license *n. (driver's)* licencia *f.* de manejar/conducir
license plate *n.* (placa *f.* de) matrícula *f.*
lid *n.* tapa *f.*
lie *n.* mentira *f.*
lie *v.i.* mentir
lie down (in the sun) *v.* tumbarse (al sol)
life *n.* vida *f.*
  in my life en mi vida
life expectancy *n.* esperanza *f.* de vida

life imprisonment *n.* cadena *f.* perpétua
life jacket *n.* salvavidas *m., sing.*
life sentence *n.* cadena *f.* perpétua
lifeguard *n.* salvavidas *m., f., sing.*
lifestyle: lead a healthy lifestyle llevar una vida sana
lift *v.t.* levantar
  lift weights levantar pesas
light *n., adj.* luz *f.;* liviano/a; ligero/a
light aircraft *n.* avioneta *f.*
light green *n., adj.* verde *m.* claro
lighter *n.* encendedor *m.*
lightning bolt *n.* rayo *m.;* relámpago *m.*
lightning rod *n.* pararrayos *m., sing.*
like *prep.* como
  What's . . . like? ¿Cómo es…?
like *v.t.* gustar
  Do you like . . . ? ¿Te gusta(n)…?
  I like . . . very much. Me encanta…
  I would like to introduce… to you. Te presento a…
  would like to tener ganas de (+ *inf.*) **I would like to visit Diamantina.** Tengo ganas de visitar Diamantina.
  Would you like to? ¿Te gustaría?
  Like father, like son. *loc.* De tal palo, tal astilla.
like this *adv.* así

likeable *adj.* simpático/a
likely: be likely that *(something will happen)* ser probable que (+ *subj.*) **It's likely that they won't arrive on time.** Es probable que no lleguen a tiempo.
likewise *adv.* igualmente
lily *n.* lirio *m.*
limb *n. (body)* miembro *m.*
limit *v.t.* limitar
limousine *n.* limusina *f.*
line *n.* línea *f.;* cola *f.* **There is a long line at the cinema.** Hay una larga cola en el cine.
   stand in/on line hacer cola
   line up hacer cola
linen *adj.* de hilo
linguist *n.* lingüista *m., f.*
linguistic *adj.* lingüístico/a
linguistics *n.* lingüística *f.*
lion *n.* león *m.*
lipstick *n.* lápiz *m.* labial; pintalabios *m., sing.*
liqueur *n.* licor *m.*
liquid *n., adj.* líquido *m.;* líquido/a
listen (to) *v.t.* escuchar
   listen to music escuchar música
   listen to the radio escuchar la radio
   Listen! *(command)* ¡Oye! *fam., sing.;* ¡Oigan! *form., pl.*
listener *n.* oyente *m., f.; (radio)* radioyente *m., f.*
literature *n.* literatura *f.*
little *adj.* pequeño/a; *adv.* poco/a

little bit *n.* pizca *f.*
Little Dipper *n.* Osa *f.* Menor
live *v.i.* vivir; residir
   live by begging vivir de limosnas
lively *adj.* vivo/a
liver *n.* hígado *m.*
living being *n.* ser *m.* vivo
living room *n.* sala *f.*
lizard *n.* lagarto *f.*
loaf (of bread) *n.* barra *f.* (de pan) *(Spain)*
loan *n.* préstamo *m.*
loan *v.* prestar
lobster *n.* langosta *f.*
located *adj.* situado/a
   be located quedar
locker room *n.* vestuario *m.*
locomotive *n.* locomotora *f.*
lodge *v.t.* alojar
lodging *n.* alojamiento *m.;* parador *m.*
log *n. (wood)* tronco *m.*, leño *m.*
long *adj.* (*length*) largo/a
   long-distance race *n.* carrera *f.* de fondo
   long jump *n.* salto *m.* de longitud *(Spain);* salto *m.* largo *(L.A.)*
long for *v.* ansiar
   long for (someone) añorar (a alguien)
longevity *n.* longevidad *f.*
longing *n.* ansia *f.*
look after oneself *v.* cuidarse
look at *v.* mirar; *(a topic)* enfocar **The program looks at the problem of homelessness.** El programa

enfoca el problema de la
falta de vivienda.
look for v. buscar
look good v. lucir
look in v. *(reference)* consultar
  I'll look in the dictionary.
  Consultaré el diccionario.
look up v. *(word)* buscar (en el
  diccionario)
lose v.t. perder (e:ie)
  lose weight adelgazar
lost adj. perdido/a
  be lost estar perdido/a
lot n. terreno m.
lot (of), a adj. mucho/a
  a lot n. sinfín m. **She still has
  a lot of things to do.** Todavía
  tiene un sinfín de cosas que
  hacer.
  a lot adv. muchas veces
loud adj. escandaloso/a
loudspeaker n. altavoz m.
lounge chair n. tumbona f.
love n. amor m.
  in love (with) adj.
  enamorado/a (de)
  fall in love (with)
  enamorarse (de)
love v.t. *(another person)*
  querer (e:ie); *(things)*
  encantar; fascinar
loyal adj. fiel
luck n. suerte f.
  be lucky tener suerte
luggage n. equipaje m.
lunch n. almuerzo m.
  have lunch almorzar (o:ue);
  comer
lung n. pulmón m.
luxurious adj. lujoso/a

luxury n. lujo m.
lying adj. mentiroso/a

M

ma'am n. señora f. (Sra.)
machine n. máquina f.
  answering machine
  contestadora f.
mad adj. enojado/a
  be hopping mad *idiom* echar
  chispas
madness n. locura f.
magazine n. revista f.
magic n. magia f.
magical adj. mágico/a
magician n. mago/a m., f.
magma n. magma m.
magna cum laude *(grade)*
  matrícula de honor
magnesium n. magnesio m.
magnet n. imán m.
magnificent adj. magnífico/a
magnifying glass n. lupa f.
mail carrier n. cartero/a m., f.
mail n. correo m. **I sent it in
  the mail.** Lo mandé por
  correo.; correspondencia f.
  You got a lot of mail.
  Recibiste mucha
  correspondencia.
  mail carrier cartero m.
mail v.t. enviar, mandar (por
  correo); echar una carta al
  buzón
mailbox n. buzón m.
main adj. principal
maintain v.t. mantener
major n. especialización f.
majority n. mayoría f.
make v.t. hacer; *(coffee)* colar

make a living *idiom* ganarse la vida **Mario makes his living writing soap opera scripts.** Mario se gana la vida escribiendo guiones de telenovela.

make a long story short *loc.* en resumidas cuentas

make one's mouth water *idiom.* hacérsele agua la boca **It smells good. It makes my mouth water.** ¡Qué bien huele! Se me hace agua la boca.

make sure *v.* asegurarse

make up *v.* maquillar

make up one's mind *v.* decidirse

makeup *n.* maquillaje *m.*
   put on makeup *v.* maquillarse; pintarse

makeup artist *n.* maquillador(a) *m., f.*

male *n.* macho *m.*

malignant *adj.* maligno/a

mall *n.* centro *m.* comercial

mammal *n.* mamífero *m.*

man *n.* hombre *m.*

manage *v.t. (business)* administrar

management *n.* administración *f.*

manager *n.* gerente *m., f.*

manicure *n.* manicura *f.*

mannequin *n.* maniquí *m.*

manufacture *n.* fabricación *f.*

manufacture *v.t.* fabricar

manufacturer *n.* fabricante *m., f.*

manure *n.* estiércol *m.*

many *adj.* muchos/as
   a great many *n.* sinfín *m.*

map *n.* mapa *m.*
   city map *n.* plano *m.*
   road map mapa *m.* de carreteras

marathon *n.* maratón *m.*

marble *n.* mármol *m.*

March *n.* marzo *m.*

margarine *n.* margarina *f.*

marital status *n.* estado *m.* civil

mark *n.* marca *f.; (imprint)* huella *f.; (grade)* nota *f.*

market *n.* mercado *m.;* supermercado *m.*
   open-air market mercado al aire libre
   street market *n.* mercadillo *m.*

marriage *n.* matrimonio *m.*

married *adj.* casado/a

marrow *n.* médula *f.*

marry: get married (to) *v.* casarse (con)

marsh *n.* pantano *m.*

martial arts *n., pl.* artes *f., pl.* marciales

marvelous *adj.* maravilloso/a

marvelously *adv.* maravillosamente

mask *n.* máscara *f.; mascarilla f.; antifaz m.*

mass produce *v.t.* fabricar en serie

mass production *n.* fabricación *f.* en serie

massage *n.* masaje *m.*

masseur *n.* masajista *m.*

masseuse *n.* masajista *f.*

master *v.t.* dominar

I am far from mastering Spanish. Estoy lejos de dominar el español.

Master's degree n. maestría (L.A.) f.

pursue a Master's degree hacer una maestría

masterpiece n. obra f. maestra

match n. cerilla f.; fósforo m.; (sports) partido m.

match (with) v.t. hacer juego (con)

match up v.i. coincidir

mate n. compañero/a m., f.

materialistic adj. materialista

maternal adj. (relative) materno/a

mathematician n. matemático/a m., f.

mathematics n. matemáticas f., pl.

matriculation n. matrícula f.

matter n. cuestión f. **She's an expert in matters of medieval history.** Es una experta en cuestiones de historia medieval.

matter v.t. importar

mattress n. colchón m.

foam mattress colchón de espuma

sprung mattress colchón de muelles

mature adj. maduro/a

maturity n. madurez f.

maximum n., adj. máximo m.; máximo/a

May n. mayo m.

maybe adv. tal vez; quizás

mayonnaise n. mayonesa f.

mayor n. alcalde m., alcaldesa f.

mayor's office n. alcaldía f.

me: It's me./That's me. Soy yo.

meal n. comida f.

mean adj. (person) malo/a

means of communication n., pl. medios m., pl. de comunicación

means: by no means de ninguna manera, de ningún modo

measles n. sarampión m.

measure v.t. medir

measurement n. medición f.; medida f.

meat n. carne f.

mechanic n. mecánico/a m., f.

mechanic's workshop n. taller m. de mecánica

mechanic's repair shop taller mecánico

mechanism n. mecanismo m.

medal n. medalla f.

media n. medios m., pl. de comunicación

medical adj. médico/a

medical insurance n. seguro m. médico

medication n. medicamento m.

medicine n. medicina f.

medicine cabinet n. botiquín m.

mediocre adj. mediocre

meditate v.i. meditar

meditation n. meditación f.

medium adj. mediano/a

meet v.t. encontrar; conocer; (each other) encontrarse; conocerse

Where shall we meet?
¿Dónde nos encontramos?
They met in Paris. Se
conocieron en París.
meeting n. reunión f.; (political)
n. mitin m.
megaphone n. megáfono m.
melon n. melón m.
melt v.t. derretir **The heat will
melt the butter.** El calor
derritirá la mantequilla.; v.i.
derretirse **The ice cream
melted.** El helado se derritió.
member n. miembro m.
membrane n. membrana f.
memorize v.t. memorizar
memory n. memoria f.
menopause n. menopausia f.
mental disorder n. trastorno m.
mental
mental hospital n. manicomio
m.
mentality n. mentalidad f.
menu n. menú m.
mercury n. mercurio m.
merit n. mérito m.
**mess around: Don't mess
around on the way to school.**
No te entretengas camino a
la escuela.
message n. mensaje m.;
(telephone) recado m.
messy adj. desarreglado/a
metabolism n. metabolismo m.
metabolize v.t. metabolizar
metal n. metal m.
metamorphosis n.
metamorfosis f.
metaphor n. metáfora f.
metaphoric adj. metafórico/a

meteorite n. meteorito m.
meteorologist n.
meteorólogo/a m., f.
meteorology n. metereología f.
method n. método m.
methodical adj. metódico/a
Mexican n., adj. mexicano/a
m., f.
Mexico n. México m.
microphone n. micrófono m.
microscope n. microscopio m.
microwave n. microonda f.
microwave oven n. horno m.
de microondas
middle age n. madurez f.
middle school n. escuela f.
secundaria
midnight n. medianoche f.
mild adj. (taste) suave
mile n. milla f.
milk n. leche f.
Milky Way n. Vía Láctea f.
mill n. molino m.
million (of) n. millón (de) m.
mind n. mente f.
keep in mind tener en
cuenta
mine n. mina f.
mine mío(s)/mía(s) poss. pron.
miner n. minero/a m., f.
mineral n. mineral m.
mining industry n. minería f.
miniskirt n. minifalda f.
minister n. (government)
ministro/a m., f.
minority n. minoría f.
mint n. menta f.
minute adj. minúsculo/a
minute n. minuto m.
minute adj. (object) diminuto/a

mirror *n.* espejo *m.*
misbehave *v.* portarse mal
miscarriage *n.* aborto *m.* espontáneo
  have a miscarriage abortar
mischief *n.* travesura *f.*
mischievous *adj.* travieso/a
miser *n.* avaro/a *m., f.*
misfortune *n.* desgracia *f.*
Miss *n.* señorita *f.* (Srta.)
miss *v.* perder (e:ie)
  miss someone *v.t.* añorar a alguien
missile *n.* misil *m.;* proyectil *m.*
missing *adj.* desaparecido/a
mistake *n.* equivocación *f.*
  make a mistake equivocarse
mistaken *adj.* equivocado/a
  be mistaken equivocarse
  You are mistaken in thinking that. Te equivocas si piensas eso.
mister *n.* señor *m.*
mix *v.t.* mezclar
mixer *n.* batidora *(Spain) f.*
mobile *adj.* móvil
mobility *n.* movilidad *f.*
modem *n.* módem *m.*
modern *adj.* moderno/a
modernize *v.t.* modernizar
modest *adj. (person)* modesto/a; *(simple)* sencillo/a
modify *v.t.* modificar
moisturizer *n.* crema *n.* hidratante; humectante *m.*
molar *n.* muela *f.*
mold *n.* moho *m.*
mom *n.* mamá *f.,* mami *f.*
moment *n.* momento *m.*

monarch *n.* monarca *m., f.*
monarchy *n.* monarquía *f.*
monastery *n.* monasterio *m.*
Monday *n.* lunes *m., sing.*
money *n.* dinero *m.*
  paper money billete *m.*
money order *n.* giro *m.* postal
monitor *n.* monitor *m.*
monk *n.* monje *m.*
monkey *n.* mono *m.*
monologue *n.* monólogo *m.*
month *n.* mes *m.*
monument *n.* monumento *m.*
mood: in a good/bad mood de buen/mal humor
moon *n.* luna *f.*
mop *n.* fregona *(Spain) f.;* trapeador *(L.A.) m.*
mop (the floor) *v.t.* trapear (el piso) *(L.A.);* fregar (el suelo) *(Spain)*
moral *n.* moral *f.*
morality *n.* moralidad *f.*
more *adj., adv.* más
  more . . . than más… que
  more than (+ number) más de (+ *number*)
moribund *adj.* moribundo/a
morning *n.* mañana *f.*
  in the morning de la mañana; por la mañana
morphology *n.* morfología *f.*
mortality *n.* mortalidad *f.*
mortality rate *n.* índice *m.* de mortalidad
mortgage *n.* hipoteca *f.*
mortgage *v.t.* hipotecar
mosque *n.* mezquita *f.*
mosquito net *n.* mosquitero *m.*
mother *n.* madre *f.*

mother-in-law *n.* suegra *f.*

motor *n.* motor *m.*

motorboat *n.* lancha *f.*

motorcycle *n.* moto *f.;* motocicleta *f.*
  go by motorcycle ir en motocicleta

motorcycling *n.* motociclismo *m.*

motorcyclist *n.* motociclista *m., f.*

motorist *n.* automovilista *m., f.*

mountain *n.* montaña *f.*

mountain range *n.* cordillera *f.* (montañosa)

mountainside *n.* ladera *f.*

mouse *n.* ratón *m.*

moustache *n.* bigote(s) *m. (pl.)*

mouth *n.* boca *f.; (river)* desembocadura *f.*

mouth-to-mouth resuscitation *n.* respiración *f.* boca a boca

move *v.i.* mudanza *f.*

move *v.i. (from one house to another)* mudarse; *(from one place to another)* desplazarse

move forward *v.i.* avanzar

movement *n.* desplazamiento *m.*

movie *n.* película *f.*
  see movies ver películas

moviemaker *n.* cineasta *m., f.*

movie star *n.* estrella *m., f.* de cine

movie theater *n.* cine *m.*

movies *n.* cine *m.*

mow the lawn *v.t.* cortar el pasto

Mr. *n.* señor *m.* (Sr.), don

Mrs. *n.* señora *f.* (Sra.)

much *adj., adv.* mucho/a

mud *n.* barro *m.;* fango *m.*

muffler *n. (car)* silenciador *m.*

mug *n.* taza *f.*

mug *v.t.* atracar

municipal *n.* municipal *m.*

murder *n.* asesinato *m.;* crimen *m.*

murderer *n.* asesino/a *m., f.*

muscle *n.* músculo *m.*

muscular *adj.* musculoso/a

museum *n.* museo *m.*

mushroom *n.* champiñón *m.*

music *n.* música *f.*
  play loud music poner la música muy alta

musical *adj.* musical

musician *n.* músico/a *m., f*

Muslim *n., adj.* musulmán *m.,* musulmana *f.*

mussel *n.* mejillón *m.*

must *v.t.* deber (+ *inf.*)
  It must be… Debe ser…

mustard *n.* mostaza *f.*

mute *adj.* mudo/a

my mi(s) *poss. adj.*

myopia *n.* miopía *f.*

myopic *adj.* miope

mysterious *adj.* enigmático/a; misterioso/a

mystery *n.* misterio *m.;* enigma *m.*
  a mystery novel una novela de misterio

N

nail *n.* clavo *m.; (finger, toe)* uña *f.*
  hit the nail on the head

idiom dar en el clavo
nail file *n.* lima *f.*
name *n.* nombre *m.*
  be named llamarse
  in the name of a nombre de
  last name apellido *m.*
  My name is . . . Me llamo…
  What's your name? *fam.*
  ¿Cómo te llamas (tú)?, *form.*
  ¿Cómo se llama usted?
name *v.t.* ponerle nombre a
nap *n.* *(afternoon)* siesta *f.*
napkin *n.* servilleta *f.*
narrator *n.* narrador(a) *m., f.*
nasty *adj.* antipático/a
national *adj.* nacional
nationalism *n.* nacionalismo *m.*
nationalist *adj.* nacionalista
nationality *n.* nacionalidad *f.*
native *adj.* indígena
natural *adj.* natural
nature *n.* naturaleza *f.*
nature reserve *n.* parque *m.*
  natural
naughty *adj.* travieso/a
nausea *n.* náusea *f.*
nauseate *v.t.* asquear,
  repugnar, dar asco
nauseated *adj.* mareado/a
nauseating *adj.* asqueroso/a,
  repugnante
navel *n.* ombligo *m.*
navy blue *n., adj.* azul *m.*
  marino
near *prep.* cerca de
neaten *v.* arreglar
necessary *adj.* necesario/a
  It's (not) necessary that…
  (No) Es necesario que…
necessity *n.* necesidad *f.*

neck *n.* cuello *m.*
necklace *n.* collar *m.*
nectarine *n.* nectarina *f.*
need *v.t.* faltar; necesitar
needle *n.* aguja *f.*
negative *adj.* negativo/a
neighbor *n.* vecino/a *m., f.*
neighborhood *n.* barrio *m.*
neither *adv.* tampoco
  neither . . . nor *conj.* ni… ni
  I eat neither meat nor fish.
  No como ni carne ni
  pescado.
nephew *n.* sobrino *m.*
nerve *n.* nervio *m.;*
  atrevimiento *m.*
  You've got some nerve! ¡Qué
  cara más dura tienes!
nervous *adj.* nervioso/a
nervous breakdown *n.* crisis *f.*
  nerviosa
network *n.* red *f.*
neuron *n.* neurona *f.*
never *adv.* nunca; jamás
new *adj.* nuevo/a; novato/a
  What's new? ¿Qué hay de
  nuevo?
newlywed *n.* recién casado/a
  m., f.
news *n.* noticias *f., pl.;*
  actualidades *f., pl.*
newscast *n.* noticiero *m.*
newsletter *n.* boletín *m.*
  informativo
newspaper *n.* periódico *m.;*
  diario *m.*
next *adj.* próximo/a
  next to *prep.* al lado de
nice *adj.* simpático/a; amable;
  agradable

nice person *idiom* buena gente
Nice to meet you. Mucho gusto.
nickname *n.* apodo *m.*
niece *n.* sobrina *f.*
nieces and nephews *n., pl.* sobrinos *m., pl.*
night *n.* noche *f.*
  at night *adv.* por la noche
  night stand *n.* mesita *f.* de noche
  night table mesa de noche
nightmare *n.* pesadilla *f.*
nine nueve
nine hundred novecientos/as
nineteen diecinueve
ninety noventa
ninth noveno *m.; adj.* noveno/a
nitrogen *n.* nitrógeno *m.*
no *adj.* ningún, ninguno/a(s)
  no one *pron.* nadie
no *adv.* no; ningún, ninguno/a(s) *adj.*
  no entry (*sign*) prohibido el paso
  no one *pron.* nadie
  no problem ningún problema
  no way de ninguna manera
nobody *pron.* nadie
noise *n.* ruido *m.*
noisy *adj.* ruidoso/a
none *adj.* ningún, ninguno/a(s)
non-fattening *adj.* que no engorda
non-resident *n.* transeúnte *m., f.*
noon *n.* mediodía *m.*
nor *conj.* ni
Nordic *adj.* nórdico/a

north *n.* norte *m.*
  to the north al norte
Northern European *n.* nórdico/a *m., f.*
nose *n.* nariz *f.*
not *adv.* no
  not any *adj.* ningún, ninguno/a(s)
  not anyone *pron.* nadie
  not anything *pron.* nada
  not bad at all nada mal
  not either *adv.* tampoco
  not ever *adv.* nunca; jamás
  Not very well. No muy bien.
note *n.* nota *f.*
notebook *n.* cuaderno *m.*
nothing *pron.* nada
  I've nothing to say. No tengo nada que decir.
nothingness *n.* nada *f.*
notice *v.t.* notar; advertir
noun *n.* sustantivo *m.*
November *n.* noviembre *m.*
now *adv.* ahora
nowadays *adv.* hoy día
nowhere a ninguna parte
nuclear *adj.* nuclear
nucleus *n.* núcleo *m.*
number *n.* número *m.; (figure)* cifra *f.*
nun *n.* monja *f.*
nunnery *n.* convento *m.*
nurse *n.* enfermero/a *m., f.*
nursery school *n.* guardería *f.*
nutcracker *n.* cascanueces *m., sing.*
nutrition *n.* nutrición *f.*
nutritionist *n.* nutricionista *m., f.*

o

o'clock: It's . . . o'clock. Son las...

It's one o'clock. Es la una.

oak tree n. roble m.

oar n. remo m.

obese adj. obeso/a

obesity n. obesidad f.

obey v.t. obedecer (c:zc)

objective adj. objetivo/a

objective n. meta f., objetivo m.

obligation n. deber m.

observant adj. observador(a)

observation n. observación f.

observatory n. observatorio m.

observe v.t. observar

obstacle course carrera de obstáculos

obtain v.t. conseguir (e:i); obtener (e:ie)

obvious adj. obvio

it's obvious es obvio

occasion n. tiempo m.

occupation n. ocupación f.

occur v.i. (happen) ocurrir, suceder, pasar, realizarse; (come to mind) ocurrir

ocean n. mar m., f.; océano m.

ocean liner n. transatlántico m.

ocher n. ocre m.

October n. octubre m.

octopus n. pulpo m.

odor n. olor m.

of prep. de

of course claro que sí; por supuesto; (idiom) desde luego

offend v.t. ofender

offer n. oferta f.

offer v.t. ofrecer (c:zc)

offering n. ofrenda f.

office n. oficina f.; (medical) consultorio m.

often adv. a menudo

Oh! interj. ¡Ay!

oil n. aceite m.; petróleo m.

OK! interj. ¡Vale! (Spain); de acuerdo

okay adj. regular

It's okay. Está bien.

old adj. viejo/a; antiguo/a

be . . . years old tener... años

How old are you? ¿Cuántos años tienes?

become old hacerse viejo/a

grow old envejecer

old age n. vejez f.

older adj. mayor

older brother/sister n. hermano/a mayor m., f.

oldest adj. el/la mayor

old-fashioned adj. anticuado/a

olive n. aceituna f.

Olympic adj. olímpico/a

Olympic Games n., pl. Juegos m., pl. Olímpicos

omelet n. tortilla (de huevo) (Spain) f.

on prep. en; sobre

on the dot en punto

on (the) one hand. . . on the other hand. . . por un lado... por otro lado...

on the other hand en cambio

on top of prep. encima de

once adv. una vez

oncologist n. oncólogo/a m., f.

one un, uno/a *m., f., sing. pron.*
  one of these days un día de estos
one hundred cien(to)
our nuestro(s)/nuestra(s) *poss. adj.; poss. pron.*
one thousand mil
one-way *n. (travel)* ida *f.*
onion *n.* cebolla *f.*
only *adj.* único/a
only *adv.* sólo, solamente
opaque *adj.* opaco/a
open *adj.* abierto/a
open *v.t.* abrir
  in the open air al aire libre
open-air dance *n.* verbena *f.*
opened *p.p.* abierto (*of* abrir)
opener *n.* abridor *m.*
opera *n.* ópera *f.*
operating room *n.* quirófano *m.*
operation *n.* operación *f.;* intervención *f.* quirúrgica
ophthalmologist *n.* oftalmólogo/a *m., f.*
opinion *n.* opinión *f.*
  express an opinion opinar
  in my opinion en mi opinión
opponent *n.* contrincante *m., f.*
opposite *prep.* en frente de
optimist *n.* optimista *m., f.*
optimistic *adj.* optimista
or *conj.* o
orange *adj.* anaranjado/a
orange *n.* naranja *f.*
orange tree *n.* naranjo *m.*
orchard *n.* huerta *f.*
orchestra *n.* orquesta *f.*
order *n.* orden *m.;* (commercial) encargo *m.*
  in order to (+ *inf.*) *prep.* para

(+ *inf.*) ; a fin de (+ *inf.*)
out of order descompuesto/a *(L.A.);* averiado/a *(Spain);* (sign) no funciona
order *v.t.* mandar; *(food)* pedir (e:i); encargar
orderly *adj.* ordenado/a
ordinal *adj.* ordinal
oregano *n.* orégano *m.*
organ *n.* órgano *m.*
organic *adj.* orgánico/a; *(food)* ecológico/a
organization *n.* organización *f.*
organize *v.t.* organizar
original *adj.* original
originality *n.* originalidad *f.*
ostrich *n.* avestruz *m.*
other *adj.* otro/a
ounce *n.* onza *f.*
our nuestro(s)/nuestra(s) *poss. adj.; poss pron.*
out *adv.* fuera, afuera
out of stock *adj.* agotado/a
outline *v.t.* delinear
outrageous *adj.* escandaloso/a
outside *adv.* (a)fuera
outskirts *n., pl.* afueras *f., pl.;* alrededores *m., pl.* **on the outskirts of Barcelona** en los alrededores de Barcelona
outstanding *adj.* sobresaliente, extraordinario, excepcional
oven *n.* horno *m.*
over *prep.* sobre
overcome *v.t.* superar
oversleep *v.i.* quedarse dormido
owl *n.* búho *m.*
own *adj.* propio/a
own *v.t.* poseer

owner n. dueño/a m., f.
oxygen n. oxígeno m.
oyster n. ostra f.

P

p.m. en la tarde, de la tarde
pacemaker n. marcapasos m.,
  sing.
pacifist n., adj. pacifista m., f.
pack (one's suitcases) v.t.
  hacer las maletas; empacar
package n. paquete m.
padded adj. acolchado/a
page n. página f.
pain n. dolor m.
  have a pain in the (knee)
  tener dolor de (rodilla)
  What pain! ¡Qué dolor!
paint v.t. pintar
painter n. pintor(a) m., f.
painting n. pintura f.
pair n. par m.
  a pair of shoes un par de
  zapatos
pajamas n., pl. pijama (Spain)
  m.; piyama (L.A.) m.
palace n. palacio m.
palate n. paladar m.
paleontologist n.
  paleontólogo/a m., f.
paleontology n. paleontología f.
palm tree n. palmera f.
pan n. (frying) sartén f.
pancreas n. páncreas m.
panic attack n. ataque m. de
  nervios
panties n., pl. bragas (Spain.)
  f., pl.; pantaletas (Venezuela)
  f., pl.; calzones (L.A.) m., pl.
pantry n. despensa f.

pants n., pl. pantalones m., pl.
pantyhose n., pl. medias f., pl.
paper n. papel m.; (report)
  informe m.; (school essay)
  trabajo m.
paperback n. libro m. de
  bolsillo
parachute n. paracaídas m.
parachuting n. paracaidismo m.
parachutist n. paracaidista m.,
  f.
parade n. desfile m.
paragraph n. párrafo m.
parakeet n. perico m.;
  periquito m.
Paralympics n., pl. Juegos m.,
  pl. Paralímpicos
parasite n. parásito m.
Pardon me. Perdón.; (May I?)
  Con permiso.
parents n., pl. padres m., pl.;
  papás m., pl.
park n. parque m.
park v.t. estacionar(se)
parking lot n. estacionamiento
  m.
parking n. estacionamiento m.
parking space n.
  estacionamiento m.
parole n. libertad f. condicional
parrot n. loro m.
parsley n. perejil m.
participate v.i. participar;
  (contest) concursar
participation n. participación
  f.; intervención f.
partner n. compañero/a m., f.;
  (business) socio/a m., f.
  (marriage, romance, sport)
  pareja f.

partnership *n.* asociación *f.*

party *n.* fiesta *f.; (political)* partido *m. (político)*

  throw a party hacer una fiesta

party pooper *n.* aguafiestas *m., f., sing.*

pass *v.t.* pasar; *(test)* aprobar

  He passed the test. Aprobó el examen.

  no passing *(traffic sign)* prohibido adelantar

  pass (a vehicle) adelantar (a un vehículo)

pass away *v.* fallecer

pass on *v. (illness)* contagiar

passed *p.p.* pasado/a *(of pasar)*

passenger *n.* pasajero/a *m., f.*

passer-by *n.* transeúnte *m., f.*

passing grade *n.* aprobado *m.*

passport *n.* pasaporte *m.*

past *n., adj.* pasado *m.;* pasado/a

pastime *n.* pasatiempo *m.*

pastry shop *n.* pastelería *f.*

paternal *adj. (relative)* paterno/a

path *n.* camino *m.;* sendero *m.; (of an object)* trayectoria *f.*

patience *n.* paciencia *f.*

patient *n., adj.* paciente *m., f.*

patio *n.* patio *m.*

patterned *adj. (fabric)* estampado/a

pay *v.t.* pagar

  pay attention atender; prestar atención

  pay in cash pagar en efectivo; pagar al contado

  pay in installments pagar a plazos

  pay the bill pagar la cuenta

pea *n.* arveja *(L.A.) f.;* chícharo *(Mexico) m.;* guisante *(Spain) m.*

peace *n.* paz *f.*

peach *n.* durazno *(L.A.) m.;* melocotón *(Spain) m.*

peak *n. (mountain)* cumbre *m.,* cima *f.;* auge *m.*

pear *n.* pera *f.*

pedagogical *adj.* pedagógico/a

pedagogue *n.* pedagogo/a *m., f.*

pedagogy *n.* pedagogía *f.*

pedal *n.* pedal *m.*

pedantic *adj.* pedante

pedestrian *n.* peatón *m.*

pedicure *n.* pedicura *f.*

peel *v.t.* pelar

peeler *n.* pelapapas *m., sing.*

pen *n.* pluma *f.;* bolígrafo *m.*

pencil *n.* lápiz *m.*

penguin *n.* pingüino *m.*

penicillin *n.* penicilina *f.*

peninsula *n.* península *f.*

penitentiary *n.* penitenciaría *f.*

penknife *n.* navaja *f.*

pensioner *n.* pensionista *m., f.*

people *n., pl.* gente *f., sing.*

pepper *n. (black)* pimienta *f.; (bell)* pimiento *m.*

percent por ciento

percentage *n.* porcentaje *m.*

perfect *adj.* perfecto/a

perfectionist *adj.* perfeccionista; detallista

perforate *v.t.* perforar

perform *v.t.* interpretar

perfume *n.* perfume *m.*
perfume shop *n.* perfumería *f.*
perhaps *adv.* quizás; tal vez
perimeter *n.* perímetro *m.*
period *n.* periodo *m.; (limited time)* plazo *m., (punctuation)* punto *m.*
permission *n.* permiso *m.;* consentimiento *m.*
permit *v.t.* permitir; consentir
persecution *n.* persecución *f.*
   He suffered persecution for his ideas. Sufrió persecuciones por sus creencias.
persist *v.i.* persistir
persistent *adj.* persistente
person *n.* persona *f.*
personality *n.* personalidad *f.*
perspiration *n.* transpiración *f.*
perspire *v.i.* transpirar
pessimist *n.* pesimista *m., f.*
pessimistic *adj.* pesimista
pesticide *n.* pesticida *m.*
petal *n.* pétalo *m.*
petrified *adj.* petrificado/a
Ph.D. *n.* doctorado *m.; (title)* Dr. *m.,* Dra. *f.*
pharmacy *n.* farmacia *f.*
pharynx *n.* faringe *f.*
pheasant *n.* faisán *m.*
phenomenal *adj.* espectacular, extraordinario; increíble; fenomenal
phenomenon *n.* fenómeno *m.*
philately *n.* filatelia *f.*
philologist *n.* filólogo/a *m., f.*
philology *n.* filología *f.*
philosopher *n.* filósofo/a *m., f.*
philosophize *v.i.* filosofar

philosophy *n.* filosofía *f.*
phonetics *n.* fonética *f.*
phonology *n.* fonología *f.*
photocopier *n.* fotocopiadora *f.*
photocopy *v.t.* fotocopiar
photograph *n.* foto(grafía) *f.*
   take photos tomar/sacar fotos
photosynthesis *n.* fotosíntesis *f., sing.*
physical (exam) *n.* chequeo *m.* (médico), revisión *f.* médica; examen *m.* médico
physician *n.* doctor(a) *m., f.,* médico/a *m., f.*
physicist *n.* físico/a *m., f.*
physics *n.* física *f.*
physique *n.* tipo *m.*
pick up *v.t.* recoger
pick up boys/girls *v.i.* ligar
pickup truck *n.* camioneta *f.*
picture *n.* cuadro *m ;* pintura *f.*
picturesque *adj.* pintoresco/a
pie *n.* pastel *m.*
pig *n.* cerdo *m.;* puerco *m.*
pilgrim *n.* peregrino/a *m., f.*
pilgrimage *n.* peregrinación *f.*
pill *n.* pastilla *f.;* píldora *f.*
pillow *n.* almohada *f.*
pimple *n.* grano *m.*
pinch *n. (quantity)* pizca *f.*
pine forest *n.* pinar *m.*
pine tree *n.* pino *m.*
pineapple *n.* piña *f.*
pink *adj.* rosado/a
pipe *n.* tubo *m.,* caño *m.;* cañería *f.,* tubería *f.*
pit *n. (fruit)* hueso *m.*
pitcher *n.* jarra *f.*
pity *n.* lástima *f.*

place *n.* lugar *m.*
place *v.t.* poner; colocar
placing *n.* colocación *f.*
plagiarism *n.* plagio *m.*
plagiarize *v.t.* plagiar
plaid *adj.* de cuadros
plan (to do something) *v.*
pensar *(+ inf.)*
plan *n.* plan *m.*
  have plans tener planes
plane *n.* avión *m.*
planet *n.* planeta *m.*
planetarium *n.* planetario *m.*
plant *n.* planta *f.*
  climbing plant enredadera *f.*
plantain *n.* plátano *m.*
plastic *n.* plástico *m.*
  made of plastic de plástico
plate *n.* plato *m.*
  license plate placa *f.*
plateau *n.* meseta *f.*
platter *n.* fuente *f.*
  platter of fried food *n.* fuente
de fritada
play *n.* drama *m.;* comedia *f.*
play *v.t.* jugar (u:ue);
  play (a musical instrument)
tocar (un instrumento
musical)
  play hooky hacer novillos
(Spain)
  play sports practicar
deportes
  play the role (of) hacer el
papel (de)
player *n.* jugador(a) *m., f.*
playwright *n.* dramaturgo/a *m.,
f.*
plead *v.i.* rogar (o:ue), suplicar
pleasant *adj.* agradable

please *interj.* por favor
  be pleased (with)
contentarse (con)
  Pleased to meet you. Mucho
gusto.; Encantado/a (de
conocerle).
pleasing: be pleasing to gustar
pleasure *n.* gusto *m.;* placer *m.*
  It's a pleasure to . . . Gusto
de *(+ inf.)*
  It's been a pleasure. Ha sido
un placer.
  The pleasure is mine. El
gusto es mío.
  What a pleasure to . . . !
¡Qué gusto (+ *inf.)*…
plot *n. (story)* argumento *m.;
(land)* terreno *m.*
plot *v.t.* tramar
pluck *v. (eyebrows)* depilarse
plum *n.* ciruela *f.*
plumber *n.* fontanero/a *(Spain)
m., f.;* plomero/a *(L.A.) m., f.*
plumbing *n.* fontanería *(Spain)
f.;* plomería *(L.A.) f.*
pluralism *n.* pluralismo *m.*
plurality *n.* pluralidad *f.*
pocket *n.* bolsillo *m.*
podium *n.* podio *m.*
poem *n.* poema *m.*
poet *n.* poeta *m., f.*
poetry *n.* poesía *f.*
point *n.* punto *m.*
polemical *adj.* polémico/a
police *n. (force)* policía *f.*
police officer *n.* policía *m.,*
mujer *f.* policía
police station *n.* comisaría *f.*
(de policía)
polish *n. (shoe)* brillo *m.* (para

zapatos); *(floor)* abrillantador
m. (para pisos/suelos)
polish *v.t.* abrillantar; encerar
polite *adj.* educado/a
political *adj.* político/a
politician *n.* político/a *m., f.*
politics *n.* política *f.*
polka dot *n.* lunar *m.*
polka-doted *adj.* de lunares
poll *n.* encuesta *f.*
pollen *n.* polen *m.*
pollinate *v.t.* polinizar
pollute *v.t.* contaminar
polluted *adj.* contaminado/a
  be polluted estar
  contaminado/a
pollution *n.* contaminación *f.*
  air/water pollution
  contaminación del aire/del
  agua
pomegranate *n.* granada *f.*
pond *n.* *(man-made)* estanque
  m.; *(natural)* charca *f.*
pony tail *n.* cola *f.* de caballo
pool: swimming pool *n.*
  piscina *f.;* alberca *(Mexico)* f.
  indoor pool piscina
  climatizada
poor *adj.* pobre
  become poor empobrecerse
  make poor empobrecer
poppy *n.* amapola *f.*
populate *v.t.* poblar
population *n.* población *f.*
porch *n.* porche *m.*
pork *n.* cerdo *m.*
pork chop *n.* chuleta *f.* de
  cerdo
port *n.* puerto *m.*
portable *adj.* portátil

portable computer *n.*
  computadora *f.* portátil
porter *n.* portero/a *m., f.*
position *n.* *(job)* puesto *m.*
possession *n.* posesión *f.*
possessive *adj.* posesivo/a
possible *adj.* posible
  it's (not) possible (no) es
  posible
post office *n.* correo *m.;*
  correos *(Spain)* m., pl.
postcard *n.* postal *f.;* tarjeta *f.*
  postal
poster *n.* cartel *m.*
postpone *v.t.* aplazar
postponement *n.* aplazamiento
  m.
pot *n.* *(cooking)* olla *f.*
potato *n.* papa *(L.A.)* f.; patata
  (Spain) f.
potato omelet *n.* tortilla *f.* de
  patatas
potter *n.* ceramista *m., f.*
pottery *n.* cerámica *f.*
pound *n.* libra *f.*
pour *v.i.* llover a cántaros
poverty *n.* pobreza *f.*
power *n.* poder *m.;* potencia *f.*
power failure *n.* apagón *m.*
power steering *n.* dirección *f.*
  asistida
powerful *adj.* poderoso/a
practice *n.* práctica *f.*
practice *v.t.* practicar;
  entrenarse
prairie *n.* llanura *f.*
praise *n.* elogio *m.*
praise *v.t.* elogiar
prank *n.* travesura *f.*
prawn *n.* langostino *m.*

pray *v.i.* rezar
predator *n.* depredador *m.*
predatory *adj.* depredador(a)
prefabricate *v.t.* prefabricar
prefabricated *adj.*
  prefabricado/a
prefer *v.t.* preferir (e:ie)
pregnant *adj.* embarazada
premiere *n. (film, play)* estreno
  m.
preparations *n., pl.*
  preparativos *m., pl.*
prepare *v.t.* preparar
preposition *n.* preposición *f.*
prescribe *v.t.* recetar
prescription *n.* receta *f.*
present *n. (gift)* regalo *m.;*
  (time) presente *m.*
present *v.t.* presentar
presenter *n.* presentador(a) *m.,*
  f.
press *n.* prensa *f.*
pressure *n.* presión *f.*
  be under (a lot of) pressure
  sufrir (muchas) presiones
pressure cooker *n.* olla *f.* a
  presión
pretend *v.t./v.i.* fingir; disimular
pretentious *adj.* pretencioso/a
pretty *adj.* bonito/a; bastante
  adv.
prevent *v.t.* prevenir; impedir;
  evitar
prevention *n.* prevención *f.*
prey *n.* presa *f.*
price *n.* precio *m.*
  What is the price? ¿Qué
  precio tiene?
pride *n.* orgullo *m.*
priest *n.* padre *m.*

primitive *adj.* primitivo/a
print *adj.* estampado
print *v.t.* imprimir
printer *n. (machine)* impresora
  f.
prison *n.* prisión *f.;* cárcel *f.*
prisoner *n.* preso/a *m., f.*
privacy *n.* intimidad *f.*
private *adj.* privado/a;
  particular; individual
prize *n.* premio *m.;* galardón *m.*
probable *adj.* probable
  it's (not) probable (no) es
  probable
problem *n.* problema *m.*
prodigy *n.* prodigio/a *m., f.*
produce *n.* frutas *f., pl.* y
  verduras *f., pl.*
produce *v.t.* fabricar
product *n.* producto *m.*
profession *n.* profesión *f.*
professor *n.* profesor(a) *m., f.;*
  catedrático/a *m., f.*
program *n.* programa *m.*
programmer *n.* programador(a)
  m., f.
prohibit *v.t.* prohibir
prohibited *p.p.* prohibido (*of*
  prohibir)
project *v.t.* proyectar
projection *n.* proyección *f.*
prolific *adj.* prolífico/a
promise *v.* prometer
promote *v.i. (work)* ascender
promotion *n. (career)* ascenso
  m.
prone to *adj.* propenso/a a
pronoun *n.* pronombre *m.*
proof *n.* demostración *f.*
proposal *n.* propuesta *f.*

propose *v.t.* proponer
protect *v.t.* proteger
protection *n.* protección *f.*
protein *n.* proteína *f.*
protest *n.* protesta *f.*
protest *v.t.* protestar
Protestant *n., adj.* protestante *m., f.*
proud *adj.* orgulloso/a
prove *v.t.* demostrar
provided (that) *conj.* con tal (de) que
provisions *n., pl.* provisiones *f., pl.;* víveres *m., pl.*
provocation *n.* provocación *f.*
provocative *adj. (dress)* atrevido/a
provoke *v.t.* provocar
psychiatrist *n.* (p)siquiatra *m., f.*
psychiatry *n.* (p)siquiatría *f.*
psychologist *n.* (p)sicólogo/a *m., f.*
psychology *n.* (p)sicología *f.*
puberty *n.* pubertad *f.*
public school *n.* escuela *f.* pública
publish *v.t.* publicar
Puerto Rican *n., adj.* puertorriqueño/a *m., f.*
Puerto Rico *n.* Puerto Rico *m.*
pull *v.t.* halar *(L.A.),* jalar *(L.A.);* tirar *(Spain)*
pull an all-nighter *idiom* quemarse las pestañas
pull out all the stops *loc.* echar la casa por la ventana
pull someone's leg *idiom* tomarle el pelo a alguien
pumpkin *n.* calabaza *f.*

punchbowl *n.* ponchera *f.*
punctual *adj.* puntual
punish *v.t.* castigar
punishment *n.* castigo *m.*
pupil *n. (eye)* pupila *f.; (student)* pupilo/a *m., f.;* alumno/a *m., f.*
purchase *n.* compra *f.,* adquisición *f.*
purchase *v.t.* comprar, adquirir
pure *adj.* puro/a
purple *n., adj.* morado *m.;* morado/a
purpose *n.* propósito *m.*
on purpose *adv.* adrede; a propósito
purse *n.* bolsa *f.*
pursue *v.t.* perseguir
pursuit *n.* persecución *f.* **The police took off in pursuit of the fugitive.** La policía salió en persecución del fugitivo.; búsqueda *f.* **the pursuit of truth** la búsqueda de la verdad
push *v.t.* empujar
put *v.t.* poner; colocar
put in a cast escayolar *(Spain);* enyesar *(L.A.)*
put *p.p.* puesto *(of* poner)
put off *v.* aplazar
put on *v. (a performance)* presentar; *(clothing)* ponerse
put out *v.t.* sofocar; extinguir **The firefighters put out the blaze.** Los bomberos extinguieron el incendio.
put something over (on somebody) *idiom* dar gato por liebre

put up *v.t. (give lodging)* alojar
put up with *v.* aguantar
puzzle, (jigsaw) *n.* rompecabezas *m., sing.*
pyramid *n.* pirámide *f.*

Q

quail *n.* codorniz *f.*
qualify *v.t./v.i.* calificarse
quality *n.* calidad *f.*
quarrel *n.* pelea *f.*
quarrel *v.i.* pelearse; discutir
They always quarrel over money. Siempre se pelean por el dinero.
quarter *n.* trimestre *m.;* cuarto *m.*
quarter after *(time)* y cuarto; y quince **It's quarter after three.** Son las tres y cuarto/quince.
quarter to menos cuarto; menos quince **It's quarter to five.** Son las cinco menos cuarto/quince.
queen *n.* reina *f.*
question *v.t.* cuestionar
question *n.* pregunta *f.*
quickly *adv.* rápido
quiet *adj.* tranquilo/a; callado/a
quit (doing something) *v.t. (habit)* dejar de (+ *inf.*); dejar
quiz *n.* prueba *f.*

R

rabbi *n.* rabino/a *m., f.*
rabbit *n.* conejo *m.*
race *n. (sport)* carrera *f.;* *(people)* raza *f.*
racecar *n.* carro *m.* de carreras
racism *n.* racismo *m.*
racist *adj.* racista
racket *n. (sport)* raqueta *f.*
radio *n. (medium)* radio *f.;* *(set receiver)* radio *m.*
radish *n.* rábano *m.*
railroad *n.* ferrocarril *m.*
railroad crossing *n.* paso *m.* a nivel
rain *n.* lluvia *f.*
rain *v.imp.* llover (o:ue)
It's raining. Llueve.
rain cats and dogs *idiom* llover a cántaros
rain forest *n.* bosque *m.* tropical
rainbow *n.* arco *m.* iris
raincoat *n.* impermeable *m.*
raise *n. (salary)* aumento *m.* de sueldo
raise *v.t. (children, animals)* criar; *(money)* recaudar (fondos)
raisin *n.* pasa *f.*
rake *n.* rastrillo *m.*
rancher *n.* ganadero/a *m., f.*
ranching *n.* ganadería *f.*
randomly *adv.* al azar
at random *adv.* al azar
ranger *n.* guarda *m., f.* forestal
raspberry *n.* frambuesa *f.*
rate *n.* índice *m.*
rather *adv.* bastante
rattlesnake *n.* serpiente *f.* de cascabel
raw *adj. (food)* crudo/a
razor *n.* máquina *f.* de afeitar; rasuradora *f.*
reach *n.* alcance

within arm's reach al alcance de la mano
reach v.t. alcanzar; llegar a; contactar, ponerse en contacto con
   reach a conclusion llegar a una conclusión
   reach an agreement llegar a un acuerdo
   How can I reach you? ¿Cómo puedo ponerme en contacto contigo?
react v.i. reaccionar
reaction n. reacción f.
read v.t. leer
   read e-mail/a newspaper/a magazine leer correo electrónico/un periódico/una revista
read p.p. leído (of leer)
reader n. lector(a) m., f.
ready adj. listo/a
   be ready estar listo/a
   get ready prepararse; arreglarse **He takes forever getting ready.** Tarda mucho en arreglarse.
real adj. auténtico/a
real estate n. bienes raíces m., pl.
realistic adj. verosímil **His characters aren't realistic.** Sus personajes no son verosímiles.
realize v.t. darse cuenta de (que) **Gustavo realized he was alone.** Gustavo se dio cuenta de que estaba solo.
reap the benefits (of) v.t. disfrutar (de)

rearview mirror n. retrovisor m.
reason n. razón f.
reason v.i. razonar
rebellious adj. rebelde
receive v.t. recibir
receptionist n. recepcionista m., f.; (hotel) conserje m., f.
recess n. recreo m.
recipe n. receta f.
recital n. recital m.
recognition n. reconocimiento m.
recognize v.t. reconocer
recommend v.t. recomendar (e:ie)
record n. (sport) marca f.; récord m.
record v.t. grabar
recreation n. diversión f.
rectangle n. rectángulo m.
rectify v.t. rectificar
recycle v.t. reciclar
recycling n. reciclaje m.
red n., adj. rojo m.; rojo/a
Red Cross n. Cruz f. Roja
reddish adj. rojizo/a
red-hair adj. pelirrojo/a
red-headed adj. pelirrojo/a
reduce v.t. reducir
   reduce stress/tension aliviar el estrés/la tensión
reduced adj. de rebaja
reef n. arrecife m.
referee n. árbitro/a m., f.
reference book n. libro m. de consulta
reflect v.t. (light) reflejar; v.i. (on something) reflexionar (sobre algo)
reform n. reforma f.

183

reform v.t. reformar
refreshing adj. refrescante
refrigerate v.t. refrigerar
refrigerator n. refrigerador m.
refund n. devolución f.
refusal n. negación f.
refuse v.i. negarse; v.t. negarse a (+ inf.)
He refused to answer. Se negó a contestar.
regarding to (con) respecto a
regards n., pl. recuerdos m., pl.; saludos m., pl.
Lila sends her regards. Lila manda saludos.
region n. región f.
register v.i. (school) matricularse; inscribirse She intends to register for the astronomy class. Pretende inscribirse en la clase de astronomía.
registration n. inscripción f.; (education) matrícula f.
registration number n. (car) matrícula f.
regret v.t. arrepentirse (de) (e:ie); lamentar; sentir (e:ie)
regular (customer) n. asiduo/a m., f.
regularization n. regularización f.
regulate v.t. regular; (temperature, etc.) graduar
rehearsal n. ensayo m.
rehearse v.t. ensayar
reign v.i. reinar
reinforce v.t. reforzar
reinforcement n. refuerzo m.
reject v.t. rechazar

rejection n. rechazo m.
rejoicing n. algarabía f.
rejuvenate v.i. rejuvenecer
rejuvenation n. rejuvenecimiento m.
relationship n. relación f.
relative adj., n. relativo/a; pariente m., f.
relatives n. familiares m., pl.; parientes m., pl.
relax v.i. relajarse
relaxation n. relajación f.
relay race n. carrera f. de relevos
release v.t. liberar; soltar; poner en libertad
relief n. alivio m.
relieve v.t. (pain) aliviar
religion n. religión f.
religious adj. religioso/a
remain v.i. quedarse
remember v.t./v.i. recordar (o:ue); acordarse (de) (o:ue)
remembrance n. conmemoración f.
remote adj. alejado/a; lejano/a
remote control m. control m. remoto
Renaissance adj. renacimento m.
Renaissance artist n. renacentista m., f.
renew v.t. renovar
renewal n. renovación f.
rent n. (payment) alquiler m.
rent v.t. alquilar
repeat v.t. repetir (e:i)
repellent n. repelente m.
replace v.t. reemplazar; sustituir They replaced the

sugar with honey.
Sustituyeron el azúcar por la miel.

report *n.* informe *m.*; reportaje *m.*; boletín *m.*; denuncia *f.*

report *v.t. (crime)* denunciar

reporter *n.* reportero/a *m., f.*

representative *n.* representante *m., f.*

repress *v.t.* reprimir

repression *n.* represión *f.*

reprimand *v.t.* regañar

reproduce *v.t.* reproducir **It's difficult to reproduce the results.** Es difícil reproducir los resultados.; *(biology)* reproducirse **Rabbits reproduce quickly.** Los conejos se reproducen rápidamente.

reptile *n.* reptil *m.*

reputation *n.* reputación *f.*; fama *f.*
have a good/bad reputation tener buena/mala fama
have a reputation for tener fama de

request *v.t.* pedir (e:i); solicitar

rescue *n.* rescate *m.*; salvamento *m.*

rescue *v.t.* rescatar

research *v.t.* investigar
do research documentarse

researcher *n.* investigador(a) *m., f.*

resentful *adj.* rencoroso/a

resentment *n.* rencor *m.*

reservation *n.* reservación *f.*

reserved *adj.* reservado/a

reservoir *n.* embalse *m.*;

pantano *m.*

reside *v.i.* residir

residence *n.* residencia *f.*

resident *n., adj.* residente *m., f.*

resign (from) *v.i.* renunciar (a)

resign *v.i.* dimitir

resignation *n.* dimisión *f.*

resist *v.t.* resistir

resistance *n.* resistencia *f.*

resolve *v.t.* resolver (o:ue)

resolved *p.p.* resuelto *(of resolver)*

resort *n. (coastal)* balneario *m.*

resource *n.* recurso *m.*
natural resource recurso natural

respect *n.* respeto *m.*

respect *v.t.* respetar

respiration *n.* respiración *f.*

respiratory failure *n.* crisis *f.* respiratoria

responsibility *n.* responsabilidad *f.* ; deber *m.*

responsible *adj.* responsable

rest *n.* reposo *m.*; descanso *m.*

rest *v.i.* descansar; reposar **He had to rest for several weeks after the operation.** Tuvo que reposar por varias semanas después de la operación.
the rest *n.* lo/los/las demás

restaurant *n.* restaurante *m.*

restore *v.t.* restaurar

restrain oneself *v.refl.* dominarse

result *n.* resultado *m.*

résumé *n.* currículum *m.* (vitae); hoja *f.* de vida *(Colombia)*

185

retire (from work) *v.i.* jubilarse
retired person *n.* pensionista *m., f.;* jubilado/a *m., f.*
retirement pension *n.* pensión *f.*
return *n. (object)* devolución *f.*
return *v.i.* regresar; volver (o:ue); *v.t. (object)* devolver (o:ue)
return trip *n.* vuelta *f.*
returned *p.p.* vuelto (*of* volver)
rewind *v.t.* rebobinar
rewind button *n.* botón *m.* de rebobinado
  push the rewind button apriete el botón de rebobinado
rhetoric *n.* retórica *f.*
rhetorical *adj.* retórico/a
rheumatism *n.* reumatismo *m.*
rhinoceros *n.* rinoceronte *m.*
rhythm *n.* ritmo *m.;* compás *m.*
rib *n.* costilla *f.*
ribbon *n.* cinta *f.*
rice *n.* arroz *m.*
rich *adj.* rico/a
  get rich enriquecerse
  make rich enriquecer
riddle *n.* adivinanza *f.*
ride *v.* pasear
ride bikes/a bike *v.i.* andar/pasear en bicicleta
ridiculous *adj.* ridículo/a
  It's ridiculous (that…) Es ridículo (que…)
right *n., adj. (direction)* derecha *f.;* derecho *m.;* derecho/a; correcto/a
  be right tener razón
  right? *interj.* ¿no?; ¿verdad?

right away *adv.* enseguida; en el acto
right here/there aquí/allí mismo
right now ahora mismo
to the right (of) a la derecha de
rights *n., pl.* derechos *m., pl*
  human rights derechos humanos
ring *n.* anillo *m.;* sortija *f.; (boxing)* cuadrilátero *m.*
  wedding ring anillo de bodas
ring *v.t. (bell)* sonar (o:ue)
rise *n. (advance)* ascenso *m.*
rise *v.i.* ascender
river *n.* río *m.*
road *n.* camino *m.*
roar *n.* rugido *m.*
roar *v.i.* rugir
roast *n.* asado *m.*
  roast chicken *n.* pollo *m.* asado
  roast lamb *n.* asado de cordero
roasted *p.p.* asado/a (*of* asar)
rob *v.t.* robar
robber *n.* ladrón *m.,* ladrona *f.*
robbery *n.* atraco *m.;* robo *m.*
robe *n.* bata *f.*
rock *n.* roca *f.,* piedra *f.*
rock *v.t.* mecer
rocket *n.* cohete *m.*
rocking chair *n.* mecedora *f.*
role *n. (movie, theater)* papel *m.*
  leading role papel principal
  supporting role papel secundario
roller skating *n.* patinaje *m.*

sobre ruedas
rollerblade v. patinar en línea
Roman n., adj. romano/a m., f.
Romanesque adj. románico/a
romantic n., adj. romántico/a m., f.
Romanticism n. romanticismo m.
room n. cuarto m.; habitación f.; sala f.
  double room habitación doble
  single room habitación individual
roommate n. compañero/a m., f. de cuarto
rooster n. gallo m.
root n. raíz f.
rope n. cuerda f.
rose n. rosa f.
rosebush n. rosal m.
rosemary n. romero m.
rough adj. (surface, skin) áspero/a; (person) grosero/a
roulette n. ruleta f.
roundtrip n., adj. de ida y vuelta
  roundtrip ticket n. pasaje m. de ida y vuelta
route n. ruta f.
routine n. rutina f.
row n. hilera f.; fila f.
row v.i. remar
rower n. remero/a m., f.
royal adj. real
royalty n. realeza f.
rubber adj. de goma
ruby n. rubí m.
rude adj. maleducado/a; grosero/a

rug n. alfombra f.
rugged adj. (terrain) accidentado/a
rule v.t. gobernar
rum n. ron m.
rumor n. rumor m.
run v.t. correr; v.i. (business) administrar
  run a red light v. pron. pasarse (el alto/el semáforo en rojo)
  run away v. fugarse
  run into v. (have an accident) chocar (con); (meet accidentally) darse con; (each other) encontrarse (o:ue)
  run out v. (supplies) agotar(se)
  run over v. derramarse
  run over (someone with a vehicle) v. atropellar (a alguien con un vehículo)
rural adj. rural; campestre
rush v.i. apurarse; darse prisa
rust n. óxido m.
rust v.i. oxidarse

S

sacred adj. sagrado/a
sad adj. triste
  It's sad (that…) Es triste (que…)
sadness n. tristeza f.
safe n. seguro m.
safe adj. seguro/a
saffron n. azafrán m.
saga n. saga f.
sage n. (herb) salvia f.
said p.p. dicho (of decir)
sail n. vela f.

sailboat *n.* velero *m.*
sailing *n.* vela *f.*
sake: for the sake of por
  for the sake of love por amor
salad *n.* ensalada *f.*
salad bowl *n.* ensaladera *f.*
salary *n.* salario *m.;* sueldo *m.*
sale *n.* rebaja *f.*
salesperson *n.* vendedor(a) *m.,*
  f.
salmon *n.* salmón *m.*
salt *n.* sal *f.*
salt shaker *n.* salero *m.*
salty *adj.* salado/a
same *adj.* mismo/a; igual
  be all the same dar lo mismo
  **It's all the same to me if she
  comes or not.** Me da lo
  mismo si viene o no.
sand *n.* arena *f.*
sandal *n.* sandalia *f.*
sandwich *n.* sándwich *m.*
sap *n.* savia *f.*
sardine *n.* sardina *f.*
Saturday *n.* sábado *m.*
sauce *n.* salsa *f.*
sauna *n.* sauna *f.*
sausage *n.* salchicha *f.*
sauté *v.t.* saltear, sofreír
save *v.t. (on a computer)*
  guardar; *(money)* ahorrar
  (dinero); salvar
savings *n.* ahorros *m., pl.*
savings account *n.* cuenta *f.*
  de ahorros
saw *n.* sierra *f.*
saw *v.t.* serrar
say *v.t.* decir (e:i); declarar
  You don't say! ¡No me
  diga(s)!

say good-bye (to) despedirse
  (de) (e:i)
saying *n.* dicho *m.;* refrán *m.*
scale *n.* balanza *f.;* báscula *f.*
scallop *n.* vieira *f.*
scalpel *n.* bisturí *m.*
scapula *n.* omoplato *m.*
scar *v.i.* cicatrizar
scarcely *adv.* apenas
  He can scarcely talk.
  Apenas sabe hablar.
scared: be scared (of) tener
  miedo (de)
scarf *n.* bufanda *f.*
scent *n.* aroma *m.*
schedule *n.* horario *m.*
scheme *v.i.* tramar
scholarship *n.* beca *f.*
school *n.* escuela *f.*
school report *n.* boletín *m.* de
  notas
science *n.* ciencia *f.*
science-fiction *n.* ciencia *f.*
  ficción; ...de ciencia ficción
scientist *n.* científico/a *m., f.*
scissors *n.* tijeras *f., pl.*
scold *v.t.* regañar
scoreboard *n.* marcador *m.*
scorpion *n.* escorpión *m.*
scream *v.i.* gritar
screen *n.* pantalla *f.*
screenplay *n.* guión *m.*
screenwriter *n.* guionista *m., f.*
screw *n.* tornillo *m.*
screwdriver *n.* destornillador
  m.
script *n.* guión *m.*
scriptwriter *n.* guionista *m., f.*
scuba dive *v.* bucear
sculpt *v.t./v.i.* esculpir

sculptor *n.* escultor(a) *m., f.*
sculpture *n.* escultura *f.*
sea *n.* mar *m.;* océano *m.*
seafood *n.* mariscos *m., pl.*
  assorted seafood mariscada *f.*
seal *n.* foca *f.*
seaquake *n.* maremoto *m.*
search *n.* búsqueda *f.*
season *n.* estación *f.;* temporada *f.*
season *v.t. (salad)* aderezar, aliñar
seasoning *n.* aderezo *m.;* aliño *m.*
seat *n.* silla *f.;* asiento *m.*
seat belt *n.* cinturón *n.* de seguridad
seaweed *n.* alga (el) *f.*
second *n., adj.* segundo *m.;* segundo/a
secretary *n.* secretario/a *m., f.*
security guard *n.* guardia *m., f.* de seguridad
sedentary *adj.* sedentario/a
sediment *n.* sedimento *m.*
sedimentation *n.* sedimentación *f.*
seduce *v.t.* seducir
seducer *n.* seductor(a) *m., f.*
seductive *adj.* seductor(a)
seductress *n.* seductor(a) *m., f.*
see *v.t.* ver; mirar
  let's see a ver; veamos
  See you. Nos vemos.
  see (you) again volver a ver(te/lo/la)
  See you later. Hasta la vista.; Hasta luego.
  See you soon. Hasta pronto.

See you tomorrow. Hasta mañana.
see-through *adj.* transparente
seed *n.* semilla *f.;* grano *m.*
seem *v.i.* parecer
seen *p.p.* visto/a (*of* ver)
select *adj.* selecto/a
select *v.t.* seleccionar
self-employed worker *n.* autónomo/a *m., f.*
self-portrait *n.* autorretrato *m.*
self-taught *adj.* autodidacta
selfish *adj.* egoísta
selfishness *n.* egoísmo *m.*
sell *v.t.* vender
semantics *n.* semántica *f.*
semester *n.* semestre *m.*
seminar *n.* seminario *m.*
senate *n.* senado *m.*
send *v.t.* enviar, mandar
sense *n.* sentido *m.*
  common sense sentido común
sense of order *n.* sentido *m.* del orden
sensible *adj.* sensato/a
sensitive *adj.* sensible
sensitivity *n.* sensibilidad *f.*
sensory organs *n., pl.* órganos *m., pl.* de los sentidos
sentimental *adj.* sentimental
separate (from) *v.* separarse (de)
separated *adj.* separado/a
September *n.* septiembre *m.*
sequence *n.* secuencia *f.*
series circuit *n.* circuito *m.* en serie
serious *adj.* serio/a; *(illness, wound)* grave

serve *v.t./v.i.* servir (e:i)
service *n.* servicio *m.*
serving *n.* porción *f.*
set *adj. (price)* fijo/a
set *n. (theater)* decorado *m.*
set *v.t.* poner, colocar
  set the table poner la mesa
set (a world record) *v.* establecer (una marca mundial)
settle *v.i.* instalarse **He settled in front of the TV and didn't budge.** Se instaló ante la tele y no se movió.
settlement *n.* colonización *f.; (agreement)* resolución *f.*
settler *n.* colono/a *m., f.*
seven siete
seven hundred setecientos/as
seventeen diecisiete
seventh séptimo *m.; adj.* séptimo/a
seventy setenta
sew *v.t./v.i.* coser
sewer *n.* cloaca *f.*
sewing machine *n.* máquina *f.* de coser
sexism *n.* sexismo *m.*
shame *n.* lástima *f.;* vergüenza *f.*
  It's a shame (that…) Es una lástima (que…)
shame *v.t.* avergonzar
shameful *adj.* vergonzoso/a
shampoo *n.* champú *m.*
shape *n.* forma *f.*
  be in good shape estar en buena forma
  stay in shape mantenerse en forma

share *v.t.* compartir
shark *n.* tiburón *m.*
sharp *adv. (time)* en punto **It starts at 4:00 sharp.** Empieza a las cuatro en punto.
sharp curve *n.* curva *f.* peligrosa
shave *v.i.* afeitarse*; (legs)* depilarse
shaving cream *n.* crema *f.* de afeitar
shawl *n.* chal *m.*
shed *n.* cobertizo *m.*
sheep *n.* oveja *f.*
sheet *n.* sábana *f.; (paper)* hoja *f.*
shellfish *n.* mariscos *m. pl.*
sherry *n.* jerez *m.*
shift *n. (work)* turno *m.*
shift gears *v.t.* cambiar de marcha
shine *v.i.* brillar
ship *n.* barco *m.*
  go by ship ir en barco
shirt *n.* camisa *f.*
shiver *n.* escalofrío *m.*
shiver *v.i.* temblar; tener escalofríos
shock *n.* choque *m.,* impacto *m.*
shock absorber *n.* amortiguador *m.*
  electric shock *n.* descarga *f.* (eléctrica)
shoe *n.* zapato *m.*
  put one's shoes on calzarse
shoe size *n.* número *m.*
  take (wear) a shoe size calzar
shoe store *n.* zapatería *f.*

shoelace *n.* cordón *m.*
shoes *n.* calzado *m.*
shoot *v.t.* disparar; *(movies)* rodar
shooting *n.* rodaje *m.*
shooting star *n.* estrella *f.* fugaz
shop *n.* tienda *f.*
shop window *n.* escaparate *(Spain) m.;* vitrina *(L.A.) f.*
shopping mall/center *n.* centro *m.* comercial
shore *n.* orilla *f.* **The house is on the seashore.** La casa está a orillas del mar.
short *adj.* *(height)* bajo/a; *(length)* corto/a
in short *loc.* en resumidas cuentas
short circuit *n.* cortocircuito *m.*
short cut *n.* atajo *m.*
short story *n.* cuento *m.*
shortage *n.* carencia *f.*
shortcoming *n.* deficiencia *f.*
shorts *n., pl.* pantalones *m., pl.* cortos
shot *n.* disparo *m.;* tiro *m.*
shotput *n.* *(sport)* lanzamiento *m.* de bala *(L.A.);* lanzamiento *m.* de peso *(Spain)*
should *(do something)* deber (+ *inf.*)
shoulder *n.* hombro *m.*
shoulder bag *n.* bolso *m.*
shovel *n.* pala *f.*
show *n.* espectáculo *m.*
show *v.t.* mostrar (o:ue); enseñar
shower *n.* ducha *f.*
shower *v.i.* ducharse, *v.t.* bañarse

shrewd *adj.* astuto/a
shrimp *n.* camarón *(L.A.)m.;* gamba *(Spain)* f.
marinated shrimp ceviche *m.* de camarón *m.*
shrub *n.* arbusto *m.*
shy *adj.* tímido/a
sick *adj.* enfermo/a
be sick estar enfermo/a
get sick enfermarse
side *n.* lado *m.*
sideburn *n.* patilla *f.*
sight *n.* *(senses)* vista *f.*
sight *v.t.* divisar
sightseeing: go sightseeing hacer turismo
sign *n.* *(board)* letrero *m.;* señal *f.*
sign *v.t.* firmar
signature *n.* firma *f.*
silence *n.* silencio *m.*
silk *n., adj.* seda *f.;* de seda
silky *adj.* sedoso/a
silly *adj.* tonto/a
silver *n., adj.* plata *f.;* plateado/a
silverware *n.* cubiertos *m., pl.*
similar *adj.* similar; semejante
simmer *v.t.* cocer a fuego lento
simple *adj.* sencillo/a, simple
sinagogue *n.* sinagoga *f.*
since *prep.* desde
sing *v.t.* cantar
singer *n.* cantante *m., f.*
single *adj.* *(unmarried)* soltero/a
single room *n.* habitación *f.* individual
singles *n.* *(sports)* individual *m.*

sink *n. (bathroom)* lavabo *m.*; lavamanos *m.*; (*kitchen*) fregadero (de la cocina) *m.*
sip *n.* sorbo *m.*
sir *n.* señor *m.* (Sr.); don
sister *n.* hermana *f.*
  younger sister hermana menor
sister-in-law *n.* cuñada *f.*
sit down *v.* sentarse (e:ie)
sitting: related to sitting sedentario/a *adj.*
six seis
six hundred seiscientos/as
sixteen dieciséis
sixth sexto *m.*; *adj.* sexto/a
sixty sesenta
size *n.* talla *f.*
  What size do you take? ¿Qué talla lleva/usa?
skate *v.i.* patinar
  skate in-line patinar en línea
skateboard *v.t.* andar en patineta
skating *n.* patinaje *m.*
skating rink *n.* pista *f.* de patinaje
skeleton *n.* esqueleto *m.*
ski *v.i.* esquiar
ski cap *n.* gorro *m.* de lana
ski slope *n.* pista *f.* de esquí
skier *n.* esquiador(a) *m., f.*
skiing *n.* esquí *m.*
skill *n.* habilidad *f.*
skillful *adj.* hábil
skimmed *adj. (dairy products)* descremado/a; desnatado/a
skin *n.* cutis *m.*; piel *f.*; (*on boiled milk*) nata *f.*
skinny *adj.* flaco/a

skirt *n.* falda *f.*
skull *n.* calavera *f.*; cráneo *m.*
sky *n.* cielo *m.*
sky blue *n., adj. (color)* azul *m.* celeste
skylight *n.* tragaluz *m.*
skyscraper *n.* rascacielos *m., sing.*
sleep *n.* sueño *m.*
sleep *v.i.* dormir (o:ue)
  fall asleep dormirse (o:ue)
  I couldn't fall asleep last night. No pude dormirme anoche.
  go to sleep dormirse (o:ue)
sleepy: be sleepy tener sueño
sleeping bag *n.* saco *m.* de dormir
sleeve *n.* manga *f.*
slender *adj. (person)* delgado/a, esbelto/a
slice *n.* trozo *m.*; rebanada *f.* **a slice of bread** una rebanada de pan; rodaja *f.* **sliced onions** rodajas de cebolla
slice *v.t.* cortar
slide *n. (photo.)* diapositiva *f.*
slim down *v.* adelgazar
slippers *n., pl.* pantuflas *f., pl.*
slope *n.* ladera *f.* **The group ascended the northern slope.** El equipo subió por la ladera norte.
slot machine *n.* tragaperras *(Spain) f., sing.*; tragamonedas *(L.A.) f., sing.*
sloth *n.* perezoso *m.*
slow *adj.* lento/a; *adv.* despacio
slowly *adv.* despacio

small *adj.* pequeño/a
small intestine *n.* intestino *m.* delgado
smallpox *n.* viruela *f.*
smart *adj.* listo/a
smell *n. (sense)* olfato *m.;* olor *m.* **The smell of gasoline makes me sick.** El olor a gasolina me da asco.
smell (like) *v.i.* oler (a) **It smells like smoke here.** Huele a humo aquí.
smile *n.* sonrisa *f.*
smile *v.i.* sonreír (e:i)
smiled *p.p.* sonreído *(of* sonreír)
smoggy: It's (very) smoggy. Hay (mucha) contaminación.
smoke *n.* humo *m.*
smoke *v.t./v.i.* fumar
 smoking section *n.* sección *f.* de fumar
 non smoking section sección de no fumar
 not to smoke no fumar
smother *v.t. (fire)* sofocar
snack *n. (in the afternoon)* merienda *f.; (at a bar)* tapa *f.*
snack *v.i.* merendar
 have an afternoon snack merendar
snail *n.* caracol *m.*
snake *n.* serpiente *f.;* culebra *f.;* víbora *f.*
sneakers *n., pl.* zapatos *m., pl.* de tenis
sneeze *v.i.* estornudar
snob *n.* esnob *m., f.*
snobbery *n.* esnobismo *m.*
snobby *adj.* esnob

snore *n.* ronquido *m.*
snore *v.i.* roncar
snorkel *n.* esnórkel *m.*
snow *n.* nieve *f.*
snow *v.imp.* nevar (e:ie)
 It's snowing. Nieva.
so *adv.* tan; *(in such a way)* así **It's so big.** Es tan grande.
 and so on y así sucesivamente
 so much *adv.* tanto
 so so *adv.* así así; regular; más o menos
 so that *conj.* para que
soap *n.* jabón *m.*
soap dish *n.* jabonera *f.*
soap opera *n.* telenovela *f.*
sob *n.* sollozo *m.*
sob *v.i.* sollozar
sober *adj.* sobrio/a
sobriety test *n.* prueba *f.* de la alcoholemia
soccer *n.* fútbol *m.*
soccer field *n.* campo *m.* de fútbol
soccer player *n.* futbolista *m., f.*
sociable *adj.* sociable
socialize *v.i.* socializar
society *n.* sociedad *f.*
sociologist *n.* sociólogo/a *m., f*
sociology *n.* sociología *f.*
sock *n.* calcetín *m.*
soda *n.* refresco *m.*
sodium *n.* sodio *m.*
sofa *n.* sofá *m.*
soft *adj. (to the touch)* suave; esponjoso/a
soft drink *n.* refresco *m.*
software *n.* programa *m.* de computación

soil *n.* tierra *f.*
solar *adj.* solar
solarium *n.* solario *m.*
soldier *n.* soldado *m., f.*
solution *n. (to a problem)* resolución *f.;* solución *f.*
solve *v.t.* resolver (o:ue); solucionar
some *pron., adj.* algún, alguno/a(s); unos/as, *m., f., pl., indef. art.*
somebody *pron.* alguien
someone *pron.* alguien
somersault *n.* salto *m.* mortal; voltereta *f.*
something *pron.* algo
  something like that algo por el estilo
sometimes *adv.* a veces
son *n.* hijo *m.*
son-in-law *n.* yerno *m.*
song *n.* canción *f.*
soon *adv.* pronto
  as soon as en cuanto; tan pronto como
  as soon as possible lo antes posible
soprano *n.* soprano *m., f.*
sorbet *n.* sorbete *m.*
sore *adj.* adolorido/a
sorry: be sorry sentir(se) (e:ie); arrepentirse
  I'm extremely sorry. Mil perdones.
  I'm sorry. Lo siento.
soul *n.* alma (el) *f.*
soup *n.* sopa *f.; (broth)* caldo *m.*
  beef soup caldo de patas
sour *adj.* agrio/a
south *n.* sur *m.*

  to the south al sur
South American *n., adj.* sudamericano/a *m., f.*
souvenir *n.* recuerdo *m.*
spa *n.* balneario *m.*
space shuttle *n.* transbordador *m.*
spaghetti *n.* espagueti *m.*
Spain *n.* España *f.*
Spaniard *n.* español(a) *m., f.*
Spanish *n., adj.* español(a) *m., f.; (language)* español
spare time *n.* ratos *m., pl.* libres; tiempo *m.* libre
spare tire *n.* rueda *f.* de recambio/repuesto
spark plug *n.* bujía *f.*
sparkling wine *n.* cava *m.*
sparrow *n.* gorrión *m.*
spatula *n.* espátula *f.*
speak *v.i.* hablar
Special Olympics *n., pl.* Olimpiadas *f., pl.* Especiales
specialist *n.* especialista *m., f.*
specialization *n.* especialización *f.*
specialize (in something) *v.i.* especializarse (en algo)
species *n.* especie *f.*
  protected species *n.* especie *f.* protegida
spectacular *adj.* espectacular
spectator *n.* espectador(a) *m., f.*
speech *n.* discurso *m.*
speed *n.* velocidad *f.*
  speed limit *n.* velocidad *f.* máxima
speed *v.* ir a exceso de velocidad

spelling *n., adj.* ortografía *f.;* ortográfico/a

spend *v.t. (money)* gastar
spend time pasar tiempo

sphere *n.* esfera *f.*

spicy *adj.* picante

spider *n.* araña *f.*

spiderweb *n.* telaraña *f.*

spill *v.t.* derramar

spill over *v.* derramarse

spinach *n.* espinaca *f.*

spinal column *n.* columna *f.* vertebral

spine *n.* columna *f.* vertebral

spleen *n.* bazo *m.*

spoiled (child) *n. (niño/a) m., f.* mimado/a/consentido/a

spokesperson *n.* portavoz *m., f.*

sponge *n.* esponja *f.*

spongy *adj.* esponjoso/a

sponsor *n.* patrocinador(a) *m., f.*

sponsor *v.t.* patrocinar

spontaneous *adj.* espontáneo/a

spoon *n. (table or large)* cuchara *f.*

sport *n.* deporte *m.*
sports-loving *adj.* deportivo/a
sports-related *adj.* deportivo/a

sporting *adj.* deportista

sporting goods *n., pl.* artículos *m., pl.* de deporte

sports car *n.* carro *m.* deportivo

sports center *n.* polideportivo *m.*

sports facilities *n., pl.* instalaciones *f., pl.* deportivas

sports-loving *adj.* deportivo/a

sportswear *n.* ropa *f.* deportiva

spouse *n.* esposo/a *m., f.*

sprain *n.* esguince

sprain (an ankle) *v.t.* torcerse (el tobillo)

sprained *adj.* torcido/a
be sprained estar torcido/a

spread *v.t. (information)* divulgar; propagar **Some papers spread rumors.** Algunos periódicos propagan rumores.; propagarse **The rumor was spreading rapidly.** El rumor se propagaba rápidamente.; *(butter, etc.)* untar

spreading *n. (news, ideas)* divulgación *f.*

spring *n. (season)* primavera *f.; (coil)* muelle *m,* resorte *m.; (water)* manantial *m.*

sprinkle *v.t. (sugar, etc.)* espolvorear

square *n.* cuadrado *m.*

square: city or town square *n.* plaza *f.*

squat *v.i.* agacharse

squid *n.* calamar *m.*

squirrel *n.* ardilla *f.*

stable *n.* establo *m.*

stack *v.t.* apilar

stadium *n.* estadio *m.*

stage *n.* etapa *f.; (theater)* escenario *m.*
the stages of life las etapas de la vida

stained-glass window *n.* vidriera *f.* (de colores)

stainless steel *n.* acero *m.* inoxidable

stair *n.* escalón *m.;* peldaño *m.*

stairs *n.* escalera *f.*

stairway *n.* escalera *f.*

stammer *v.i.* tartamudear

stamp *n.* estampilla *(L.A.) f.;* sello *(Spain) m.*

stamp collecting *n.* filatelia *f.*

stand *v.i. (person)* estar parado *(L.A.);* estar de pie

stand in line *v.* hacer cola

stand out *v.* sobresalir

stand somebody up *v.* dejar a alguien plantado/a

star *n.* estrella *f.*

starry *adj.* estrellado/a

start *v.t. (vehicle)* arrancar; *(begin)* empezar (e:ie), comenzar (e:ie)

state *n.* estado *m.*

station *n. (train, bus)* estación *f.*

statue *n.* estatua *f.*

status: marital status estado *m.* civil

stay *n.* estancia *f.* **Our stay in La Coruña was magnificent.** Nuestra estancia en La Coruña fue magnífica.

stay *v.i.* quedarse; *(hotel)* alojarse

stay up all night *v.* trasnochar

steady *adj.* fijo/a

steak *n.* bistec *m.*

steal *v.t.* robar

steam *n.* vapor *m.*

steel *n.* acero *m.*

steering wheel *n.* volante *m.*

step *n.* etapa *f.;* paso *m.; (stair)*

escalón *m.,* peldaño *m.*

stepbrother *n.* hermanastro *m.*

stepdaughter *n.* hijastra *f.*

stepfather *n.* padrastro *m.*

stepmother *n.* madrastra *f.*

stepsister *n.* hermanastra *f.*

stepson *n.* hijastro *m.*

stereo *n.* estéreo *m.*

sterile *adj.* estéril

sterilize *v.t.* esterilizar

stethoscope *n.* estetoscopio *m.*

stew *n.* guiso *m.*

stick *v.t.* pegar

stifling *adj. (heat)* sofocante, agobiante **The heat is stifling.** Este calor es agobiante.

still *adv.* todavía, aún, ya

stingy *adj.* tacaño/a

stir *v.t.* remover

stockbroker *n.* bolsista *m., f.;* corredor(a) *m., f.* de bolsa

stockings *n.* medias *f., pl.*

stomach *n.* estómago *m. f.* **get an upset stomach** empacharse

stomach disorder *n.* trastorno *m.* estomacal

stone *n.* piedra *f.*

stool *n.* taburete *m.*

stop *v.i.* parar(se)

stop (doing something) *v.* dejar de (+ *inf.*)

stop sign *n.* señal *m.* de alto

storage *n.* almacenamiento *m.*

store *n.* tienda *f.*

store *v.t.* almacenar

stork *n.* cigüeña *f.*

storm *n.* tormenta *f.*

story *n.* cuento *m.;* historia *f.*

stove n. estufa f.; cocina (Spain) f.
straight adj. derecho/a; recto/a; (hair) lacio/a
straight adv. derecho
  straight ahead (todo) derecho
straighten up v. arreglar
strain v.t. colar
strange adj. extraño/a
  It's strange (that…) Es extraño (que…)
straw n. paja f.; (drinking) pajita f., popote m.
  That's the last straw! loc. ¡Esto es el colmo!
strawberry n. fresa f., frutilla (Ecuador) f.
stream n. riachuelo m.
streamer n. serpentina f.
street n. calle m.
  street light n. semáforo m.
stress n. estrés m.; tensión f.
  under stress adj. estresado/a
stress v.t. destacar, enfatizar, recalcar
stressful adj. estresante
stretch v.t. estirar
stretcher n. camilla f.
stretching n. estiramiento m.
  do stretching exercises hacer ejercicios m., pl. de estiramiento
strike n. (labor) huelga f.
striker n. huelguista m., f.
stripe n. raya f.
striped adj. de rayas
stroke n. (swimming) estilo m.
stroll v.i. pasear
strong adj. fuerte

struggle (for/against; to + inf.) v. luchar (por/contra; para + inf.)
stubborn adj. testarudo/a
student n., adj. estudiante m., f.; estudiantil
  student desk n. pupitre m.
studious adj. estudioso/a
study v.t./v.i. estudiar
stuff v.t. (culinary) rellenar
stuff oneself v. hartarse
stuffed adj. relleno/a
  I love stuffed chilies. Adoro los chiles rellenos.
stuffed-up adj. congestionado/a
stuffing n. relleno m.
stunned adj. atontado/a
stupendous adj. estupendo/a
stutter v.i. tartamudear
style n. estilo m.
subject matter n. temática f.
subject n. (university) disciplina f.; tema m.
subjective adj. subjetivo/a
submarine n. submarino m.
substance n. sustancia f.
substitute n. sustituto/a m., f.
substitute v.t. sustituir
  He substituted coffe for tea. Sustituyó el café por el té.
subterranean adj. subterráneo/a
suburbs n. afueras f., pl.
subway n. metro m.
  go by subway ir en metro
subway station n. estación f. del metro
succeed v.i. triunfar
success n. éxito m.

be successful tener éxito
successively adv. sucesivamente
such as [tal(es)] como
  She used words such as justice and freedom. Usó palabras (tales) como justicia y libertad.
suddenly adv. de repente
suffer v.t. sufrir
  suffer an illness sufrir una enfermedad
suffer from v. (disease) padecer de **He suffers from heart problems.** Padece del corazón.
suffering n. padecimiento m.
sufficient adj. bastante
suffocation n. sofoco m.
sugar n. azúcar m.
sugar bowl n. azucarero m.
suggest v.t. sugerir (e:ie)
suggestion n. sugerencia f.
suicide n. suicidio m.
  commit suicide suicidarse
suit n. traje m.
suit v.t. (clothes) sentar
  That jacket suits you. Esa chaqueta te sienta bien.
suitable adj. apto/a
suitcase n. maleta f.
summer n. verano m.
summer v.i. veranear
  She summers in the mountains. Veranea en las montañas.
summit n. cima f.
sumptuous adj. suntuoso/a
sun n. sol m.
sunbathe v.i. tomar el sol; tumbarse al sol
Sunday n. domingo m.
sunflower n. girasol m.
sunglasses n., pl. lentes m., pl. de sol; gafas f., pl. oscuras/negras/de sol
sunny adj. soleado/a
  It's (very) sunny. Hace (mucho) sol.
sunrise n. salida f. del sol
sunset n. puesta f. de(l) sol
sunshade n. sombrilla f.
suntan lotion n. bronceador m.
sun-tanned adj. bronceado/a
supermarket n. supermercado m.
superstition n. superstición f.
superstitious adj. supersticioso/a
supervise v.t. supervisar
supper n. cena f.
supplier n. suministrador(a) m., f.
supplies n., pl. provisiones f., pl.; víveres m., pl.
supply n. suministro m.
supply v.t. suministrar
support v.t. apoyar; sostener; soportar; respaldar
suppose v.t. suponer
Supreme Court n. Corte f. Suprema (L.A.); Tribunal m. Supremo (Spain)
sure adj. seguro/a
  be sure estar seguro/a
surf (the Internet) v.i. navegar (en Internet)
surgeon n. cirujano/a m., f.
surgery n. cirugía f.
surprise n. sorpresa f.

What a surprise! ¡Qué
sorpresa!
surprise *v.t.* sorprender
be surprised sorprenderse
He was surprised to see me.
Se sorprendió al verme.
surrounding area *n.*
alrededores *m., pl.*
survey *n.* encuesta *f.*
survival *n.* supervivencia *f.*
survivor *n.* superviviente *m., f.*
suspect *v.t.* sospechar
suspenders *n., pl.* tirantes *m., pl.*
suspense: in suspense *adj.*
intrigado/a
suspension bridge *n.* puente *f.*
colgante
suspicion *n.* sospecha *f.*
suspicious *adj.* sospechoso/a
swallow *v.t./v.i.* tragar
swamp *n.* pantano *m.;* ciénaga
f.
swan *n.* cisne *m.*
swear *v.t.* jurar
sweat *v.i.* sudar
sweater *n.* suéter *m.*
sweaty *adj.* sudado/a
sweep (the floor) *v.t.* barrer (el
piso/suelo)
sweet *adj.* dulce
sweets *n., pl.* dulces *m., pl.*
swim *v.i.* nadar
swimmer *n.* nadador(a) *m., f.*
swimming *n.* natación *f.*
synchronized swimming
natación sincronizada
swimming pool *n.* piscina *f.;*
alberca *(Mexico) f.*
swimming suit *n.* traje *m.* de
baño

symbiosis *n.* simbiosis *f.*
symbolize *v.t.* simbolizar
symphonic *adj.* sinfónico/a
symphony *n.* sinfonía *f.*
symphony orchestra *n.*
sinfónica *f.*
symptom *n.* síntoma *m.*
synonym *n.* sinónimo *m.*
synonymous *adj.* sinónimo/a
syntax *n.* sintaxis *f.*
syringe *n.* jeringa *f.*
syrup *n.* almíbar *m.*
system *n.* sistema *f.*

T
table *n.* mesa *f.*
tablecloth *n.* mantel *m.*
tablespoon *n.* cuchara *f.*
tablet *n. (pill)* pastilla *f.*
tactful *adj.* diplomático/a
tactless *adj.* indiscreto/a
tail *n.* cola *f.*
tailor *n.* sastre *m.*
take *v.t.* llevar; tomar; traer
take a bath *v. pron.* bañarse
take a shower *v. pron.*
ducharse
take a trip *v.* hacer un viaje
take someone somewhere
llevar
take advantage of *v.*
aprovecharse de
take back *v.t.* devolver
take care of cuidar
take care of oneself
cuidarse
take care of clients *v.i.*
atender a los clientes
take off *v. (clothes)* quitarse;
(airplane, rocket) despegar

take off one's shoes descalzarse
take-off *n.* despegue *m.*
take offense *v.* ofenderse
take out (the trash) *v.* sacar (la basura)
take out (walk) the dog sacar al perro a pasear
take the risk *v.* arriesgarse
take up *v. (hobby)* aficionarse
talented *adj.* talentoso/a
talk *v.i.* hablar; conversar
talk show *n.* programa *m.* de entrevistas
talkative *adj. (person)* hablador(a); charlatán, charlatana
tall *adj.* alto/a
tan *v.t.* broncear; *v.i.* broncearse
tangerine *n.* mandarina *f.*
tangy *adj.* ácido/a
tank *n.* depósito *m.;* tanque *m.*
tanned *adj.* moreno/a
tantrum *n.* berrinche *m.*
 throw tantrums hacer berrinches
tape *n.* cinta *f.*
tape recorder *n.* grabadora *f.*
tapestry *n.* tapiz *m.*
target shooting *n.* tiro *m.* al blanco
tart *adj.* ácido/a
taste *n. (senses)* gusto *m.*
taste *v.t.* probar (o:ue)
tasteless *adj.* soso/a
tasty *adj.* rico/a, sabroso/a
tax *n.* impuesto *m.*
taxi(cab) *n.* taxi *m.*
 go by taxi ir en taxi

tea *n.* té *m.*
 herbal tea *n.* infusión *f.* (de hierbas)
teabag *n.* bolsita *f.* de té
teach *v.t.* enseñar
teacher *n.* profesor(a) *m., f.; (elementary school)* maestro/a *m., f.*
team *n.* equipo *m.*
 technical team equipo de técnicos
teapot *n.* tetera *f.*
tear *n.* lágrima *f.*
tear gas *n.* gas *m.* lacrimógeno
technician *n.* técnico/a *m., f.*
teddy bear *n.* osito *m.* de peluche
telecommuting *n.* teletrabajo *m.*
teleconference *n.* videoconferencia *f.*
telephone *n.* teléfono *m.*
 cellular telephone teléfono celular
 by phone por teléfono
telescope *n.* telescopio *m.*
television *n.* televisión *f.; (set)* televisor *m.*
tell *v.* decir; contar
temperament *n.* temperamento *m.*
temperature *n.* temperatura *f.*
 take (someone's) temperature tomar la temperatura (a alguien)
temple *n.* templo *m.*
ten diez
tendency *n.* tendencia *f.*
tender *adj. (meat; loving)* tierno/a
tendon *n.* tendón *m.*

tennis *n. (sport)* tenis *m.; (sneakers)* tenis *m.*
tennis court *n.* pista *f.* de tenis
tennis player *n.* tenista *m., f.*
tennis shoes *n.* zapatillas *f., pl.* de deporte; zapatos *m., pl.* de tenis
tenor *n.* tenor *m.*
tension *n.* tensión *f.*
tent *n.* tienda *f.* (de campaña)
tenth décimo *m.; adj.* décimo/a
terrace *n.* terraza *f.*
terrible *adj.* terrible
  It's terrible (that…) Es terrible (que…)
terrific *adj.* genial, fantástico, estupendo, chévere
terrorist *n., adj.* terrorista *m., f.*
terrorist attack *n.* atentado *m.* terrorista
test *n.* examen *m.;* prueba *f.;* evaluación *f.*
  placement test prueba de nivel
  aptitude test prueba de aptitud
test *v.t.* evaluar
thanks *interj.* gracias
  Thank you. Gracias.
  Thank you very much. Muchas gracias.
  Thank you very, very much. Muchísimas gracias.
  Thanks (a lot). (Muchas) gracias.
  Thanks again. Gracias una vez más.
  Thanks for everything. Gracias por todo.
that (one) ése, esa, eso *pron.;*

ese, esa *adj.*
that (over there) aquél, aquélla, aquello *pron.;* aquel, aquella *adj.*
that *conj.* que
that which *conj.* lo que
that's why por eso
theater *n.* teatro *m.;* auditorio
theft *n.* robo *m.*
their su(s) *poss. adj.;* suyo(s)/suya(s) *poss. pron.*
thematic *adj.* temático/a
theme *n.* tema *m.*
then *adv. (afterward)* después (de); *(as a result)* entonces; *(next)* luego, pues
theorize *v.i.* teorizar
theory *n.* teoría *f.*
therapeutic *adj.* terapéutico/a
therapy *n.* terapia *f.*
there *adv.* allí
  There is/are… Hay…
  There is/are not… No hay…
therefore *adv.* por eso; por lo tanto
thermostat *m.* termostato
these estos, estas *adj.;* éstos, éstas *pron.*
thesis *f.* tesis
thief *n.* ladrón *m.,* ladrona *f.*
thigh *n.* muslo *m.*
thin *adj.* delgado/a
thing *n.* cosa *f.*
think *v.t.* pensar (e:ie); *(believe)* creer
  What do you think? *form.* ¿Qué le/les parece?
  think about *v.* pensar en
third tercio *m.; adj.* tercer, tercero/a

third-world country n. país m. tercermundista

thirst n. sed f.

 be thirsty tener sed

thirsty adj. sediento/a

thirteen trece

thirty treinta; (minutes past the hour) y treinta, y media

 It's six thirty. Son las seis y treinta/media.

this este, esta adj.; éste, ésta, esto pron.

 This is he/she. (on the phone) Con él/ella habla.

thorn n. espina f.

those esos, esas adj.; ésos, ésas pron.

thread n. hilo m.

threat n. amenaza f.

threaten v.t. amenazar

three tres

three hundred trescientos/as

thrilled adj. ilusionado/a

throat n. garganta f.

through prep. por; a través de

throw n. lanzamiento m.

throw v.t. echar; tirar; lanzar

throw away v.t. (leftovers) desechar, tirar

thunder n. trueno m.

Thursday n. jueves m., sing.

thus adv. así

thyme n. tomillo m.

ticket n. (show) boleto (L.A.) m.; entrada (Spain) f.; (trip) pasaje; (fine) multa f.

tidal wave n. maremoto m.

tidy adj. arreglado/a

tie n. (clothing) corbata f.; (sports) empate m.; (bond)

lazo m., vínculo m

 family ties lazos familiares

tie v.t. atar; (sports) empatar

tiger n. tigre m.

tile n. (ceramic) azulejo m.; (floor) baldosa f.; (roof) teja f.

time n. tiempo m.; (occasion) vez f.

 We have time. Tenemos tiempo.

 We had a great time. Lo pasamos de película/super bien.

 What time is it? ¿Qué hora es?

 ahead of time con anticipación

 full-time tiempo completo

 many times muchas veces

 on time a tiempo

 one more time una vez más

 one time una vez

 part-time tiempo parcial

time trial n. carrera n. contra reloj

timid adj. tímido/a

tinfoil n. papel m. de aluminio

tiny adj. minúsculo/a

tip n. propina f.

 leave a tip dejar una propina

tire n. llanta f.; neumático m.

tire oneself out v. cansarse

tired adj. cansado/a

 be tired estar cansado/a

tissue n. (anat.) tejido m.; pañuelo m. de papel

title n. título m.

to prep. a

toad n. sapo m.

toast n. pan m. tostado;

tostada *f.; (drinking)* brindis *m.*

toast *v.t.* tostar; *(drinking)* brindar (por)

toasted *adj.* tostado/a
toasted bread pan tostado

toaster *n.* tostadora *f.*

today *adv.* hoy
Today is… Hoy es…

toe *n.* dedo *m.* (del pie)

together *adj.* juntos/as

toilet *n.* inodoro *m.*

toiletry kit *n.* neceser *m.*

toilet paper *n.* papel *m.* higiénico

tolerance *n.* tolerancia *f.*

tolerant *adj.* tolerante

tolerate *v.t.* tolerar

tomato *n.* tomate *m.*

tomorrow *adv.* mañana

tongs *n., pl.* tenazas *f., pl.*

tonight *adv.* esta noche

tonsil *n.* amígdala *f.*

too *adv.* también

too much *adv.* demasiado; en exceso

tool *n.* herramienta *f.*

tooth *n.* diente *m.; (back)* muela *f.*
pull a tooth sacar una muela
I had a tooth pulled. Me sacaron una muela.

toothbrush *n.* cepillo *m.* de dientes

toothpaste *n.* pasta *f.* de dientes

toothpick *n.* mondadientes *m., sing.;* palillo *m.* (de dientes)

top *n.* cima *f.*

torch *n.* antorcha *f.*

tornado *n.* tornado *m.*

tortilla *n.* tortilla *f.*

toss *v.t.* tirar; mezclar

touch *n. (sense)* tacto *m.*

touch *v.t.* tocar

tour *n.* visita *f.* turística; viaje *m.*
go on a tour hacer una excursión
tour around an area excursión *f.*

tourism *n.* turismo *m.*

tourist *adj.* turístico/a

tourist *n.* turista *m., f.*

toward *prep.* hacia

towel *n.* toalla *f.*

towel bar *n.* toallero *m.*

tower *n.* torre *f.*

town *n.* pueblo *m.*

town square *n.* plaza *f.* mayor

toy *n.* juguete *m.*

toy store *n.* juguetería *f.*

track *n.* pista *f.; (sport)* pista de atletismo; *(railroad)* vía *f.*
indoor track *n.* pista *f.* cubierta

track and field *n.* atletismo *m.*

trade *n.* oficio *m.*

tradition *n.* tradición *f.*

traffic *n.* circulación *f.;* tráfico *m.*

traffic (in) *v.t.* traficar (en)

traffic jam *n.* atasco *m.;* embotellamiento *m.* (de tráfico) *(Spain)*

traffic sign *n.* señal *f.* de tráfico

traffic signal *n.* semáforo *m.*

tragedy *n.* tragedia *f.*

tragic *adj.* trágico/a

203

trail n. sendero m.
trailer n. caravana f.
trailhead n. sendero m.
train n. tren m.
  go by train ir en tren
train station estación f. de tren
train v.i. entrenarse
trainer n. entrenador(a) m., f.;
  monitor(a) m., f.
training n. entrenamiento m.;
  capacitación f.
traitor n. traidor(a) m., f.
trajectory n. trayectoria f.
transfer n. transferencia f.
transfusion n. transfusión f.
translate v.t. traducir
translation n. traducción f.
translator n. traductor(a) m., f.
transparent adj. transparente
transplant n. transplante m.
transport v.t. transportar
transportation n. transporte m.
trapshooting n. tiro m. al plato
trash n. basura f.
travel v.i. viajar; desplazarse
travel agency n. agencia f. de
  viajes
travel agent n. agente m., f. de
  viajes
travel document n. documento
  m. de viaje
traveler n. viajero/a m., f.
traveler's check n. cheque m.
  de viajero
treacherous adj. traicionero/a,
  traidor(a); peligroso/a
treachery n. traición f.
treadmill cinta caminadora
treason n. traición f.
treasure n. tesoro m.

tree n. árbol m.
trendy: be trendy ir a la moda
trial n. juicio m.
triangle n. triángulo m.
tribute n. homenaje m.
tricycle n. triciclo m.
trigger n. (firearm) gatillo m.
trigonometry n. trigonometría f.
trimester n. trimestre m.
trip n. viaje m.; desplazamiento
  m.
  go on/take a trip hacer un
  viaje
tripod n. trípode m.
triviality n. trivialidad f.
trivialize v.t. trivializar
trout n. trucha f.
truck n. camión m.
truck driver n. camionero/a m.,
  f.
true adj. verdadero/a; cierto
  it's (not) true (no) es verdad
true-to-life adj. verosímil
trunk n. baúl m.; (car) maletero
  (Spain) m.; (live tree) tronco
  m.
truth n. verdad f.
try n. intento m.
try v.t. intentar; probar (o:ue);
  (to do something) tratar de
  (+ inf.)
try hard v. esforzarse
try on v. (clothes) probarse
  (o:ue)
try out v.t./v.i. experimentar
t-shirt n. camiseta f.
tube n. tubo m.
tuberculosis n. tuberculosis f.
Tuesday n. martes m., sing.
tulip n. tulipán m.

tuna *n.* atún *m.*
tune up *v.t.* afinar
  out of tune *adj.* desafinado/a
tunnel *n.* túnel *m.*
turbine *n.* turbina *f.*
turkey *n.* pavo *m.*
turn *n.* giro *m.;* turno *m.;* vuelta *f.*
turn *v.t./v.i.* doblar; girar;
  dar(se) la vuelta **Turn left at
  the next corner.** Gira
  a la izquierda en la próxima
  esquina.
turn off *v.t.*
  (electricity/appliance)
  apagar
turn on *v.t.*
  (electricity/appliance) poner,
  encender; prender
turn over *v.t. (tortilla, cup)*
  voltear *(L.A.)*
turn signal *n. (car)* intermitente
  m
turquoise *n.* turquesa *f.*
turtle *n.* tortuga *f.*
tutor *n.* profesor(a) *m., f.*
  particular
tweezers *n., pl.* pinzas *f., pl.*
  (para depilar)
twelve doce
twenty veinte
twenty-eight veintiocho
twenty-five veinticinco
twenty-four veinticuatro
twenty-nine veintinueve
twenty-one veintiún, veintiuno/a
twenty-seven veintisiete
twenty-six veintiséis
twenty-three veintitrés
twenty-two veintidós
twice *adv.* dos veces

twin *n.* gemelo/a *m., f.;*
  mellizo/a *m., f.*
twisted *adj.* torcido/a
  be twisted estar torcido/a
two dos
  two times dos veces
two hundred doscientos/as
two weeks *n., pl.* quincena *f.*
type *n.* especie *f.*
type *v.i.* escribir a máquina;
  teclear
typewriter *n.* máquina *f.* de
  escribir
typist *n.* mecanógrafo/a *m., f.*

U

**UFO (Unidentified Flying
  Object)** *n.* OVNI *m.* (Objeto
  Volador No Identificado)
ugly *adj.* feo/a
umbrella *n.* paraguas *m.*
umbrella stand *n.* paragüero *m.*
umpire *n.* árbitro/a *m.*
unbearable *adj.* insoportable
unblock *v.t.* desatascar
uncertainty *n.* incertidumbre *f.*
uncle *n.* tío *m.*
under *adv.* bajo, debajo (de)
undergo *v.t. (test, examination)*
  someterse a
underground *adj.*
  subterráneo/a
underlined *adj.* subrayado/a
understand *v.t.* comprender;
  entender (e:ie)
understanding *n.* comprensión
  f.
underwear *n.* ropa *f.* interior
  long underwear *n.*
  calzoncillos *m., pl.* largos

undress *v.i.* desvestirse
unemployment *n.* desempleo *m.*
unexpected *adj.* inesperado/a
unfair *adj.* injusto/a
unfavorable *adj.* desfavorable
unforgettable *adj.* inolvidable
unfortunate *adj.* desgraciado/a
unfortunately *adv.* desafortunadamente; desgraciadamente
unfriendly *adj.* antipático/a; arisco/a
ungrateful *adj.* desagradecido/a
unhappy *adj.* infeliz; desgraciado/a
United States *n., pl.* Estados *m., pl.* Unidos
universe *n.* universo *m.*
university *n.* universidad *f.*
unkempt *adj. (appearance)* desarreglado/a
unless *adv.* a menos que
unlikely *adj.* improbable, poco probable
  be unlikely that *(something will happen)* ser poco probable que (+ *subj.*) **It's unlikely that they will arrive on time.** Es poco probable que lleguen a tiempo.
unmarried *adj.* soltero/a
unnoticed *adj.* inadvertido/a
unpack *v.t.* desempacar
unpleasant *adj.* desagradable; *(person)* antipático/a
unresolved *adj.* pendiente
unsociable *adj.* insociable
unsuccessful *adj.* fracasado/a

unthinkable *adj.* impensable
until *adv.* hasta (que)
until *prep.* hasta
  until now hasta ahora
unusual *adj.* inusual, poco corriente; insólito/a
unwillingly *adv.* de mala gana
up *adv.* arriba
  up to date al día, al corriente
  bring someone up to date *idiom* poner a uno al día/al corriente
upset enojado/a; molesto/a
urgent *adj.* urgente
  It's (not) urgent that… (No) Es urgente que…
urinate *v.i.* orinar
urine *n.* orina *f.*
use *v.t.* usar
  make good use of aprovechar
useful *adj.* útil; práctico/a
usually *adv.* soler (o:ue) +*inf.*
  I usually study at night. Suelo estudiar por la noche.
utensil *n.* utensilio *m.*
uterus *n.* útero *m.*

V

vacation *n.* vacaciones *f., pl.*
  be on vacation estar de vacaciones
  go on vacation ir(se) de vacaciones
vacationer *n. (summer)* veraneante *m., f.*
vacuum *v.i.* pasar la aspiradora
vacuum cleaner *n.* aspiradora *f.*
vain *adj.* presumido/a

valley n. valle m.
value n. valor m.
value v.t. valorar
vanilla n. vainilla f.
vapor n. vapor m.
variation n. variación f.
varied adj. variado/a
variety n. surtido m.
various adj. varios/as
vary v.i. variar
vase n. florero m.; jarrón m.
VCR n. videocasetera f.
veal n. ternera f.
vegetables n., pl. verduras f., pl.
vegetation n. vegetación f.
vehicle n. vehículo m.
vein n. vena f.
velodrome n. velódromo m.
velvet n. terciopelo m.
verb n. verbo m.
verisimilitude n. verosimilitud f.
vermillion n. bermellón m.
vermouth n. vermut m.
versatile adj. versátil
vertebra n. vértebra f.
vertebrate n., adj. vertebrado m.; vertebrado/a
very adv. muy
  Very good, thank you. Muy bien, gracias.
very well adv. muy bien
very much adv. muchísimo/a
vest n. chaleco m.
veterinarian n. veterinario/a m., f.
veterinary science n. veterinaria f.
vibrate v.i. vibrar

vibration n. vibración f.
video n. video (L.A.) m.; vídeo (Spain) m.
video(cassette) n. video(casete) m.
video camera n. cámara f. de video
videoconference n. videoconferencia f.
visor n. visera f.
view n. vista f.
village n. aldea f.
vinegar n. vinagre m.
violence n. violencia f.
visit v.t. visitar
  visit monuments visitar monumentos
visiting team n. (sports) equipo m. visitante
visitor n. visitante m., f.
visor n. visera f.
vitamin n. vitamina f.
vocational training n. formación f. profesional
volcano n. volcán m.
volleyball n. vóleibol m.
volume n. volumen m.
voluntary adj. voluntario
volunteer n. voluntario/a m., f.
vomit v.i. vomitar
vote n. voto m.
vote v.i. votar
vulture n. buitre m.

W

wage n. sueldo m.
waist n. cintura f.
wait (for) v.i. esperar
  be waiting estar pendiente

I'm waiting for Woody to call me. Estoy pendiente de que Woody me llame.
waiter *n.* camarero *m.;* mesero *m.;* mozo *m. (L.A.)*
waitress *n.* camarera *f.;* mesera *f.;* moza *f. (L.A.)*
wake up *v.i.* despertarse (e:ie)
walk *v.i.* caminar
  go for a walk dar un paseo
  take a walk pasear
  walk around the city/the town pasear por la ciudad/el pueblo
walking stick *n.* bastón *m.*
Walkman *n.* walkman *m.*
wall *n.* pared *f.;* muro *m.*
wallet *n.* cartera *f.*
walnut *n.* nuez *f.*
walnut tree *n.* nogal *m.*
want *v.t.* querer (e:ie)
  I don't want to. No quiero.
war *n.* guerra *f.*
wardrobe *n.* ropero *m.;* vestuario *m.*
warm (oneself) up *v.* calentarse (e:ie)
warranty *n.* garantía *f.*
wart *n.* verruga *f.*
wash *v.t.* lavar; *v.ref. (oneself)* lavarse
  wash one's face/hands lavarse la cara/las manos
  wash the floor lavar el piso
washing machine *n.* lavadora *f.*
wasp *n.* avispa *f.*
waste *v.t.* malgastar
wastebasket *n.* papelera *f.*
watch *n.* reloj *m.*

watch *v.t./v.i.* mirar; ver
  watch television mirar (la) televisión
  watch out *interj.* cuidado
water *n.* agua (el) *f.*
  drinking water agua potable
  fresh water agua dulce
  holy water agua bendita
  mineral water agua mineral
  salt water agua salada
water *v.t. (plants)* regar
water park *n.* parque *m.* acuático
water skiing *n.* esquí *m.* acuático
waterfall *n.* catarata *f.*
watering can *n.* regadera *f.*
watermelon *n.* sandía *f.*
waterproof *adj.* impermeable
waterskiing *n.* esquí *m.* acuático
wave *n. (water)* ola *f.; (physics, radio)* onda *f.*
wax *n.* cera *f.*
wax *v.t.* encerar; *(legs)* depilarse
way *n.* manera *f.;* camino *m.*
weak *adj.* débil
weapon *n.* arma (el) *f.*
wear *v.t.* llevar; usar; ponerse
  wear a costume disfrazarse de
  wear for the first time estrenar
wear oneself out *v.* fatigarse
weary *adj.* fatigado/a
weather *n.* tiempo *m.*
  It's nice/bad weather. Hace buen/mal tiempo.
  What's the weather like?

¿Qué tiempo hace?
weaving n. tejido m.
Web n. red f.
website n. sitio m. web
wedding n. boda f.
  wedding ring n. anillo m. de
  bodas
Wednesday n. miércoles m.,
  sing.
week n. semana f.
  next week semana entrante,
  semana que viene
weekdays, (on) entre semana
weekend n. fin m. de semana
weigh oneself v. pesarse
weight n. pesa f.; peso m.
weightless adj. ingrávido/a
weightlifting n. (sport)
  halterofilia f.
welcome adj. bienvenido/a(s)
  You're welcome.
  (responding to thanks) De
  nada; No hay de qué
weld v.t. soldar
welding n. soldadura f.
well adv. bien; pues; bueno
well n. pozo m.
well-being n. bienestar m.
well-known adj. conocido/a
  be well-known for tener
  fama de
well-mannered adj. educado/a
well-organized adj.
  ordenado/a
west n. oeste m.
  to the west al oeste
western adj. (genre) ...de
  vaqueros
  a western una (película) de
  vaqueros

wet adj. mojado/a
wet v.t. mojar
  get wet mojarse
whale n. ballena f.
wharf n. embarcadero m.
what rel. pron. lo que
what? adj., pron. ¿qué?
  What did you say? ¿Cómo?
  What's going on? ¿Qué
  pasa?
  What a . . . ! ¡Qué…!
  What a drag! loc. ¡Qué lata!
wheat n. trigo m.
wheel n. rueda f.
wheel chair n. silla f. de
  ruedas
wheelbarrow n. carretilla f.
when adv., conj. cuando
when? adv. ¿cuándo?
  when all's said and done
  loc. a fin de cuentas
where prep. donde
where? adv. (destination)
  ¿adónde?; (location) ¿dónde?
  Where are you from? (fam.)
  ¿De dónde eres?; (form.) ¿De
  dónde es Ud.?
  Where is . . . ? ¿Dónde
  está...?
which? adj., pron. ¿cuál(es)?;
  ¿qué?
  which one(s)? ¿cuál(es)?
while adv. mientras
whim n. antojo m.; capricho m.
whine v.i. lloriquear
whisk v.t. batir
whisk n. batidor m.
whistle n. silbato m.
whistle v.i. silbar
white n., adj. blanco m.;

blanco/a

who *pron.* que **Is there anyone who speaks English?** ¿Hay alguien que hable inglés?; quien(es)

who? *pron.* ¿quién(es)?
Who is . . . ? ¿Quién es...?
Who is calling? *(on telephone)* ¿De parte de quién?
Who is speaking? *(on telephone)* ¿Quién habla?

whole *adj.* todo/a

whole-wheat bread *n.* pan *m.* integral

whose? *adj., pron.* ¿de quién(es)?

why? *adv.* ¿por qué?

wicker *n.* mimbre *m.*

widow *adj.* viuda

widowed *adj.* viudo/a

widower *adj.* viudo

wife *n.* esposa *f.*

wig *n.* peluca *f.*

wild *adj. (animal)* salvaje; *(plant)* silvestre

willingly *adv.* de buena gana

win *v.t.* ganar; vencer

wind *n.* viento *m.*
It's (very) windy. Hace (mucho) viento.

window *n.* ventana *f.*; cristal *m.*

windshield *n.* parabrisas *m., sing.*

windshield wiper *n.* limpiaparabrisas *m., sing.*

wine *n.* vino *m.*
bottle of wine *n.* botella *f.* de vino

red/white wine vino tinto/blanco

wine cellar *n.* bodega *f.*

wineglass *n.* copa *f.*

wink (one's eye) *v.t.* guiñar(le) (el ojo) (a alguien)

winter *n.* invierno *m.*

wire netting *n.* tela *f.* metálica

wisdom *n.* sabiduría *f.*

wisdom tooth *n.* muela *f.* del juicio

wise *adj.* sabio/a

wise person *n.* sabio/a *m., f.*

wish *n.* deseo *m.*

wish *v.t.* desear; esperar
I wish (that) *interj.* Ojalá (que)

with *prep.* con
with me conmigo
with you *fam.* contigo
with regard to con respecto a

withdrawn *adj. (person)* retraído/a

within *prep.* dentro de

without *conj.* sin que

without *prep.* sin

withstand *v.t.* soportar, resistir, aguantar

witness *n.* testigo *m., f.*

wolf *n.* lobo *m.*

woman *n.* mujer *f.*

womanizer *n.* donjuán *m.*; mujeriego *m.*

womb *n.* útero *m.*

wool *n.* lana *f.*
made of wool de lana

wool cap *n.* gorro *m.* de lana

word *n.* palabra *f.*

work *n.* trabajo *m.; (of art,*

literature, music, etc.) obra *f.*
work *v.i.* trabajar; funcionar
  not working *adj.*
  descompuesto/a
work out *v.i.* hacer gimnasia
workshop *n.* taller *m.;*
  (mechanic's) taller de
  mecánica
world *n.* mundo *m.*
worldwide *adj.* mundial
worm *n.* gusano *m.*
worried (about) *adj.*
  preocupado/a (por);
  inquieto/a
worry (about) *v.* preocuparse
  (por); inquietar(se)
  Don't worry. No se/te
  preocupe/s.
worrysome *adj.* inquietante
worse *adj.* peor
worse than *adv.* peor que
worst *adj.* el/la peor, lo peor
  the worst *n.* el/la peor *m., f.*
  lo peor
worth *n.* valor
  be worth the trouble valer la
  pena
wound *n.* herida *f.*
wrap *v.t.* envolver
wretch *n.* desgraciado/a *m., f.*
wrist *n.* muñeca *f.*
write *v.t.* escribir
  **write a letter/postcard/e-
  mail message** escribir una
  carta/una (tarjeta) postal/un
  mensaje electrónico
writer *n.* escritor(a) *m., f.*
written *p.p.* escrito/a (*of*
  escribir)
wrong *adj.* equivocado/a

be wrong no tener razón
What's wrong? ¿Qué pasa?

X

X-ray *n.* radiografía *f.*

Y

yam *n.* ñame *m.*
yard *n.* jardín *m.;* patio *m.*
year *n.* año *m.*
yearning *n.* añoranza *f.*
yeast *n.* levadura *f.*
yellow *n., adj.* amarillo *m.;*
  amarillo/a
yellowish *adj.* amarillento/a
yes *interj.* sí
  Yes, sure! ¡Sí, vale!
yesterday *adv.* ayer
yet *adv.* todavía
yield (the right of way) *v.*
  ceder el paso
yoga *n.* yoga *m.*
yogurt *n.* yogur *m.*
young *adj.* joven
young person *n.* joven *m., f.;*
  chico/a *m., f.*
younger *adj.* menor
youngest *n.* el/la menor *m., f.*
your su(s) *poss. adj. form.;* tu(s)
  poss. adj. fam. sing.;
  vuestro(s)/vuestra(s) *poss.
  adj. form. pl.;* suyo(s)/suya(s)
  poss. pron. form.;
  tuyo(s)/tuya(s) *poss. fam.
  sing.*
youth *n.* juventud *f.;* joven *m., f.*
youth hostel *n.* albergue *m.*
  juvenil
youthful *adj.* juvenil

z

zebra *n.* cebra *f.*
zero *n.* cero *m.*
zipper *n.* cremallera *f.*
zoo *n.* zoológico *m.*
zoologist *n.* zoólogo/a *m., f.*

Useful Expressions

The *Useful Expressions* section of the **Vista Higher Learning Introductory Spanish Pocket Dictionary & Language Guide** puts at your fingertips a great variety of useful language organized according to situations similar to those in your textbook. This section of the dictionary provides numerous models of natural and expressive Spanish and covers all the conversational situations likely to come up as you progress through your book.

To use *Useful Expressions* for your class work, look for situations similar to those in the lesson you are studying, read through the section, copy out sentences and expressions that interest you, review them several times, and write new sentences modeled on them. Before you know it, you will find that you have acquired the new vocabulary, expressions, and language structures. This section can not only help you make yourself understood, it can help you express yourself, your opinions, and your personality in fluent and natural Spanish.

USEFUL EXPRESSIONS

SALUDOS, PRESENTA-CIONES Y DESPEDIDAS	GREETINGS, INTRODUC-TIONS, AND FAREWELLS
Buenos días.	Good morning.
¿Hay alguien?	Is anyone there?
¿Se puede pasar?	May I come in?
Pues claro, adelante.	Of course, come in.
Pasa./Pase./Pasen.	Come in.
Es (todo) un placer conocerle.	It's a (great) pleasure to meet you.
El placer es mío.	The pleasure is mine.
(Muchísimas) Gracias.	Thank you (very much).
Quiero presentarle a la Sra. Paredes.	I would like you to meet Mrs. Paredes.

ENCUENTROS / UPON MEETING

¡Cuánto tiempo sin verte/verlo/verla/verlos/verlas!	Long time no see!
¡Qué alegría volver a verte!	How nice to see you again!
¿Qué (te) cuentas?	What's going on?/What's up?
Ha pasado mucho tiempo.	What a long time it's been.
¡Cómo vuela el tiempo!	How time flies!
¿Cómo va la vida?	How's life?
Bien, muy bien.	Good, very good.
Todo va sobre ruedas.	Everything's going smoothly.
Y tú, ¿qué tal?	How are things with you?
No me puedo quejar.	I can't complain.
Me alegro de volver a verte.	I'm so glad to see you again.
Es estupendo verte otra vez.	It's great to see you again.

Igualmente.	Likewise./The same to you.
Lo mismo digo.	Same here.

EXPRESIONES CORTESES Y SERVICIALES
EXPRESSIONS OF COURTESY AND HELPFULNESS

Con permiso.	Excuse me.
Permítame.	Allow me.
¡A la orden!	At your service.
No hay de qué.	Don't mention it./You're welcome.
Con gusto.	With pleasure.
¡Para servirle!	At your service./You're welcome.
Perdone.	Pardon me./Excuse me.
Perdóneme.	Pardon me./Excuse me.
Sin falta.	By all means.
Ahora mismo.	Right away.
Al minuto.	Right away.
No faltaba más.	Of course./No problem.
¿Cómo no?	But of course./Sure.
Enseguida.	Right away.

EXPRESIONES DE TIEMPO
EXPRESSIONS OF TIME

¿A cuántos estamos? A doce de agosto.	What's the date? The twelfth of August.
¿A qué día estamos hoy? A seis.	What's the date today? The sixth.
¿Qué día es hoy? Miércoles veinticuatro.	What day is it? Wednesday, the twenty-fourth.
¡Uy, qué tarde es!	Oh, it's so late!
Se me ha hecho tarde.	I'm late.
¡Ya es mediodía!	It's already noon!

Tengo mucha prisa.	I'm in a big hurry.
¡Qué contratiempo! No tengo reloj.	What a nuisance! I don't have a watch.
¡Qué inconveniente!	How inconvenient!
Son las dos de la tarde.	It's two in the afternoon.
Son las tres de la madrugada.	It's three in the morning.
Es la una de la noche.	It's one in the morning.
Son las siete de la tarde.	It's seven in the evening.
¿Tiene (Ud.) hora, por favor?	Do you have the time, please?
¿Qué hora tiene?	What time do you have?
¿Me dice la hora?	Can you tell me the time?
¿Podría Ud. decirme qué hora es?	Could you please tell me what time it is?
Pasan diez minutos de las once.	It's ten minutes past eleven.
Llego justito.	I'm just in the nick of time.
Falta (un) cuarto para las dos.	It's (a) quarter to two.
Tengo tiempo de tomar un café.	I have time for a cup of coffee.
Es la una y media.	It's one thirty.
Aún es temprano.	It's still early.
Son las tres en punto.	It's three on the dot.
Aún falta una hora.	There's still an hour to go.
Son las seis menos cuarto.	It's a quarter to six.
No llego, no llego.	I'll never make it.
Se me/nos ha ido el día en tonterías.	I/We have fiddled away the entire day.
Son las cinco cuarenta y cinco.	It's five forty-five.
Ya llego tarde.	I'm already late.

¡Cómo vuela/pasa el tiempo!	How time flies!
El tiempo vuela.	Time flies.
¿Te das cuenta de lo rápido que pasa el tiempo?	Do you realize how fast time goes by?
¡Qué de prisa/despacio pasan las horas!	The hours pass so quickly/ slowly!
Vamos, date prisa/apresúrate que llegamos tarde.	Let's go! Hurry up or we'll be late.
Siempre de prisa./Siempre con prisas.	Always in a hurry./Always in a rush.

DE VIAJE — TRAVELING

¡Por fin (nos) vamos de viaje!	At last we're going on a trip!
Nos vamos.	We're leaving.
Es hora de irse/partir.	It's time to leave.
¡Todos a bordo!	All aboard!
Vamos de excursión.	We're going on a field trip/day trip.
¡Vámonos!	Let's go!
Estamos listos.	We're ready.
Buen viaje.	Have a good trip!/Bon voyage!
¡Que (te/le/les) vaya bien!	Have a nice time!/Hope it goes well!
¡Que lo pases/pasen bien!	Have a nice time!/Hope it goes well!
¡Que disfrutes/disfrute/disfruten!	Enjoy yourself/yourselves!
Nada de despedidas.	No goodbyes.
Feliz viaje y hasta la vuelta.	Have a nice trip. See you when you get back.

Nos vemos a la vuelta.	We'll see each other when you/we/I return.
¡Que se divierta/diviertan!	Have fun!
No olviden mandar una postal.	Don't forget to send a postcard.
A ver si nos escribes unas líneas.	Drop a line.

DE REGRESO

BACK HOME

¡Estamos de vuelta!	We're back!
Aquí estamos, sanos y salvos.	Here we are, safe and sound.
Bienvenidos.	Welcome.
¡Qué alegría!	Great!/Wonderful!
¿Qué tal el viaje?	How was your trip?
Indescriptible. Inolvidable.	Indescribable. Unforgettable.
¿Cómo (te/le/les) fue?	How was it?
Lo pasé/pasamos en grande.	I/We had a great time.
Lo pasé/pasamos super bien.	I/We had a terrific time.
No hay nada como volver a casa.	There's no place like home./It's great to be home.
Me alegro de que estés/esté/estén de vuelta.	I'm glad you're back.
Me alegra volver a verte/verlo/verlos.	It's nice to see you again.
Ya te/los echaba de menos./Ya te/los extrañaba.	I missed you.
¿Me/Nos echaste de menos?/¿Me/Nos extrañaste?	Did you miss me/us?
Te/Los eché muchísimo de menos./Te/Los extrañé muchísimo.	I missed you a lot.

Pues claro que te/los extrané.	Of course I missed you.
Estamos impacientes por ver las fotos.	We can't wait to see the pictures.
Hogar, dulce hogar.	Home sweet home.

EN CLASE

IN CLASS

Buenos días, clase.	Good morning, class.
Ahora voy a pasar lista.	Now I'll take the roll/attendance.
A ver… ¿Adams?	Let's see, Adams?
Presente.	Present./Here.
Ahora, presten atención.	Now pay attention.
Fíjense bien.	Pay attention.
¡Qué profe tan estupendo/a!	What a terrific professor!
La profesora de historia del arte es buenísima.	The art history professor is great.
Sabe muchísimo y además explica muy bien.	She knows a lot and explains everything so well.
Sus clases son muy interesantes, y aprendo mucho.	Her classes are really interesting, and I learn a lot.
¡Qué profe tan pesado/a!	That professor is a pain in the neck!
Siempre habla de lo mismo.	He/She says the same thing over and over again.
¡Qué clase más/tan aburrida!	What a boring class!
El próximo semestre (no) voy a tomar geografía.	Next semester I'm (not) going to take geography.
Las fechas no son mi fuerte.	I don't have a head for dates.
Tengo ganas de que se acabe/termine el curso.	I can't wait until this course is over.

Yo también tengo ganas de ir de vacaciones.	I also want a vacation.
Tranquilo, hombre. Sólo faltan los exámenes finales.	Take it easy, man. Just the final exams are left.
Uf, no quiero ni pensarlo.	Ugh, I don't even want to think about it.
Tengo que presentar un trabajo el próximo martes.	I have to hand in a paper next Tuesday.
Es sobre la sociología de las masas.	It's on the sociology of the masses.
Tengo tanto/tantísimo trabajo.	I have so much work.
No sé por dónde empezar.	I don't know where to begin.
No te preocupes.	Don't worry.
Vas a sacar unas notas de fábula, como siempre.	You're going to get excellent grades, as always.
Ya lo verás.	You'll see.
Tú siempre apruebas todos los exámenes.	You always pass all your exams.
Y además con buena nota.	And with a good grade to boot.

DESPUÉS DE CLASE

AFTER CLASS

Ay, dormilón/dormilona, ¿de dónde sales?	Hey, sleepyhead, where have you been?
¿Dónde estabas esta mañana?	Where were you this morning?
¿Se te pegaron las sábanas?	Couldn't you drag yourself out of bed?
La clase de historia estuvo muy interesante; como siempre.	History class was very interesting, as always.
Anoche no pegué ojo.	I didn't sleep a wink last night.
Estoy/Voy atrasado/a en álgebra.	I'm behind in algebra.
Soy fatal para las matemáticas.	I'm lousy in math.

A mí se me dan muy bien las ciencias en general.	I do very well in science, in general.
Si necesitas ayuda, te hecho una mano.	If you need help, I'll give you a hand.
Laura es una sabihonda, ¡se cree que lo sabe todo!	Laura is a know-it-all; she thinks she knows everything!
Su nombre de pila es Eduardo; su apodo es Dudu.	His given name is Eduardo; his nickname is Dudu.
¿Por qué estudia tanto ese individuo?	Why does that guy study so much?
Quiere (llegar a) ser presidente.	He/she wants to be president (some day).
Tiene fama de ambicioso.	He/she has a reputation for being ambitious.
No me digas. ¿En serio? ¿Me tomas el pelo?	You don't say. Seriously? Are you pulling my leg?
¿Cómo te fue en el examen de química?… Fatal./Estupendo.	How was the chemistry exam?… Terrible./Great.
El examen fue pan comido.	The exam was a piece of cake.
Tengo que ponerme al día en biología.	I need to catch up in biology.
No quiero suspender otra vez.	I don't want to flunk again.
Los exámenes finales ya están cerca.	Final exams are getting close.
Sí, están a la vuelta de la esquina.	Yes, they're just around the corner.
No sé qué me pasa.	I don't know what's happening to me.
No me puedo concentrar.	I can't concentrate.
Estoy lleno/a de dudas.	I'm full of doubts.

221

No me gusta nada la computación.	I don't like computer science at all.
A mí tampoco.	Neither do I.
A mí se me dan muy bien los idiomas.	I do very well with languages.
¡Qué casualidad! A mí también.	What a coincidence! Me too.
¡Qué coincidencia! Compartimos el mismo interés por las lenguas.	What a coincidence! We share an interest for languages.
Tengo mucho interés en las lenguas clásicas.	I'm very interested in classical languages.
¡Genial! A mí me interesa muchísimo el latín.	Great! I'm really interested in Latin.
El único inconveniente es que no tengo con quién practicarlo.	The only drawback is that I don't have anyone to practice with.
¿Te importa dejarme tus apuntes de literatura?	Would you mind lending me your literature notes?
En absoluto./Pues claro que no./Aquí los tienes./Aquí están.	Not at all. /Of course not./Here you go./Here they are.
Espero que entiendas mi letra.	I hope you can read my writing.
Tengo una letra horrible/ilegible.	My handwriting is terrible/illegible.
Pero están muy completos.	But they're very complete.

LA FAMILIA

YOUR FAMILY

¿Todos bien?	Is everyone well?
Sí, todos bien, gracias a Dios.	Yes, everyone's well, thank goodness.
¿Tienes muchos hermanos/parientes/sobrinos?	Do you have a lot of brothers and sisters/relatives/nieces and nephews?
¿Dónde viven tus padres?	Where do your parents live?

222

¿Visitas muy a menudo a tus familiares/parientes?	Do you visit your family/relatives often?
¿Son tus padres muy mayores?	Are your parents very old?
¿Vives con tus padres?	Do you live with your parents?
¿Quién es mayor, tu padre o tu madre?	Who is older, your father or your mother?
¿A qué se dedica tu padre/madre?	What does your father/mother do for a living?
¿Qué estudia tu hermano mayor?	What does your older brother study?
¿Tienen bisnietos tus abuelos?	Do your grandparents have great-grandchildren?
¿Conoces a todos tus primos?	Do you know all your cousins?
¿Son tus padres de la misma nacionalidad?	Are your parents of the same nationality?
¿Hablan tus padres español?	Do your parents speak Spanish?
¿Te llevas bien con tus hermanos?	Do you get along well with your brothers and sisters?
¿Dónde se conocieron tus padres?	Where did your parents meet?
¿Tienes familiares en el extranjero?	Do you have relatives abroad?
¿Dónde nacieron tus padres?	Where were your parents born?
¡Qué dicha ver a toda la familia junta!	What good fortune to see the whole family together!
Con una familia tan grande, siempre hay de qué/con quién hablar.	With such a big family, there is always something to talk about/someone to talk to.

EL OCIO

¿Dónde vas a ir este sábado?

¿Vas a hacer algo especial el domingo?

¿Tienes algún pasatiempo favorito/preferido?

¿Cuál es tu pasatiempo favorito/preferido?

¿Qué vas a hacer después de clase?

¿Qué vas a hacer este fin de semana?

Creo que voy a ir al zoológico.

La entrada es gratuita los fines de semana.

¿Puedes creerlo?

Y tú, ¿qué? ¿Vas a ir al cine este fin de semana?

Bah, ya estoy harto/a de ir al cine.

No hay ninguna película interesante.

¿Ves mucho la televisión?

¡Que va! Es terrible. Siempre hacen lo mismo.

Me gusta divertirme sin gastar mucho dinero.

Me gustan las actividades que no cuestan dinero.

LEISURE

Where are you going this Saturday?

Are you going to do anything special on Sunday?

Do you have a favorite pastime?

What is your favorite pastime?

What are you doing after class?

What are you doing this weekend?

I think I'll go to the zoo.

Admission is free on weekends.

Can you believe it?

What about you? Are you going to go to the movies this weekend?

I'm tired/sick of going to the movies.

There aren't any interesting movies.

Do you watch a lot of television?

No way! It's awful. It's always the same thing.

I like to have fun without spending too much money.

I like activities that don't cost money.

Oye, ¿por qué no vienes conmigo al zoológico?	Hey, why don't you come to the zoo with me?
Estupendo. ¡Decidido, pues!	Great. It's decided, then!
El domingo vamos los dos al zoológico. ¡Y no se hable más!	On Sunday the two of us will go to the zoo. That's settled!
A partir de ahora voy a comprar la guía del ocio todas las semanas.	From now on I'm going to buy the city entertainment guide every week.
Quiero estar informado de todas las actividades que tienen lugar en la ciudad.	I want to know about all the activities that take place in the city.
No quiero perderme nada, sobre todo si es gratis.	I don't want to miss anything, especially if it's free.
Nos vemos en el zoológico.	We'll see each other at the zoo.
¡Que se diviertan en el zoológico!	Have a good time at the zoo!

EXPRESIONES DEL TIEMPO

WEATHER EXPRESSIONS

¡Qué buen día hace hoy!	What a nice day it is today!
Hoy hace un día espléndido.	It's a beautiful day today.
El cielo está totalmente despejado.	The sky is perfectly clear.
No hay ni una nube.	There's not a cloud in the sky.
El hombre del tiempo pronosticó lluvia para el fin de semana.	The weatherman predicted rain for the weekend.
Afortunadamente, ¡se equivocó!	Fortunately, he was wrong!
Me pregunto qué tiempo va a hacer mañana.	I wonder what the weather will be like tomorrow.
¡Últimamente el tiempo es tan variable!	The weather has been so variable lately!
Sí, es imprevisible. No es fácil adivinar/predecir.	Yes, it's unpredictable. It's not easy to predict.

USEFUL EXPRESSIONS

Mañana (dicen que) va a caer un aguacero.	Tomorrow (they say that) there will be a downpour.
Llueve a cántaros.	It's raining cats and dogs.
Y yo sin paraguas. ¡Qué contratiempo!	And me without an umbrella. How annoying!
No salgas sin paraguas.	Don't leave/go out without an umbrella.
Si llueve y hace sol, va a salir el arco iris.	If it rains and the sun comes out, there will be a rainbow.
¡Qué emoción! Me fascinan los arco iris.	Cool! I love rainbows.
A ver si vemos uno bien grande.	Maybe we'll see a nice big one.
¡Qué lunes tan horrible!	What a horrible Monday!
Hace viento y hace frío.	It's windy and it's cold.
¡Qué día tan feo! Es feo con ganas.	What an awful day! It's awful and then some.
Hay mucha niebla y no se ve nada.	There's a lot of fog and you can't see anything.
Hoy hace un día para no salir de casa/para quedarse en casa.	Today is a nice day to stay home.
¡Que pase/tenga un buen día!	Have a nice day!
Igualmente.	Same to you.

EN LA AGENCIA DE VIAJES

AT THE TRAVEL AGENCY

Bueno, ¡menos mal! Parece que hoy está abierto.	Okay, great! It looks like it's open today.
Quisiéramos dos pasajes para Octopulco, ida y vuelta.	We'd like two round-trip tickets to Octopulco.
En primera clase, por supuesto.	In first class, of course.
Cómo no.	But of course.

¿Para qué día?	For what day?
¿Cuándo quieren regresar?	When would you like to return?
Queremos hospedarnos en un hotel de cinco estrellas/hotel barato.	We'd like to stay in a five-star hotel/an inexpensive hotel.
¿Cuántos días van a quedarse?	How many days will you stay?
Nos vamos a quedar quince días.	We're going to stay two weeks.
¿Quieren alquilar un auto?	Do you want to rent a car?
No, no hace falta.	No, we don't need one.
La isla es pequeña. Podemos ir en bicicleta.	The island is small. We can get around by bike.
Aquí tienen sus pasajes.	Here are your tickets.

EN EL AEROPUERTO

AT THE AIRPORT

¿Dónde está la aerolínea Gavilán?	Where is Gavilán Airlines?
Vuelo 8778	Flight 8778
Destino Octopulco	Destination: Octopulco
¿Cancelado?… No, retrasado.	Canceled? . . . No, delayed.
Bueno, pues a esperar.	Okay, then we'll wait.
¡Estoy cansado/a de esperar en los aeropuertos!	I'm tired of waiting in airports!
¿Debemos facturar el equipaje ahora?	Should we check our luggage now?
Me olvidé el itinerario.	I forgot the itinerary.
Al menos es un vuelo directo, sin escalas.	At least it's a direct flight, without any stopovers.
¿Dónde está la tienda libre de impuestos?	Where is the duty-free shop?

USEFUL EXPRESSIONS

Da igual. No tenemos tiempo. Ya vamos a embarcar.	It doesn't matter. We don't have time. We're going to board now.
Esta maleta pesa demasiado/es demasiado pesada.	This suitcase weighs too much/is too heavy.
Voy a buscar un carrito.	I'm going to look for a cart.
Yo prefiero viajar ligero de equipaje.	I prefer to travel light.
A la vuelta debemos pasar por la aduana.	On the way back we have to go through customs.
¿Algo que declarar?	Anything to declare?
No, nada.	No, nothing.

EN EL HOTEL

AT THE HOTEL

Bienvenidos al hotel Miramar.	Welcome to the Hotel Miramar.
Por fin llegamos.	Finally we're here.
¿Tuvieron un vuelo agradable?	Did you have a good flight?
¡Qué vuelo tan largo!	What a long flight!
Lo sentimos, pero el ascensor/el elevador no funciona hoy.	We're sorry, but the elevator is out of order today.
Deben subir por las escaleras.	You need to take the stairs.
Por suerte están Uds. en el primer piso.	Luckily you're on the second floor.
Ésta es la mejor habitación con vista(s) al mar.	This is the best room with an ocean view.
Esperamos que todo sea de su agrado.	We hope that everything will be to your liking.
Cualquier cosa que necesiten, llamen a recepción.	If you need anything, call the front desk.
Gracias por hospedarse en/elegir nuestro hotel.	Thank you for staying in/choosing our hotel.

228

Esperamos que tengan una estancia agradable.	We hope you have an enjoyable stay.
¡Que tengan una feliz estancia!	Have a nice stay!

EN LA PLAYA

AT THE BEACH

¡Qué belleza de paisaje!	What beautiful scenery!
Pues, espera a ver el atardecer.	Wait until you see the sunset.
Dicen que es de película.	They say it's fantastic.
¡Qué paz!	What peace!
¡Qué aire tan puro y fresco!	What pure, fresh air!
No hay nada como la brisa del mar.	There's nothing like a sea breeze.
¡Qué calor!	It's so hot!
Este verano no quiero quemarme.	This summer I don't want to get sunburned.
¡Cuánta gente!	What a lot of people!
Pensaba que veníamos a una isla desierta.	I though we were going to a desert island.
¡Qué tonto/a! Me olvidé el traje de baño.	How stupid! I forgot my bathing suit.
Hoy no me apetece hacer nada.	Today I'm not in the mood to do anything.
Voy a contemplar el paisaje y pasear por la orilla.	I'm going to contemplate the scenery and take a walk along the shore.

¿QUÉ ME PONGO PARA LA FIESTA DEL SÁBADO?

WHAT SHOULD I WEAR TO THE PARTY SATURDAY?

¡Qué problema!	What a problem!
No tengo nada que ponerme.	I don't have anything to wear.
Necesito renovar mi vestuario.	I need a new wardrobe.

No tengo nada que me guste.	I don't have anything that I like.
Estoy harta de ponerme siempre la misma ropa.	I'm tired of always wearing the same clothes.
Lo que necesitas es un cambio de imagen.	You need a new image.
Sí, tienes razón.	Yes, you're right.
Es justo lo que necesito.	It's just what I need.
¿Quieres ser mi asesor de imagen?	Would you like to be my image consultant?
Esta misma tarde voy a ir al centro (comercial) a ver qué encuentro.	This afternoon I'm going to the mall/downtown to see what I can find.
Esta semana hay unas rebajas espectaculares.	This week there are some great discounts.
No me gustan los mercados; odio regatear.	I don't like markets; I hate to haggle.

EN LA TIENDA DE ROPA PARA DAMAS

IN THE WOMEN'S CLOTHING STORE

¡Cuánta variedad! ¡Cuánto colorido!	What variety! So many colors!
Va a ser difícil decidir.	It's going to be hard to decide.
Quiero un vestido bien llamativo.	I want an attractive dress.
Señorita, ¿podría probarme este vestido?	Miss, may I try on this dress?
Naturalmente. El probador está al fondo a la derecha.	Of course. The fitting room is in the back to the right.
Uy, me queda un poco justo.	Aw, it's a little too small.
Necesito una talla más grande.	I need a bigger size.
¿Qué talla quiere?	What size do you want?
La mediana, por favor.	Medium, please.

Sí, éste me sienta bien/mejor.	Yes, this one fits me well/better.
¿Cuál te gusta más, el rojo o el negro?	Which do you like better, the red or the black?
El negro te va como anillo al dedo.	The black one suits you to a "T."
El color negro te favorece.	You look good in black.
Te ves más delgada.	It makes you look thinner.
Sí, el rojo no me sienta tan bien.	Yes, the red one doesn't fit me as well.
Te ves muy atractiva con ese vestido.	You look very attractive in that dress.
¡Y qué suave es!	And it's so soft!
¡Buena compra!	A good buy!
Ahora necesitas otro bolso.	Now you need another purse.
Ese bolso no va (bien) con el vestido.	This purse doesn't go (well) with this dress.
Y también unos zapatos a juego.	And also shoes to match.
Espérame, voy a pagar el vestido y nos vamos a una zapatería.	Wait, I'll pay for the dress, then we'll go to a shoe store.
¿Cuánto vale?	How much does it cost?
Uy, baratísimo.	Oh, really inexpensive/cheap.
¡Hoy es mi día de suerte!/¡Hoy estoy de suerte!	Today is my lucky day!
¿Vamos a la zapatería?	Shall we go to the shoe store?

EN LA TIENDA DE ROPA PARA CABALLEROS

IN THE MEN'S CLOTHING STORE

Necesito un traje bien elegante.	I need an elegant suit.
¿De qué color lo quiere?	What color would you like?

231

No sé... ¿Qué me sugiere Ud.?	I don't know . . . What would you suggest?
Un color oscuro le quedará/sentará bien.	You'd look good in a dark color.
Venga por aquí, joven.	Come over hear, young man.
¿Qué talla usa?	What size do you wear?
No sé, es mi primer traje.	I don't know. It's my first suit.
Bueno, Ud. debe usar la talla 52 para la chaqueta... y la talla 32 para los pantalones.	Well, you should wear a size 52 jacket . . . and size 32 pants.
A ver, pruébese este traje azul marino... ¿Qué tal?	Let's see. Try on this dark blue suit. What do you think?
Le queda perfecto.	It fits you perfectly.
Parece hecho a su medida.	It looks like it was made for you.
Ahora necesita una bonita camisa.	Now you need a nice shirt.
¿La prefiere blanca o azul?	Would you like white or blue?
¿Blanca?	White?
Muy bien. Tenga, pruébese ésta.	Okay. Here you are. Try on this one.
Es la talla 16.	It's size 16.
Sí, me gusta...¡Qué tela más fina!	Yes, I like it. . . . What nice material!
Ahora sólo falta el último toque... ¡la corbata!	Now all you need is the last touch . . .a tie!
¿Qué tal esta roja?	How about this red one?
Ni hablar... demasiado llamativa.	Don't even suggest it . . . too flashy.
Necesitamos un color más suave.	We need a more muted color.

Azul celeste… Confíe en mí.	Light blue . . . trust me.
Mire, pruébese ésta… Es de seda italiana.	Look, try this one on. It's Italian silk.
Está Ud. impecable.	You are impeccable.
Pues sí, parezco otra persona.	Yes, I look like another person.
No sabía que era tan guapo.	I didn't know I was so handsome.
Muchísimas gracias por su ayuda.	Thanks so much for your help.
¿Cuánto le debo?	How much do I owe you?

LA RUTINA DIARIA — DAILY ROUTINE

¿Necesitas simplificar tu vida?	Do you need to simplify your life?
¿A qué hora te levantas?	What time do you get up?
¿Qué es lo primero que haces al levantarte?	What's the first thing you do when you get up?
¿Desayunas en casa?	Do you have/eat breakfast at home?
¿Qué desayunas? ¿Tostadas con mantequilla?	What do you have/eat for breakfast? Toast with butter?
¿Desayunas lo mismo todos los días?	Do you have/eat the same thing for breakfast every day?
¿Te vistes antes de desayunar o desayunas primero y luego te vistes?	Do you get dressed before breakfast or do you eat breakfast first and then get dressed?
¿A qué hora sales de casa?	What time do you leave the house?
¿Cuánto tiempo necesitas para prepararte por la mañana?	How much time do you need to get ready in the morning?
¿Te gusta ir de prisa o te tomas las cosas con calma?	Do you like to be quick or do you take your time?
¿A qué hora almuerzas?	What time do you eat lunch?

¿Dónde? ¿Con quién?	Where? With whom?
¿Te gusta almorzar solo o acompañado/a?	Do you like to eat lunch alone or with other people?
¿Estudias, trabajas o haces las dos cosas?	Are you studying, working, or both?
¿Qué haces de las 3 a las 5 de la tarde?	What do you do from 3:00 to 5:00 in the afternoon?
¿Qué haces después de las clases/después del trabajo?	What do you do after class/after work?
¿A qué hora regresas a casa?	What time do you get home?
¿Llegas muy tarde a casa por la noche?	Do you get home very late at night?
¿Qué es lo primero que haces al llegar a casa?	What's the first thing you do when you get home?
¿A qué hora cenas?	What time do you eat/have dinner?
¿Qué haces después de cenar?	What do you do after dinner?
¿Cuántas veces al día te lavas los dientes?	How many times a day do you brush your teeth?
¿A qué hora te vas a dormir/te acuestas?	What time do you go to sleep/to bed?
¿Qué es lo último que haces antes de acostarte?	What is the last thing you do before going to bed?
¿Cuántas horas duermes?	How many hours do you sleep?
¿Crees que duermes pocas horas?	Do you think you don't get enough sleep?
¿Es necesaria la rutina?	Is routine necessary?
¿Estás contento/a con tu rutina?	Are you happy with your routine?
¿Pierdes mucho tiempo por las mañanas?	Do you waste a lot of time in the morning?

¿Cuál es tu secreto para ganar tiempo libre?

What is your secret for finding free time?

EN EL RESTAURANTE

AT THE RESTAURANT

¿Mesa para dos?

Table for two?

¡Qué ambiente más selecto!

What an exclusive place!

Este lugar es muy acogedor.

This place is very cozy.

Está decorado con mucho gusto.

This place is decorated in very good taste.

Sin duda es el restaurante más caro de la ciudad.

Without a doubt, this is the most expensive restaurant in the city.

Tiene fama de ser excelente… y de ser carísimo.

It is supposed to be excellent . . . and very expensive.

Todo el mundo habla muy bien de este sitio.

Everyone speaks very well of this place.

Los cubiertos son de plata.

The silverware is real silver.

A ver el menú.

Let's look at the menu.

Aquí tienen el menú.

Here's the menu.

Mmm, se me hace la boca agua.

Mmm, it makes my mouth water.

No sé qué pedir.

I don't know what to order.

¿Qué nos sugiere?

What do you suggest?

Pidan lo que más les guste.

Order whatever you like the best.

Todo es exquisito, sin excepción.

Everything is superb, without exception.

Esta carne está en su punto.

This meat is just right.

¡Qué ensalada más original!

What an original salad!

Sí, combina frutas y verduras.

Yes, it combines fruit and vegetables.

El aderezo/aliño es divino.

The dressing is divine.

¿Nos trae la carta de vinos, por favor?	Would you bring us the wine list, please?
No me gusta el vino tinto; prefiero el vino blanco.	I don't like red wine; I prefer white wine.
Yo no puedo tomar vino de ningún color; enseguida me emborracho.	I can't drink wine of any color; it goes right to my head.
Tenemos una selección de postres que les va a encantar.	You're going to love our dessert selection.
¡Qué carta de postres más creativa!	What a creative dessert menu!
Tiremos la casa por la ventana.	Let's go all out.
Probémoslos todos.	Let's try everything.
Camarero/a, nos trae la cuenta (cuando pueda), por favor.	Waiter, please bring us the check (when you can).
¿Cuánto se debe?	How much is it?
Quédese con el cambio.	Keep the change.
Nos quedamos sin plata/dinero.	We're broke.
¡Qué velada más/tan agradable!	What a pleasant evening!
¿A quién vamos a recomendar este restaurante?	To whom are we going to recommend this restaurant?

EL ALMUERZO — LUNCH

Spanish	English
¡A comer!	Lunch is ready!
¿Qué hay para comer?	What is there/do we have to eat?
¡Qué hambre tengo!	I'm so hungry!
Estoy muerto/a de hambre./Me muero de hambre.	I'm starved.
Tengo un hambre feroz.	I'm famished./I could eat a horse.
Yo me lo como todo.	I'll eat anything.

236

Pues yo no. Estoy harto/a de lentejas.	Well, not me. I'm tired of lentils.
¿Otra vez lo mismo?	The same thing again?
No tengo (nada de) hambre.	I'm not hungry (at all).
¡Mmm, qué bien huele!	Mmm, it smells good!
Este estofado sabe a gloria.	This casserole tastes heavenly.
Esta sopa quema.	This soup is burning hot.
¡Pues sopla!	So blow on it!
Por favor, ¿me pasas la sal?	Please pass the salt.
¿Qué es esto rojo?	What's this red stuff?
Esta carne no me la como, está cruda.	I won't eat this meat, it's raw.
No me gusta este pescado, tiene muchas espinas.	I don't like this fish, it has lots of bones.
Esta salsa es demasiado picante/pica demasiado.	This sauce is too spicy.
¿Qué hay de postre?	What's for dessert?
Yo estoy lleno/a.	I'm full.
Claro, te comiste todo el pan.	Of course, you ate all the bread.
Voy a explotar.	I'm going to explode.
Mejor dejo el postre para la noche.	I'd better leave dessert until later tonight.
¡Coman, coman!	Eat up!
¡Buen provecho!/¡Que aproveche!	Enjoy your meal!

CELEBRACIONES

¡Estamos de fiesta!	Let's celebrate!
¿Qué se celebra?	What is being celebrated?

CELEBRATIONS

EL NACIMIENTO DE NUESTRO HIJO

	THE BIRTH OF OUR SON
Mi esposa dio a luz a nuestro tercer hijo.	My wife gave birth to our third child/son.
¿Cuándo nació?	When was he born?
El 1º de enero.	January first.
¡Enhorabuena! ¡Felicidades!	Congratulations!
¡Es un niño precioso!	What a beautiful child!

EL CUMPLEAÑOS DE MI HERMANO JORGE

	MY BROTHER JORGE'S BIRTHDAY
¿Cuántos años cumple?	How old is he?
Dieciocho. Ya es mayor de edad.	Eighteen. He's of legal age now.
¡Cuántos amigos y amigas tiene tu hermano!	Your brother has so many friends!
En esta fiesta no cabe ni un alfiler.	This party is packed.
¡Muchísimas felicidades, Jorge!	Best wishes, Jorge!
¡Y que cumplas muchos más!	And may you have many more!

LA GRADUACIÓN DE MARGARITA

	MARGARITA'S GRADUATION
Es nuestra hija más pequeña.	She's our youngest daughter.
Se acaba de graduar en geología.	She's just graduated with a degree in geology.
Estamos muy orgullosos de ella.	We're very proud of her.
¡Felicidades!	Congratulations!
¡Por un futuro brillante!	To a bright future!

EL ANIVERSARIO DE BODAS DE MIS PADRES

	MY PARENTS' ANNIVERSARY
¿Cuántos años hace que se casaron?	How many years have they been married?

Cincuenta. Celebran sus bodas de oro.	Fifty. They are celebrating their golden anniversary.
Y aún se quieren como cuando eran recién casados.	They still love each other as much as they did when they were newlyweds.
¡Qué maravilla!	How wonderful!
¡Feliz aniversario!	Happy anniversary!
¡Y que celebren muchos más!	May you have many more!
La boda de mi tía Carolina	*My aunt Carolina's wedding*
¡Qué dicha!	What good fortune!
¡Que sean muy felices!	May they be very happy!
¡Que se besen los novios!	A kiss!
Un brindis por los recién casados.	A toast to the newlyweds.
¡Vivan los novios!	Long live the newlyweds!
DAR EL PÉSAME	GIVING CONDOLENCES
Estamos de luto.	We're in mourning.
¡Qué desgracia!	How unfortunate!
Murió Roberto.	Roberto died.
¡Qué lastima!	What a shame!
Pobre Roberto, era tan joven.	Poor Roberto, he was so young.
Estamos todos muy apenados/tristes.	We're all very sad.
Le acompaño en el sentimiento.	My thoughts are with you.
Reciba nuestro más sincero pésame.	Our deepest sympathies.
No sé qué decir.	I don't know what to say.
Sólo puedo llorar.	I can only cry.

239

USEFUL EXPRESSIONS

Lo vamos a echar mucho de menos.	We're going to miss him very much.
EN EL CONSULTORIO	IN THE DOCTOR'S OFFICE
¡Me duele todo el cuerpo!	My whole body aches!
¿Cuál es el problema?	What is the problem?
¿Qué le pasa?	What's the matter?
¿Dónde le duele?	Where does it hurt?
¿Qué síntomas tiene?	What are your symptoms?
¿Cuáles son sus síntomas?	What are your symptoms?
¿Cómo se encuentra hoy?	How are you feeling today?
Mejor./Peor.	Better./Worse.
Doctor, parece que no mejoro.	Doctor, it seems like I'm not getting better.
¿Se encuentra mejor hoy?	Are you feeling better today?
Al contrario, cada día estoy peor.	No, just the opposite, every day I'm worse.
¿Qué dicen los resultados de los análisis?	What do the test results show?
Tiene Ud. el colesterol muy alto/por las nubes.	Your cholesterol is very high/sky-high.
¿(Le) Duele?	Does it hurt?
Sólo va a notar un pinchazo.	You'll only feel a pinch.
¿Me va a doler, doctor?	Will it hurt, doctor?
Esto le va a doler un poco.	This will hurt a little.
Ay, creo que me voy a desmayar.	Oh, I think I'm going to faint.
Me aterran las agujas.	I'm afraid of needles.
No va a sentir ningún dolor.	You won't feel any pain.

Le vamos a operar con aneste-sia local/general.	We'll operate with local/general anesthesia.
¡Qué valiente es Vicente!	Vicente is so brave!
¿Hay que operar?	Do you have to operate?
¿Me quedará cicatriz?	Will I have/it leave a scar?
¿Podré volver a caminar/andar?	Will I be able to walk again?
¿Cuánto dura el tratamiento?	How long will the treatment last?
Doctor, ¿puede recetarme algo para el dolor?	Doctor, can you prescribe me something for the pain?
Inyecciones no, por favor.	Please, no shots.
¿No hay otra solución?	There's no other solution?
Le recomiendo que siga el tratamiento al pie de la letra.	I recommend that you follow the treatment to the letter.
¿Qué efectos secundarios tiene este medicamento?	What are the side effects of this medication?
Produce vómito y somnolencia.	It causes vomiting and drowsi-ness.
¿Qué opciones tengo?	What options do I have?
¿Va a tomarme la presión?	Are you going to take my blood pressure?
Tiene Ud. la presión/tensión muy alta/baja.	You have very high/low pressure.
¿Cuándo empezó a fumar?	When did you start smoking?
¿Cuántos años hace que fuma?	How many years have you been smoking?
Debe dejar de fumar YA.	You must stop smoking NOW.
Le aconsejo que deje de fumar cuanto antes.	I advise you to stop smoking immediately.
El tabaco perjudica la salud.	Tobacco jeopardizes your health.

Durante el embarazo no debe fumar ni consumir alcohol.	While you're pregnant, you shouldn't smoke or drink alcohol.
Debe Ud. ver a un especialista.	You need to see a specialist.
Es una enfermedad muy grave.	It's a very serious illness.
Conocemos los síntomas, pero no las causas.	We are familiar with the symptoms, but not the causes.
El pronóstico es grave/favorable.	The prognosis is serious/good.
Lo que yo necesito es reposo indefinido.	What I need is a prolonged rest.

LA COMUNICACIÓN TELEFÓNICA

TELEPHONING

¿Con quién hablo?	With whom am I speaking?
Soy el vecino de al lado…	I'm the next-door neighbor.
¿Quién es? ¿Quién?	Who is it? Who?
Hable más fuerte. No oigo./No oigo nada.	Please, speak up. I can't hear you/a thing.
Soy Juan, tu vecino.	It's Juan, your neighbor.
¿Te importaría bajar el volumen del radio, por favor?	Would you mind turning the radio down, please?
¿Podría hablar con el director?	May I speak with the director?
Por favor, me pone con el Sr. Ramos.	May I speak with Mr. Ramos, please?
¿De parte de quién? ¿Quién lo llama?	May I tell him/ask who's calling?
Dígale que lo llama Ruti, su primo.	Tell him that his cousin Ruti is calling.
Espere un momentito, ahora pongo.	Just a minute, here he is.
No cuelgue por favor, ahora paso.	Don't hang up, please; here he is.

Oiga, el Sr. Ramos salió a almorzar.	Oh, Mr. Ramos is out to lunch.
¿Quiere dejar un mensaje?	Would you like to leave a message?
No, yo vuelvo a llamar mañana.	No, I'll call back tomorrow.
Dígale que me llame, por favor.	Tell him to call me, please.
¿Quiere que le devuelva la llamada cuando regrese?	Would you like me to have him call you when he gets back?
Pues sí. Gracias.	Yes, thanks.
Mire, mi número es el 001-1100.	My number is 001-1100.
¿Es éste el 010-0110?	Is this 010-0110?
Lo siento, se ha equivocado de número.	I'm sorry, you have the wrong number.
Disculpe.	Oh, excuse me./I'm sorry.
Vuelva a marcar.	Try dialing again.
Estoy esperando una llamada importante.	I'm expecting an important call.
¡Ese teléfono no para de sonar!	That phone won't stop ringing/is ringing off the hook!
¿Quieres hacer el favor de contestar el teléfono?	Would you please answer the phone?
¿Cómo? ¿No tienes contestador automático?	What? You don't have an answering machine?
Señora, tiene una llamada a cobro revertido. ¿Acepta Ud. la llamada?	Ma'am, you have a collect call. Will you accept the call?
Hago un sinfín de llamadas de larga distancia e internacionales.	I make a ton of long distance and international calls.

USEFUL EXPRESSIONS

243

La factura del teléfono me cuesta cada mes una fortuna/un dineral.	My phone bill costs a fortune each month.
Ring, riiiing,... riiiiiiing. No contestan.	Ring, ring, riiing. No answer.
Parece que la línea está ocupada.	It seems that the line is busy.
Llama/e a la operadora.	Call the operator.
¿A qué número llama?	What number are you calling?
Ay, olvidé el número.	Oh, I forgot the number.
Llame a información. Marque el 003.	Call information. Dial 003.
Para más información, llame al 1-800-289-1948.	For more information, call 1-800-289-1948.
Las líneas están abiertas 24 horas al día, siete días a la semana.	The lines are open 24 hours a day, seven days a week.

LOS APARATOS

MECHANICAL DEVICES

¿Cómo funciona esto?	How does this thing work?
¿Y me preguntas a mí?	You're asking me?
¡Qué sé yo!	What do I know?
¿Y a mí me lo preguntas?	You're asking me?
No tengo ni (la más mínima) idea.	I have no idea./I haven't the foggiest idea.
Las máquinas me asustan.	Machines frighten me.
Las instrucciones me aburren.	Instructions bore me.
¿No hay una versión abreviada?	Isn't there a shorter version?
¿Cuándo viene el técnico a arreglar la antena?	When is the repair man coming to fix the antenna?

Hace semanas que no funciona el televisor.	It's been weeks since the television worked.
Me vuelvo loco/a sin la caja tonta.	I'm going crazy without the idiot box.
Creo que quiero una computadora portátil.	I think I want a laptop.
Están de moda.	They are in style.
Son prácticas, ¿no?	They're practical, aren't they?
¿Cómo se pone en marcha este trasto?	How do you get this thing/piece of junk to work?
Esta máquina de coser funciona a las mil maravillas.	This sewing machine works like a dream.
No sé qué haría sin ella.	I don't know what I would do without it.
En fin, ¿qué más?	So, what else?

LOS AUTOMÓVILES

CARS

¿Necesito carro?	Do I need a car?
A lo mejor me compro uno de segunda mano.	Maybe I should get a used one.
Cuanto más barato sea, mejor, ¿no?	The cheaper the better, no?
Total, ¿qué más da? Se va a estropear/descomponer igual.	Bah, what does it matter? It will break down just the same.
Al menos si me cuesta barato, no me preocupo tanto.	At least if it's cheap, I won't worry too much.
Un carro puede durar muchos años si lo cuidas bien.	A car can last many years if you take good care of it.
Creo que voy a vender mi carro viejo y me voy a comprar uno nuevo.	I think I'll sell my old car and buy a new one.

245

USEFUL EXPRESSIONS

Pero no puedo tomar una decisión sin ton ni son.	But I can't make a decision willy nilly.
Esto es un asunto serio.	This is a serious matter.
Debo pensarlo bien.	I should think it over well.
A ver, ¿qué tipo de carro me conviene más?	Let's see, what kind of car is best for me?
¿Uno automático o uno de marchas?	An automatic or manual transmission?
¿Uno deportivo o uno familiar?	A sports car or a family car?
¿Uno de lujo o uno todo terreno?	A luxury car or an all-terrain vehicle?
¿Cuánto dinero me quiero gastar?	How much money do I want to spend?
¿Qué es lo más importante a la hora de comprar un carro?	What is the most important thing when it comes time to buy a car?
¿Cuál es mi máxima necesidad/prioridad?	What is my top priority?
¿Una carretera sin baches?	A road without potholes?
Pero pensándolo bien/mejor, ¿para qué necesito yo un carro?	But, on second thought, what do I need a car for?
¿Qué sé yo de mecánica?	What do I know about mechanics?

LAS AVERÍAS

BREAKDOWNS

Otra vez al mecánico.	To the mechanic again.
Este carro es un tremendo dolor de cabeza.	This car is a big headache.
Se estropea/descompone cada dos por tres.	It breaks down all the time.
Cuando no es una cosa es otra.	If it's not one thing, it's another.
El mes pasado eran los frenos.	Last month it was the brakes.

Hace dos meses, el cambio de marchas.	Two months ago, the gear shift.
Ayer, el intermitente delantero izquierdo.	Yesterday, the front left directional signal.
Ya te digo, me da más problemas que alegrías/satisfacciones.	I'm telling you, it's more trouble than it's worth.
Cada reparación me cuesta una fortuna/un ojo de la cara.	Every repair costs a fortune/an arm and a leg.
Además, es dificilísimo encontrar un buen mecánico en quien poder confiar.	And it's so hard to find a good, trustworthy mechanic.
Encontrar un buen mecánico es como buscar una aguja en un pajar.	Finding a good mechanic is like finding a needle in a haystack.
Ahora llevo el tubo de escape colgando y, cuando llueve, no hay quien lo ponga en marcha.	Now my exhaust pipe is hanging, and when it rains the car won't start.

EN LA CARRETERA

ON THE HIGHWAY

Iba yo conduciendo tan tranquilo/a y me paró la policía.	I was just driving along and the police pulled me over.
Me paró un policía de tráfico…	A traffic cop stopped me…
Aparentemente, por ir demasiado despacio.	Apparently, for driving too slowly.
La velocidad límite era de 65 millas por hora.	The speed limit was 65 miles per hour.
Yo iba a 15 millas por hora.	I was going 15 miles per hour.
Le dije que no tenía gasolina.	I told him that I didn't have gas.
El policía se hizo el sordo y me puso una multa.	The policeman didn't listen and gave me a fine.
Fue inútil discutir.	It was pointless to argue about it.

247

Me pregunto quién la va a pagar.	I'm wondering who is going to pay it.
¿Dónde hay una estación de servicio?	Where is there a service station?
Necesito llenar el tanque/el depósito.	I need to fill the tank.

UNA VIVIENDA DESASTROSA

A DISASTROUS HOUSE

¡Esta casa es un desastre!	This house is a disaster!
¡Qué casa, madre mía! Un frigorífico en invierno y un horno en verano.	What a house! A refrigerator in the winter and an oven in the summer.
Las luces se encienden y se apagan cuando les da la gana.	The lights turn on and off when they feel like it.
¿Electrodomésticos? ¿Para qué?	Appliances? For what?
Por la noche hay que tener las velas preparadas.	At night we have to have candles ready.
Siempre hay que estar prevenido (por lo que pueda pasar).	You always have to be prepared (for what may happen).
Ninguna puerta cierra bien; ninguna ventana abre bien.	None of the doors close tight; none of the windows open easily.
Las paredes son de papel.	The walls are paper thin.
No existe la intimidad.	There is no privacy.
El gato que tenía se ha mudado.	The cat I had has moved.
La ropa sale de la lavadora tal y como estaba.	The clothes come out of the washing machine the same as they went in.
Las goteras inundan el altillo.	The leaks flood the attic.
El día que llueve es todo un espectáculo.	When it rains, it's a show.

248

No queda pintura en la fachada.

There's no paint left on the outside.

Y esta escalera de caracol es una pesadilla a cualquier hora del día.

And this spiral staircase is a nightmare at any time of day.

Las sorpresas no faltan viviendo en tal casa.

We have no lack of surprises living in such a house.

¿Por qué no vienen Uds. mañana?

Why don't you come over tomorrow?

LA VIVIENDA PERFECTA

THE PERFECT HOUSE

¡Qué ilusión me hace tener una casa!

How I'd love to own a house!

Una casa bien grande, con jardín y con terraza.

A fairly large house, with a garden and a patio.

Siempre he querido ser ama de casa.

I have always wanted to be a housewife.

Limpiar, ordenar y lavar a todas horas del día.

Cleaning, straightening up, and washing at all hours of the day.

Cantar y cantar mientras preparo la comida.

Singing and singing while I prepare the meals.

Tener una cocina moderna y práctica a la vez.

I'd have a kitchen that was both modern and practical.

Tener electrodomésticos de todos los colores y tamaños.

I'd have appliances of all shapes and colors.

Pues no son sólo trastos; algunos te echan una mano.

They're not just pieces of junk; some help you out.

Y con un lavaplatos, todo está limpio y ordenado.

And with a dishwasher, all is clean and organized.

¡Qué maravilla! ¡Qué sueño de vida!

How wonderful! What a dream of a life!

MEDIO AMBIENTE Y ECOLOGÍA

Parece que la contaminación del aire crece a un ritmo alarmante.

El dióxido de carbono es cada vez más abundante en la atmósfera.

La sequía es un grave problema en muchos países de África.

Las aguas de los ríos, océanos y mares están cada vez más contaminadas.

El agujero de la capa de ozono sigue creciendo.

Los incendios forestales y las inundaciones están a la orden del día.

ENVIRONMENT AND ECOLOGY

It seems that air pollution is growing at an alarming rate.

There is more and more carbon dioxide in the atmosphere.

Drought is a serious problem in many African countries.

Rivers, oceans, and seas are becoming more and more polluted.

The hole in the ozone layer keeps growing.

Forest fires and floods are everyday events.

PREGUNTAS SOBRE ECOLOGÍA

¿Está en peligro la vida en la Tierra?

¿A quién afecta la destrucción del medio ambiente?

¿Qué predicen los científicos para dentro de cincuenta años?

¿Qué consecuencias puede tener el calentamiento global de la Tierra?

¿Es posible que se deshielen los casquetes polares?

ENVIRONMENTAL QUESTIONS

Is life on earth in danger?

Who does the destruction of the environment affect?

What do scientists predict for the next fifty years?

What can the consequences of global warming be?

Is it possible that the polar caps will melt?

¿Crees que hay solución a los problemas actuales de contaminación?

Do you think there's a solution to the current pollution problems?

¿Cuáles son las condiciones medioambientales óptimas que garantizan la existencia de los seres vivos en la Tierra?

What are the optimal environmental conditions that guarantee the existence of living beings on earth?

¿Qué medidas se pueden tomar para poner marcha atrás al problema de la contaminación atmosférica? ¿Y de la contaminación del agua?

What measures can be taken to reverse the problem of atmospheric pollution? And of water pollution?

¿Qué medidas generales se pueden adoptar para conservar la naturaleza?

What general measures can be adopted to conserve nature?

¿Qué países producen más basura? ¿Cuáles consumen más recursos naturales?

What countries produce the most garbage? Consume more natural resources?

¿Perteneces a alguna organización dedicada a la conservación del medio ambiente?

Do you belong to an organization dedicated to environmental conservation?

¿Crees que son exagerados los datos sobre el calentamiento global del planeta?

Do you think the global warming data is exaggerated?

¿Crees que es todo una farsa? ¿Una exageración de los Verdes?

Do you think it is all a farce? An exaggeration of the Green Party?

¿Cómo afecta la tala de árboles al ecosistema?

How does the cutting of trees affect the ecosystem?

¿Cuáles son en tu opinión las principales causas del creciente deterioro medioambiental?

In your opinion, what are the main causes of the increasing environmental degradation?

¿De qué modo colaboras tú en la conservación de la naturaleza?

In what way do you help in the conservation of nature?

¿Quién tiene la culpa del deterioro medioambiental? ¿Hay algún culpable?

Whose fault is environmental degradation? Is anyone at fault?

DAR Y PEDIR DIRECCIONES

GIVING AND ASKING FOR DIRECTIONS

¿Por dónde se va al centro?

How do I get downtown?

Sigan todo recto/derecho hasta el final de esta calle.

Keep going straight until you get to the end of this street.

Luego doblen/giren a la derecha.

Then turn right.

Sigan tres cuadras y ya están en pleno centro.

Go three blocks and you'll be right downtown.

Señor, ¿sabe cómo llegar al Museo Nacional de Arte Contemporáneo?

Sir, do you know how to get to the National Museum of Contemporary Art?

Está en la otra punta de la ciudad.

It's on the other side of the city.

Está demasiado lejos para ir caminando.

It's too far to walk.

Tienen que tomar el metro.

You need to take the subway.

Tomen la línea roja en dirección Colinas.

Take the red line towards Colinas.

Deben bajarse en la última parada.

You should get off at the last stop.

Luego deben tomar la línea amarilla en dirección Paseo Coral.

Then you need to take the yellow line towards Paseo Coral.

Y bajarse en la penúltima parada.

Get off at the next-to-last stop.

Todo el trayecto les tomará casi una hora y cuarto.

The whole trip should take you about an hour and a quarter.

Al salir del metro verán el Museo Nacional justo enfrente.

When you get out of the subway, you'll see the National Museum right in front of you.

Señora, ¿le importaría decirnos cómo llegar al Ayuntamiento?

Ma'am, would you mind telling us how to get to City Hall?

Es que somos turistas y queremos verlo todo.

We're tourists and we want to see everything.

Es mejor que no vayan caminando.

It's better not to walk.

Les recomiendo que tomen un taxi.

I recommend that you take a taxi.

¡Qué paciencia tiene con nosotros la gente de esta ciudad!

The people in this city are so patient with us!

Creo que debemos dejar de preguntar.

I think we should stop asking questions.

Esta ciudad es monstruosa, gigantesca y complicada.

This city is monstrous, gigantic, and complicated.

Y una de dos, o compramos un mapa o tomamos un autobús turístico.

One or the other: do we buy a map or take a tour bus?

Si es que queremos llegar a algún sitio.

If we want to get anywhere.

¿Qué opinas?

What do you think?

Me parece buena la idea del autobús turístico.

I think the tour bus idea is a good idea.

PREGUNTAS SOBRE NUTRICIÓN

QUESTIONS ABOUT NUTRITION

¿Cuántas calorías tiene este plato preparado?

How many calories does this prepared meal have?

¿Qué porcentaje de sodio tiene una lata de frijoles?

What percentage of sodium does a can of beans have?

253

¿Cuántos gramos de azúcar suele tener más o menos un jugo envasado?	How many grams of sugar, more ore less, does a container of juice have?
¿Qué alimentos son ricos en Vitamina A?	What foods are rich in Vitamin A?
¿Es verdad que el aceite de hígado de bacalao contiene Vitamina D?	Is it true that cod liver oil has Vitamin D?
¿Es verdad que la falta de hierro en la sangre causa anemia?	Is it true that a lack of iron in the blood causes anemia?
¿Para qué es importante la Vitamina C?	What is Vitamin C important for?
¿Por qué necesita el cuerpo vitaminas y minerales?	Why does the body need vitamins and minerals?
¿Es bueno ingerir fibra para evitar el estreñimiento?	Is it good to eat fiber to avoid constipation?
¿Por qué es mejor comer pan integral que pan blanco?	Why is it better to eat whole-wheat bread than white bread?
¿Qué alimentos son esenciales para llevar una dieta equilibrada?	What foods are essential to a balanced diet?
¿Qué alimentos deben ingerirse diariamente?	What foods should you eat daily?
¿Qué alimentos deben consumirse con moderación?	What foods should you eat in moderation?
¿Qué desventajas tiene la dieta vegetariana?	What drawbacks does a vegetarian diet have?
¿Qué ventajas tiene la dieta mediterránea?	What advantages does a Mediterranean diet have?
¿Qué alimentos constituyen la base de la dieta mediterránea?	What are the basic foods in a Mediterranean diet?
¿Qué dieta proporciona mayores ventajas para la salud?	What diet offers the most health advantages?

¿Qué es el colesterol?	What is cholesterol?
¿Qué alimentos son ricos en colesterol?	What foods are high in cholesterol?
¿Qué alimentos contienen elevados índices de colesterol?	What foods have high amounts of cholesterol?
¿Cuáles son los inconvenientes de la comida rápida?	What are the drawbacks of fast food?
¿Qué tipo de alimentación favorece el buen funcionamiento del organismo?	What kind of nutrition promotes the proper functioning of the body?
¿Qué sustancias son perjudiciales para la salud?	What substances are harmful to your health?
¿Qué comían nuestros antepasados?	What did our ancestors eat?
¿Cómo han evolucionado los hábitos alimenticios a lo largo de la historia?	How have nutritional habits evolved throughout history?

PREGUNTAS SOBRE LA FORMA FÍSICA Y MENTAL

QUESTIONS ABOUT PHYSICAL AND MENTAL WELL-BEING

¿Es el estar en forma una moda o un estilo de vida?	Is being in shape a fashion or a lifestyle?
¿Hasta qué punto es importante estar en forma?	How important is it to be in shape?
¿Qué es aconsejable hacer para mantenerse en forma?	What activities are advisable for staying in shape?
¿Qué es recomendable hacer para perder peso?	What is recommended for losing weight?
¿Hasta qué punto es importante mantener un peso adecuado?	How important is it to maintain an adecuete weight?
¿Por qué es aconsejable realizar algún tipo de actividad física?	Why is it advisable to keep up some kind of physical activity?

255

¿Es la obesidad una cuestión estética o un grave problema de salud?

Is obesity an issue of appearance or a serious health problem?

¿Qué inconvenientes presenta para la salud el estilo de vida de los países industrializados?

What disadvantages does the lifestyle of industrialized countries have to health?

¿Qué es el estrés?

What is stress?

¿Qué papel juega el estrés en la salud de la sociedad actual?

What role does stress play in the health of society today?

¿En qué medida puede afectar el medio ambiente a la salud?

To what extent can the environment affect health?

¿Qué condiciones medioambientales son perjudiciales para la salud?

What environmental conditions are hazardous to our health?

¿Debo preocuparme por lo que como/bebo?

Should I worry about what I eat/drink?

¿Qué puedo hacer para mantenerme en forma?

What can I do to stay in shape?

¿Debo vigilar mi peso?

Should I watch my weight?

¿Soy un fanático/una fanática de la nutrición?

Am I a nutrition fanatic?

¿Qué me preocupa más, el número de calorías que ingiero al día o el valor nutritivo de los alimentos que tomo?

What should I worry about more, the number of calories I take in every day or the nutritional value of the foods I eat?

¿Quiero vivir cien años? ¿Por qué?

Do I want to live a hundred years? Why?

PREGUNTAS SOBRE EL FUTURO LABORAL

QUESTIONS ABOUT YOUR FUTURE IN THE WORKPLACE

¿Qué piensas hacer cuando te gradúes?

What do you think you'll do after you graduate?

¿Piensas en el futuro o vives al día?	Do you think about the future, or do you live day to day?
¿Has pensado seriamente en tu futuro?	Have you thought seriously about your future?
¿De qué color lo ves?	And how do you see it?/What do you think it will be like?
¿Eres optimista o pesimista?	Are you an optimist or a pessimist?
¿Te gustan los retos?	Do you like challenges?
¿Te interesa correr riesgos?	Are you interested in taking risks?
¿Cuál es tu trabajo/profesión ideal?	What is your ideal job/ profession?
¿Qué buscas en un trabajo? ¿Y en un jefe o jefa?	What do you look for in a job? And in a boss?
¿Qué alicientes crees que ofrece el mundo del trabajo?	What incentives/attractions do you think the working world offers?
¿Quieres ganar mucho dinero?	Do you want to earn a lot of money?
¿Podrías vivir sin dinero?	Could you live without money?
¿Qué tipo de trabajo buscas?	What kind of job are you looking for?
¿En qué tipo de ambiente laboral piensas?	What kind of work atmosphere are you thinking about?
¿Estás impaciente por salir de la universidad e incorporarte al mundo laboral?	Are you eager to leave school and enter the working world?
¿Eres una persona responsable?	Are you a responsible person?
¿Crees que trabajar es más interesante que estudiar?	Do you think working is more interesting than studying?

USEFUL EXPRESSIONS

257

¿Has asistido ya a alguna entrevista de trabajo?	Have you gone on a job interview yet?
¿Cuáles consideras tus puntos fuertes?	What do you consider your strong points to be?
¿Cuáles crees que son tus puntos débiles?	What do you think your weak points are?
¿Buscas un trabajo creativo, de atención al público o de dirección?	What kind of job are you looking for, a creative one, one where you have to work with the public, or a managerial one?
¿Buscas un trabajo vocacional o uno puramente lucrativo?	Are you looking for a job you love, or just one that will make a lot of money?
¿Para qué tipo de trabajo crees que estás mejor preparado?	For what type of job do you think you are best prepared?
¿Qué crees que puedes ofrecer?	What do you think you have to offer?
¿Qué esperas recibir a cambio?	What do expect to get in return?
¿Cuál es tu meta u objetivo principal?	What is your main goal or objective?
¿Hasta dónde quieres llegar?	How far do you want to go?
¿Qué estás dispuesto/a a arriesgar para conseguirlo?	What are you willing to risk to get there?
¿Qué precio estás dispuesto/a a pagar?	What price are you willing to pay?
¿Cuáles serían tus prioridades?	What would your priorities be?
¿Estarías interesado/a en trabajar horas extras?	Would you be interested in working extra hours?
En caso afirmativo, ¿esperarías algo a cambio?	If so, would you expect something in return?
¿Por qué cualidades te gustaría ser recordado?	For what qualities would you like to be remembered?

258

¿Cómo te gustaría pasar a la historia?	How would you like to go down in history?
¿O prefieres vivir tranquilo/a y pasar desapercibido/a?	Or do you prefer to live quietly and go unnoticed?

LAS ARTES

THE ARTS

¿Para qué sirve el arte?	What is art for?
¿Qué significa el término artista?	What does the term "artist" mean?
¿Para qué usa el arte el/la "artista"?	What does an artist use art for?
¿Cuál es la misión del/de la artista?	What is the artist's mission?
¿Son los artistas egocentristas?	Are artists egocentric/self-centered?
¿Son realistas los artistas?	Are artists realists?
¿Envidias la vida del/de la artista?	Do you envy the life of an artist?
¿Tienes tú madera de artista?	Do you have what it takes to be an artist?
¿Qué significa la expresión "trabajar por amor al arte"?	What does the expression "to work for the love of art" mean?
¿Por qué llaman al cine el séptimo arte?	Why do they call film the seventh art?
¿Crees que una imagen vale más que mil palabras?	Do you think a picture is worth a thousand words?
¿Te gusta ver películas extranjeras en versión original subtitulada?	Do you like to see foreign films in the original language with subtitles?
¿Cómo expresas lo que piensas, lo que sientes, lo que quieres, lo que te gusta?	How do you express what you think, feel, want, and like?

¿Eres aficionado/a a la pintura?	Are you a painting aficionado?
¿Estás familiarizado/a con el surrealismo? ¿Y con el cubismo?	Are you familiar with surrealism? With cubism?
¿Qué otras tendencias artísticas conoces? ¿Cuáles te interesan más? ¿Por qué?	What other artistic movements do you know about? Which ones interest you the most? Why?
¿Te gusta o te gustaría coleccionar objetos de arte?	Do you or would you like to collect works of art?
¿Pagarías cincuenta millones de dólares por un original de Picasso?	Would you pay fifty million dollars for a Picasso original?
¿Eres amante de la música?	Are you a music lover?
¿A qué sentidos seduce la música?	Which senses does music affect?
¿Qué se necesita para disfrutar del arte?	What do you need to enjoy art?
¿Hace falta un sexto sentido?	Do you need a sixth sense?
¿Sin cuál de los cinco sentidos no podrías vivir?	Which of the five senses could you not live without?
¿Qué tipo de música está de moda entre la juventud actual?	What kind of music is popular with today's youth?
Y por último, la pregunta del millón, ¿Beatles o Rolling Stones?	And finally, the million-dollar question, the Beatles or the Rolling Stones?

PREGUNTAS SOBRE LAS ACTUALIDADES

QUESTIONS ABOUT CURRENT EVENTS

¿Estás al día?	Are you up to date?
¿Qué dicen hoy los periódicos?	What do the newspapers say today?
¿Has leído las últimas noticias?	Have you read the latest news?

¿Te interesa la política? ¿Por qué?	Are you interested in politics? Why?
¿Estás al día de lo que pasa en tu país? ¿Y en el resto del mundo?	Are you up to date with what's happening in your country? And in the rest of the world?
¿Qué temas sociales y políticos te preocupan?	What social and political topics concern you?
Si fueras político/a, ¿qué medidas tomarías para solucionar los problemas actuales del medio ambiente?	If you were a politician, what measures would you take to solve the current environmental problems?
¿Sigues de cerca la actualidad (política)?	Do you follow current events (politics) closely?
¿Lees las noticias internacionales?	Do you read international news?
¿Te interesa la política exterior?	Does foreign politics interest you?
¿(Te) Crees todo lo que lees en los periódicos?	Do you believe everything you read in the newspapers?
¿Te consideras una persona bien informada?	Do you consider yourself well-informed?
¿Crees que estamos bien informados?	Do you think we are well-informed?
¿Cómo es posible digerir tanta información?	How can one take in so much information?
En tu opinión, ¿qué cualidades debe tener un buen político/una buena política?	In your opinion, what qualities should a good politician have?
¿Qué harías si fueras presidente de los Estados Unidos?	What would you do if you were president of the United States?
¿Cuáles crees que son las causas principales de la violencia?	What do you think the principal causes of violence are?

¿Qué opinas de las campañas electorales/publicitarias?	What do you think of electoral/publicity campaigns?
¿Crees que los políticos tienen demasiado poder?	Do you think politicians have too much power?
¿Crees que el poder corrompe?	Do you think that power corrupts?
¿Qué opinas de la sociedad actual?	What do you think about present-day society?
¿Cómo valoras los últimos avances de la tecnología?	What do you think of/How do you rate the latest technology advances?
¿Ha avanzado el ser humano al mismo ritmo que la tecnología?	Have human beings advanced at the same rate as technology?
¿Qué avances positivos se lograron a lo largo del siglo XX?	What positive advances were made over the course of the 20th century?
¿Qué cuestiones te gustaría ver resueltas en el siglo XXI?	What issues would you like to see resolved in the 21st century?
¿Confías en los líderes políticos de tu país?	Do you trust the political leaders of your country?
¿Qué papel crees que juega el dinero en la sociedad actual?	What role do you think money plays in present-day society?
¿Hasta qué punto crees que los medios de comunicación influyen en la visión que tenemos del mundo?	To what extent do you think that the media influence our world view?
¿Crees que está bien repartida la riqueza del planeta?	Do you think the wealth of the planet is well distributed?
¿Hay problemas de discriminación en tu ciudad y/o país?	Are there discrimination problems in your city and/or country?
¿Crees que vivimos en un mundo justo y solidario?	Do you think we live in a just and supportive world?

¿Qué medidas tomarías para
que el mundo fuera un lugar
mejor para todos?

What measures would you take
so that the world would be a
better place for everyone?

¿Quién tiene la última palabra?

Who has the last word?

Verb conjugation tables

The verb lists

The list of verbs below and the model-verb tables that start on page 270 show you how to conjugate every verb taught in **VISTAS, AVENTURAS,** and **INVITACIONES.** Each verb in the list is followed by a model verb that is conjugated according to the same pattern. The number in parentheses indicates where in the tables you can find the conjugated forms of the model verb. If you want to find out how to conjugate **divertirse,** for example, look up number 33, **sentir,** the model for verbs that follow the e:ie stem-change pattern.

abrazar (z:c) like cruzar (37)

abrir like vivir (3) *except* past participle is abierto

aburrir(se) like vivir (3)

acabar de like hablar (1)

acampar like hablar (1)

aceptar like hablar (1)

acompañar like hablar (1)

aconsejar like hablar (1)

acordarse (o:ue) like contar (24)

acostarse (o:ue) like contar (24)

adelgazar (z:c) like cruzar (37)

afeitarse like hablar (1)

ahorrar like hablar (1)

alegrarse like hablar (1)

aliviar like hablar (1)

almorzar (o:ue) like contar (24) *except* (z:c)

alquilar like hablar (1)

andar like hablar (1) *except* preterite stem is anduv-

anunciar like hablar (1)

apagar (g:gu) like llegar (41)

aplaudir like vivir (3)

apreciar like hablar (1)

aprender like comer (2)

apurarse like hablar (1)

armar like hablar (1)

arrancar (c:qu) like tocar (43)

arreglar like hablar (1)

asistir like vivir (3)

aumentar like hablar (1)

ayudar(se) like hablar (1)

bailar like hablar (1)

bajar(se) like hablar (1)

bañarse like hablar (1)

barrer like comer (2)

beber like comer (2)

besar(se) like hablar (1)

borrar like hablar (1)

brindar like hablar (1)

bucear like hablar (1)

buscar (c:qu) like tocar (43)

caber (4)

caer(se) (5)

calentarse (e:ie) like pensar (30)

calzar (z:c) like cruzar (37)

cambiar like hablar (1)

caminar like hablar (1)

cantar like hablar (1)

casarse like hablar (1)

castigar like hablar (1)

cazar (z:c) like cruzar (37)

celebrar like hablar (1)

cenar like hablar (1)

How to use the verb tables

In the tables you will find the infinitive, present and past participles, and all the simple forms of each model verb. The formation of the compound tenses of any verb can be inferred from the table of compound tenses, pages 270–271, either by combining the past participle of the verb with a conjugated form of **haber** or by combining the present participle with a conjugated form of **estar**.

cepillarse like hablar (1)
cerrar (e:ie) like pensar (30)
chocar (c:qu) like tocar (43)
cobrar like hablar (1)
cocinar like hablar (1)
colorear like hablar (1)
comenzar (e:ie) (z:c) like empezar (26)
comer (2)
compartir like vivir (3)
oomprar like hablar (1)
comprender like comer (2)
comprometerse like comer (2)
comunicarse (c:qu) like tocar (43)
conducir (c:zc) (6)
confirmar like hablar (1)
conocer (c:zc) (35)
conseguir (e:i)
  like seguir (32)
conservar like hablar (1)
consumir like vivir (3)
contaminar like hablar (1)
contar (o:ue) (24)
controlar like hablar (1)
correr like comer (2)
cortar like hablar (1)
costar (o:ue) like contar (24)
creer (y) (36)
cruzar (z:c) (37)

cubrir like vivir (3) *except* past participle is cubierto
cuidar(se) like hablar (1)
cumplir like vivir (3)
dañar like hablar (1)
dar(se) (7)
deber like comer (2)
decidir like vivir (3)
decir (e:i) (8)
declarar like hablar (1)
dejar like hablar (1)
depositar like hablar (1)
desarrollar like hablar (1)
desayunar like hablar (1)
descansar like hablar (1)
descargar like hablar (1)
descomponer(se) like poner(se) (15)
describir like vivir (3) *except* past participle is descrito
descubrir like vivir (3) *except* past participle is descubierto
desear like hablar (1)
despedirse (e:i) like pedir (29)
despertarse (e:ie)
  like pensar (30)
destruir (y) (38)
dibujar like hablar (1)
dirigir (g:j) like vivir (3) *except* (g:j)
discutir like vivir (3)

disfrazar(se) like hablar (1)

disfrutar like hablar (1)

divertirse (e:ie) like sentir (33)

divorciarse like hablar (1)

doblar like hablar (1)

doler (o:ue) like volver (34) *except* past participle is regular

dormir(se) (o:ue) (25)

ducharse like hablar (1)

dudar like hablar (1)

durar like hablar (1)

echar like hablar (1)

elegir (e:i) like pedir (29) *except* (g:j)

embarazarse like hablar (1)

emitir like vivir (3)

empezar (e:ie) (z:c) (26)

empujar like hablar (1)

enamorarse like hablar (1)

encantar like hablar (1)

encontrar(se) (o:ue) like contar (24)

enfermarse like hablar (1)

engordar like hablar (1)

enojarse like hablar (1)

enseñar like hablar (1)

ensuciar like hablar (1)

entender (e:ie) (27)

entrar like hablar (1)

entregar like hablar (1) *except* (g:gu)

entrenarse like hablar (1)

entrevistar like hablar (1)

enviar (envío) (39)

escalar like hablar (1)

escoger (g:j) like proteger (42)

escribir like vivir (3) *except* past participle is escrito

escuchar like hablar (1)

esculpir like vivir (3)

esperar like hablar (1)

esquiar (esquío) like enviar (39)

establecer (c:zc) like conocer (35)

estacionar(se) like hablar (1)

estar (9)

estornudar like hablar (1)

estudiar like hablar (1)

evitar like hablar (1)

explicar (c:qu) like tocar (43)

explorar like hablar (1)

faltar like hablar (1)

fascinar like hablar (1)

firmar like hablar (1)

frenar like hablar (1)

fumar like hablar (1)

funcionar like hablar (1)

ganar like hablar (1)

gastar like hablar (1)

grabar like hablar (1)

graduarse (gradúo) (40)

guardar like hablar (1)

gustar like hablar (1)

haber (hay) (10)

hablar (1)

hacer (11)

iluminar like hablar (1)

importar like hablar (1)

imprimir like vivir (3)

informar like hablar (1)

insistir like vivir (3)

interesar like hablar (1)

invertir (e:ie) like sentir (33)

invitar like hablar (1)

ir(se) (12)

jubilarse like hablar (1)

jugar (u:ue) (g:gu) (28)

juntar(se) like hablar (1)

lastimarse like hablar (1)

lavar(se) like hablar (1)

leer (y) like creer (36)

levantar(se) like hablar (1)

limpiar like hablar (1)

llamar(se) like hablar (1)

llegar (g:gu) (41)

llenar like hablar (1)

llevar(se) like hablar (1)

llover (o:ue) like volver (34) *except* past participle is regular

luchar like hablar (1)

mandar like hablar (1)

manejar like hablar (1)

mantener(se) (e:ie) like tener (20)

maquillarse like hablar (1)
mejorar like hablar (1)
merendar (e:ie) like pensar (30)
mirar like hablar (1)
molestar like hablar (1)
montar like hablar (1)
morir (o:ue) like dominar (25) *except* past participle is muerto
mostrar (o:ue) like contar (24)
mudarse like hablar (1)
nacer (c:zc) like conocer (35)
nadar like hablar (1)
navegar (g:gu) like llegar (41)
necesitar like hablar (1)
negar (e:ie) like pensar (30) *except* (g:gu)
nevar (e:ie) like pensar (30)
obedecer (c:zc) like conocer (35)
obtener (e:ie) like tener (20)
ocurrir like vivir (3)
odiar like hablar (1)
ofrecer (c:zc) like conocer (35)
oír (13)
olvidar like hablar (1)
pagar (g:gu) like llegar (41)
parar(se) like hablar (1)
parecer (c:zc) like conocer (35)
pasar(se) like hablar (1)
pasear like hablar (1)
patinar like hablar (1)
pedir (e:i) (29)
pegar like hablar (1) *except* (g:gu)
peinarse like hablar (1)
pelearse like hablar (1)
pensar(se) (e:ie) (30)
perder (e:ie) like entender (27)
pescar (c:qu) like tocar (43)
pintar(se) like hablar (1)
planchar like hablar (1)
poder (o:ue) (14)
ponchar(se) like hablar (1)
poner(se) (15)
portar(se) like hablar (1)
practicar (c:qu) like tocar (43)
preferir (e:ie) like sentir (33)

preguntar like hablar (1)
preocuparse like hablar (1)
preparar like hablar (1)
presentar like hablar (1)
prestar like hablar (1)
probar(se) (o:ue) like contar (24)
prohibir like vivir (3)
prometer like comer (2)
proteger (g:j) (42)
publicar (c:qu) like tocar (43)
quedar(se) like hablar (1)
quemar like hablar (1)
querer (e:ie) (16)
quitar(se) like hablar (1)
rasurar(se) like hablar (1)
recetar like hablar (1)
recibir(se) like vivir (3)
reciclar like hablar (1)
recoger (g:j) like proteger (42)
recomendar (e:ie) like pensar (30)
recordar (o:ue) like contar (24)
reducir (c:zc) like conducir (6)
regalar like hablar (1)
regañar like hablar (1)
regatear like hablar (1)
regresar like hablar (1)
reír(se) (e:i) (31)
relajarse like hablar (1)
renunciar like hablar (1)
repetir (e:i) like pedir (29)
resolver (o:ue) like volver (34)
respirar like hablar (1)
revisar like hablar (1)
rogar (o:ue) like contar (24) *except* (g:gu)
romper(se) like comer (2) *except* past participle is roto
saber (17)
sacar (c:qu) like tocar (43)
sacudir like vivir (3)
salir(se) (18)
saltar like hablar (1)
saludar(se) like hablar (1)
secar(se) (c:q) like tocar (43)
seguir (e:i) (32)

sentarse (e:ie) like pensar (30)
sentir(se) (e:ie) (33)
separarse like hablar (1)
ser (19)
servir (e:i) like pedir (29)
solicitar like hablar (1)
sonar (o:ue) like contar (24)
sonreír (e:i) like reír(se) (31)
sorprender like comer (2)

subir(se) like vivir (3)
sudar like hablar (1)
sufrir like vivir (3)
sugerir (e:ie) like sentir (33)
suponer like poner (15)
temer like comer (2)
tener (e:ie) (20)
terminar like hablar (1)
tocar (c:qu) (43)

tomar like hablar (1)
torcerse (o:ue) like volver (34)
except (c:z) and past participle is
regular; e.g. yo me tuerzo
toser like comer (2)
trabajar like hablar (1)
traducir (c:zc) like conducir (6)
traer (21)
transmitir like vivir (3)
tratar like hablar (1)

usar like hablar (1)
vender like comer (2)
venir (e:ie) (22)
ver (23)
vestirse (e:i) (44)
viajar like hablar (1)
visitar like hablar (1)
vivir (3)
volver (o:ue) (34)
votar like hablar (1)

Regular verbs: simple tenses

		INDICATIVE			
Infinitive		Present	Imperfect	Preterite	Future
1 hablar		hablo	hablaba	hablé	hablaré
		hablas	hablabas	hablaste	hablarás
Participles:		habla	hablaba	habló	hablará
hablando		hablamos	hablábamos	hablamos	hablaremos
hablado		habláis	hablabais	hablasteis	hablaréis
		hablan	hablaban	hablaron	hablarán
2 comer		como	comía	comí	comeré
		comes	comías	comiste	comerás
Participles:		come	comía	comió	comerá
comiendo		comemos	comíamos	comimos	comeremos
comido		coméis	comíais	comisteis	comeréis
		comen	comían	comieron	comerán
3 vivir		vivo	vivía	viví	viviré
		vives	vivías	viviste	vivirás
Participles:		vive	vivía	vivió	vivirá
viviendo		vivimos	vivíamos	vivimos	viviremos
vivido		vivís	vivíais	vivisteis	viviréis
		viven	vivían	vivieron	vivirán

All verbs: compound tenses

PERFECT TENSES					
INDICATIVE					
Present Perfect		Past Perfect		Future Perfect	
he		había		habré	
has		habías		habrás	
ha	hablado	había	hablado	habrá	hablado
hemos	comido	habíamos	comido	habremos	comido
habéis	vivido	habíais	vivido	habréis	vivido
han		habían		habrán	

INDICATIVE	SUBJUNCTIVE		IMPERATIVE
Conditional	Present	Past	
hablaría	hable	hablara	
hablarías	hables	hablaras	habla (no hables)
hablaría	hable	hablara	hable
hablaríamos	hablemos	habláramos	hablemos
hablaríais	habléis	hablarais	hablad (no habléis)
hablarían	hablen	hablaran	hablen
comería	coma	comiera	
comerías	comas	comieras	come (no comas)
comería	coma	comiera	coma
comeríamos	comamos	comiéramos	comamos
comeríais	comáis	comierais	comed (no comáis)
comerían	coman	comieran	coman
viviría	viva	viviera	
vivirías	vivas	vivieras	vive (no vivas)
viviría	viva	viviera	viva
viviríamos	vivamos	viviéramos	vivamos
viviríais	viváis	vivierais	vivid (no viváis)
vivirían	vivan	vivieran	vivan

PERFECT TENSES

INDICATIVE	SUBJUNCTIVE	
Conditional Perfect	Present Perfect	Past Perfect
habría	haya	hubiera
habrías	hayas	hubieras
habría } hablado	haya } hablado	hubiera } hablado
habríamos } comido	hayamos } comido	hubiéramos } comido
habríais } vivido	hayáis } vivido	hubierais } vivido
habrían	hayan	hubieran

	PROGRESSIVE TENSES		
	INDICATIVE		
Present Progressive	Past Progressive		Future Progressive
estoy	estaba		estaré
estás	estabas		estarás
está hablando	estaba	hablando	estará hablando
estamos comiendo	estábamos	comiendo	estaremos comiendo
estáis viviendo	estabais	viviendo	estaréis viviendo
estan	estaban		estarán

Irregular verbs

		INDICATIVE			
Infinitive	Present	Imperfect	Preterite	Future	
4 caber	**quepo**	cabía	**cupe**	**cabré**	
	cabes	cabías	**cupiste**	**cabrás**	
Participles:	cabe	cabía	**cupo**	**cabrá**	
cabiendo	cabemos	cabíamos	**cupimos**	**cabremos**	
cabido	cabéis	cabíais	**cupisteis**	**cabréis**	
	caben	cabían	**cupieron**	**cabrán**	
5 caer(se)	**caigo**	**caía**	**caí**	caeré	
	caes	**caías**	**caíste**	caerás	
Participles:	cae	**caía**	**cayó**	caerá	
cayendo	caemos	**caíamos**	**caímos**	caeremos	
caído	caéis	**caíais**	**caísteis**	caeréis	
	caen	**caían**	**cayeron**	caerán	
6 conducir	**conduzco**	conducía	**conduje**	conduciré	
(c:zc)	conduces	conducías	**condujiste**	conducirás	
Participles:	conduce	conducía	**condujo**	conducirá	
conduciendo	conducimos	conducíamos	**condujimos**	conduciremos	
conducido	conducís	conducíais	**condujisteis**	conduciréis	
	conducen	conducían	**condujeron**	conducirán	

PROGRESSIVE TENSES

	SUBJUNCTIVE	
Conditional Progressive	Present Progressive	Past Progressive
estaría estarías estaría } hablando estaríamos comiendo estaríais viviendo estarían	esté estés esté } hablando estemos comiendo estéis viviendo estén	estuviera estuvieras estuviera } hablando estuviéramos comiendo estuvierais viviendo estuvieran

	SUBJUNCTIVE		IMPERATIVE
Conditional	Present	Past	
cabría	quepa	cupiera	
cabrías	quepas	cupieras	cabe (no quepas)
cabría	quepa	cupiera	quepa
cabríamos	quepamos	cupiéramos	quepamos
cabríais	quepáis	cupierais	cabed (no quepáis)
cabrían	quepan	cupieran	quepan
caería	caiga	cayera	
caerías	caigas	cayeras	cae (no caigas)
caería	caiga	cayera	caiga
caeríamos	caigamos	cayéramos	caigamos
caeríais	caigáis	cayerais	caed (no caigáis)
caerían	caigan	cayeran	caigan
conduciría	conduzca	condujera	
conducirías	conduzcas	condujeras	conduce (no conduzcas)
conduciría	conduzca	condujera	conduzca
conduciríamos	conduzcamos	condujéramos	conduzcamos
conduciríais	conduzcáis	condujerais	conducid (no conduzcáis)
conducirían	conduzcan	condujeran	conduzcan

	Infinitive	INDICATIVE			
		Present	Imperfect	Preterite	Future
7	dar	**doy**	daba	**di**	daré
		das	dabas	**diste**	darás
	Participles:	da	daba	**dio**	dará
	dando	damos	dábamos	**dimos**	daremos
	dado	dais	dabais	**disteis**	daréis
		dan	daban	**dieron**	darán
8	decir (e:i)	**digo**	decía	**dije**	**diré**
		dices	decías	**dijiste**	**dirás**
	Participles:	**dice**	decía	**dijo**	**dirá**
	diciendo	decimos	decíamos	**dijimos**	**diremos**
	dicho	decís	decíais	**dijisteis**	**diréis**
		dicen	decían	**dijeron**	**dirán**
9	estar	**estoy**	estaba	**estuve**	estaré
		estás	estabas	**estuviste**	estarás
	Participles:	**está**	estaba	**estuvo**	estará
	estando	estamos	estábamos	**estuvimos**	estaremos
	estado	**estáis**	estabais	**estuvisteis**	estaréis
		están	estaban	**estuvieron**	estarán
10	haber	**he**	había	**hube**	habré
		has	habías	**hubiste**	habrás
	Participles:	**ha**	había	**hubo**	habrá
	habiendo	**hemos**	habíamos	**hubimos**	habremos
	habido	habéis	habíais	**hubisteis**	habréis
		han	habían	**hubieron**	habrán
11	hacer	**hago**	hacía	**hice**	**haré**
		haces	hacías	**hiciste**	**harás**
	Participles:	hace	hacía	**hizo**	**hará**
	haciendo	hacemos	hacíamos	**hicimos**	**haremos**
	hecho	hacéis	hacíais	**hicisteis**	**haréis**
		hacen	hacían	**hicieron**	**harán**
12	ir	**voy**	**iba**	**fui**	iré
		vas	**ibas**	**fuiste**	irás
	Participles:	**va**	**iba**	**fue**	irá
	yendo	**vamos**	**íbamos**	**fuimos**	iremos
	ido	**vais**	**ibais**	**fuisteis**	iréis
		van	**iban**	**fueron**	irán
13	oír (y)	**oigo**	oía	**oí**	oiré
		oyes	oías	**oíste**	oirás
	Participles:	**oye**	oía	**oyó**	oirá
	oyendo	**oímos**	oíamos	**oímos**	oiremos
	oído	oís	oíais	**oísteis**	oiréis
		oyen	oían	**oyeron**	oirán

	SUBJUNCTIVE		IMPERATIVE
Conditional	Present	Past	
daría	dé	diera	
darías	des	dieras	da (no des)
daría	dé	diera	dé
daríamos	demos	diéramos	demos
daríais	deis	dierais	dad (no deis)
darían	den	dieran	den
diría	diga	dijera	
dirías	digas	dijeras	di (no digas)
diría	diga	dijera	diga
diríamos	digamos	dijéramos	digamos
diríais	digáis	dijerais	decid (no digáis)
dirían	digan	dijeran	digan
estaría	esté	estuviera	
estarías	estés	estuvieras	está (no estés)
estaría	esté	estuviera	esté
estaríamos	estemos	estuviéramos	estemos
estaríais	estéis	estuvierais	estad (no estéis)
estarían	estén	estuvieran	estén
habría	haya	hubiera	
habrías	hayas	hubieras	
habría	haya	hubiera	
habríamos	hayamos	hubiéramos	
habríais	hayáis	hubierais	
habrían	hayan	hubieran	
haría	haga	hiciera	
harías	hagas	hicieras	haz (no hagas)
haría	haga	hiciera	haya
haríamos	hagamos	hiciéramos	hayamos
haríais	hagáis	hicierais	haced (no hayáis)
harían	hagan	hicieran	hayan
iría	vaya	fuera	
irías	vayas	fueras	ve (no vayas)
iría	vaya	fuera	vaya
iríamos	vayamos	fuéramos	vayamos
iríais	vayáis	fuerais	id (no vayáis)
irían	vayan	fueran	vayan
oiría	oiga	oyera	
oirías	oigas	oyeras	oye (no oigas)
oiría	oiga	oyera	oiga
oiríamos	oigamos	oyéramos	oigamos
oiríais	oigáis	oyerais	oíd (no oigáis)
oirían	oigan	oyeran	oigan

	Infinitive	INDICATIVE			
		Present	Imperfect	Preterite	Future
14	poder (o:ue)	**puedo**	podía	**pude**	**podré**
		puedes	podías	**pudiste**	**podrás**
	Participles:	**puede**	podía	**pudo**	**podrá**
	pudiendo	podemos	podíamos	**pudimos**	**podremos**
	podido	podéis	podíais	**pudisteis**	**podréis**
		pueden	podían	**pudieron**	**podrán**
15	poner	**pongo**	ponía	**puse**	**pondré**
		pones	ponías	**pusiste**	**pondrás**
	Participles:	pone	ponía	**puso**	**pondrá**
	poniendo	ponemos	poníamos	**pusimos**	**pondremos**
	puesto	ponéis	poníais	**pusisteis**	**pondréis**
		ponen	ponían	**pusieron**	**pondrán**
16	querer (e:ie)	**quiero**	quería	**quise**	**querré**
		quieres	querías	**quisiste**	**querrás**
	Participles:	**quiere**	quería	**quiso**	**querrá**
	queriendo	queremos	queríamos	**quisimos**	**querremos**
	querido	queréis	queríais	**quisisteis**	**querréis**
		quieren	querían	**quisieron**	**querrán**
17	saber	**sé**	sabía	**supe**	**sabré**
		sabes	sabías	**supiste**	**sabrás**
	Participles:	sabe	sabía	**supo**	**sabrá**
	sabiendo	sabemos	sabíamos	**supimos**	**sabremos**
	sabido	sabéis	sabíais	**supisteis**	**sabréis**
		saben	sabían	**supieron**	**sabrán**
18	salir	**salgo**	salía	salí	**saldré**
		sales	salías	saliste	**saldrás**
	Participles:	**sale**	salía	salió	**saldrá**
	saliendo	salimos	salíamos	salimos	**saldremos**
	salido	salís	salíais	salisteis	**saldréis**
		salen	salían	salieron	**saldrán**
19	ser	**soy**	**era**	**fui**	seré
		eres	**eras**	**fuiste**	serás
	Participles:	**es**	**era**	**fue**	será
	siendo	**somos**	**éramos**	**fuimos**	seremos
	sido	**sois**	**erais**	**fuisteis**	seréis
		son	**eran**	**fueron**	serán
20	tener (e:ie)	**tengo**	tenía	**tuve**	**tendré**
		tienes	tenías	**tuviste**	**tendrás**
	Participles:	**tiene**	tenía	**tuvo**	**tendrá**
	teniendo	tenemos	teníamos	**tuvimos**	**tendremos**
	tenido	tenéis	teníais	**tuvisteis**	**tendréis**
		tienen	tenían	**tuvieron**	**tendrán**

	SUBJUNCTIVE		IMPERATIVE
Conditional	Present	Past	
podría	pueda	pudiera	
podrías	puedas	pudieras	puede (no puedas)
podría	pueda	pudiera	pueda
podríamos	podamos	pudiéramos	podamos
podríais	podáis	pudierais	poded (no podáis)
podrían	puedan	pudieran	puedan
pondría	ponga	pusiera	
pondrías	pongas	pusieras	pon (no pongas)
pondría	ponga	pusiera	ponga
pondríamos	pongamos	pusiéramos	pongamos
pondríais	pongáis	pusierais	poned (no pongáis)
pondrían	pongan	pusieran	pongan
querría	quiera	quisiera	
querrías	quieras	quisieras	quiere (no quieras)
querría	quiera	quisiera	quiere
querríamos	queramos	quisiéramos	queramos
querríais	queráis	quisierais	quered (no queráis)
querrían	quieran	quisieran	quieran
sabría	sepa	supiera	
sabrías	sepas	supieras	sabe (no sepas)
sabría	sepa	supiera	sepa
sabríamos	sepamos	supiéramos	sepamos
sabríais	sepáis	supierais	sabed (no sepáis)
sabrían	sepan	supieran	sepan
saldría	salga	saliera	
saldrías	salgas	salieras	sal (no salgas)
saldría	salga	saliera	salga
saldríamos	salgamos	saliéramos	salgamos
saldríais	salgáis	salierais	salid (no salgáis)
saldrían	salgan	salieran	salgan
sería	sea	fuera	
serías	seas	fueras	sé (no seas)
sería	sea	fuera	sea
seríamos	seamos	fuéramos	seamos
seríais	seáis	fuerais	sed (no seáis)
serían	sean	fueran	sean
tendría	tenga	tuviera	
tendrías	tengas	tuvieras	ten (no tengas)
tendría	tenga	tuviera	tenga
tendríamos	tengamos	tuviéramos	tengamos
tendríais	tengáis	tuvierais	tened (no tengáis)
tendrían	tengan	tuvieran	tengan

		INDICATIVE			
Infinitive		Present	Imperfect	Preterite	Future
21 traer		**traigo**	**traía**	**traje**	traeré
		traes	**traías**	**trajiste**	traerás
Participles:		trae	**traía**	**trajo**	traerá
trayendo		traemos	**traíamos**	**trajimos**	traeremos
traído		traéis	**traíais**	**trajisteis**	traeréis
		traen	**traían**	**trajeron**	traerán
22 venir (e:ie)		**vengo**	venía	**vine**	**vendré**
		vienes	venías	**viniste**	**vendrás**
Participles:		**viene**	venía	**vino**	**vendrá**
viniendo		venimos	veníamos	**vinimos**	**vendremos**
venido		venís	veníais	**vinisteis**	**vendréis**
		vienen	venían	**vinieron**	**vendrán**
23 ver		**veo**	**veía**	**vi**	veré
		ves	**veías**	viste	verás
Participles:		ve	**veía**	vio	verá
viendo		vemos	**veíamos**	vimos	veremos
visto		veis	**veíais**	**visteis**	veréis
		ven	**veían**	**vieron**	verán

Stem-changing verbs

		INDICATIVE			
Infinitive		Present	Imperfect	Preterite	Future
24 contar (o:ue)		**cuento**	contaba	conté	contaré
		cuentas	contabas	contaste	contarás
Participles:		**cuenta**	contaba	contó	contará
contando		contamos	contábamos	contamos	contaremos
contado		contáis	contabais	contasteis	contaréis
		cuentan	contaban	contaron	contarán
25 dormir (o:ue)		**duermo**	dormía	dormí	dormiré
		duermes	dormías	dormiste	dormirás
Participles:		**duerme**	dormía	**durmió**	dormirá
durmiendo		dormimos	dormíamos	dormimos	dormiremos
dormido		dormís	dormíais	dormisteis	dormiréis
		duermen	dormían	**durmieron**	dormirán
26 empezar (e:ie) (c)		**empiezo**	empezaba	**empecé**	empezaré
		empiezas	empezabas	empezaste	empezarás
		empieza	empezaba	empezó	empezará
Participles:		empezamos	empezábamos	empezamos	empezaremos
empezando		empezáis	empezabais	empezasteis	empezaréis
empezado		**empiezan**	empezaban	empezaron	empezarán

	SUBJUNCTIVE		IMPERATIVE
Conditional	Present	Past	
traería	traiga	trajera	
traerías	traigas	trajeras	trae (no traigas)
traería	traiga	trajera	traiga
traeríamos	traigamos	trajéramos	traigamos
traeríais	traigáis	trajerais	traed (no traigáis)
traerían	traigan	trajeran	traigan
vendría	venga	viniera	
vendrías	vengas	vinieras	ven (no vengas)
vendría	venga	viniera	venga
vendríamos	vengamos	viniéramos	vengamos
vendríais	vengáis	vinierais	venid (no vengáis)
vendrían	vengan	vinieran	vengan
vería	vea	viera	
verías	veas	vieras	ve (no veas)
vería	vea	viera	vea
veríamos	veamos	viéramos	veamos
veríais	veáis	vierais	ved (no veáis)
verían	vean	vieran	vean

	SUBJUNCTIVE		IMPERATIVE
Conditional	Present	Past	
contaría	cuente	contara	
contarías	cuentes	contaras	cuenta (no cuentes)
contaría	cuente	contara	cuente
contaríamos	contemos	contáramos	contemos
contaríais	contéis	contarais	contad (no contéis)
contarían	cuenten	contaran	cuenten
dormiría	duerma	durmiera	
dormirías	duermas	durmieras	duerme (no duermas)
dormiría	duerma	durmiera	duerma
dormiríamos	durmamos	durmiéramos	durmamos
dormiríais	durmáis	durmierais	dormid (no durmáis)
dormirían	duerman	durmieran	duerman
empezaría	empiece	empezara	
empezarías	empieces	empezaras	empieza (no empieces)
empezaría	empiece	empezara	empiece
empezaríamos	empecemos	empezáramos	empecemos
empezaríais	empecéis	empezarais	empezad (no empecéis)
empezarian	empiecen	empezaran	empiecen

		INDICATIVE			
Infinitive	**Present**	**Imperfect**	**Preterite**	**Future**	
27 entender (e:ie)	**entiendo**	entendía	entendí	entenderé	
	entiendes	entendías	entendiste	entenderás	
	entiende	entendía	entendió	entenderá	
Participles:	entendemos	entendíamos	entendimos	entenderemos	
entendiendo	entendéis	entendíais	entendisteis	entenderéis	
entendido	**entienden**	entendían	entendieron	entenderán	
28 jugar (u:ue) (gu)	**juego**	jugaba	**jugué**	jugaré	
	juegas	jugabas	jugaste	jugarás	
	juega	jugaba	jugó	jugará	
Participles:	jugamos	jugábamos	jugamos	jugaremos	
jugando	jugáis	jugabais	jugasteis	jugaréis	
jugado	**juegan**	jugaban	jugaron	jugarán	
29 pedir (e:i)	**pido**	pedía	pedí	pediré	
	pides	pedías	pediste	pedirás	
Participles:	**pide**	pedía	**pidió**	pedirá	
pidiendo	pedimos	pedíamos	pedimos	pediremos	
pedido	pedís	pedíais	pedisteis	pediréis	
	piden	pedían	**pidieron**	pedirán	
30 pensar (e:ie)	**pienso**	pensaba	pensé	pensaré	
	piensas	pensabas	pensaste	pensarás	
Participles:	**piensa**	pensaba	pensó	pensará	
pensando	pensamos	pensábamos	pensamos	pensaremos	
pensado	pensáis	pensabais	pensasteis	pensaréis	
	piensan	pensaban	pensaron	pensarán	
31 reír(se) (e:i)	**río**	reía	reí	reiré	
	ríes	reías	reíste	reirás	
Participles:	**ríe**	reía	**rió**	reirá	
riendo	reímos	reíamos	reímos	reiremos	
reído	reís	reíais	reísteis	reiréis	
	ríen	reían	**rieron**	reirán	
32 seguir (e:i) (gu)	**sigo**	seguía	seguí	seguiré	
	sigues	seguías	seguiste	seguirás	
	sigue	seguía	**siguió**	seguirá	
Participles:	seguimos	seguíamos	seguimos	seguiremos	
siguiendo	seguís	seguíais	seguisteis	seguiréis	
seguido	**siguen**	seguían	**siguieron**	seguirán	
33 sentir (e:ie)	**siento**	sentía	sentí	sentiré	
	sientes	sentías	sentiste	sentirás	
Participles:	**siente**	sentía	**sintió**	sentirá	
sintiendo	sentimos	sentíamos	sentimos	sentiremos	
sentido	sentís	sentíais	sentisteis	sentiréis	
	sienten	sentían	**sintieron**	sentirán	

| | SUBJUNCTIVE | | IMPERATIVE |
Conditional	Present	Past	
entendería	**entienda**	entendiera	
entenderías	**entiendas**	entendieras	**entiende** (no **entiendas**)
entendería	**entienda**	entendiera	**entienda**
entenderíamos	entendamos	entendiéramos	entendamos
entenderíais	entendáis	entendierais	entended (no entendáis)
entenderían	**entiendan**	entendieran	**entiendan**
jugaría	**juegue**	jugara	
jugarías	**juegues**	jugaras	**juega** (no **juegues**)
jugaría	**juegue**	jugara	**juegue**
jugaríamos	**juguemos**	jugáramos	**juguemos**
jugaríais	**juguéis**	jugarais	jugad (no **juguéis**)
jugarían	**jueguen**	jugaran	**jueguen**
pediría	**pida**	**pidiera**	
pedirías	**pidas**	**pidieras**	**pide** (no **pidas**)
pediría	**pida**	**pidiera**	**pida**
pediríamos	**pidamos**	**pidiéramos**	**pidamos**
pediríais	**pidáis**	**pidierais**	pedid (no **pidáis**)
pedirían	**pidan**	**pidieran**	**pidan**
pensaría	**piense**	pensara	
pensarías	**pienses**	pensaras	**piensa** (no **pienses**)
pensaría	**piense**	pensara	**piense**
pensaríamos	pensemos	pensáramos	pensemos
pensaríais	penséis	pensarais	pensad (no penséis)
pensarían	**piensen**	pensaran	**piensen**
reiría	**ría**	**riera**	
reirías	**rías**	**rieras**	**ríe** (no **rías**)
reiría	**ría**	**riera**	**ría**
reiríamos	**riamos**	**riéramos**	**riamos**
reiríais	**riáis**	**rierais**	reíd (no **riáis**)
reirían	**rían**	**rieran**	**rían**
seguiría	**siga**	**siguiera**	
seguirías	**sigas**	**siguieras**	**sigue** (no **sigas**)
seguiría	**siga**	**siguiera**	**siga**
seguiríamos	**sigamos**	**siguiéramos**	**sigamos**
seguiríais	**sigáis**	**siguierais**	seguid (no **sigáis**)
seguirían	**sigan**	**siguieran**	**sigan**
sentiría	**sienta**	**sintiera**	
sentirías	**sientas**	**sintieras**	**siente** (no **sientas**)
sentiría	**sienta**	**sintiera**	**sienta**
sentiríamos	**sintamos**	**sintiéramos**	**sintamos**
sentiríais	**sintáis**	**sintierais**	sentid (no **sintáis**)
sentirían	**sientan**	**sintieran**	**sientan**

		INDICATIVE		
Infinitive	Present	Imperfect	Preterite	Future
34 volver (o:ue) Participles: volviendo **vuelto**	**vuelvo** **vuelves** **vuelve** volvemos volvéis **vuelven**	volvía volvías volvía volvíamos volvíais volvían	volví volviste volvió volvimos volvisteis volvieron	volveré volverás volverá volveremos volveréis volverán

Verbs with spelling changes and reflexive verbs

		INDICATIVE		
Infinitive	Present	Imperfect	Preterite	Future
35 conocer (c:zc) Participles: conociendo conocido	**conozco** conoces conoce conocemos conocéis conocen	conocía conocías conocía conocíamos conocíais conocían	conocí conociste conoció conocimos conocisteis conocieron	conoceré conocerás conocerá conoceremos conoceréis conocerán
36 creer (y) Participles: **creyendo** **creído**	creo crees cree creemos creéis creen	creía creías creía creíamos creíais creían	**creí** **creíste** **creyó** **creímos** **creísteis** **creyeron**	creeré creerás creerá creeremos creeréis creerán
37 cruzar (c) Participles: cruzando cruzado	cruzo cruzas cruza cruzamos cruzáis cruzan	cruzaba cruzabas cruzaba cruzábamos cruzabais cruzaban	**crucé** cruzaste cruzó cruzamos cruzasteis cruzaron	cruzaré cruzarás cruzará cruzaremos cruzaréis cruzarán
38 destruir (y) Participles: **destruyendo** destruido	**destruyo** **destruyes** **destruye** destruimos destruís **destruyen**	destruía destruías destruía destruíamos destruíais destruían	destruí destruiste **destruyó** destruimos destruisteis **destruyeron**	destruiré destruirás destruirá destruiremos destruiréis destruirán
39 enviar (envío) Participles: enviando enviado	**envío** **envías** **envía** enviamos enviáis **envían**	enviaba enviabas enviaba enviábamos enviabais enviaban	envié enviaste envió enviamos enviasteis enviaron	enviaré enviarás enviará enviaremos enviaréis enviarán

	SUBJUNCTIVE		IMPERATIVE
Conditional	Present	Past	
volvería	**vuelva**	volviera	
volverías	**vuelvas**	volvieras	**vuelve** (no **vuelvas**)
volvería	**vuelva**	volviera	**vuelva**
volveríamos	volvamos	volviéramos	volvamos
volveríais	volváis	volvierais	volved (no volváis)
volverían	**vuelvan**	volvieran	**vuelvan**

	SUBJUNCTIVE		IMPERATIVE
Conditional	Present	Past	
conocería	**conozca**	conociera	
conocerías	**conozcas**	conocieras	conoce (no **conozcas**)
conocería	**conozca**	conociera	**conozca**
conoceríamos	**conozcamos**	conociéramos	**conozcamos**
conoceríais	**conozcáis**	conocierais	conoced (no **conozcáis**)
conocerían	**conozcan**	conocieran	**conozcan**
creería	crea	**creyera**	
creerías	creas	**creyeras**	cree (no creas)
creería	crea	**creyera**	crea
creeríamos	creamos	**creyéramos**	creamos
creeríais	creáis	**creyerais**	creed (no creáis)
creerían	crean	**creyeran**	crean
cruzaría	**cruce**	cruzara	
cruzarías	**cruces**	cruzaras	cruza (no **cruces**)
cruzaría	**cruce**	cruzara	**cruce**
cruzaríamos	**crucemos**	cruzáramos	**crucemos**
cruzaríais	**crucéis**	cruzarais	cruzad (no **crucéis**)
cruzarían	**crucen**	cruzaran	**crucen**
destruiría	**destruya**	**destruyera**	
destruirías	**destruyas**	**destruyeras**	destruye (no **destruyas**)
destruiría	**destruya**	**destruyera**	**destruya**
destruiríamos	**destruyamos**	**destruyéramos**	**destruyamos**
destruiríais	**destruyáis**	**destruyerais**	destruid (no **destruyáis**)
destruirían	**destruyan**	**destruyeran**	**destruyan**
enviaría	**envíe**	enviara	
enviarías	**envíes**	enviaras	**envía** (no **envíes**)
enviaría	**envíe**	enviara	**envíe**
enviaríamos	**enviemos**	enviáramos	enviemos
enviaríais	**enviéis**	enviarais	enviad (no enviéis)
enviarían	**envíen**	enviaran	**envíen**

283

	Infinitive	INDICATIVE			
		Present	Imperfect	Preterite	Future
40	graduarse (gradúo) **Participles:** graduando graduado	**gradúo** **gradúas** **gradúa** graduamos graduáis **gradúan**	graduaba graduabas graduaba graduábamos graduabais graduaban	gradué graduaste graduó graduamos graduasteis graduaron	graduaré graduarás graduará graduaremos graduaréis graduarán
41	llegar (gu) **Participles:** llegando llegado	llego llegas llega llegamos llegáis llegan	llegaba llegabas llegaba llegábamos llegabais llegaban	**llegué** llegaste llegó llegamos llegasteis llegaron	llegaré llegarás llegará llegaremos llegaréis llegarán
42	proteger (j) **Participles:** protegiendo protegido	**protejo** proteges protege protegemos protegéis protegen	protegía protegías protegía protegíamos protegíais protegían	protegí protegiste protegió protegimos protegisteis protegieron	protegeré protegerás protegerá protegeremos protegeréis protegerán
43	tocar (qu) **Participles:** tocando tocado	toco tocas toca tocamos tocáis tocan	tocaba tocabas tocaba tocábamos tocabais tocaban	**toqué** tocaste tocó tocamos tocasteis tocaron	tocaré tocarás tocarás tocaremos tocaréis tocarán
44	vestirse (e:i) **Participles:** **vistiendo** vestido	**me visto** **te vistes** **se viste** nos vestimos os vestís **se visten**	me vestía te vestías se vestía nos vestíamos os vestíais se vestían	me vestí te vestiste **se vistió** nos vestimos os vestisteis **se vistieron**	me vestiré te vestirás se vestirá nos vestiremos os vestiréis se vestirán

	SUBJUNCTIVE		IMPERATIVE
Conditional	Present	Past	
graduaría	**gradúe**	graduara	
graduarías	**gradúes**	graduaras	**gradúa** (no **gradúes**)
graduaría	**gradúe**	graduara	**gradúe**
graduaríamos	graduemos	graduáramos	graduemos
graduaríais	**graduéis**	graduarais	graduad (no **graduéis**)
graduarían	**gradúen**	graduaran	**gradúen**
llegaría	**llegue**	llegara	
llegarías	**llegues**	llegaras	llega (no **llegues**)
llegaría	**llegue**	llegara	**llegue**
llegaríamos	**lleguemos**	llegáramos	**lleguemos**
llegaríais	**lleguéis**	llegarais	llegad (no lleguéis)
llegarían	**lleguen**	llegaran	**lleguen**
protegería	**proteja**	protegiera	
protegerías	**protejas**	protegieras	protege (no **protejas**)
protegería	**proteja**	protegiera	**proteja**
protegeríamos	**protejamos**	protegiéramos	**protejamos**
protegeríais	**protejáis**	protegierais	proteged (no **protejáis**)
protegerían	**protejan**	protegieran	**protejan**
tocaría	**toque**	tocara	
tocarías	**toques**	tocaras	toca (no **toques**)
tocaría	**toque**	tocara	**toque**
tocaríamos	**toquemos**	tocáramos	**toquemos**
tocaríais	**toquéis**	tocarais	tocad (no **toquéis**)
tocarían	**toquen**	tocaran	**toquen**
me vestiría	me vista	me vistiera	
te vestirías	te vistas	te vistieras	vístete (no te vistas)
se vestiría	se vista	se vistiera	vístase
nos vestiríamos	nos vistamos	nos vistiéramos	vistámonos
os vestiríais	os vistáis	os vistierais	vestíos (no os vistáis)
se vestirían	se vistan	se vistieran	vístanse Uds.

Sección de consulta
Reference Section

MATERIAS	ACADEMIC SUBJECTS
la administración de empresas	business administration
la agronomía	agriculture
el alemán	German
el álgebra	algebra
la anatomía	anatomy
la antropología	anthropology
la arqueología	archaeology
la arquitectura	architecture
el arte	art
la astronomía	astronomy
la biología	biology
la bioquímica	biochemistry
la botánica	botany
el cálculo	calculus
el chino	Chinese
las ciencias políticas	political science
la computación	computer science
las comunicaciones	communications
la contabilidad	accounting
la danza	dance
el derecho	law
la economía	economics
la educación	education
la educación física	physical education

la enfermería	nursing
el español	Spanish
la filosofía	philosophy
la física	physics
el francés	French
la geografía	geography
la geología	geology
el griego	Greek
el hebreo	Hebrew
la historia	history
la informática	computer science
la ingeniería	engineering
el inglés	English
el italiano	Italian
el japonés	Japanese
el latín	Latin
las lenguas clásicas	classical languages
las lenguas romances	romance languages
la lingüística	linguistics
la literatura	literature
las matemáticas	mathematics
la medicina	medicine
el mercadeo/la mercadotecnia	marketing
la música	music
los negocios	business
el periodismo	journalism

287

el portugués	Portuguese
la psicología	psychology
la química	chemistry
el ruso	Russian
los servicios sociales	social services
la sociología	sociology
el teatro	theater
la trigonometría	trigonometry
la zoología	zoology
LOS ANIMALES	**ANIMALS**
la abeja	bee
la araña	spider
la ardilla	squirrel
el ave (f.), el pájaro	bird
la ballena	whale
el burro	donkey
la cabra	goat
el caimán	alligator
el camello	camel
la cebra	zebra
el ciervo, el venado	deer
el cocodrilo	crocodile
el cochino, el cerdo, el puerco	pig
el conejo	rabbit
el coyote	coyote
la culebra, la serpiente,	snake

la víbora	
el elefante	elephant
la foca	seal
la gallina	hen
el gallo	rooster
el gato	cat
el gorila	gorilla
el hipopótamo	hippopotamus
la hormiga	ant
el insecto	insect
la jirafa	giraffe
el lagarto	lizard
el león	lion
el lobo	wolf
el loro, la cotorra, el papagayo, el perico	parrot
la mariposa	butterfly
el mono	monkey
la mosca	fly
el mosquito	mosquito
el oso	bear
la oveja	sheep
el pato	duck
el perro	dog
el pez	fish
la rana	frog

el ratón	mouse
el rinoceronte	rhinoceros
el saltamontes, el chapulín	grasshopper
el tiburón	shark
el tigre	tiger
el toro	bull
la tortuga	turtle
la vaca	cow
el zorro	fox

EL CUERPO HUMANO Y LA SALUD
THE HUMAN BODY AND HEALTH

El cuerpo humano
The Human Body

la barba	beard
el bigote	mustache
la barriga, la panza, la guata	belly, tummy
la boca	mouth
el brazo	arm
la cabeza	head
la cadera	hip
la ceja	eyebrow
el cerebro	brain
la cintura	waist
el codo	elbow
el corazón	heart
la costilla	rib
el cráneo	skull

el cuello	neck
el dedo	finger
el dedo del pie	toe
la espalda	back
el estómago	stomach
la frente	forehead
la garganta	throat
el hombro	shoulder
el hueso	bone
el labio	lip
la lengua	tongue
la mandíbula	jaw
la mejilla	cheek
el mentón, la barba	chin
la muñeca	wrist
el músculo	muscle
el muslo	thigh
las nalgas, el trasero, las asentaderas	buttocks
la nariz	nose
el nervio	nerve
el oído	(inner) ear
el ojo	eye
el ombligo	navel, belly button
la oreja	(outer) ear
la pantorrilla	calf

el párpado	eyelid
el pecho	chest
la pestaña	eyelash
el pie	foot
la piel	skin
la pierna	leg
el pulgar	thumb
el pulmón	lung
la rodilla	knee
la sangre	blood
el talón	heel
el tobillo	ankle
el tronco	torso, trunk
la uña	fingernail
la uña del dedo del pie	toenail
la vena	vein

LOS CINCO SENTIDOS	*THE FIVE SENSES*
el gusto	taste
el oído	hearing
el olfato	smell
el tacto	touch
la vista	sight

LA SALUD	*HEALTH*
el accidente	accident
alérgico/a	allergic
el antibiótico	antibiotic

la aspirina	aspirin
el ataque cardiaco, el ataque al corazón	heart attack
el cáncer	cancer
la cápsula	capsule
la clínica	clinic
congestionado/a	congested
el consultorio	doctor's office
la curita	adhesive bandage
el/la dentista	dentist
el/la doctor(a), el/la médico/a	doctor
el dolor (de cabeza)	(head)ache, pain
embarazada	pregnant
la enfermedad	illness, disease
el/la enfermero/a	nurse
enfermo/a	ill, sick
la erupción	rash
el examen médico	physical exam
la farmacia	pharmacy
la fiebre	fever
la fractura	fracture
la gripe	flu
la herida	wound
el hospital	hospital
la infección	infection
la inyección	injection

el insomnio	insomnia
el jarabe	(cough) syrup
mareado/a	dizzy, nauseated
el medicamento	medication
la medicina	medicine
las muletas	crutches
la operación	operation
el/la paciente	patient
el/la paramédico/a	paramedic
la pastilla, la píldora	pill, tablet
los primeros auxilios	first aid
la pulmonía	pneumonia
los puntos	stitches
la quemadura	burn
el quirófano	operating room
la radiografía	X-ray
la receta	prescription
el resfriado	cold (illness)
la sala de emergencia(s)	emergency room
saludable	healthy, healthful
sano/a	healthy
el seguro médico	medical insurance
la silla de ruedas	wheelchair
el síntoma	symptom
el termómetro	thermometer
la tos	cough

la transfusión	transfusion
la vacuna	vaccination
la venda	bandage
el virus	virus
cortar(se)	to cut (oneself)
curar	to cure, to treat
desmayar(se)	to faint
enfermarse	to get sick
enyesar	to put in a cast
estornudar	to sneeze
guardar cama	to stay in bed
hinchar(se)	to swell
internar(se) en el hospital	to check into the hospital
lastimarse (el pie)	to hurt (one's foot)
mejorar(se)	to get better; to improve
operar	to operate
quemar(se)	to burn
respirar (hondo)	to breathe (deeply)
romperse (la pierna)	to break (one's leg)
sangrar	to bleed
sufrir	to suffer
tomarle la presión a alguien	to take someone's blood pressure
tomarle el pulso a alguien	to take someone's pulse
torcerse (el tobillo)	to sprain (one's ankle)
vendar	to bandage

REFERENCE

EXPRESIONES ÚTILES PARA LA CLASE

USEFUL CLASSROOM EXPRESSIONS

PALABRAS ÚTILES

USEFUL WORDS

ausente	absent
el departamento	department
el dictado	dictation
la conversación, las conversaciones	conversation(s)
la expresión, las expresiones	expression(s)
el examen, los exámenes	test(s)
la frase	sentence
la hoja de actividades	activity sheet
el horario de clases	class schedule
la oración, las oraciones	sentence(s)
el párrafo	paragraph
la persona	person
presente	present
la prueba	quiz
siguiente	following
la tarea	homework

EXPRESIONES ÚTILES

USEFUL EXPRESSIONS

Abra(n) sus libros.	Open your book(s).
Cambien de papel.	Change roles.
Cierre(n) su(s) libro(s).	Close your books.
¿Cómo se dice ___ en español?	How do you say ___ in Spanish?
¿Cómo se escribe ___ en español?	How do you write ___ in Spanish?

¿Comprende(n)?	Do you understand?
(No) comprendo.	I (don't) understand.
Conteste(n) las preguntas.	Answer the questions.
Continúe(n), por favor.	Continue, please.
Escriba(n) su nombre.	Write your name.
Escuchen la cinta (el disco compacto).	Listen to the tape (compact disc).
Estudie(n) la lección tres.	Study lesson three.
Haga(n) la actividad (el ejercicio) número cuatro.	Do activity (exercise) number four.
Lea(n) la oración en voz alta.	Read the sentence aloud.
Levante(n) la mano.	Raise your hand(s).
Más despacio, por favor.	Slower, please.
No sé.	I don't know.
Páse(n)me los exámenes.	Pass me the tests.
¿Qué significa ___?	What does ___ mean?
Repita(n), por favor.	Repeat, please.
Siénte(n)se, por favor.	Sit down, please.
Siga(n) las instrucciones.	Follow the instructions.
¿Tiene(n) alguna pregunta?	Do you have any questions?
Vaya(n) a la página dos.	Go to page two.

COUNTRIES & NATIONALITIES

PAÍSES Y NACIONALIDADES (GENTILICIOS)

NORTH AMERICA / NORTEAMÉRICA

Canada	**Canadá**	canadiense
Mexico	**México**	mexicano/a
United States	**Estados Unidos**	estadounidense

CENTRAL AMERICA / CENTROAMÉRICA

Belize	**Belice**	beliceño/a
Costa Rica	**Costa Rica**	costarricense
El Salvador	**El Salvador**	salvadoreño/a
Guatemala	**Guatemala**	guatemalteco/a
Honduras	**Honduras**	hondureño/a
Nicaragua	**Nicaragua**	nicaragüense
Panama	**Panamá**	panameño/a

THE CARIBBEAN / EL CARIBE

Cuba	**Cuba**	cubano/a
Dominican Republic	**República Dominicana**	dominicano/a
Haiti	**Haití**	haitiano/a
Puerto Rico	**Puerto Rico**	puertorriqueño/a

SOUTH AMERICA / AMÉRICA DEL SUR

Argentina	**Argentina**	argentino/a
Bolivia	**Bolivia**	boliviano/a
Brazil	**Brasil**	brasileño/a
Chile	**Chile**	chileno/a
Colombia	**Colombia**	colombiano/a

Ecuador	**Ecuador**	**ecuatoriano/a**
Paraguay	**Paraguay**	**paraguayo/a**
Peru	**Perú**	**peruano/a**
Uruguay	**Uruguay**	**uruguayo/a**
Venezuela	**Venezuela**	**venezolano/a**
EUROPE	*EUROPA*	
Armenia	**Armenia**	**armenio/a**
Austria	**Austria**	**austríaco/a**
Belgium	**Bélgica**	**belga**
Bosnia	**Bosnia**	**bosnio/a**
Bulgaria	**Bulgaria**	**búlgaro/a**
Croatia	**Croacia**	**croata**
Czech Republic	**República Checa**	**checo/a**
Denmark	**Dinamarca**	**danés, danesa**
England	**Inglaterra**	**inglés, inglesa**
Estonia	**Estonia**	**estonio/a**
Finland	**Finlandia**	**finlandés, finlandesa**
France	**Francia**	**francés, francesa**
Germany	**Alemania**	**alemán, alemana**
Great Britain (United Kingdom)	**Gran Bretaña (Reino Unido)**	**británico**
Greece	**Grecia**	**griego/a**
Hungary	**Hungría**	**húngaro/a**
Iceland	**Islandia**	**islandés, islandesa**
Ireland	**Irlanda**	**irlandés, irlandesa**
Italy	**Italia**	**italiano/a**

Latvia	**Letonia**	letón, letona
Lithuania	**Lituania**	lituano/a
Netherlands (Holland)	**Países Bajos (Holanda)**	holandés, holandesa
Norway	**Noruega**	noruego/a
Poland	**Polonia**	polaco/a
Portugal	**Portugal**	portugués, portuguesa
Romania	**Rumania**	rumano/a
Russia	**Rusia**	ruso/a
Scotland	**Escocia**	escocés, escocesa
Serbia	**Serbia**	serbio/a
Slovakia	**Eslovaquia**	eslovaco/a
Slovenia	**Eslovenia**	esloveno/a
Spain	**España**	español(a)
Sweden	**Suecia**	sueco/a
Switzerland	**Suiza**	suizo/a
Ukraine	**Ucrania**	ucranio/a, ucraniano/a
Wales	**Gales**	galés, galesa
Yugoslavia	**Yugoslavia**	yugoslavo/a
ASIA	*ASIA*	
Bangladesh	**Bangladesh**	bangladesí
Cambodia	**Camboya**	camboyano/a
China	**China**	chino/a
India	**India**	indio/a
Indonesia	**Indonesia**	indonesio/a

Iran	**Irán**	**iraní**
Iraq	**Iraq, Irak**	**iraquí**
Israel	**Israel**	**israelí**
Japan	**Japón**	**japonés, japonesa**
Jordan	**Jordania**	**jordano/a**
Korea	**Corea**	**coreano/a**
Kuwait	**Kuwait**	**kuwaití**
Lebanon	**Líbano**	**libanés, libanesa**
Malaysia	**Malaisia**	**malaisiano/a**
Pakistan	**Pakistán**	**pakistaní**
Russia	**Rusia**	**ruso/a**
Saudi Arabia	**Arabia Saudí**	**saudí**
Singapore	**Singapur**	**singapurés, singapuresa**
Syria	**Siria**	**sirio/a**
Taiwan	**Taiwán**	**taiwanés, taiwanesa**
Thailand	**Tailandia**	**tailandés, tailandesa**
Turkey	**Turquía**	**turco/a**
Vietnam	**Vietnam**	**vietnamita**
AFRICA	*ÁFRICA*	
Algeria	**Argelia**	**argelino/a**
Angola	**Angola**	**angolano/a**
Cameroon	**Camerún**	**camerunés, camerunesa**
Congo	**Congo**	**congolés, congolesa**
Egypt	**Egipto**	**egipcio/a**
Equatorial Guinea	**Guinea Ecuatorial**	**ecuatoguineano**

Ethiopia	**Etiopía**	etíope
Ivory Coast	**Costa de Marfil**	ivoriano/a
Kenya	**Kenia, Kenya**	keniano/a
Libya	**Libia**	libio/a
Mali	**Malí**	malinqués, malinquesa
Morocco	**Marruecos**	marroquí
Mozambique	**Mozambique**	mozambicano
Nigeria	**Nigeria**	nigeriano/a
Rwanda	**Ruanda**	ruandés, ruandesa
Somalia	**Somalia**	somalí
South Africa	**Sudáfrica**	sudafricano/a
Sudan	**Sudán**	sudanés, sudanesa
Tunisia	**Tunicia, Túnez**	tunecino/a
Uganda	**Uganda**	ugandés, ugandesa
Zambia	**Zambia**	zambiano/a
Zimbabwe	**Zimbabue**	zimbabuense

AUSTRALIA AND THE PACIFIC	***AUSTRALIA Y EL PACÍFICO***	
Australia	**Australia**	australiano/a
New Zealand	**Nueva Zelanda**	neozelandés, neozelandesa
Philippines	**Filipinas**	filipino/a

MONEDAS DE LOS PAÍSES HISPANOS

CURRENCIES OF SPANISH-SPEAKING COUNTRIES

PAÍS Country	*MONEDA* Currency
Argentina	el peso
Bolivia	el boliviano
Chile	el peso
Colombia	el peso
Costa Rica	el colón
Cuba	el peso
Ecuador	el sucre, el dólar estadounidense
El Salvador	el colón, el dólar estadounidense
España	el euro
Guatemala	el quetzal, el dólar estadounidense
Honduras	el lempira
México	el peso
Nicaragua	el córdoba
Panamá	el balboa, el dólar estadounidense
Paraguay	el guaraní
Perú	el sol
Puerto Rico	el dólar estadounidense
República Dominicana	el peso
Uruguay	el peso
Venezuela	el bolívar

303

EXPRESIONES Y REFRANES

EXPRESIONES Y REFRANES CON PARTES DEL CUERPO

EXPRESSIONS & SAYINGS

EXPRESSIONS & SAYINGS WITH PARTS OF THE BODY

A cara o cruz	Heads or tails
A corazón abierto	Open heart
A lo hecho, pecho	What's done is done./Don't cry over spilled milk.
A ojos vistas	Clearly, visibly
Al dedillo	Like the back of one's hand
¡Choca/Vengan esos cinco!	Put it there!/Give me five!
Codo con codo	Very closely/Cheek by jowl
Con las manos en la masa	Red handed
Costar un ojo de la cara	To cost an arm and a leg
De rodillas	On one's knees
Duro de oído	Hard of hearing
En cuerpo y alma	In body and soul
En la punta de la lengua	On the tip of one's tongue
Darle a la lengua	To chatter/To gab
En un abrir y cerrar de ojos	In a blink of the eye
Entrar por un oído y salir por otro	In one ear and out the other
Estar con el agua al cuello	To be up to one's neck with/in
Estar para chuparse los dedos	To be delicious/To be finger-licking good
Hablar entre dientes	To mutter/To speak under one's breath
Hablar por los codos	To talk a lot
Hacer la vista gorda	To turn a blind eye on something

Hombro con hombro	Shoulder to shoulder
Llorar a lágrima viva	To sob/To cry one's eyes out
Metérsele (a alguien) algo entre ceja y ceja	To put an idea in someone's head
Mirar por encima del hombro	To look over one's shoulder
No pegar ojo	Not to be able to sleep/To stay up all night
No tener corazón	Not to have a heart
No tener dos dedos de frente	Not to have an ounce of common sense
Ojos que no ven, corazón que no siente	Out of sight, out of mind
Perder la cabeza	To lose one's head
Quedarse con la boca abierta	To be thunderstruck
Romper el corazón	To break someone's heart
Tener buen/mal corazón	Have a good/bad heart
Tener un nudo en la garganta	Have a knot in your throat
Tomarse algo a pecho	To take something too seriously
Venir como anillo al dedo	To fit like a charm/To suit perfectly
EXPRESIONES Y REFRANES CON ANIMALES	*EXPRESSIONS & SAYINGS WITH ANIMALS*
A caballo regalado no le mires el diente.	Don't look a gift horse in the mouth.
Comer como un cerdo	To eat like a pig
Cuando menos se piensa, salta la liebre.	Things happen when you least expect it.
Es una mosquita muerta.	Butter wouldn't melt in his/her mouth.

305

Llevarse como el perro y el gato	To fight like cats and dogs
Perro ladrador, poco morde-dor./Perro que ladra no muerde.	His/her bark is worse than his/her bite.
¿Quién le pone el cascabel al gato?	Who will bell the cat?
Ser una tortuga	To be a slowpoke

EXPRESIONES Y REFRANES CON ALIMENTOS	*EXPRESSIONS AND SAYINGS WITH FOOD*
Agua que no has de beber, déjala correr.	If you're not interested, don't ruin it for everybody else.
Al pan, pan y al vino, vino.	Not to mince words.
Como agua para chocolate	Ready to explode/At the boiling point
Con pan y vino se anda el camino.	Things never seem as bad after a good meal.
Contigo pan y cebolla.	You are all I need.
Dame pan y dime tonto.	I don't care what you say, as long as I get what I want.
Descubrir el pastel	To let the cat out of the bag
Dulce como la miel	Sweet as honey
Estar en el ajo	To be in the know
Estar en la higuera	To take the lid off something
Estar más claro que el agua	To be clear as a bell
Ganarse el pan	To earn a living/To earn one's daily bread
No hay miel sin hiel.	There's no rose without a thorn./There's always a catch.
No sólo de pan vive el hombre.	Man doesn't live by bread alone.

Pan con pan, comida de tontos.	Variety is the spice of life./All work and no play makes Jack a dull boy.
Ser agua pasada	To be water under the bridge
Ser más bueno que el pan	To be gorgeous
Temblar como un flan	To shake/tremble like a leaf

EXPRESIONES Y REFRANES CON COLORES	*EXPRESSIONS AND SAYINGS WITH COLORS*
Estar verde	To be inexperienced/wet behind the ears
Poner los ojos en blanco	To roll one's eyes
Ponerle a alguien un ojo morado	To give someone a black eye
Ponerse rojo de ira	To turn red with anger
Ponerse rojo	To turn red/To blush
Ponerse verde de envidia	To be green with envy
Quedarse en blanco	To go blank
Verlo todo de color de rosa	See the world through rose-colored glasses

REFRANES	*SAYINGS*
A buen entendedor, pocas palabras bastan.	A word to the wise is sufficient.
Ande o no ande, caballo grande.	Bigger is always better.
A quien madruga, Dios le ayuda.	The early bird catches the worm.
Cuídate, que te cuidaré.	Take care of yourself, and then I'll take care of you.
De tal palo tal astilla.	A chip off the old block.
Del dicho al hecho hay mucho trecho.	Easier said than done.

Spanish	English
Dime con quién andas y te diré quién eres.	A man is known by the company he keeps.
El saber no ocupa lugar.	You can never know too much.
Lo que es moda no incomoda.	No discomfort is too great in the name of fashion.
Más vale maña que fuerza.	Brains is better than brawn.
Más vale prevenir que curar.	Prevention is better than cure.
Más vale solo que mal acompañado.	Better alone than with a bad companion.
Más vale tarde que nunca.	Better late than never.
Mucho ruido y pocas nueces.	All talk and no action.
No es oro todo lo que reluce.	All that glitters is not gold.
Poderoso caballero es don Dinero.	Money talks.
Por la boca muere el pez.	Talking too much can be dangerous.
Vale más una imagen que mil palabras.	A picture is worth a thousand words.

COMMON FALSE FRIENDS

False friends are Spanish words that look similar to English words but have very different meanings. While recognizing the English relatives of unfamiliar Spanish words you encounter is an important way of constructing meaning, there are some Spanish words whose similarity to English words is deceptive. Here is a list of some of the most common Spanish false friends.

actualmente ≠ actually

actualmente = nowadays, currently

actually = **de hecho, en realidad, en efecto**

aprobar ≠ approve

aprobar = to pass (an exam)

approve = **consentir, estar de acuerdo**

argumento ≠ argument

argumento = plot

argument = **discusión, pelea**

armada ≠ army

armada = navy

army = **ejército**

asistir ≠ assist

asistir = to attend, to go to

assist = **ayudar, colaborar**

balde ≠ bald

balde = pail, bucket

bald = **calvo/a**

batería ≠ battery

batería = drum set

battery = **pila**

bravo ≠ brave

bravo = wild, fierce

brave = **valiente**

cándido/a ≠ candid

cándido/a = innocent

candid = **sincero/a**

carbón ≠ carbon

carbón = coal

carbon = **carbono**

casual ≠ casual

casual = coincidental

casual = **informal, despreocupado/a**

309

REFERENCE

casualidad ≠ casualty

casualidad = coincidence

casualty = **víctima**

colegio ≠ college

colegio = school

college = **universidad**

collar ≠ collar

collar = necklace

collar = **cuello (de camisa)**

comprensivo/a ≠ comprehensive

comprensivo/a = understanding

comprenhensive = **completo, extensivo**

constipado ≠ constipated

estar constipado/a = to have a cold

to be constipated = **estar estreñido/a**

crudo/a ≠ crude

crudo/a = raw, undercooked

crude = **burdo/a; grosero/a**

desgracia ≠ disgrace

desgracia = misfortune

disgrace = **deshonra, vergüenza**

divertir ≠ divert

divertirse = to enjoy oneself

to divert = **desviar**

educado/a ≠ educated

educado/a = well-behaved

educated = **culto/a, instruido/a**

embarazada ≠ embarrassed

estar embarazada = to be pregnant

to be embarrassed = **tener vergüenza**

eventualmente ≠ eventually

eventualmente = possibly

eventually = **finalmente, al final**

éxito ≠ exit

éxito = success

exit = **salida**

físico/a ≠ physician

físico/a = physicist

physician = **médico/a**

fútbol ≠ football

fútbol = soccer

football = **fútbol americano**

lectura ≠ lecture
lectura = reading
lecture = **conferencia**

librería ≠ library
librería = bookstore
library = **biblioteca**

máscara ≠ mascara
máscara = mask
mascara = **rímel**

molestar ≠ to molest
molestar = to bother, to annoy
molest = **abusar**

oficio ≠ office
oficio = trade, occupation
office = **oficina**

rato ≠ rat
rato = while
rat = **rata**

realizar ≠ realize
realizar = to do
to realize = **darse cuenta**

red ≠ red
red = net
red = **rojo**

remover ≠ remove
remover = to stir; to turn over
remove = **sacar, quitar**

revolver ≠ revolver
revolver = to stir; to rummage through
revolver = **revólver**

sensible ≠ sensible
sensible = sentitive
sensible = **sensato/a, razonable**

suceso ≠ success
suceso = event
success = **éxito**

sujeto ≠ subject
sujeto = fellow, guy
subject = **tema, asunto**

LOS ALIMENTOS

FOODS

FRUTAS

FRUITS

la aceituna	olive
el aguacate	avocado
el albaricoque, el damasco	apricot
la banana, el plátano	banana
la cereza	cherry
la ciruela	plum
el dátil	date
la frambuesa	raspberry
la fresa, la frutilla	strawberry
el higo	fig
el limón	lemon, lime
el melocotón, el durazno	peach
la mandarina	tangerine
el mango	mango
la manzana	apple
la naranja	orange
la papaya	papaya
la pera	pear
la piña	pineapple
el pomelo, la toronja	grapefruit
la sandía	watermelon
las uvas	grapes

VEGETALES	*VEGETABLES*
la alcachofa	artichoke
el apio	celery
la arveja, el guisante	pea
la berenjena	eggplant
el brócoli	broccoli
la calabaza	squash, pumpkin
la cebolla	onion
el champiñón, la seta	mushroom
la col, el repollo	cabbage
la coliflor	cauliflower
los espárragos	asparagus
las espinacas	spinach
los frijoles, las habichuelas	beans
las habas	lima beans
las judías verdes, los ejotes	string beans, green beans
la lechuga	lettuce
el maíz, el choclo, el elote	corn
la papa, la patata	potato
el pepino	cucumber
el pimentón	bell pepper
el rábano	radish
la remolacha	beet
el tomate, el jitomate	tomato
la zanahoria	carrot

EL PESCADO Y LOS MARISCOS	*FISH AND SHELLFISH*
la almeja	clam
el atún	tuna
el bacalao	cod
el calamar	squid
el cangrejo	crab
el camarón, la gamba	shrimp
la langosta	lobster
el langostino	prawn
el lenguado	sole, flounder
el mejillón	mussel
la ostra	oyster
el pulpo	octopus
el salmón	salmon
la sardina	sardine
la vieira	scallop
LA CARNE	*MEAT*
la albóndiga	meatball
el bistec	steak
la carne de res	beef
el chorizo	hard pork sausage
la chuleta de cerdo	pork chop
el cordero	lamb
los fiambres	cold cuts; food served cold
el filete	fillet
la hamburguesa	hamburger

el hígado	liver
el jamón	ham
el lechón	suckling pig; roasted pig
el pavo	turkey
el pollo	chicken
el puerco	pork
la salchicha	sausage
la ternera	veal
el tocino	bacon

OTRAS COMIDAS	*OTHER FOODS*
el ajo	garlic
el arroz	rice
el azúcar	sugar
el batido	milkshake
el budín	pudding
el cacahuete, el maní	peanut
el café	coffee
los fideos	noodles, pasta
la harina	flour
el huevo	egg
el jugo, el zumo	juice
la leche	milk
la mermelada	marmalade; jam
la miel	honey
el pan	bread
el queso	cheese

la sal	salt
la sopa	soup
el té	tea
la tortilla	omelet (Spain); tortilla (Mexico)
el yogur	yogurt
CÓMO DESCRIBIR LA COMIDA	*WAYS TO DESCRIBE FOOD*
a la plancha, a la parrilla	grilled
ácido/a	sour
al horno	baked
amargo/a	bitter
caliente	hot
dulce	sweet
duro/a	tough
frío/a	cold
frito/a	fried
fuerte	strong, heavy
ligero/a	light
picante	spicy
sabroso/a	tasty
salado/a	salty

DÍAS FESTIVOS

ENERO
Año Nuevo (1)
Día de los Reyes Magos (6)
Día de Martin Luther King, Jr.

FEBRERO
Día de San Blas (Paraguay) (3)
Día de San Valentín, Día de los Enamorados (14)
Día de los Presidentes
Carnaval

MARZO
Día de San Patricio (17)
Nacimiento de Benito Juárez (México) (21)

ABRIL
Semana Santa
Pésaj
Pascua
Declaración de la Independencia de Venezuela (19)
Día de la Tierra (22)

HOLIDAYS

JANUARY
New Year's Day
Three Kings Day (Epiphany)
Martin Luther King, Jr. Day

FEBRUARY
St. Blas Day (Paraguay)
Valentine's Day

Presidents' Day
Carnival (Mardi Gras)

MARCH
St. Patrick's Day
Benito Juárez's Birthday (Mexico)

APRIL
Holy Week
Passover
Easter
Declaration of Independence of Venezuela

Earth Day

Mayo	*May*
Día del Trabajo (1)	Labor Day
Cinco de Mayo (5) (Mexico)	Cinco de Mayo (May 5th)
Día de las Madres	Mother's Day
Independencia Patria (Paraguay) (15)	Independence Day (Paraguay)
Día Conmemorativo	Memorial Day

Junio	*June*
Día de los Padres	Father's Day
Día de la Bandera (14)	Flag Day
Día del Indio (Perú) (24)	Native People's Day

Julio	*July*
Día de la Independencia de los Estados Unidos (4)	Independence Day (United States)
Día de la Independencia de Venezuela (5)	Independence Day (Venezuela)
Día de la Independencia de la Argentina (9)	Independence Day (Argentina)
Día de la Independencia de Colombia (20)	Independence Day (Colombia)
Nacimiento de Simón Bolívar (24)	Simón Bolívar's Birthday
Día de la Revolución (Cuba) (26)	Revolution Day (Cuba)
Día de la Independencia del Perú (28)	Independence Day (Peru)

AGOSTO

Día de la Independencia de Bolivia (6)

Día de la Independencia del Ecuador (10)

Día de San Martín (Argentina) (17)

Día de la Independencia del Uruguay (25)

AUGUST

Independence Day (Bolivia)

Independence Day (Ecuador)

San Martín Day (anniversary of his death)

Independence Day (Uruguay)

SEPTIEMBRE

Día del Trabajo (EE. UU.)

Día de la Independencia de Costa Rica, El Salvador, Guatemala, Honduras y Nicaragua (15)

Día de la Independencia de México (16)

Día de la Independencia de Chile (18)

Año Nuevo Judío

Día de la Virgen de las Mercedes (Perú) (24)

SEPTEMBER

Labor Day (U. S.)

Independence Day (Costa Rica, El Salvador, Guatemala, Honduras, Nicaragua)

Independence Day (Mexico)

Independence Day (Chile)

Jewish New Year

Day of the Virgin of Mercedes (Peru)

OCTUBRE

Día de la Raza (12)

Noche de Brujas (31)

OCTOBER

Columbus Day

Halloween

NOVIEMBRE	*NOVEMBER*
Día de los Muertos (2)	All Souls Day
Día de los Veteranos (11)	Veterans' Day
Día de la Revolución Mexicana (20)	Mexican Revolution Day
Día de Acción de Gracias	Thanksgiving
Día de la Independencia de Panamá (28)	Independence Day (Panama)

DICIEMBRE	*DECEMBER*
Día de la Virgen (8)	Day of the Virgin
Día de la Virgen de Guadalupe (México) (12)	Day of the Virgin of Guadalupe (Mexico)
Januká	Chanukah
Nochebuena (24)	Christmas Eve
Navidad (25)	Christmas
Año Viejo (31)	New Year's Eve

NOTE: In Spanish, dates are written with the day first, then the month. Christmas Day is **el 25 de diciembre**. In Latin America and in Europe, abbreviated dates also follow this pattern. Halloween, for example, falls on 31/10. You may also see the numbers in dates separated by periods: 14.2.01. When referring to centuries, roman numerals are always used. The 16th century, therefore, is **el siglo XVI**.

PESOS Y MEDIDAS

WEIGHTS & MEASURES

Longitud

Length

El sistema métrico
Metric system

El equivalente estadounidense
U.S. equivalent

milímetro	**= 0,001 metro**		= 0.039 inch
millimeter	= 0.0001 meter		
centímetro	**= 0,01 metro**		= 0.39 inch
centimeter	= 0.01 meter		
decímetro	**= 0,1 metro**		= 3.94 inches
decimeter	= 0.1 meter		
metro			= 39.4 inches
meter			
decámetro	**= 10 metros**		= 32.8 feet
dekameter	= 10 meters		
hectómetro	**= 100 metros**		= 328 feet
hectometer	= 100 meters		
kilómetro	**= 1.000 metros**		= .62 milc
kilometer	= 1,000 meters		

U.S. system
El sistema estadounidense

Metric equivalent
El equivalente métrico

inch			= 2.54 centimeters
pulgada			**= 2,54 centímetros**
foot	= 12 inches		= 30.48 centimeters
pie	**= 12 pulgadas**		**= 30,48 centímetros**
yard	= 3 feet		= 0.914 meter
yarda	**= 3 pies**		**= 0,914 metro**
mile	= 5,280 feet		= 1.609 kilometers
milla	**= 5.280 pies**		**= 1,609 kilómetros**

SUPERFICIE

El sistema métrico
Metric system

metro cuadrado
square meter

área	=	**100 metros cuadrados**
are	=	100 square meters

hectárea	=	**100 áreas**
hectare	=	100 ares

U.S. system
El sistema estadounidense

SURFACE AREA

El equivalente estadounidense
U.S. equivalent

= 10.764 square feet

= 0.025 acre

= 2.471 acres

Metric equivalent
El equivalente métrico

yarda cuadrada = 9 pies cuadrados = 0,836 metros cuadrados
square yard = 9 square feet = 0.836 square meters

acre = 4.840 yardas cuadradas = 0,405 hectáreas
acre = 4,840 square yards = 0.405 hectares

CAPACIDAD

El sistema métrico
Metric system

CAPACITY

El equivalente estadounidense
U.S. equivalent

mililitro	=	**0,001 litro**
milliliter	=	0.001 liter

= 0.034 ounces

centilitro	=	**0,01 litro**
centiliter	=	0. 01 liter

= 0.34 ounces

decilitro	=	**0,1 litro**
deciliter	=	0.1 liter

= 3.4 ounces

litro
liter

= 1.06 quarts

decalitro	=	**10 litros**
dekaliter	=	10 liters

= 2.64 gallons

| **hectolitro** | = | **100 litros** | |
| hectoliter | = | 100 liters | = 26.4 gallons |

| **kilolitro** | = | **1.000 litros** | |
| kiloliter | = | 1,000 liters | = 264 gallons |

| *U.S. system* | | *Metric equivalent* |
| **El sistema estadounidense** | | **El equivalente métrico** |

| ounce | | | = 29.6 milliliters |
| **onza** | | | = 29,6 mililitros |

| cup | = | 8 ounces | = 236 milliliters |
| **taza** | = | **8 onzas** | = **236 mililitros** |

| pint | = | 2 cups | = 0.47 liters |
| **pinta** | = | **2 tazas** | = **0,47 litros** |

| quart | = | 2 pints | = 0.95 liters |
| **cuarto** | = | **2 pinta** | = **0,95 litros** |

| gallon | = | 4 quarts | = 3.79 liters |
| **galón** | = | **4 cuartos** | = **3,79 litros** |

PESO		*WEIGHT*
El sistema métrico		**El equivalente estadounidense**
Metric system		U.S. equivalent

| **miligramo** | = | **0,001 gramo** | |
| **milligram** | = | **0.001 gram** | |

| **gramo** | | | |
| gram | | | = 0.035 ounce |

| **decagramo** | = | **10 gramos** | |
| dekagram | = | 10 grams | = 0.35 ounces |

| **hectogramo** | = | **100 gramos** | |
| hectogram | = | 100 grams | = 3.5 ounces |

| **kilogramo** | = | **1.000 gramos** | |
| kilogram | = | 1,000 grams | = 2.2 pounds |

tonelada (métrica)	**=**	**1.000 kilogramos**	
metric ton	=	1,000 kilograms	= 1.1 tons

U.S. system			*Metric equivalent*
El sistema estadounidense			***El equivalente métrico***

ounce			= 28.35 grams
onza			*= 28,35 gramos*
pound	=	16 ounces	= 0.45 kilograms
libra	**=**	**16 onzas**	*= 0,45 kilogramos*
ton	=	2,000 pounds	= 0.9 metric tons
tonelada	**=**	**2,000 libras**	*= 0,9 toneladas métricas*

TEMPERATURA

Grados centígrados
Degrees Celsius

To convert from Celsius to Fahrenheit, multiply by 9/5 and add 32.

TEMPERATURE

Grados Fahrenheit
Degrees Fahrenheit

To convert from Fahrenheit to Celsius, subtract 32 and multiply by 5/9.

Centígrados °C	°F	**Fahrenheit**
Celsius		Fahrenheit
50°	122°	
45°	113°	
40°	104°	
37°	98.6°	
35°	95°	
30°	86°	
25°	75°	
20°	68°	
15°	59°	
10°	50°	
5°	41°	
0°	32°	
-5°	23°	
-10°	14°	

NOMBRES DE PILA ESPAÑOLES

SPANISH PERSONAL NAMES

Note: Not all Spanish names have English equivalents.

NOMBRES FEMENINOS	WOMEN'S NAMES
Alba	Elba
Alicia	Alice, Alicia
Amanda	Amanda
Ana	Ann, Anne
Araceli (Celi)	
Asunción (Asun)	
Asunta	
Aurora	Aurora, Dawn
Beatriz (Bea, Beti, Biata)	Beatrice
Belén	
Berta	Bertha
Blanca	Blanche
Carlota	Charlotte
Carolina (Carol)	Caroline
Catarina (Cati)	Catherine, Catharine
Cecilia	Cecile
Celia	Celia
Claudia	Claudia
Consuelo	
Diana	Diane
Dorotea	Dorothy
Elena	Helen, Ellen

Elia	
Elvira	Elvira
Emilia	Emily
Encarna	
Ester	Esther
Estrella	Stella, Estelle
Eva	Eve
Gemma	
Gertrudes	Gertrude
Gloria	Gloria
Inés	Inez
Irene	Irene
Isabel	Elizabeth
Josefa	
Josefina (Pepi, Fina)	Josephine
Juana	Joan, Joanne, Jane
Judith	Judith
Julia	Julia, Julie
Julieta	Juliet, Juliette
Laura	Laura
Leonor	Leonore
Lidia	Lydia
Lourdes	
Luisa	Louise
Manuela (Manola, Manoli)	
Margarita (Marga)	Margaret

María	Mary, Marie
Marta	Martha
Mercedes (Merche)	
Mónica	Monica, Monique
Montserrat (Montse)	
Noelia	
Norma	Norma
Olga	Olga
Paloma	
Patricia (Pati)	Patricia
Paula	Paula
Raquel	Rachel
Rocío	
Rosa	Rose
Rosalía	Rosalie
Rosana	Rosana, Roseanne
Rosario	
Sandra	Sandra
Sara	Sarah
Silvia	Sylvia
Sofía	Sophia
Sonia	Sonya
Susana (Susi)	Susan
Teresa	Theresa
Verónica	Veronica
Victoria (Vicki)	Victoria

REFERENCE

Violeta	Violet
Zoe	Zoe
NOMBRES MASCULINOS	*MEN'S NAMES*
Alberto	Albert
Alejandro	Alexander
Álex	Alex
Alfonso	Alphonse
Alfredo	Alfred
Andrés	Andrew
Ángel	
Antonio (Toni)	Anthony
Aquiles	Achilles
Arturo	Arthur
Augusto	August
Bernardo	Bernard
Camilo	
Carlos	Charles
César	
Cristiano	Christian
Cristóbal	Christopher
Damián	Damian
David	David
Diego	James
Eduardo	Edward
Emilio	Emil
Enrique	Henry, Eric

Ernesto	Ernest
Esteban	Stephen
Eugenio	Eugene
Evaristo	
Federico (Fede)	Frederick
Felipe	Philip
Fernando	
Francisco (Paco)	Francis
Gerardo	Gerard
Gregorio	Gregory
Guillermo	William
Gustavo	Gustav
Ignacio (Nacho)	Ignatius
Jaime	James
Javier (Javi)	Xavier
Jeremías	Jeremiah, Jeremy
Jesús	
Joaquín	
Jorge	George
José (Pepe)	Joseph
Juan	John
Julián	Julian
Julio	Julius
Justino	Justin
León	Leo, Leon
Leonardo	Leonard

Lucas	Luke
Luis	Louis
Manolo	
Manuel	
Marcelo	Marcel
Marcos	Mark
Mariano	
Miguel	Michael
Oscar (Óscar)	Oscar
Pablo	Paul
Patricio	Patrick
Pedro	Peter
Rafael (Rafa)	Raphael
Raimundo	Raymond
Ramón	Raymond
Ricardo	Richard
Roberto	Robert
Santiago	James
Sebastián	Sebastian
Sergio	Serge
Simón	Simon
Sixto	
Teodoro	Theodore
Tomás	Thomas
Vicente	Vincent

COMPOUND WOMEN'S NAMES

In Spanish-speaking countries women frequently have names that are a combination of **María** and another name, as in **María Dolores** or **Ana María**, for example. Women with such names are rarely known as **María** but are addressed using the second name in the combination or a nickname derived from both names. **María del Carmen**, therefore, might be called **Carmen** or perhaps **Maricarmen**. Below are listed common combinations with **María**, followed by nicknames derived from them.

Note: **María** is not strictly a woman's name in the Spanish-speaking world. Some men's names contain **María**. **José María**, for example, is a common name.

María Ana (Ana, Mariana)

María Antonia (Antonia, Tonia, Toñi)

María Concepción (Concha)

María Cristina (Cristina, Cris, Tina)

María de los Ángeles (Ángeles, Mariángeles)

María del Carmen (Carmen, Maricarmen, Mámen)

María del Mar (Marimar)

María Dolores (Dolores, Mariló, Loles, Lola, Lolita)

María Elena (Elena)

María Eugenia (Eugenia, Maru, Genia)

María Inmaculada (Inma)

María Isabel (Isabel, Isa, Maribel, Mabel)

María Luisa (Luisa, Marilú)

María Nieves (Nieves, Marinieves)

María Pilar (Pilar, Pili, Maripili, Mapi)

María Reyes (Reyes, Marirreyes)

María Rosa (Marisa)

REFERENCE

María Soledad (Marisol)
María Teresa (Teresa, Tere, Maritere, Maite)
Ana María (Ana, Anamari)
Ángela María (Ángela)
Eva María (Eva)
Rosa María (Rosa, Rosamari)

COMPOUND MEN'S NAMES

José Manuel (Josema)
José María (Josema, Chema)
José Miguel
Juan Antonio
Juan Carlos (Juanca)
Juan José (Juanjo)
Juan Luis (Juanlu)
Juan Manuel (Juanma)
Juan Pablo (Juanpa)
Miguel Ángel

NÚMEROS

NÚMEROS ORDINALES

primero/a	1º/1ª
segundo/a	2º/2ª
tercero/a	3º/3ª
cuarto/a	4º/4ª
quinto/a	5º/5ª
sexto/a	6º/6ª
séptimo/a	7º/7ª
octavo/a	8º/8ª
noveno/a	9º/9ª
décimo/a	10º/10ª

FRACCIONES

$\frac{1}{2}$	un medio, la mitad
$\frac{1}{3}$	un tercio
$\frac{1}{4}$	un cuarto
$\frac{1}{5}$	un quinto
$\frac{1}{6}$	un sexto
$\frac{1}{7}$	un séptimo
$\frac{1}{8}$	un octavo
$\frac{1}{9}$	un noveno
$\frac{1}{10}$	un décimo
$\frac{2}{3}$	dos tercios
$\frac{3}{4}$	tres cuartos
$\frac{5}{8}$	cinco octavos

NUMBERS

ORDINAL NUMBERS

first	1st
second	2nd
third	3rd
fourth	4th
fifth	5th
sixth	6th
seventh	7th
eighth	8th
ninth	9th
tenth	10th

FRACTIONS

one half	
one third	
one fourth (quarter)	
one fifth	
one sixth	
one seventh	
one eighth	
one ninth	
one tenth	
two thirds	
three fourths (quarters)	
five eighths	

DECIMALES		*DECIMALS*	
un décimo	0,1	one tenth	0.1
un centésimo	0,01	one hundredth	0.01
un milésimo	0,001	one thousandth	0.001

OCUPACIONES	**OCCUPATIONS**
el/la abogado/a	lawyer
el actor, la actriz	actor
el/la administrador(a) de empresas	business administrator
el/la agente de bienes raíces	real estate agent
el/la agente de seguros	insurance agent
el/la agricultor(a)	farmer
el/la arqueólogo/a	archaeologist
el/la arquitecto/a	architect
el/la artesano/a	artisan
el/la auxiliar de vuelo	flight attendant
el/la basurero/a	garbage collector
el/la bibliotecario/a	librarian
el/la bombero/a	firefighter
el/la cajero/a	bank teller, cashier
el/la camionero/a	truck driver
el/la cantinero/a	bartender
el/la carnicero/a	butcher
el/la carpintero/a	carpenter
el/la científico/a	scientist
el/la cirujano/a	surgeon

el/la cobrador(a)	bill collector
el/la cocinero/a	cook, chef
el/la comprador(a)	buyer
el/al consejero/a	counselor, advisor
el/la contador(a)	accountant
el/la corredor(a) de bolsa	stockbroker
el/la diplomático/a	diplomat
el/la diseñador(a) (gráfico/a)	(graphic) designer
el/la electricista	electrician
el/la empresario/a de pompas fúnebres	funeral director
el/la especialista en dietética	dietician
el/la fotógrafo/a	photographer
el/la higienista dental	dental hygienist
el hombre/la mujer de negocios	businessperson
el/la ingeniero/a en computación	computer engineer
el/la intérprete	interpreter
el/la juez	judge
el/la maestro/a	elementary school teacher
el/la marinero/a	sailor
el/la obrero/a	manual laborer
el/la oficial de prisión	prision guard
el/la obrero/a de la construcción	construction worker
el/la optometrista	optometrist
el/la panadero/a	baker
el/la paramédico/a	paramedic

335

el/la peluquero/a	hairdresser
el/la piloto	pilot
el/la pintor(a)	painter
el/la plomero/a	plumber
el/la político/a	politician
el/la programador(a)	computer programer
el/la psicólogo/a	psychologist
el/la quiropráctico/a	chiropractor
el/la redactor(a)	editor
el/la reportero/a	reporter
el/la sastre	tailor
el/la secretario/a	secretary
el/la supervisor(a)	supervisor
el/la técnico/a (en computación)	(computer) technician
el/la fisioterapeuta	physical therapist
el/la vendedor(a)	sales representative
el/la veterinario/a	veterinarian